Enemy Lines

A

Philip E. Lilienthal

■   ■   ■

B O O K

Enemy Lines

Childhood, Warfare, and Play in Batticaloa

Margaret Trawick

UNIVERSITY OF CALIFORNIA PRESS

Berkeley / Los Angeles / London

University of California Press, one of the most distinguished university presses in the United States, enriches lives around the world by advancing scholarship in the humanities, social sciences, and natural sciences. Its activities are supported by the UC Press Foundation and by philanthropic contributions from individuals and institutions. For more information, visit www.ucpress.edu.

University of California Press
Berkeley and Los Angeles, California

University of California Press, Ltd.
London, England

Library of Congress Cataloging-in-Publication Data
Trawick, Margaret.
    Enemy lines : childhood, warfare, and play in Batticaloa / Margaret Trawick.
        p.   cm.
    Includes bibliographical references and index.
    ISBN-13: 978-0-520-24515-0 (alk. paper)
    ISBN-13: 978-0-520-24516-7 (pbk. : alk. paper)
    1. Tamil (Indic people) — Wars — Sri Lanka — Batticaloa District.
2. Tamil (Indic people) — Sri Lanka — Batticaloa District — Social
conditions.   3. Children — Sri Lanka — Batticaloa District — Social
conditions.   4. Children and war — Sri Lanka — Batticaloa District.
5. Children and violence — Sri Lanka — Batticaloa District.   6. Batticaloa
District (Sri Lanka) — Social conditions.   7. Tamirira Viḍutalaipppulikaḷ
(Association).   I. Title.
DS432.T3T728   2007
940.9303'2 — dc22   2006024689

Manufactured in the United States of America

15   14   13   12   11   10   09   08   07
10   9   8   7   6   5   4   3   2   1

This book is printed on New Leaf EcoBook 50, a 100% recycled fiber
of which 50% is de-inked postconsumer waste, processed chlorine free.
EcoBook 50 is acid free and meets the minimum requirements of
ANSI/ASTM D5634-01 (*Permanence of Paper*).

In loving memory of Dharmeratnam Sivaram (Taraki),
fighter, friend

Contents

Acknowledgments

Thanks to J. Bernard Bate, Erika Büky, Isabelle Clark-Deces, Stan Goff, Ann Grodzins Gold, Don Handelman, Suzanne Knott, Patricia Lawrence, Malathy Naguleswaran, Mike Roguski, Martha Ann Selby, Avis Sri-Jayanta, D. S. Sivaram, Alison Thwaites, and Jim Wilce for their valuable comments on early drafts and portions of this book.

Thanks to the Jesuit Fathers of Batticaloa for their astute criticisms of my work and their unfailing compassion for those who suffer.

Thanks to the American Institute of Sri Lankan Studies for funding my research in Sri Lanka from November 1997 through June 1998.

Thanks to Massey University for allowing me to conduct this research.

Thanks to the government of Sri Lanka and the Liberation Tigers of Tamil Eelam for enabling this research.

Thanks to all the people of Batticaloa town and the Paduvankarai area for welcoming me into their company and assisting me in my efforts to learn and document the events of the time I was with them.

Special thanks to the people I have called Vasanta, Rosa, Menan, Sita, Alagar, Inbam, and Rudrakumaran for their kindness, wisdom, and good humor.

Extra-special thanks to S. George Rajmenan for his insightful paintings and for his continuing friendship. The painting on the cover of this book is his.

Thanks, love, and blessings to all the girls in the LTTE whom I met, most especially the two I have called Vidya and Nalini. I hope they are alive and unharmed.

Love to the mother of the one I have called Sita, and love to the mother of the ones I have called Rosa and Vasanta.

Love to the memory of Das.

Thanks to Ken Butler, Dan Egnor, and Abe Egnor for their patience and trust.

I alone am responsible for any mistakes I may have made in the process of researching and writing this book.

Tamil Transliterations

The phonetic and phonological systems of Tamil are different from those of English, which means that the sounds are different, and no one-to-one correspondence exists between letters in the Tamil alphabet and letters in the English alphabet. Also, no single standard conversion system exists, and therefore transliteration is always a problem.

I have tried to employ as simple a system as possible for the transliteration of Tamil words and phrases, so that Tamil speakers will know what each transliterated word is meant to be. For non-Tamil speakers, I offer a brief introduction to the Tamil sound system, which probably will be of no use at all.

Tamil does not distinguish between voiced and unvoiced consonants. In English transliterations, Tamil consonants are therefore assigned voiced or unvoiced values according to context, except for nasals, which are always voiced. Vowels are either long (extended in duration of utterance) or short (not extended in duration). Consonants may be geminate (double) and held longer or nongeminate and not held longer. Several points of articulation are part of the system, including retroflex, which means that the tip of the tongue curls back and touches the roof of the mouth when a retroflex consonant is uttered. The use of diacritical marks is as follows:

A vowel with a line over it is a long vowel.

A vowel with no line over it is a short vowel.

A consonant with an underdot is retroflex.

An unmarked *r* is a single flap.

An *r* with an underdot is retroflex, likewise an *l* with an underdot.

An underlined *r* is "hard," and when it has no consonant behind it, sounds like an unmarked *r*.

When preceded by an *n,* hard *r* sounds like English *dr*.

An underlined double *tt* is a double "hard" *rr* and sounds like English *tr*.

Tamil words that have conventional English spellings, such as *Batticaloa* or *Tamil*, are given those conventional English spellings in this book. Most of the names of people and places appearing in this book have also acquired assorted English spellings as they have appeared in assorted English-language news sites. When in doubt about preferred English spellings of Tamil proper nouns, I have followed *TamilNet* usage.

CHAPTER I

Introduction

This book is based on field notes and interviews I did in the Batticaloa District of Sri Lanka from November 1997 through June 1998, plus material from briefer visits in 1996 and 2002. Most of the interviews and notes were recorded in the Paduvankarai area, just across a narrow lagoon from the town of Batticaloa. The narrow coastal peninsulas on which the town of Batticaloa and other main towns of the district are situated were and are held by the Sri Lankan army. Batticaloa District, which contains Batticaloa city and Paduvankarai, is a Tamil-majority area within Sri Lanka. *Paḍuvān-karai* in Tamil means "the side where it goes down." What goes down on that side is the sun, and Paduvankarai is known for its beautiful sunsets. Indeed, the whole landscape is gorgeous. But some people say that Paduvankarai has its name because so many bad things have happened there. During the time of my work there, the Paduvankarai area was under the control of the Liberation Tigers of Tamil Eelam (LTTE), the Tamil rebel army that is fighting for the independence of Sri Lankan Tamils from the Sinhala-dominated government of Sri Lanka. Sinhala people constitute the great majority (70 to 75 percent) of the population of that country. Tamils are the largest ethnic minority there, and they have been subjected to harassment and persecution at the hands of the government, the armed forces, and civilians. Armed resistance and terrorist acts on the part of the LTTE have been met with increased persecution and violent reprisals on the part of the government. Many people have disappeared without a trace, or their bodies have been found much later. And so the conflict has escalated. From early 1997 through late 1998, the war was at a climax.

The main body of this book consists of a series of narratives, most of them based on my own observations and experiences in the Paduvankarai area, but two of which are verbatim narratives of the war by civilians. Others recount conversations I had with civilians and with members of the LTTE. Still others describe adventures they shared with me. I chose the title, *Enemy Lines,* because of the sharp divide, geographically marked by the lagoon, between army-held territory and Tiger-held territory. The difference in appearance, way of life, and shared and sharable knowledge between the two sides was striking, even though many people had to cross the divide every day. Other lines were less visible but equally sharp and dangerous — for instance, the line between those who sympathized with the Tigers and those who did not. Many people in Paduvankarai had to tread this line very carefully to avoid alienating one side or the other. Another dangerous line was the one marking off the stage of innocent childhood from the stage of maturity, responsibility, and combat capability.

The subtitle, *Childhood, Warfare, and Play in Batticaloa,* reflects the intent of my project, which was to understand the nature of childhood in this particular war-torn environment, to see how children addressed the circumstances of the war, and to understand the worldviews of young people who had never known a life outside of war. I was more interested in finding out about children's agency than in recording the many obvious ways in which children are victimized by warfare. An important decision facing each child on entering his or her teens is whether to join the LTTE. Conversations with young female members of the LTTE and with high school students in the LTTE-controlled area illuminated the nature of their decision making on this matter. The issue of child combatants is an emotionally fraught one. This book attempts, among other things, to offer a realistic, nonsensationalistic assessment of the situation in which young members of the LTTE live, the reasons why they join the LTTE, the global and local forces impinging upon them, and, finally, what the young people I met were like as individual human beings.

The word *play* appears in the title because I found that many adult members of the LTTE presented themselves to me as playful and entertaining people. They were in the habit of doing and saying things to make me laugh. Whether this was just the nature of my relationship with them, or whether they were this way with others, I do not know, although one of them told me they were this way with others, and with each other also. But, in addition, entertainments and sports events were constantly being organized by the Tigers for the civilians; the civilians participated with enthusiasm. Laughter and play were essential to everyday life. So was make-believe. Combat was referred to by the combatants themselves as a game or sport (*vilaiyāḍḍu*), even as they engaged in it with full serious-ness and were always surrounded by death. The deep connections between warfare and play were revealed to me as real, with some young people participating in both. Finally, adult Tigers sometimes represented themselves as children. In general, they were called *iyakkappiḷḷaikaḷ*, "chil-dren of the movement," regardless of their age. Because members of the LTTE fed me meals, one elderly civilian woman said it meant I was their *piḷḷai*, their child. I was in my late forties at the time. Clearly the concept of childhood was much different for people of that area, and more flex-ible than the concept of childhood with which I grew up.

While the war was being waged right around us, it was also being waged in the media. Civilians — both adults and children — assiduously fol-lowed newspaper, radio, and television accounts of war-related events. So, of course, did the Tigers. The most bloody and protracted campaign of the war was going on in the Vanni District, a jungle area just south of the Jaffna peninsula (but many miles north of Batticaloa), with the army trying to capture a stretch of highway that ran through Tiger territory, and the Tigers fighting them back in a series of set-piece battles. The war had become what some people call conventional: one large, well-organized, well-equipped army hurling itself directly against another, again and again. The Tigers planned better than the army and were less afraid of death. In the end, the Tigers defeated the army campaign, but at a high price. The area through which the contested highway ran was devastated by bombing, the civilian population was impoverished, and many lives were lost.

It became apparent that the whole terrible campaign, called Operation Jayasikurui (Victory Assured) by the Sri Lankan army, was more than any-thing else a spectacle staged by the government to muster civilian support. The Tigers countered with spectacles of their own. At the peak of this long campaign, and intimately bound up with it, was the celebration of the fiftieth anniversary of Sri Lanka's independence, which the govern-ment tried to make into a glorious affair, while the Tigers tried to foil it and largely succeeded.

Many members of the LTTE who came from the Batticaloa District, and from Paduvankarai itself, were sent north to fight in Jayasikurui. Some came back down to their home villages or bases nearby to rest and then returned north again to fight. Many families had sons and daughters fighting in the north, and the anxiety they felt for their kin who were fighting, or for the souls of those who had perished in battle, was made poignantly manifest in the June temple festivals, where people made vows, undertook penances, and gave offerings to the temple to protect a named relative who was fighting in the north.[1] The amount of each offering, the name of the offerer, and the name of the person for whom protection was sought were announced over a loudspeaker; at one such festival the announcements continued all night long. Meanwhile, smaller battles were being waged within earshot of where we were, sometimes simultaneously with celebrations. The sounds of gunfire and loud explosions a mile or so away did not have any effect on the celebrations at all that I could see.

It was all very surreal. But I am not the first to observe that warfare is surreal.

Throughout this book, readers will notice a certain degree of reflexivity on my part, and some may be annoyed by it. This book is not a confession, and it is not about me. I was part of the scene that I was describing. I observed myself among others, recording my own feelings and words, with a certain detachment from myself. Those feelings and words were not professional views, and the opinions of that person in the field are not necessarily shared by the person now finishing this book. I am responsible for my own words and actions, of course, whether they happened today or ten years ago. It is just that feelings are ephemeral and change with context, and my views and understandings, and the ways I make sense of people, events, and my own experiences, have all changed over time, as I have learned new things and my mind has shifted and settled into new configurations.

Some people have called me a Tiger sympathizer. Until recently, that charge would have been true. I did, and still do, sympathize with the overall aims of the LTTE, and I did, and still do, care for the rank and file of the movement. At the same time, I could not then, and cannot now, condone everything that they do. I did and still do hate terrorism — the targeting of random civilians for destruction, the attempt to inflict terror on a population — and see no point in it. All these views of mine are in accord with the views of most Sri Lankan Tamil civilians, I think. But the terrorist acts of the LTTE pale in comparison to the terrorist acts committed in the name of my own country, the United States.[2] The terrorist acts of the Sri Lankan government have likewise been monstrous. And until recently, I have been able to believe that the Tiger leadership, despite the assassinations and the bombings it has ordered, has internal integrity and acts in what it sincerely believes are the best interests of the Sri Lankan Tamil people as a nation. The ceasefire initiated by the LTTE in 2001, and joined by the SLA in 2002, brought hope to many, including LTTE members themselves. But more recent events have shaken my (already reserved and provisional) confidence in the leadership of the LTTE. In March 2004, a split occurred between the head of the LTTE, Velupillai Prabhakaran, and Karuna, the commander of the LTTE forces in the east. My friends in the LTTE, who lived and worked in the east and had fought the army both in the east and in the north, had either to surrender to Prabhakaran and become enemies of their former commander Karuna or stay loyal to Karuna and become enemies of Prabhakaran, to whom they had previously sworn allegiance. To become an enemy of either side meant to be targeted for killing by that side. About three thousand members of the LTTE, most of them recent recruits, chose to leave after the split, only to find themselves in a civilian limbo. Long-time members of the LTTE did not have the option of returning to civilian life. Since the split, there have been hundreds of murders in the northeast, with no end to the killing in sight. My sympathy remains with the people of Batticaloa, including those who worked and fought on the side of the LTTE for many years and now are in danger of being killed by their former comrades. I do not know the details of the Prabhakaran-Karuna split, nor which of the two men is more at fault. But I feel it would have been better for all concerned if the leader of the LTTE and his eastern commander had worked things out between themselves somehow, rather than suddenly turning from close and trusting friendship to mortal enmity.

Developing Theories

When I started this project and went to Sri Lanka, I had no special theory in mind, except that children exercise agency — they knowingly act on their worlds to change those worlds — and they do so in warfare as well as in peace. This is, however, a trivial theory, in the sense that one can easily prove it.[3] I thought that under the challenges and pressures of warfare, the ability of children to change their worlds might emerge more clearly than it does in easier situations.[4] This was not so much a theory as something I thought might be possible. However, what I saw of childhood in war-torn Paduvankarai was different from what I was looking for. It did not contradict my conscious expectations; it was just different. The people I was with led me to see what was important to them, which was not quite the same thing as what was important to me. They led me off the path I was following onto other paths. When this happened, I had to put things together in some other way than the way I had thought, develop a new conceptual framework to organize what I had learned, and answer the "So what?" question. This and the following chapters trace the reorganization of that conceptual framework. My account is not an effort to describe the world as the people I was with would describe it. It is rather an effort to describe it to myself, and to you, the reader, in a way that hangs together and has some degree of plausibility to me, to you, and to the people I write about.

Childhood and play are often linked in modern imaginations. Warfare and play are likewise strongly linked. But the concepts of warfare and childhood repel each other. Or, to state this formulation more cautiously, people of a certain cosmopolitan, universalist, fundamentally Western mind-set desire to keep warfare and childhood separate. This is because children are seen as not fully competent, not capable of exercising the skills that warfare requires; because their relative newness to the world is interpreted as a deficiency of the wisdom supposedly forged by experience; because they are seen as more easily damaged than adults; because they are seen as innocent, untainted by sin and guilt, and therefore deserving to be kept pure; because many people consider warfare to be the most horrible thing that people do, hope that someday warfare may cease to be, and want to protect children from it; because children represent the future, and many adults hope that children will not carry the seeds of warfare with them into that future, to repeat the horrible mistakes of their forebears; and because, although they are mere potential now, children will someday become the next producers, the next harvesters, the next harvest.[5] Children must be saved up for the future, whereas warfare destroys lives wantonly, with no regard for the future. In addition, for many the waging of war is a distinguishing mark of manhood, the absolute fulfillment of manhood; and if even children (and women) can be warriors, this distinguishing mark will be taken away from those men for whom it is essential to their identity as men. And perhaps there are other reasons for keeping childhood and warfare separate, having to do with the origins of sacrifice.[6]

But most of these reasons are subject to debate, or at best are valid only in certain contexts and not in others. A special danger is perceived, a special fear arises in the hearts of some adults, when warfare and childhood mix. For instance, many middle-class Western parents are troubled when their children play war games on their computers. They fear that the enjoyment of war games reflects violent fantasies that the child may act out in real life, however unlikely the prospect. Likewise, Western middle-class parents are likely to deny real or toy guns to their children, even when the parents themselves own guns. And quite recently (since around 1989) the United Nations passed a series of resolutions barring children (those under the age of eighteen) from involvement in warfare. The existence of child soldiers is seen as unnatural and immoral. And yet, despite such concerns, young people, especially adolescents, have always been involved in warfare; and warfare and childhood do mix, perhaps more now than ever before in history.

Each of these three worlds — warfare, childhood, and play — is, conceptually, if not in fact, a world set apart, in which the rules of the ordinary, or "real," world are suspended, and other rules apply.[7] These three states might therefore be called liminal.[8] They are not contained within the ordinary, stable categories of life and are therefore not expected to obey the ordinary rules. Because the liminal is by definition extraordinary, it is often ascribed a sacred status — and so are warfare, childhood, and play. But to call them liminal is to say both too much and too little about these three modes of being and action. *Liminal* literally means "on the threshold" — neither fully inside nor fully outside the house. It is an unstable and transitional state, on the way from one well-defined position to another. In liminal states, things are turned upside down, and chaos threatens. But we are all, always, in some kind of transition; chaos is always nearby, on the edge of the shadows. And warfare, childhood, and play are all definite, well-defined categories in themselves.

I prefer to say of these three states of being that they are supernatural conditions — in a different sense, however, from the sense usually borne by the word *supernatural,* with its connotations of psychic or spectral phenomena. When I call certain states supernatural, I mean these states are beyond and above the rules governing everyday human life, whatever these rules might be. They challenge people's understanding of (human) nature, whatever that understanding might be. They are more natural than nature itself. They show that nature, most of all human nature, is far more than is commonly supposed. Supernatural states and the beings who occupy them coexist with and interact closely with the "natural" (everyday, rule-bound) world, to the extent of being almost inextricable from it, and necessary to it, as it is to them. But they do not follow the rules of the natural world. They are unpredictable, uncontrollable, powerful, and dangerous. You might say that the natural world itself is just that, but then you are thinking of something called "nature" as a wild and untamed set of forces: the nature side of the Lévi-Straussian nature/culture dichotomy, where culture is whatever human beings make and control, and nature is everything else. But I am thinking of nature in another sense, as something subject to "natural laws" and therefore predictable, inasmuch as the laws of nature can be known; nature in this sense is subject to complete understanding by human knowledge, and therefore amenable to human control. Being amenable to and for the most part under the control of knowledge, nature can be taken for granted, half-forgotten, allowed to run itself regularly and predictably.[9] If it fails, it can be wrested back into control. I am not asserting that nature "really is" one thing or another. I am talking about a way of thinking only. In this way of thinking, nature is the world of the habitual. And once something is a habit, one need not think about it. The supernatural, conversely, forces itself into consciousness and forces people to think about it.

In addition to being supernatural, warfare, play, and childhood are modes of being and action that, to be done well, require intense concentration, heightened awareness, and the expenditure of great energy. In each of these three states, you concentrate on the moment, on your immediate surroundings, and on how each element of the here and now is part of what you are doing and being. The future and the past are forgotten. The small and the enormous meet as equals. Time and space are different from what they are in the habitual world; objects and forces are different; personhood is different. Reality in such a state is different: it is strange and impossible, even though it is indisputably real; it is surreal, beyond the real, more real than real. It stands out, and forces you to look for reason in it, but when you try, you cannot. The ordinary, natural world fades into the background, and ceases to exist on the surface of consciousness.

Such a mode of being and action cannot be sustained indefinitely. We are mortal, finite, embodied creatures. And for this reason only, warfare, childhood, and play are transitory states. If they were not, we might do them always. These are all states of being that people can move in and out of. Players are not always in a state of play, warriors are not always in a state of war, and children are not always in a state of childhood. I don't mean this third statement in the sense that children grow out of childhood, but in the sense that children are not always allowed to be children. They have to follow the rules of adults, or imposed by adults, much of the time.

CHILDHOOD

Given that no child is always in the state of childhood, how shall we define this state? I will give a definition congruent with both Tamil and Western idealizations of childhood. In the state of (ideal) childhood, one is free, and unconstrained by more powerful people (including other children). Nobody is more powerful than the ideal child. There may be threats, either animate or existential or both, but in the state of ideal childhood one can outmaneuver them and ultimately defeat them. Peter Pan exemplifies such a state. The runaway Huckleberry Finn seeks and to a certain degree attains it. Pippi Longstocking, perhaps more than any other, is in such a state, and so is Harry Potter. Ender of *Ender's Game* is in such a state, although he must struggle with its implications — above all, the possibility that he will lose his humanity.

Outside the state of ideal childhood, a real-life child must do as authority dictates. A real-life child must be good. But the ideal child is amoral. He or she can get into all kinds of mischief, can wreak bloody havoc, and still do no wrong, still be adored. The real-life child is small, inconsequential, and dirty; a real-life child constantly stumbles, makes mistakes, and is subject to shame and punishment. A real-life child may have to go hungry. An ideal child is flawlessly beautiful and irresistibly attractive, suffers no unfulfilled desires, and possesses perfect grace. Who would not wish to live in the state of ideal childhood? I would not, but only because I know such a state must be an illusion, from which, if one entertains it, one must eventually fall and be hurt. It might be called an infantile fantasy.[10] But do any infants really have this fantasy? Maybe a few.

In Tamil there is a word, *summā,* that etymologically means "without burden." I translate it sometimes as "just kidding." People would make up stories that I took for true, and then, when I asked if they meant what they were saying, they would tell me they just said it *summā*. Or if I asked what someone was doing, they would say *summā,* which in that context might mean "for no particular purpose," or it might mean "just wait (and you will see and understand)." One might say to a harassing person, *nān summā irukkaddum* (just let me be). Or, to an impatient child, *summā iru* (just be, or be still). Although nobody has ever said this to me, I imagine that a fundamental aspect of Tamil childhood is *summā*. Not *summā* in the sense of being still and waiting, but *summā* in the sense of just being and doing, without burden.

There is a genre of poetry in the Tamil countries called *piḷḷaittamiṛ,* "child-Tamil."[11] It is a sort of praise poetry, in which the person praised is placed in a state of ideal childhood somewhat as I have described it above. All the known *piḷḷaittamiṛ* poems were composed by men, but all are animated by the voice of a woman or girl caring for the child. Each verse of a *piḷḷaittamiṛ* poem is based on some action of the child or done with respect to the child. These actions include the caregiver's beseeching the moon to come and play with the child or asking a god or gods to protect the child. Some involve requesting actions of the child: asking the child to come, move her tongue (say "la la"), rock her body back and forth, give the caregiver a kiss, or clap her hands. The poems may entreat a girl child to play in water or on a swing, or ask a boy child to beat his little drum or drive his little toy chariot. Girl children playing together may plead with a boy child not to knock down the little sand houses they've made on the beach. These are all things we can imagine children doing, with their caregivers acting as an appreciative audience. One can even in real life, in modern times, see doting caregivers beg children to do cute things that they like to do anyway: "Bat your big eyes," "Pretend you're a photographer taking a picture," "Sing [a particular song]," "Dance [a particular dance]." I have seen this both in India and in Sri Lanka. But the *piḷḷaittamiṛ* poems take us far beyond any conventional childhood and carry us into worlds of myth and fantasy.

The being who inhabits a *piḷḷaittamiṛ* poem is charmingly innocent but not unsexed; she or he can be the most erotic of creatures. The same being is also not merely an object of adoration and indulgence. In Paula Richman's words, "These little babies wield salvific power."[12] With a wave of her hand, a *piḷḷaittamiṛ* child can create and destroy the universe. If we can accept the idea that some babies, and some older people, too, may have fantasies of omnipotence, then we can perhaps understand how it would please an actual person to have such a poem written for them. If we can further accept the idea that among Tamil (and many other) people, little children are typically adored, then we may understand how an adult may be pleased to be likened to a little child.[13] And even before the *piḷḷaittamiṛ* was invented, many gods were worshipped as children.

Your childhood ends as your fantasies end. As you must give more of your thought and energy to the tasks and problems of real life, and lose the habits of play and pretense, you become an adult. Some individuals never become adults, and some never know childhood, but almost all of us live in a mix of play and necessity. Both are essential to human existence, and neither is better than the other. When you are very young, you distinguish clearly between play and not-play; but as you grow older, the distinction dissolves between what you must do and what you do for no purpose. Sport becomes grimly purposeful. War is waged over what-if.

PLAY

In a state of play you delineate a space and a time within which the ordinary rules of life are suspended, and other rules are created and brought into force. You must forget the ordinary world, which distracts you from the play. All kinds of reasons have been imagined for play: for instance, that it is juvenile practice for adult life. However, the reason I will go with here is that it has no reason beyond itself. As with dreaming, we need to do it, but nobody knows why. Sometimes, but not always, it involves competition. Sometimes, but not always, it involves fantasy. Always, though, players must transcend themselves, be what they are not; in this sense they are impossible, yet they exist, and therefore they are supernatural. In the form of play called theater, as well as in cinema and computer-based transformations of what can be seen and (momentarily, at least) believed, and in art as a form of play where anything is possible, the surreal is always present. In the form of play called sport — closely related to organized warfare, as Johan Huizinga and others have noted — people push themselves to and beyond their physical limits, exciting crowds into frenzy, for no apparent reason except perhaps the transient glory bestowed by the crowds (and the status and money afforded professional players in modern days). In the form of play called sex, desire is provoked and fulfillment postponed to a point beyond bearing. Engaged in this play, people do remarkable things that could by no stretch of the imagination be called natural. Imagination itself is taxed to exhaustion.

In Tamil the word for play is *vilaiyāḍḍu*. This is a combination of two roots: *vilai* means grow and flourish; *āḍḍu* means movement or dancing. Thus play — *vilaiyāḍḍu* — is the dance of growth and flourishing. It is something done by the young, and by gods. Tamil *tiruvilaiyāḍḍu* (Sanskrit *lila*) is the play of the gods — the sexual play between male and female, which can build up so much heat that it threatens to burn everything down, as well as the playful building and demolition of the universe. In Tamil India, certain diseases that cause internal bleeding are considered the mischievous play (*cēḍḍai*) of the goddess (*amman*). When play is irresponsible, it can cause damage. An energetic, playful child can dismantle and destroy many kinds of things. A playful god will do likewise.

In and around Batticaloa, when I asked young people what their favorite *vilaiyāḍḍu* was, they would name some organized team sport, such as cricket or football. Sports generated great enthusiasm, and much care and energy went into organizing them. In the spring, the Tigers helped organize sports contests, *vilaiyāḍḍuppōḍḍi,* in which everybody, young and old, was involved. Spontaneous, comedic events took place. Laughter and excitement brought everyone together, refreshed everyone.

WAR

In the state of war as in the state of play, imagination is taxed. I have never been in combat. Many of those who have describe it as an extraordinary experience. Stan Goff observes: "Everyone wants to focus on that luminous adrenaline Eucharist when the 'game' is on, when tomorrow is inscrutable — the delicious dread of chaos, of not knowing when or how that next bifurcation will hit."[14]

Warfare involves life-or-death struggles between enormously powerful, conscious, and sentient forces. War can only be waged between groups of human beings, or, in some mythologies, between gods. We sometimes speak of individual human beings waging war against other individuals (as in war between a husband and wife), but this is just a metaphorical use of the word *war*, unless the individuals in question mobilize whole armies to kill and die for their sakes.

Warfare is a numinous, social event. Things happen in war that the mind cannot comprehend. Your close companion of many years who was living, acting, and vital until just a moment ago is suddenly — something else. In warfare, human bodies are torn open, their insides revealed shining red in the light of day. Fiery explosions blossom like flowers. Corpses soften and emit their sweet stench.

Both Tamil and Sinhala civilizations have long histories and elaborate mythologies of warfare, but none of this has prepared the people for the kind of war being waged on the island today. Most of the history and mythology of war has either proved irrelevant to the present situation, or, if mobilized, has been twisted and forced into use as propaganda, though it has not succeeded in that purpose. Moreover, careful reading of the old texts reveals a serious questioning of the institution of warfare. These old texts and the questions they raise are explored in chapter 2.

Unlike the texts used as propaganda, one old Tamil text about war, the *Kalingattuparani*, resonates deeply with modern representations of warfare as created by the Tamil Tigers themselves.[15] In fact, it resonates with some Western twentieth-century portrayals of warfare, such as Joseph Heller's *Catch-22*, in that the grisly and the comedic meet in a surreal space that threatens to spill into madness. In the *Kalingattuparani*, however, the madness that would otherwise arise from the intense, prolonged suffering of war is evaded by the fact that the only suffering depicted is the hunger of demons, who are soon to be sated with the corpses lying on a battlefield, and the sexual frustration of women, who are about to be filled with the lust of their young men returning fresh from the battle.

The Tiger films, street theater, and other performances I have seen, while avoiding the topic of sex, were upbeat about death, with no trace of bitterness or irony. Films examined corpses on the battlefield with clinical enthusiasm. The filmmakers watched and commented on the quality of the films, while I watched the filmmakers, who knew I was watching them and were evidently quite comfortable with the situation. Other performances were even more heavily laminated, so that the questions of what was real and what was representation, what was inside and what was outside, were rendered completely unanswerable, and so we ceased to ask such questions. Live performances were Halloweenish, complete with dancing skeletons (dancers wearing skeleton costumes) jumping out from the dark at the audience of children and adults, who jumped back, startled, and then laughed.

I cannot know how the Tigers experienced actual battle. But they represented it to me and other civilians as child's play — fully intense, concentrated, and serious, but also elevated above the mundane world, and fun.

CHAPTER 2

The Past

Some Metaphors

It is not the aim of this book to explain or make sense of the war in Sri Lanka.[1] Many millions of words have been written on this topic by people more knowledgeable than I. For me, this war is a context in which certain aspects of being human are illuminated in unique combinations of lights. Sri Lanka has been called a laboratory for the study of ethnic conflict, but it is not that for me. In a laboratory, conditions are controlled. In Sri Lanka, they are not. The violence in Sri Lanka, at the magnitude and intensity it has maintained for more than twenty years, is a severe affliction upon the people who make up Sri Lankan society, most of all the poor of all regions and all ethnicities. I would like to think this book may somehow ameliorate that affliction, but I know better than to expect such an outcome. I do not intend to make any prescriptions.

The aim of this book is to examine childhood, warfare, and play, as related and intersecting states of being, in the context of Batticaloa and Paduvankarai during the most intense phase of the Sri Lankan conflict so far. But the ramifications of the small, local events recounted in the ethnographic chapters of this book will not be evident to general readers in the absence of some description of how the overall war is configured.

Such a description cannot refer only to the actions of people in a closely circumscribed locality and period of time. In that sense, it cannot be purely ethnographic. It must be historical, shown as emerging from long social processes, patterns, and habits, to be understood in something like the way the parties to the conflict understand it. Chronologically ordered chains of cause and effect, however, are not what this chapter is about. History is not the same thing as what happened in the past. History includes only the events that get recorded and the records that receive later attention. And these records are not mirrors of events; they are interpretations. Records from a thousand years ago may receive more attention from people in the present, and be much more influential, than records from an intervening period. To the extent that it is read and heard by people in the present, a historical document is a thing existing in the present; and in this chapter I treat historical documents that way. The ones to which I devote the most attention are among the ones best known by the parties to the current conflict. On the foundation of such documents, both ancient and recent, they build their arguments for continuing the struggle.

My description in this chapter is a compilation and digest of information from multiple sources. None of the information or interpretation is original. I have put the description in my own words to give it coherence. Some of my own thoughts are added; I have dwelt at length on details that I believe are of special significance in the present moment, and I have only touched on certain historical eras to which whole books have been devoted. Rather than focusing on political economy and assuming this to be the foundation of all warfare, I focus on ideology, because I believe that the current war in Sri Lanka is principally a war of ideology. I do not like to label this conflict an "ethnic" war: that is too simple a concept, and very misleading. But it is also certainly not a class war; it is not a war between different ways of life (such as farming versus herding, or agriculture versus industry); and it is not primarily a war over resources, although the question of who controls what resources is obviously of great importance, as it always has been. Much as I would like to say that the war in Sri Lanka is strictly a modern phenomenon, having no deep roots, I am no longer persuaded that this is the case. There are deep roots. These roots have nothing to do with one "tribe" in conflict with another, still less with one "civilization" versus another. They have to do with a habit of intellectual, emotional, and physical struggle over issues profound and trivial, funny and deadly, that human beings engage in. They have to do with tortuous streams of thought, and long, multistranded threads of conversation and argument drifting over time from one topic to another, seemingly unrelated one, merging and diverging, with early participants wandering out and new participants wandering in. Sometimes these threads get caught together and snarled into knots.

One way to imagine the war in Sri Lanka, then, is as a giant knot made of many smaller knots, all tangled together and pulled tight. Efforts to untie the knot create new knots that get pulled into the whole. Simplified representations do not help, and cutting the knot is not an option, as the entire society has become inseparable from the knot that binds it. By "cutting the knot" I do not mean partitioning of the island into two or more sovereign states. This is in principle an option, but in practice it is not possible at present because of the powerful voices demanding that all the people of the island live under one strong central government. The resistance to devolution of power is a tightening force. Such a force is not good or evil in itself: it is merely an intrinsic and intractable part of the knot. Once someone has attained a level of power, such as control or the illusion of control over a whole country, they will be unwilling, and indeed unable, to relinquish it. It must be wrested from them. The need for control in frightening and unpredictable times adds ferocity to the insistence on nondevolution of power and maintenance of central control, or some facsimile of control, on the island. But even more powerful forces than the need for central control pull against the tightening, most importantly the human need to be free of subjugation, humiliation, impoverishment, separation from loved people and places, murder, torture, and predation. Last but not least is the vital importance to individuals and local communities of control over the circumstances of their own lives. The smaller knots that have been drawn into the larger one are petty personal quarrels and feuds, fights over resources, and the delusions of power, pride, and raw greed.

A more abstract way of imagining the conflict in Sri Lanka is to posit that it is historically overdetermined. An event is historically overdetermined if it has several contributing causes, any one of which could have led to the event or something much like it. Rather than causes, one might more accurately speak of historical vectors or forces, including intentional human movements with specific goals. A single vector may split into two or more vectors traveling in different directions, and two or more vectors may merge into one. If it is possible to speak of turbulence in the interaction of vectors, then the war may be considered a site of giant turbulence, a storm.

This storm broke in July 1983. A newcomer to the study of Sri Lanka must learn this first of all. The Tamil Tigers up to that moment were a small band of young men who used guns and explosives to register their views. They had few civilian supporters. Then one night they blew up a government military vehicle in Jaffna, killing nineteen soldiers. Word of the event reached Colombo. Cries, falsely proclaiming, "The Tigers are coming [here, to Colombo]," hit the streets. Crowds panicked. Every Tamil person was suddenly not just under suspicion of being a Tiger but convicted immediately of being a dangerous monster. Hundreds of ordinary Tamil civilians were massacred by gangs of Sinhalese men. The victims were cut down with knives and machetes, beaten to death with clubs or slabs of concrete, or doused in kerosene and burned alive. The violence spread to the hill country, where, as in Colombo, Tamils lived and worked among Sinhalese. Some of the killers carried voter lists indicating which houses were Tamil — thus some acts of anti-Tamil destruction were probably planned in advance.[2] But the madness went beyond whatever may have been centrally planned. Individuals took advantage of the chaos to rob, batter or destroy their own real or perceived enemies. Mobs coalesced. "The rioters were the denizens of downtown: men in sarongs; youths in trousers; women in skirts, saris, or traditional wraps; bureaucrats in office clothes; some white-hair elders." Such mobs of people from all walks of life converged upon groups of Tamils and killed them.[3] When the killers saw people on the road, they murdered anyone, rich or poor, man, woman, or child, whom they determined (by speech or identity cards) to be Tamil. Police assisted in the anti-Tamil violence, or stood idly by. In addition to the destruction of life, millions of dollars worth of property owned by Tamils — homes, stores, hotels, and industries — went up in flames.[4]

The events of July 1983 were not the first manifestation of violence against Tamils in which the government was complicit, but they were the worst. The mobsters, looters, and killers were not representative of Sinhala society as a whole. But they prevailed, and there was no organized protection against them.

Before July 1983, both Tamils and Sinhalese thought of their country as a civilized place. Afterward, most Sinhalese went into denial about the enormity of what had happened. Some expressed the view that the Tamils had it coming. And Tamils who had previously been pacifists — from middle-class professionals and wealthy traders to landless laborers — decided that war against the Sri Lankan government was the only option left to them if they wanted to be free of Sinhala domination and its accompanying horrors. They mobilized their physical, material and intellectual resources toward this end. The conflict between the LTTE and the Sri Lankan government has been raging ever since.

To understand how and why this storm broke and how and why it has followed this particular course, one must consider myriad factors. Here

I describe just a few of the features that constitute Sinhala and Tamil cultures and try to indicate the roles they have played in the current war.

Ancient History

The first human beings set foot on the land now called Sri Lanka perhaps as early as fifty thousand years ago. Recent evidence suggests that India may have been settled first from the south, instead of from the north, as was previously assumed.[5] Thus the island of Lanka may have been settled many millennia before *Homo sapiens sapiens* ventured into central and northern India. Even if the first human settlers came from the north, it is certain that the people of Lanka and southern India raised their children, became familiar with the landscape, the flora and fauna, and developed their cultures, their technologies, their languages, their arts, and their spirits and minds long before anyone spoke of Siva or Buddha or Tamil or Sinhala or Sanskrit.

The earliest written inscriptions known from that area were created only about two and a half thousand years ago. But before written history, there would have been many waves of migration into and through the island, which is accessible by coastal sea routes from the Arabian peninsula and Southeast Asia and from the Indian mainland. Since its first settlement so long ago, the island has always been awash in the currents of the wide world.

Language, Religion, and Myth

LANGUAGE

The main difference between Sinhala and Tamil people is that they speak different languages. This difference is not trivial. The language you know structures the world you see and feel as real. If you know more than one language, you know more than one world. If you do not, you may have difficulty accepting that your way of understanding the world is not the only valid way. More Sinhalese and Tamils know English than know each other's languages. Few Sinhalese are motivated to learn Tamil. Some urban Tamils take the trouble to learn at least spoken Sinhalese, in large part to facilitate their getting along in a country where Sinhalese-speaking people constitute a majority.

The majority of Tamil-speaking people live not in Sri Lanka but in southern India. There are also old Tamil communities in Malaysia, Fiji, Mauritius, and other places. More recent Tamil communities, collectively called the Tamil diaspora, have developed in Western countries. There are presently about seventy million Tamil speakers in the world. There are only about ten million Sinhalese, of whom the great majority live in Sri Lanka.

The origins of the Sinhala language are enshrined in legend. The word *Sinhala* (*sihala* in Pali) means "people of the lion." The first written use of this word as a name for the island or the people on it came in the chronicles *Dīpavāmsa* and *Mahāvāmsa* of the fourth to fifth centuries A.D. The *Mahāvāmsa* traces the descent of the Sinhala people to a lion, hence their name.

Linguistic evidence suggests that the Sinhala language is related to the languages of central India. Hence the Sinhala language, together with north and central Indian languages generally, may be ultimately derived from Sanskrit, in combination with other, more local languages. It is said that the Sinhala language is remarkably homogeneous throughout the island — that is, relatively free of dialect variation — perhaps partly because the Sinhala nationalist movement of the late nineteenth and early twentieth centuries entailed the promotion of "pure" Sinhala.[6] (There was a pure-Tamil movement among Tamils also). The pure-Sinhala movement, like the pure-Tamil movement, never caught on among the masses, but it did result in a standardized orthography and grammar for written Sinhalese. Because a large proportion of Sinhalese people are literate and educated, the standardization of the written language would have conduced to reduction in dialect variation throughout the island. Literacy and standardization of forms in turn allowed the development of what Benedict Anderson calls print nationalism.[7] "From 1860 to 1900, there were hundreds of Sinhala newspapers and periodicals. After that, it became thousands."[8]

The Tamil language and the people who speak it have no mythological origin. Tamil is one of a group of languages spoken in southern India known as Dravidian languages. These are grammatically and phonetically distinct from languages spoken in the north but very similar to one another. Analysis of inscriptions from the Indus Valley civilization of 2500 B.C. indicates that the people there spoke some kind of proto-Dravidian language. This evidence does not necessarily contradict the theory that the first South Asian settlers came from the south, or that Dravidian languages originated there. To the best of modern historical knowledge,

Tamil-speaking people have lived in southern India for as long as there have been Tamil-speaking people. It is not unlikely that they settled in Lanka, together with any other peoples already there, before writing was introduced to the area. Inscriptional evidence puts Tamil Buddhist monks on the island of Lanka from the early centuries A.D.

The earliest extant Tamil literature is called Sangam literature because it is believed to have arisen from academies or gatherings (*sangam*) of scholars and poets. Extant Sangam literature is dated from about the first through about the fifth century A.D. Most Sangam literature consists of collections of short poems about either love or war. This poetry is naturalistic and humanistic in tone and usually bears no overt religious agenda. Features of the natural landscape, together with small but telling details of daily human, animal, and plant life, are woven into the poetry to indicate different emotional moods.[9]

RELIGION

Religious differences among Tamils and Sinhalese are more complicated than linguistic differences: in popular practice there is no sharp line between Sinhala religion and Tamil religion. Most Sinhalese subscribe to a variant of Theravada Buddhism currently called Sinhala Buddhism. Theravada Buddhism is based on early Buddhist texts written in Pali. It includes the idea that only a monk following the path of the Buddha can achieve spiritual liberation. Laypeople can improve their karma in various ways, including by feeding monks; but without joining the *sangha* (the community of monks), they cannot attain enlightenment. Theravada keeps itself separate from Mahayana Buddhism, which developed about eight hundred years after the life and death of the Buddha. According to Mahayana teachings, you do not have to be a monk to achieve spiritual liberation. They also raise the bar of spiritual achievement: the highest level of enlightenment is not *arhat* (someone who has achieved personal liberation) but *bodhisattva* (someone who refuses to be free until all other creatures are free and who works for the liberation of others from suffering). Mahayana supplanted Theravada in India and thence spread north to Tibet, Mongolia, China, Korea, and Japan. Theravada persists in Sri Lanka, Burma, Thailand, Vietnam, Laos, and Cambodia. Buddhism was supplanted in India by Islam, in conjunction with other religious forces: Saivism (the worship of Siva), Vaishnavism (the worship of Vishnu), and Christianity. Sri Lanka is therefore now geographically isolated from other predominantly Buddhist countries.

Tamil people practice any religion they want or none at all. Most Sri Lankan Tamils who have religion are either Saivas or Christians (some Catholics, some Protestants). Sri Lankan Muslims are the second-largest minority after Tamils. They speak Tamil at home and among themselves, but they do not consider themselves ethnic Tamils. They are descended from Arab traders who came first to southwestern India and later settled in eastern Lanka, marrying local women. In India, Tamil-speaking Muslims consider themselves to be culturally both Tamil and Muslim.

Sinhala Buddhist religious history is entirely confined to the island of Sri Lanka, and little is known about indigenous island religion before the Buddhist chronicles. Sri Lankan Tamil religious history is merged with South Indian religious history. The latter in turn developed continuously from local indigenous religious practices to participation in pan–South Asian religious practices, stories, and philosophies.

From about the eighth century A.D., fierce verbal and sometimes physical feuds among Buddhists, Jains, Saivas, and Vaishnavas in southern India took place. These feuds roughly coincided with the rise of religious devotionalism (Tamil *pattu;* Sanskrit *bhakti*) in southern India and the flowering of many kinds of devotional poetry.

The word *devotion* does not entirely capture the meaning of *pattu* or *bhakti*. It is passionate and total, agonizing and struggle-ridden, ego-annihilating devotion. All the Tamil religions, including Christianity as practiced in the Tamil countries, contain an element of *pattu*. The philosophical idea behind the religious practice of *pattu/bhakti* is that the natural human emotions can be a vehicle for spiritual liberation and dissolution of self into the divine. This idea was alien to ascetic philosophies, which taught that the passions are enemies and obstacles on the path to spiritual release. Buddhism taught that there is no eternal self or soul (*ātmā*), nor is there an eternal God. This idea too was anathema to those for whom the whole aim of life was personal devotion to a personal god, an eternal bond between the soul of the worshipper and the soul of the god. One can see how South Indian theologians, in the mode of academics today, could get into nasty disputes and even come to blows over which approach was correct.

Mahayana Buddhism developed through the thought of the great philosopher Nagarjuna, who lived in southern India during the second or third century A.D. One can see in Mahayana a reconciliation between the insistent passionlessness of Theravada Buddhism and the passionate devotionalism of Tamil *pattu*.

Liberation in Buddhist thought consists in the realization that nothing exists in itself: everything we experience as enduringly real is only a construct, a temporary conglomeration of other things. The knowledge that all creatures are ephemeral constructs with no real existence in themselves should, logically, disable all feeling for them. One cannot have feeling for something one knows to be an illusion. For instance, when one awakens from a dream containing an illusory lover, one's passion for that lover dissolves. Nevertheless, in Mahayana, compassion for creatures is, paradoxically, equivalent to ultimate knowledge in the person of the *bodhisattva,* the "truly enlightened," who postpones his or her own extinction and release from the world in order to stay and save other creatures, including of course human beings, from the suffering of sentient existence. The motivation for this stay is not reason but compassion, or love, a natural human sentiment.

Buddhism flourished in southern India alongside other religions for a number of centuries before being scattered and absorbed by non-Buddhist religious institutions there and eventually disappearing from India altogether. Mahayana Buddhism became "corrupted" (in the view of some scholars) by *pattu/bhakti.* People came to believe that all they had to do to be saved was call out to the Bodhisattva to save them. After all, the Bodhisattva remained among sentient beings only to save them. The Bodhisattva is the manifestation of purest love. An individual person therefore does not need to go through all the mental exercises prescribed by early Buddhism to attain enlightenment: one need only trust in the love of the Bodhisattva and one will be saved, depart this world of suffering, and be born again into a perfect and heavenly world — the closest thing to nirvana that ordinary people were thought capable of imagining.[10]

Pattu-enraptured Buddhism, though it disappeared from India, resurfaced in China in the form of devotion to the female *bodhisattva* Kwan Yin, who remains the favorite deity of the Chinese people. Kwan Yin, like the *pattu*-inspiring deities of South India, is available to anyone who calls her, regardless of rank or social station.

It is generally accepted that Buddhism first came to Sri Lanka during the reign of King Asoka in northern India in the third century B.C. — three centuries after the life of the Buddha. This was before Mahayana schools of thought arose, but there were already bitter disagreements among different groups of Buddhists. Asoka was a powerful proponent of Buddhism who sought to restore peace among the disagreeing factions and promoted the spread of the religion throughout South Asia.

The earliest extant Lankan Buddhist texts, the *Dīpavaṃsa* and the *Mahāvaṃsa,* were composed in Pali between the fourth and fifth centuries A.D. The *Dīpavaṃsa* is considered a crude early chronicle; the *Mahāvaṃsa* is said to be more coherent and is more frequently cited in teaching and debate. Modern Sinhala Buddhist nationalists think of the *Mahāvāmsa* as a sacred text.

MYTH

The *Mahāvāmsa* recounts the genealogies and lives of the first Buddhist kings on the island. It also describes the mythological origin of the Sinhala people. The *Mahāvāmsa* makes it clear that Sinhala Lankan kings were from the start immoral people. Even though they were willed by the Buddha to be protectors of Buddhism on the island, their behavior was in violation of everything Buddhism stands for. Thus the chroniclers demonstrate to readers that they have taken on, or been assigned (we don't know which), an impossible task: to marry the Buddhist religion to the history of kingship on the island. They could have portrayed the kings as exemplars of virtue, but they chose the opposite route. Perhaps (again, we will never know) the chroniclers were warning their readers that this marriage would lead to trouble. And in fact it has, in the modern age. The current conflict is exacerbated by, or might even not have happened without, this marriage.

The very first story of the Sinhala people tells us that their originating ancestors, who were savage troublemakers before they arrived on the island, became civilizing proponents of Buddhism after they entered the island. Vijaya, the eldest grandson of a lion and an amorous princess, is of evil conduct, and so is expelled with his followers to sea. They land on an island from which they are expelled, as before, for troublemaking. Then they arrive on the island of Lanka.

The *Mahāvāmsa* contains exciting war stories about the conquering Buddhist kings. The most famous of the Sinhala warrior kings is Duttagamani, who is fated before he is born to make war against Damilas (the Sinhala name for Tamils), defeat the Tamil king Elara, and unify the island so that "the doctrine [of Buddhism] will shine brightly." Defeating and killing Elara becomes an obsession with him.

Elara is not represented as evil. He shows compassion for the smallest creature and is fanatically evenhanded. He also shows a unique propensity for self-sacrifice. His *tapas* — the intensity of his self-punishment — is so powerful that it overcomes the whole hierarchy of supernatural authorities, including Buddha, in whom Elara does not even believe; and in this way he gets his desire, which is for the rain to fall at just the right times and places in his kingdom.

Elara is destined to be killed so that dharma will prevail. His killer is the violent and headstrong Duttagamani. Against the will of his parents, Duttagamani goes to war first against his loyal brother, and then against the righteous Elara. In a great battle, Duttagamani defeats Elara's armies and kills Elara. He immediately builds a monument honoring Elara and commands that the monument be kept as a place of worship forever.

After the great battle is over, Duttagamani grieves because of the millions of deaths he has caused. But the *bhikkus* (Buddhist monks) comfort him by saying that really he has taken only one and a half human lives, because, of all those he killed, only one had embraced the Three Refuges, and one had adopted the Five Precepts.[11] The others killed do not matter so much because they did not worship the Buddha and were therefore no better than animals.

The fact that Buddhist doctrine forbids destroying *any* life, human or animal, adds irony to the story, as the compilers of these legends surely must have seen.[12] But it is more than just irony. Duttagamani's story embodies the dilemma faced by all kings who must shed blood to defend a religion that denounces bloodshed as foul and immoral.[13]

And it is not only kings who face a dilemma. The *bhikkus* face one even worse. Are they to follow the Buddhist precepts and advise the king accordingly, or are they to placate him? By cynically advising the king that in killing countless creatures he has committed no great sin, the *bhikkus* show the reader (or the chroniclers show us) how corrupt they have already become. The *Mahāvāmsa* seems to assume that unification of a large territory under a single flag entails warfare and bloodshed. In a unified state, ideally, there is no violent conflict. In fact, unity is almost synonymous with peace in this worldview, and both are conjoined with a notion of justice. But violent conflict is necessary to establish the unified state in the first place. Again the message seems to be that a king cannot be a Buddhist, that, in general, kingship and Buddhism cannot be reconciled. But today, as then, the idea of a unified Sri Lanka is sacred to Sinhalese Buddhists, and they cite the *Mahāvāmsa* in support of their claim that the island belongs to them alone.

The *Mahāvāmsa* also presupposes that an ambitious king needs someone to conquer. Thus Duttagamani goes on conquering rampages, even heedlessly killing some of his own men. He insists that his warfare is not selfish but intended to spread the doctrine of the Buddha.

After the great battle in which Elara is defeated and the island united, Duttagamani hands out honors to the warriors who have fought for him. One warrior refuses to accept any reward. When asked why, the warrior answers, "This is war." Duttagamani further asks the warrior, "When a single realm is created, what war is there?" And the warrior answers, "I will do battle with those rebels, the passions, wherein victory is hard to win." And the warrior thus renounces worldly life. This incident illustrates that the passions are viewed as rebels and mortal enemies. It also underlines the point already made about the incompatibility of kingship, when it entails war, and Buddhism.

Although Duttagamani has been absolved of any serious wrongdoing by the *bhikkus*, he is still not certain of his own salvation, because he remembers that, having vowed never to take a meal without the *bhikkus*, he once ate a pepper pod, leaving none for the *bhikkus*, and for this lapse he must make reparation. He builds a great monastery to house *bhikkus* and *bhikkunis* (female renouncers). This incident reveals that failure to share even a morsel with the *bhikkus* is a worse sin than slaying countless people and animals without cause. But certainly this episode, which need not have been recounted, is another comment by the chroniclers about the corruption of Buddhism.

The king gives numerous costly treasures to the *bhikkus*. The chapter ends with the comment, "Treasures which, in truth, bear on them the blot of the five faults become, if they be acquired by people who are gifted with special wisdom, possessed of the five advantages, therefore let the wise man strive to have them thus." It becomes apparent that *bhikkus* in Buddhist Lanka played the same role as Brahmans in Hindu South India — they accepted gifts from a king who had obtained them by violent and polluting means, including warfare, and by their acceptance of the gifts purified the king of his sin.

The *Mahāvāmsa* is not about good versus evil. Nor is it about Sinhalese versus Tamils. It is an effort to reconcile the bloody history of kingship and conquest on the island with institutionalized Buddhism: to give divine sanction to the lineage of kings and the stories of their exploits and to portray the community of *bhikkus* as indispensable to legitimate governance by Sinhala kings. On a broader level, it is about warfare, dharma, human destinies, and human flaws, and in this respect it has some things in common with the *Mahābhārata*. It is a complex work. I have suggested that the chroniclers deliberately revealed the contradictions inherent in the alliance between *bhikkus* and kings. Alternatively, one may argue that the chroniclers lived in a world where ethical contradictions were not perceived. But I don't believe the chroniclers were so ignorant.

The *Mahāvāmsa* was composed in Lanka before the period of intense religious antagonisms in the Tamil region in India, at a time when Buddhism, Jainism, and the worship of what would now be called Hindu gods were not so much at odds with each other. Prince Vijaya in the *Mahāvāmsa* sought and received a princess for himself and wives for his ministers from a south Indian king. But even by the time the *Mahāvāmsa* was written, Theravada Buddhism in India was losing ground to Mahayana Buddhism. Although the *Mahāvāmsa* never mentions other forms of Buddhism, one of the motives for its composition may have been to shore up the position of Theravada monastic communities in relation to Lankan kingly states, as these monastic communities found themselves losing the patronage of Indian kings to other religions.

If the dating is correct, then the *Mahāvāmsa* would have been composed around the end of the Sangam period in southern India. It is possible that while the *Mahāvāmsa* was being put into writing in Lanka, the Tamil Jain and Buddhist stories of *Silappadikāram* and *Maṇimēkalai* (dated between the third and seventh centuries A.D.) were being put into writing in southern India. I say "put into writing" because all three texts would have had oral precursors that went much further back in time. Whereas *Silappadikāram* is not about any specific, named religion (the Saiva goddess Minakshi is the most important but not the only deity in the story, one of the principal and most sympathetic characters is a Buddhist nun, and the book was written by a Jain ascetic), *Maṇimēkalai* is very specifically about Mahayana Buddhism. Both books are also about the power of women, most of all the power of girls in their teens. This theme remains salient in Tamil culture, but not among Sinhalese.

The story of *Silappadikāram* (The Ankle Bracelet) is still well known and exists in multiple oral and written variants in southern India and Lanka. The heroine of the story, Kannaki, marries at the age of twelve. Her husband is the young Kovalan. Sometime after their marriage, Kovalan takes up with the courtesan Madhavi, who is also twelve years old and trained in all the arts. Kovalan later returns to Kannaki, all his wealth spent. The couple travel to the city of Madurai to sell Kannaki's golden ankle bracelet and make a new start. There, Kovalan is unjustly accused of theft and killed by order of the city's king. Kannaki goes mad with rage, tears off her left breast, and hurls it into the dust. The city bursts into flame. She wanders through the countryside in a state of distraction for fourteen days, after which she is taken to heaven by the gods.

The Chera king Senguttuvan, learning Kannaki's story, vows to honor her by traveling to the Himalayas, carving out a block of stone there, and bringing it back to his own country to turn it into a monument.[14] En route he will conquer all the kings of the north. Senguttuvan's chief minister tells him, "No one can stop you if you choose to impose Tamil rule over the whole sea-encircled world." The minister further advises the king to carry with him a baked clay seal on which are stamped all the emblems of all the Tamil kings, so that all the great northern kings will know of his coming.

This story contains the first mention of the concept of Tamil political unity, as well as of world conquest by a Tamil king.[15] The idea of world conquest seems to have been in the air at that time. In Theravada Buddhism, the Buddha had come to be seen as a king and world conqueror.[16] Alexander the Great entered northern India in 327 B.C. with world conquest on his mind. But in northern India, his expedition faltered, and Alexander with his armies returned westward.

Where Alexander failed, it is unlikely that Senguttuvan could have succeeded, and have conquered all of north India. But that is not the issue. The point is the story and the precedent it may set. As he is about to go on his expedition northward, Senguttuvan is angered by rumors of kings who disparage him, and he wants to attack them. One of the king's counselors, the Brahman Madalan, seeks to rein in his ambition through diplomacy, by telling him that words disparaging him could only have been spoken by the Chola and Pandyan kings. No northern king would dare oppose him. "Therefore, appease your wrath."[17] The implication here seems to be that even if the Chola and Pandyan kings speak disrespectfully of him, they are really on his side, because they are southern and Tamil, like him. Also, the kings of the north are considered weaker and easier to conquer than the kings of the south. Hence his minister advises him to "be firm in your resolve" and attack the northern kings but to leave the southern kings alone.

Both the Brahman Madalan and the king himself desire unity among the southern kings. But for Senguttuvan, this unity consists in nobody's criticizing him, whereas for Madalan the unity of the Tamil kings consists in their not fighting each other.

Senguttuvan returns victorious from his expedition to the north. But again some of the southern kings criticize him, this time for mistreating his captives. Again Senguttuvan grows angry with them, "his eyes casting flames." Again he contemplates war against his critical neighbors, and again Madalan talks him out of it.

"King of the sea-encircled world," says Madalan, "give up anger." He reminds Senguttuvan that he is aging and that during fifty years of rule he has made no sacrifices to please the gods and protect the land. He has only "contributed to the hecatombs of war." Madalan persuades Senguttuvan to give up his thoughts of war and instead prepare a great sacrifice. Senguttuvan starts the preparations for the sacrifice and frees the enemy kings he has imprisoned. He thereby shows he has accepted the criticism of the southern kings and righted the wrong they justly accused him of. Here the poet cites a proverb: "The virtue of women is of no use where the king has failed first to establish the reign of justice."

How is one to interpret this proverb in this context? That virtuous women alone cannot ensure the well-being of a country? That a woman's virtue is of no use to her, when she lives beneath an unjust king? This second interpretation would certainly have applied to Kannaki. But the poet continues, apparently speaking in his own voice, to point out that the injustice done to Kannaki resulted in a series of tragedies far exceeding the suffering of this one woman, culminating in the conquering expedition of Senguttuvan and the killing of many people. The story of Senguttuvan is only incidentally connected to that of Kannaki. If there is a deeper connection, it may be that the anger of Kannaki is transferred somehow to the already combative Senguttuvan and empowers him to go on his not entirely justifiable conquering mission. We are left to ponder the value of anger.

The sequel to the *Silappadikāram* is the *Manimēkalai*. Manimekalai is the daughter, by Kovalan, of the courtesan Madhavi. She is expected to follow in her mother's footsteps, but she does not. Threatened with rape by a powerful prince, she must flee and hide. Like her mother, she is only twelve when the turning point of her life arrives.

Manimekalai is destined to receive a magic bowl, always filled with an infinite supply of the best food, so that the possessor of the bowl can feed as many people or creatures as come her way. The bowl has been thrown into a lake by the king Aputra, who received it from the goddess of learning. Aputra discarded the bowl in despair when deprived of people and creatures to feed, and then starved himself to death in solitude. When Manimekalai approaches the lake, the bowl flies into her hands. The goddess of the sea, Manimekalai's namesake and protector, then delivers a lecture on hunger:

Hunger is the most hateful of maladies. It degrades the most noble beings. It is the cause of all crime and kills all human feeling. . . . I cannot find words of sufficient praise to recount the merits of those generous beings who dedicate themselves to delivering man from the curse of starvation. . . . Food offered to those capable of providing it for themselves is really only a kind of exchange made under the pretext of charity. Only those who distribute food out of pure charity, expecting no return, are protectors of life in this world, which is but a temporary assembly of atoms.[18]

The suffering caused by hunger and the question of how to feed the hungry are two of the major themes of the book. In the midst of wealth and celebration, hunger is a constant presence and famine a constant threat. The god Indra, who controls the rain, may withhold it for years for no apparent reason, out of sheer malice. The only legitimate motivation to feed the hungry at that time would be pure compassion, as the author of the work makes clear. For Aputra, feeding the hungry becomes a kind of obsession. He cannot live without feeding others. And poor Manimekalai has all she can do just to keep from being raped, let alone perform acts of charity.

The related themes of rain and food, drought and famine, and the terrible power of hunger recur throughout Tamil literature. The *Tirukkural,* one of the earliest and most highly praised Tamil works, devotes one of its first sections to rain, because without rain there is no food, no life. In the *Purananuru,* bards seeking the patronage of kings describe in realistic detail the ravages of hunger on women and children.[19]

While in the *Manimekalai* the need to feed the hungry, whether humans or animals or birds, motivates the narrative, in the *Mahāvāmsa,* the imperative of feeding *bhikkus* is a constant refrain.[20] But the motivations are entirely different. An equally important theme in both the *Manimekalai* and the *Silappadikāram* is the unsurpassable power of a virtuous young girl.[21]

A large section of the *Manimekalai* is devoted to the exposition of Buddhist principles as they were learned by Manimekalai from her teachers. Alain Danielou, a modern translator of *Manimēkalai* into English, considers that Manimekalai was a historical figure and that her main preceptor, Aravana Adigal, was none other than the great Nagarjuna. The written narrative that bears Manimekalai's name contains stories within stories within stories and dwells on descriptive details of everyday life. Both the authors clearly enjoy writing narrative poetry. The exquisite beauty of life and the need to renounce enjoyment of this beauty for the very sake of all the beautiful living things on earth are themes common to the two books.

The *Mahāvāmsa* and *Silappadikāram-Manimēkalai* are not only seminal narratives in their respective cultures but also originate from approximately the same place and time. The place was the area within a radius of three hundred miles from Adam's Bridge, a series of islands connecting Sri Lanka with India. The time was a period of about three hundred years when Mahayana Buddhism was at its height in the Tamil country and Theravada Buddhism was coming into its own on the island of Lanka.

Despite the numerous differences between the Tamil and the Pali or Sinhala texts, their representations of kingship have some points in common. For instance, in both, valorous and virtuous enemies are praised: the composer of the text, Ilango, praises the brave "Aryan" warriors who fought against Senguttuvan, and the chroniclers of the *Mahāvāmsa* praise Elara, the chief enemy of Duttagamani.

As a character in a story, the Tamil Senguttuvan, like the Sinhala Duttagamani, is someone who can scarcely control his anger. Ilango states it straight out: "Senguttuvan was a quarrelsome person." Senguttuvan's innate anger is stressed in the *Silappadikāram*, just as Duttagamani's anger is stressed in the *Mahāvāmsa*. His very name, altered from plain Gamani to Duttagamani because of his childhood behavior, means "angry Gamani." Both kings put their anger to use by conquering other kings and sacking their cities, bringing riches back to their people, and reaping praise for themselves. For Duttagamani, "crossing the river" means defeating one Tamil king in Anuradhapura and then a large number of other kings, and thereby uniting the island of Lanka. For Senguttuvan it means crossing the Ganges far to the north, defeating all the kings in northern India, and thereby achieving dominion over the whole world. Both Senguttuvan and Duttagamani, having gone on brutal wars of conquest, are finally appeased, see that they must renounce their anger, and build great monuments to increase their merit.

Something, however, remains unsettled. Their deeds cannot be reconciled with the pacificist religions to which they subscribe. They are cruel men who suffer no punishment, whereas Elara and Aputra are good men who suffer cruel fates. In both the Sinhala and Tamil texts, the deep moral ambiguity, perhaps even absolute evil, of warfare is acknowledged, together with the arrogance and destructive anger of warrior kings. And yet these kings are praised, for they are perceived as necessary to the survival of their subjects.

Thus Sinhala and Tamil civilizations share the legend of a conquering, angry, and morally ambiguous, if not downright evil, king. The precedents set by these legends come into play in the current conflict.

On the female side, Kannaki of the *Silappadikāram* is considered by many modern Tamils to be an exemplar of perfect Tamil womanhood. She stands at the center of what some Tamils refer to as *tamiṛ paṇbāḍu*, Tamil culture. Neither Manimekalai nor her mother, the courtesan Madhavi, can serve as a perfect role model, for a traditional Tamil woman is expected above all else to be the chaste servant of her husband.[22] Manimekalai refuses to marry, and her mother, Madhavi, being a courtesan, is not chaste. However, Madhavi has honor and intelligence. She is skilled to perfection in all the fine arts. She is blessed with bewitching beauty, but she is no witch; she is thoroughly human.

Most important, Madhavi, like Kannaki, is very young, just twelve years old, when she enters the world of men. At that moment, she represents human perfection. We can know by a bit of extrapolation from the timing of her affair with Kovalan that she bore her daughter, Manimekalai, when she was no older than fourteen. Manimekalai is likewise perfect when she steps into the world, a pure, beautiful, highly educated twelve-year-old girl. This girl makes a hard decision to act against the tradition into which she was born, and her adherence to this decision leads her to enlightenment.

Although the authors of the *Mahāvāmsa* and *Silappadikāram-Maṇimēkalai* apparently did not know each other's works, the story of Kannaki was brought from southern India to Sri Lanka, where she became the Buddhist goddess Pattini. Gananath Obeyesekere states that Kannaki is no longer the basis of a cult in India but has been absorbed into other goddess cults there.[23] But although Kannaki is not the center of a cult in the modern Indian state of Tamil Nadu, it would be hard to find a literate adult Tamil person (and perhaps even an unlettered one) who does not know her story. Among Sinhalese people in southern Sri Lanka, Pattini is the center of a well-developed cult, with elaborate rituals incorporating stories and symbolism that are not present in the *Silappadikāram*. In addition, the Tamils of Batticaloa on the east coast of Sri Lanka continue to worship Kannaki and have temples and rituals dedicated to her. Thus the values and emotions this goddess represents are apparently shared to some degree by Sinhala and Tamil people. The terrible power of anger is certainly something that both sides respect, fear, and mobilize against real and perceived injustices.

The *Mahāvāmsa* and the texts of the Sangam period are invoked by Sinhala and Tamil nationalists to support their competing, mutually incompatible causes. But the use of these texts as propaganda tools obscures their subtexts, their ambiguities, and their thinly veiled criticisms of the existing social order. That warring kings are evil and that warfare is unconscionable may have been among the messages the writers most strongly wished to convey. One thing is clear: dynasties, religions, and birth categories of people can be made to inhere in each other only tenuously, through the sheerest and most illogical of fictions.

The early Lankan chronicles are said to have shown virulent antagonism to Tamils. However, in the *Mahāvāmsa*, this antagonism seems to be ascribed to certain characters in the texts rather than harbored by the texts' compilers and authors. No motivation for hatred of Tamils is ever offered. According to the *Mahāvāmsa,* the hero of these chronicles, Duttagamani, united under one banner a previously disunited island. This unification was seen as a good thing, but bringing it about entailed terrible evil. Tamils as a race are not described in the first Lankan chronicles one way or the other. It is not even entirely clear what the term *Damila* means in these texts: Someone who speaks the Tamil language? Who belongs to a certain society? Who has a certain lineage? Who behaves in a certain way? For that matter, it is not clear what *Sinhala* means when it refers to people.[24] Conflicts were between kings, and not between different categories of human being.

In the medieval Tamil Saiva texts, Buddhists (*bauttarkal*) were not equated with Sinhala people. Buddhists were seen by Saivas as exponents of a rival religion, and not inhabitants of a specific geographic region. Conflicts in the Tamil country, too, were between kings, who adopted one or another religious persuasion. There were also conflicts between religious communities, each carrying the banner of a different god. In fact, gods *were* kings, and kings were gods. Nevertheless, conflicts between flesh-and-blood kings, as far as can be told, primarily involved territory, whereas the conflicts between proponents of different gods involved ideas, and the winning of human followers. The god Siva was represented as a powerful conquering king; he was also represented as the very essence of love. Vaishnavas and Saivas were mutual antagonists. There were sometimes violent conflicts between proponents of different religions, all of which preached abstention from violence. All of this had little if anything to do with any naturalized categories of people. An individual's religion was a matter of personal choice. The different religions, like different political parties, tried to win people from each other. Bards and poets composed praise songs for kings as well as for gods. They could also withhold praise, or not so covertly criticize a king or chieftain for his cruelty or selfishness.[25] A good praise song for a king could win the king's patronage, and it could also serve as good publicity for the king. A good argument in favor of religion A could win followers over from religion B. That the songs and the debates had political value did not mean that they had no aesthetic, spiritual, or emotional value. They had all of these. That is why they were powerful.

Although kings fought kings and gods fought gods, and although kings were gods and gods (including the Buddha as represented in Theravada) were kings, the conflicts between gods or religions did not necessarily align with the conflicts between kings or polities. Some kings patronized only their favorite religions; others patronized all religions. In this respect, the kings of yore were not unlike modern Sri Lankan and South Indian people, who are often religiously eclectic.

The development of *pattu*-based worship in South India ultimately was not dependent on religious or political rivalries. It was and remains popular because it is available to all and because it aims for the heart. It is accessible to anyone who knows the language in which its literature was composed, and the languages of *pattu* and *bhakti* poets were the local vernaculars.

This mode of worship did not, however, catch on among people who identified themselves as Sinhalese. This may be because the very concept of Sinhalese arose as an integral part of Lankan-Buddhist historical mythology. The *Mahāvāmsa* is the only origin story and the only foundational history the Sinhala people have. There are no alternative versions. Their very identity as Sinhalese ties them to Theravada Buddhism. To have embraced South Indian–style devotionalism, even toward the Buddha, would have been a betrayal of their heritage, and most of all a betrayal of the *bhikkus*, who, like Hindu priests, mediated between common people and the divine. *Bhakti* made such mediators unnecessary: it posited a direct connection between a worshipper and the god. *Bhikkus* could not have endured a style of worship that rendered them unnecessary; they depended for their survival on laypeople's belief in their holiness.

But just as references to Buddhism were not essential to the development of Saiva devotionalism, except perhaps as a kind of foil, references to Tamils in the earliest Lankan chronicles were arguably not essential to the aim of those texts, which was to document the history of kingship in relation to Buddhism on the island, somehow finding a way to weave the two together. In both the *Mahāvāmsa* and the *Silappadikāram*, the most lauded kings are those who are driven by something deep inside them to conquer, and thus necessarily to kill. The most lauded king seeks the worthiest opponent, takes over all that is his, and thereby enriches the people at the center of the conqueror's dominion.

For all their shared values, the value of passion was and remains quite different between Tamil and Sinhalese people. In Sinhalese Buddhism, passion is a destructive and selfish force. Passion is beyond control: it is part of the dangerous wild. It is attributed to the *yakku*, the creatures of the wild, who are constantly threatening the order and equanimity of people's lives and must be kept under control.[26] Demons, gods beneath the

Buddha, and kings, the wielders of earthly power, are allowed to experience passion. In fact, they own it. Aspirants to spiritual peace and freedom, however, renounce it. *Bhikku*s are, in the ideal, passionless people.

In contrast, a strong current in Tamil and other South Indian literature
portrays passion as a beautiful but dangerous gift. It is there to be channeled and mobilized for the sake of the highest good. Without passion,
nothing can be done. Nature (which includes the dangerous wild) is
beautiful, to be embraced and enjoyed.

If one considers the *Mahāvāmsa,* the *Silappadikāram,* and *Maṇimēkalai*
as threads in the knot, or as streams drawn into the storm of the current
armed conflict in Sri Lanka, it is essential to view these books not as
accounts of "what really happened" so long ago, but rather to think of
them as stories, or collections of stories, that have endured over time or
have been "rediscovered," in part because they have been written down.
But then again, were they not written down, and kept over all these years,
because they are great stories? Stories can have tremendous power in
moving people to think in certain ways and act in certain ways.

One scholar has aptly suggested that the *Mahāvāmsa* is not so much
about the victory of "Sinhala protonationalism" over "Dravidian imperi-
alism" as it is about "the first real success of centripetalism over centrifu-
galism in Sri Lanka's history."[27] Setting aside the question of whether the
Mahāvāmsa is history or something else, the observation about central-
ization versus decentralization, pulling in versus letting go, pertains to the
metaphorical knot that I posited at the beginning of this chapter.[28] Still,
it is not entirely clear that these two forces are at work in the ancient
chronicle. The idea of the conquering hero, whose cruelty and destructive
power are employed in service to the Buddha, strikes me as a more central theme of the text. A second major theme, repeatedly stressed, is the
importance of maintaining the entire island under Sinhala Buddhist rule.

The models of kingship developed in the old Sinhala and Tamil texts
were preserved in the texts throughout the years of colonization; but the
practice of kingship, with all its unwritten rules, its compromises, its
checks and balances, was washed away. In the mid-twentieth century, at
the time of independence, these models were revived and deployed, but
the new versions were missing the balances and compromises that may
have existed before. Some of the modern, democratically elected leaders
of Lanka have been nothing but powermongers for whom neither
dharma nor any modern notion of fairness and justice was ever a concern.
(Of course, this is true of many modern, democratically elected leaders in
other nations, too.)

Medieval History

After the early chronicles, Sinhala-Buddhist-Lankan and Tamil-Saiva histories continue, not surprisingly, to focus on kings and conquests. In both Lanka and India, dynasties were established, and small and large kingdoms grew like mushrooms after rain. The more powerful and aggressive rulers expanded their dominions. Strategic alliances were formed, and great empires were built. Raiding parties and regular armies from the mainland of India sometimes invaded the territories of kings on the island of Lanka, and vice versa. Sinhala armies helped Tamil kings defeat other Tamil kings in battle, and Tamil armies helped Sinhala kings defeat other Sinhala kings.[29]

Lankan civilization is traditionally considered to have been at its peak in the two cities of Anuradhapura and Polonnaruwa. Anuradhapura was established in the fourth century B.C. and is said to have remained a seat of power for more than two thousand years. A cutting from the Bodhi tree, under which the Buddha achieved enlightenment, is said in the Lankan chronicles to have been planted in that city. To modern Sinhalese, Anuradhapura symbolizes the pride of their heritage. But although — or because — the city was always a center of power, it was frequently fought over, within ruling families and between different kings. Sometimes Tamil kings occupied the throne, sometimes Sinhala kings. At the end of the tenth century A.D., Rajaraja Chola, the king of the most powerful and largest Tamil empire ever, captured and sacked Anuradhapura. Rajaraja's son, Rajendra, expanded the Chola empire still further. The Cholas moved the capital of Lanka from Anuradhapura to the nearby city of Polonnaruwa, which was more defensible militarily. The Cholas ruled the whole island of Lanka for seventy-five years as a province of their far-flung empire.

The Cholas were Saivas and supported the Saiva religion. Under Chola rule, Tamil arts and civilization flourished, and great Saiva temples were built. Present-day Tamils still look back to the Chola empire as a time of glory. Long, romantic historical novels are written about it. But for Lankan Buddhists, the Chola "occupation" of Lanka was not a good time. In 1070, a Sinhala king drove the Cholas out of Lanka, and Sinhala rule was reestablished.

The Anuradhapura-Polonnaruwa age in Sri Lanka is most celebrated for the irrigation systems built and sustained during that period. A large irrigation project requires extensive organization, expertise, and cooperation. One reason why unification of diverse peoples and lands is often held to be a good thing is that political unification facilitates consolidation of resources, allowing the building of resource-intensive projects for the common good.[30] In addition, historians sometimes suggest that internal unity is necessary to withstand external pressures. When a great kingdom or empire is invaded and conquered by armies from the outside, the defeat is a sign that the kingdom or empire was already vulnerable because of internal decline and dissension. Without such internal vulnerabilities, it might have withstood the external challenges.

The flip side of this argument has been made by the anthropologist Mary Douglas: when a society faces serious external challenges, it reinforces not only its city walls but also its conceptual walls, and any internal heterodoxy is viewed as foreign and therefore dangerous. Mass paranoia can then result, and harmless people can be destroyed. Obviously, such a response does not help the society under challenge but only renders it more vulnerable.

From yet another point of view, if a society is unified by force, as for instance by military conquest or slavery, it can be hard to hold together except by continuous applications of more force, which sap the society's resources. This is exactly the situation in Sri Lanka today. Present-day Sinhala nationalists argue that unity is necessary because the unity of the island is sacred. But the current fear of Tamils as "outsiders" is a classic reaction of the sort identified by Douglas. Tamils are blamed for all the internal problems faced by Sinhalese. Extremists believe that if only Tamils were eliminated, the society would be whole and perfect "again." But war against the Tamils exacerbates problems and quarrels within Sinhalese society. The idealized unity of the past is not the same as the sought-after unity of the present.

After the Chola rulers were driven out of Lanka, Sinhala civilization rallied. Over the next hundred years in Lanka, Buddhism was revived, renewed, and restored. Great new water tanks and irrigation canals were built, and Polonnaruwa became a center of artistic and architectural achievement. The period from 1070 to about 1200 was marked by several good kings who nurtured the society and intermittent periods of political instability. At the end of the twelfth century, it became mandatory for the Sinhala king to be a Buddhist.[31]

The deathblow to the Anuradhapura-Polonnaruwa age in Lanka was dealt not by any Tamil but by Magha of Kalinga. Kalinga was a long-established dynastic civilization in the area of east India now called Orissa and the home of the great-grandmother of Prince Vijaya of the *Mahāvamsa*. Thus we may assume travel and communications between Kalinga and the Sinhala country from at least the beginning of Sinhala written history. Much later in history, Kalinga kings harassed the Tamil Chola kings and invaded their territory south of Kalinga. Thus Kalingas were enemies both of the Chola Tamils and of the Sinhalese. Historians concur that Magha's rule in Polonnaruwa, from 1215 to 1236, was devastating. Some Sinhalese blame the Cholas for the defeat and destruction of Polonnaruwa, but actually it was their mutual enemy the Kalingas who accomplished this task.

After Magha died, Polonnaruwa was gradually abandoned. The irrigation canals of the central dry zone could not be maintained, malaria-bearing mosquitoes bred in the deserted tanks and waterways, and the Sinhalese residents migrated to the lush southwest of the island. A Tamil kingdom had been established in the north of the island, deriving wealth from the pearl fisheries around the Jaffna peninsula. The formerly irrigated dry zone in the north-central area turned to jungle and formed a buffer between the Tamils and the Sinhalese.[32] By the mid-fifteenth century, the Sinhalese kingdom of Kotte had grown up in the south, deriving wealth from the cinnamon trade. The independent kingdom of Kandy developed in the central mountainous region. When Europeans arrived, they found these three separate kingdoms.

Recent History

EUROPEAN INROADS

The Portuguese arrived in 1505. They were more interested in establishing coastal trade than in exploring the interior. They were also interested in propagating Catholicism, and they engaged in both activities aggressively and violently. Although they were few in number, they had superior firepower. After the Portuguese took over Kotte on the southwest coast and Jaffna in the north, the central mountain kingdom of Kandy became a refuge for Buddhist monks and others who could not or would not live under Portuguese domination.

Portuguese conversions to Catholicism angered both Sinhalese and Tamils, even though converts were numerous among both groups. These conversions were linked with military aggression and transparent ambitions for appropriating the wealth of the island. The initial target of the Portuguese had been Muslim traders, who, in addition to holding a near-monopoly over commerce in the Indian Ocean after the decline of the Chola maritime trade, practiced a religion hated by Catholics. After the

Portuguese established control over the coastal trading areas, they turned their religious attentions to both Buddhism and Saivism, whose adherents they persecuted with zeal.

A third interest of the Portuguese was education, as giving children a Catholic education was a good way of gaining converts. They took away the Sinhala heir to the throne when he was a child on the pretext of protecting him from his father's enemies, had him educated by Catholic priests, and thus converted him to Catholicism, alienating him from his people and rendering him dependent on his Portuguese advisers.

After 150 years of Portuguese domination, the Dutch drove them out and took over the maritime provinces. The Dutch, although they were kinder and more tolerant than the Portuguese, were fiercely Protestant, and they persecuted Catholics. Thus the people of the island were subjected to a double dose of religious warfare, European style. If the combination of military conquest, religious persecution, and aggressive conversions had not previously been recognized on the island as a strategy of political domination, it now would have become readily apparent. After another 150 years, around 1800, the British took over from the Dutch, who put up little resistance.

BRITISH RULE

One determining cause of the current conflict in Sri Lanka is the legacy of British colonial policy. The policy of the British in South Asia included the principle of knowing their subjects.[33] To this end, the colonizers classified the colonized according to caste, physical type, religion, language, region, kinship patterns, means of subsistence, level of savagery, degree of manliness, and so forth. The classification was held to be a precise and accurate record of natural fact. It aimed to be scientific: to quantify, measure, standardize, and categorize. It was pragmatic, ascertaining which categories of people would be useful and in what ways. Existing customs, habits, and organizations were allowed to continue if they were not considered harmful to the inhabitants or to the British government; all others were suppressed or abolished. Other precepts of colonial rule included the following: Keep the traditions you approve of as they have been — that is, as you believe they have been, or as your trusted native informants tell you they have been — from time immemorial. Disambiguate ambiguities. Maintain clear distinctions. Give names to categories that have no name, or many names. Recruit servants from among the most educable of the population, those who most resemble you, or can be most easily made to resemble you, but will not seek to be your rivals. Let missionaries and others collect knowledge about your subjects for you. Let missionaries and others found schools to educate the people in your language, your values, and your means of social organization.

The British colonial governments created systems of knowledge intended to contain, in both the cognitive and the political senses, the diverse peoples they governed. In creating these systems of knowledge, they transformed existing realities and created new ones, sometimes knowingly but at other times quite unwittingly. Systems of government were knowingly transformed, whereas the transformation of such categories as caste, religion, kinship, and language was on the whole unwitting.

Even where they did not significantly change the realities, British and other European influences radically changed the metarealities. The concept of nation, with its related concept of a bounded nation-state, was perhaps the most profoundly unsettling metareality introduced to South Asia from the West. Whereas previously a kingdom had been defined by its center, and the outermost limits of a kingdom or empire were not always precise, now strict geographical boundaries were drawn between polities. In order to govern in their own fashion, the British colonists had to make maps and draw lines so that every bit of land and every human settlement was accounted for. This emphasis on boundaries remains a factor exacerbating the conflict between ethnic groups on the island.

India was too vast for Britain to comprehend, manage, contain, govern, or mold to its own image, even with its brilliant apparatus of knowledge and control. But Britain had in common with Sri Lanka that it was an island, within a day's sailing distance of a great continent, and had a long history of warfare and conquest, wealth and trade, fierce foreign armies storming the shores, legends of glorious kingdoms and kings, a blooded aristocracy, and (unlike precolonial India) a definite sense of its own distinctiveness. Perhaps Britain saw a certain tropical likeness of itself in Sri Lanka, and a flattering likeness at that, for Sri Lanka has a beauty and grace, an abundance of natural life, a mystery and a warmth that Britain might covet. Perhaps this is why Britain treated Sri Lanka so (relatively) kindly.

By the same token, Sri Lanka gave the British a relatively easy time. The maritime provinces had been colonized for three hundred years already and were thus in a sense prepared for the British arrival. Only the highland kingdom of Kandy could not be easily annexed. The Dutch had tried and failed to gain control over it, and the initial British efforts likewise met with failure. The mountain terrain was rough, and the trails were set with traps. Advancing troops were either killed by Kandyan warriors on the way in or else succumbed to disease on the way out.

The Kandyan kingdom was unique also in that it was a Tamil-Sinhalese hybrid. It was not unknown for Sinhala kings to take wives from ruling families of South India.[34] Vijaya was the first to do so: because there were no women of high enough rank on the island for him to marry, he procured a properly royal consort from the Tamil city of Madurai. Later kings occasionally followed suit. When the kingdom of Kandy remained the only true kingdom on the island, the lowland kingdoms having fallen under the dominion of European and British colonists, the kings of Kandy also sought and procured their queens from Madurai. In addition to the need for a fresh infusion of royal blood, the Kandyan kings had another reason to take their wives from abroad: they ruled over a collection of stroppy chiefdoms, and there was some danger that a coalition of chieftains could overthrow the king in favor of a leader more to their liking. To keep themselves separate from and higher than the Kandyan chiefly nobility, the kings took wives from outside that nobility. If the chiefs rose against the king, he could call for assistance from his powerful South Indian in-laws. Because the Kandyan kings had received military assistance from the Tamil ruling family of Nayaks in Madurai to help fight off the Portuguese, alliances between Kandy and Madurai were already established. In the seventeenth and eighteenth centuries, marital alliances between Kandyan kings and Nayak princesses became a matter of policy.

However, as the Nayak kingdom in the Tamil country lost ground to more powerful forces seeking control of South India, when a Nayak princess married a Kandyan king, she brought all her relatives with her. The Kandyan kingdom came to have a strong South Indian flavor. Whereas the Kandyan Sinhalese were patrilineal, the Nayak family had a strong matrilineal tradition. Thus, when one Sinhalese Kandyan king died without offspring by his queen, a brother of his Tamil queen assumed the throne even though the king had had offspring by a secondary, Kandyan wife. These children were not even considered heirs to the throne. The Sinhalese Kandyan aristocracy had no problem with this new form of succession. Either they wanted only pure royal blood on the throne, or else patriliny and Sinhalese blood were not of great importance to them in choosing a king. Thus, in 1739, the Tamil Nayak dynasty came to rule the kingdom of Kandy. Subsequent Nayak kings of Kandy followed tradition and took their wives from among their kin in India. At least one Nayak king married four Madurai princesses, each of whom brought her relatives with her.

It was not until 1815 that the Sinhalese nobles rebelled, apparently in response to the unwise and cruel rule of the current Nayak boy king. The British stepped in at this point, made a deal with the chiefs, and gained control of Kandy. The deposed king and all his male relatives were sent back to India.

The agreement with the Sinhala chieftains stipulated that "the Dominion of the Kandyan Provinces is vested in the Sovereign of the British Empire under King George III and to being exercised through the Governors of Ceylon for the time being"; that "the native headmen" (the Sinhala chieftains) would continue to enjoy "the rights and priviledges and powers of the respective offices"; and that there would be accorded "to all other classes of people, the safety of their persons and property with their civil rights and immunities according to the laws Institutions and Customs established and in force among them."

The meaning of the term *dominion*, along with that of *for the time being*, may not have been entirely clear. It would have been clear that the Sinhala Kandyan people were being guaranteed the right to maintain their customary social order and protection against violent attacks from outsiders — essentially what they expected of a good king. Another part of the agreement with the Sinhala chieftains was that "the Religion of the Boodoo professed by the Chiefs and inhabitants of these Provinces is declared inviolable, its Rites, Ministers and Places of Worship are to be maintained and protected."[35] The treaty was not honored as the Kandyans expected, and, a mere three years later, the Kandyan Sinhala chieftains rebelled against British rule. But it was already too late to unseat the British, whose annexation of Kandy had given them control over the whole island and the strength to put down any local rebellion.

One lesson to be gleaned from this story is that Tamils and Sinhalese in the Kandyan kingdom during the eighteenth century had no problem intermarrying or even being ruled by one another. One may reasonably surmise that until the nineteenth century, the two groups got along together fine as long as they did not step on one another's toes, which in general they had no reason to do. They shared certain understandings of good governance and the nature of kingship. These shared understandings were, however, challenged and disrupted by their new rulers.

By one skillful act, in Kandy, of playing one side against the other — a strategy they employed regularly in South Asia — the British consolidated their rule over the island of Lanka. And this event leads to another general lesson. The British created animosities of whole birth categories of people against whole other birth categories of people where there were no such animosities before. They essentialized what they considered to be races and then, deliberately or not, set those races against each other. The

British, along with other Western Europeans and Americans, at that time genuinely believed in the essential qualities of races and of birth categories. Although there might have been disagreement over what constituted the essential qualities of a particular race, such as Brahmans or Red Indians, there was little or no disagreement over the reality of distinct races, each with its essential, heritable qualities. This concept of essential qualities of one or another race haunts Sri Lanka still, and is what makes the war between Tamils and Sinhalese conceivable.

British rule and administration completely transformed the island's cultures and civilizations. Old categories were eliminated and new ones created. High-country Sinhalese, from the Kandyan area, were distinguished from low-country Sinhalese, from the rich southern agricultural area. Sri Lankan Tamils, who had lived for many generations on the island, were distinguished from Indian Tamils, who had been imported by the British to work in the tea and coffee plantations. New export crops — coffee, tea, and rubber — were developed. Education and literacy — until then the preserve of a few — became a route to economic and political advancement to which all were in principle entitled. Kings and kingship were eliminated (except for the British monarchy), and democratic egalitarianism, economic liberalism, a modern constitution, and the rule of law were introduced in their stead. Sri Lankans were recruited into the civil service, and a Westernized elite was created.

With the disappearance of monarchy, the *bhikkus* saw their position imperiled: for hundreds of years, they had obtained support from the king in exchange for the divine legitimacy they bestowed on him. They now had to struggle for protection and privilege. The monks, all sons of Sinhala families, encountered new enemies: in addition to the British colonial rulers, who fostered Christian missionary activities, they felt themselves to be in conflict with Sri Lankan Tamils, who were predominantly Saiva, with a large contingent of Christians and few if any Buddhists. The Sinhala people by and large had no reason to oppose the Buddhist monastic tradition of the island and many reasons to support it.

After Sri Lanka attained independence, all the island's prior history was reinterpreted as much as possible in terms of a conflict between Sinhala and Tamil.

GLOBAL CAPITAL AND ITS LOCAL EFFECTS

The transformations caused by colonial, and in particular British, rule of the island contributed to the current conflict by creating sources of discord among Tamils and Sinhalese, even though there is no reason to think that the British colonial administrators (at least after they had established stable rule over the island) intended or desired such tensions. Internal conflict, after all, does not make for an easily governed country.

By the time of independence in 1948, the people of Sri Lanka were very well off in comparison to people of other Third World countries. Sri Lanka became a model for the provision of "basic human needs."[36] Infant mortality was low, life expectancy was high, food was abundant, and the educational system was good and available to most children. The literacy rate was and remains very high. India, by contrast, was and remains home to massive poverty and illiteracy.

The independent Sri Lankan government started out with a liberal, modernist, multiethnic and nationalist bent under the United National Party (UNP). In 1952, a World Bank study noted that 35 percent of the budget of Sri Lanka was spent on social and welfare services — a proportion that the bank considered too high.[37] The prime minister's bending to the bank's will caused increases in food prices and reductions in food subsidies and other social benefits. Nationwide protests at such changes led to the defeat of the UNP government in the 1956 elections.

The subsequent Sri Lanka Freedom Party (SLFP) government, led by S. W. R. D. Bandaranaike, expanded pension plans, medical care, nutrition programs, and food and fuel subsidies. Foreign investment was restricted, critical industries were nationalized, and land-reform measures nationalized plantations and redistributed land to the peasants.[38] Despite the disapproval of foreign aid agencies, for twenty-nine years after independence, through several administrations, Sri Lanka grew as a welfare state.

Effectively, the parties competing for power on the national stage had little choice but to continue to increase social benefits for the majority, as any given politician's continuance in office depended on his or her ability to woo the majority of voters, and the majority wanted all the benefits from the government they could get. No government, however, could meet all the demands of the voters without amassing a mountain of debt and incurring the displeasure of international investors and aid agencies, which in turn meant reductions in aid and thus in social benefits. Some degree of economic turmoil was inevitable. The people were already highly politicized and prepared to take to the streets to protest any perceived injustice.

Very early in the postindependence period, economic troubles were transformed into ethnic antagonisms. Nascent discontent with the transethnic ruling class, which had taken over government from the British, was deflected onto the ethnic minorities. Tamils, the largest ethnic minority, came to be defined as malicious and their interests inimical to those of Sinhalese. The ruling class, which controlled both major parties and thereby the government, was let off the hook.

Because the vast majority of people in the country were Sinhalese, the Sinhalese were competitively courted in every election. And in courting the Sinhalese people as though they were all ethnonationalists, the post-independence politicians gave a sharp edge to that nationalism and may have instilled it in many who would otherwise have remained indifferent to it.[39]

Control of the government shifted back and forth between two major political parties, the conservative and Western-oriented UNP and the more leftist-nationalist SLFP. Both parties used Buddhist imagery and terminology to appeal to Sinhalese voters. Sri Lankan national pride was identified with Sinhala pride. Tamils were labelled as exogenous invaders. Sinhala people were encouraged by both major parties to direct their hostilities against Tamils, who in turn resisted their marginalization. Sinhalese interpreted even peaceful resistance as threatening to their perceived control of the island, and thus to their economic well-being. Initially, Tamil resistance took the form of *satyagrāhas* — Gandhian-style, nonviolent demonstrations. As marginalization turned into violent oppression, however, Tamil resistance, too, gradually became violent.

Until the 1970s, the main Sinhalese grudge against Tamils was that they were economically and politically privileged. This claim was based on the fact that Tamils were disproportionately represented in government, the professions, and the universities. Overlooked were the facts that Tamils were still a minority in government and had no leverage there, and that the majority of Tamil people were no better off educationally or economically than the majority of Sinhala people.

In the early 1970s, the Sinhala Marxist militant Janatha Vimukthi Peramuna (People's Liberation Front, or JVP) arose in the south of the island, and militant Tamil youth movements began to emerge in the Jaffna peninsula in the north. In 1971, when the JVP attempted a coup against the government, it was met with massive and merciless military destruction. In 1975, the LTTE assassinated the mayor of Jaffna, who supported the SLFP.

Even as late as the mid-1970s, few people would have advocated all-out civil war. If the government had managed to keep the country economically stable; if there had been strong, enduring transpartisan will to quell racist sentiment; and if murderous ethnic riots had been stopped in their tracks and met with genuine justice, perhaps the simmering strife might have subsided. But this is mere speculation.

In 1978, elections brought a change of government from the left-wing SLFP to the more conservative UNP, resulting in a change of development policy from welfare socialism to a liberalized, open economy. Welfare socialism and free-market liberalism are two radically different ways of managing the wealth of a country, accompanied by two radically different ways of governing a people. The former, in principle, takes it as its top priority to ensure the welfare of all those who live in the country, regardless of individual productivity. The poor in particular are looked after. Internal economic self-sufficiency is promoted, foreign investment is discouraged, and private industry is nationalized — in principle, to ensure that the wealth of the country belongs to the public domain and is not taken up by private or overseas interests. Two disadvantages of such a system are a lack of incentives for increasing productivity and problems with ensuring government accountability. Money meant for public welfare may be channeled through bureaucratic agencies to the bureaucrats' friends and families.

The main priority of free-market liberalism is to expand a nation's economy by fostering greater productivity through unregulated competition. In practice this means that the overall monetary wealth of a country may grow, but there are definite winners and definite losers, with little protection for individuals and families against poverty or even starvation. Under a neoliberal economy, success in obtaining wealth is rewarded with opportunities to compound that wealth, and just as in a welfare economy, corrupt and illegal activities on the part of the powerful may rob people lower on the economic hierarchy of their savings and livelihoods, among other things.

International development agencies applauded the 1978 shift in Sri Lanka's economic priorities. Large infusions of foreign capital became available for massive public works projects, which were expected to improve the country's infrastructure and thereby support industrial development. The most important such work was the Mahaveli River Development Scheme, which aimed to bring new land under irrigation while also providing hydroelectric power. Jobs were created by this project. In addition, the Mahaveli project was a matter of cultural pride, because it evoked images of the ancient irrigation-based civilization of Anuradhapura and Polonnaruwa, the golden age of Sinhala history.

When jobs on this project were handed out, the existing system of patronage politics was strengthened. The ruling class benefited. The influx of foreign capital enabled individuals in key political positions to enrich themselves. As Ronald Herring points out, "Fortunes were made." Not only did some individuals increase their wealth, as might reasonably be expected, but they amassed fortunes out of foreign aid. Since all foreign aid money was channeled through the state, the state's power expanded. Deficit spending increased, and foreign investors urged less social and welfare expenditure. But spending on public salaries and wages — which Herring identifies as "one important measure of patronage" — increased. USAID-funded housing programs also served the interests of political patronage. Houses, like jobs, were traded for votes. When newly irrigated land was up for distribution, the same rule applied. Inevitably, according to Herring, "the lion's share of boons appeared in Sinhala areas."[40] In addition, Sinhala people from the south were resettled in the Mahaveli area. Repeated references were made to Sinhala national pride: "Inspired by engineering feats of an ancient kingdom and hailed as the world's largest foreign aid project, the Mahaveli scheme was to be a symbol of progress and national identity."[41]

Tamils were left out of this scheme and its accompanying vision, not only symbolically but also economically. The nationalism celebrated by the Mahaveli project was specifically Sinhala nationalism, and the beneficiaries were Sinhalese also. Tamil resentment was compounded because Tamils considered that the newly irrigated and resettled land was traditionally Tamil land. They felt that they were being colonized by the Sinhalese and that their numbers in their own territory were being diluted. In fact, resettlement of Sinhalese in Tamil-majority areas had begun immediately after independence, but the Mahaveli project accelerated this process. Tamil people's chances of acquiring local political strength — control over a large, contiguous, legally defined section of the country in which Tamils would form a solid majority — were reduced. Sinhalese settlers in that area were viewed by Tamils somewhat as Jewish settlers on the West Bank are viewed by Palestinians. Additionally, some of the Sinhalese settlers were people who were not wanted in the south: people who did not know how to farm, some of whom were criminals. Subsequent ethnic violence in these areas was fierce, brutal, and personal.

The flames of ethnic antagonism had already been fanned by the SLFP government under Sirimavo Bandaranaike (prime minister from 1960 to 1965 and from 1970 to 1977), who combined welfare socialism with a vehement and emotional pro-Sinhala ethnonationalist stance — despite the fact that her husband, when he was prime minister, had been assassinated by a Sinhala ethnonationalist. Tamils were branded as capitalists, although, "objectively, economic position did not track ethnicity closely. . . . [There was no] neat ethnic division of labor."[42] Because educated Jaffna Tamils had benefited under British colonial rule and were favored as administrators, Tamils were also branded as "loyalists" to the British, and therefore as traitors to the Sri Lankan nation. Some say that the favoring of Jaffna Tamils by colonial governors was part of England's "divide and rule" policy. Others say that Jaffna Tamils were favored because they already had a tradition of educated professionalism, which tradition in turn was a consequence of the fact that Jaffna's soil was not hospitable to agriculture, so the Jaffna Tamils had turned to trade and the professions as alternative means of accruing wealth. Meanwhile, Tamil people who hailed not from Jaffna but from the east or the hill country lived primarily by farming, fishing, and wage labor, just as most Sinhalese people did.

In the mid-1970s, Tamil leaders united to form a single political party to contest the coming 1977 elections. The platform of this party, called the Tamil United Liberation Front (TULF), was the Vaddukkoddai Resolution of 1976, mandating an independent, separate state for Tamils. During the 1977 elections, the TULF won an overwhelming majority of Tamil votes from the north and east. During the same period, Tamil youth stepped up their agitation for a separate state. "An apparently false rumor that Sinhalese policemen had died at the hands of Tamil terrorists, combined with other rumors of alleged anti-Sinhalese statements made by Tamil politicians, sparked brutal communal rioting that engulfed the island within two weeks of the new government's inauguration. The rioting marked the first major outbreak of communal violence in the nineteen years since the riots of 1958. Casualties were many, especially among Tamils, both the Sri Lankan Tamils of Jaffna and the Indian Tamil plantation workers. The Tamil Refugee Rehabilitation Organization estimated the death toll at 300."[43] Tamils were not the only people who suffered from the political and economic transformations of the postindependence period, nor were they the first to turn to active militancy.

A radical Sinhala left wing, originally Marxist but later allying with the Sinhala Buddhist nationalist right wing, has also been a force to contend with. In 1971, the Sinhala far Left, or JVP, driven by youths who had been educated for white-collar employment but then denied jobs or higher education, staged a violent insurrection whose aim was to overthrow the government. The insurrection was brutally suppressed by the Sri Lankan Army (SLA). Later JVP insurgencies in 1981 and 1987–89 were likewise met with harsh military action. Tens of thousands of people were killed, including many who had nothing to do with the insurgency. Elderly Tamils who are now in the diaspora remember the bodies of massacred Sinhala youths lying in piles on the roadsides, and any Sinhala youth was held suspect by the government, just as Tamil youths are today. The JVP also massacred people, mostly Sinhalese youths belonging or suspected of belonging to rival factions or groups.

Such factional violence in the south continues, although at a lower level than before.[44] Meanwhile, the JVP has become a regular political party, holding seats in the Sri Lankan parliament. It has been among those Sinhala ethnonationalist parties that blame Tamils for the ills of the country; they strongly favor war against the LTTE and oppose a negotiated peace settlement.

The JVP insurgencies were a direct reaction to changes in economic and social policy. Hence the JVP directly attacked the government, and the government retaliated. But other, equally murderous riots in which the government was not a target, culminating in the giant pogroms against Tamils in 1983, met with no government opposition.

The severely destabilizing effect of the transition from socialist to neoliberal policies, combined with the ethnically biased political management of foreign aid capital during the 1970s, helped propel Sri Lanka into total war. The conjecture that economic liberalization has independently aggravated the war in Sri Lanka is supported by the fact that similar policies have helped to precipitate armed ethnic conflict in other countries.[45] Other causes are also at work in these conflicts: no social or economic force operates in a vacuum. But global capitalism is more powerful than any ethnic nationalism, and it turns what might have been liberating social forces against themselves, while creating others that are lethal from their inception.

Two Nationalisms

A third cause of the present conflict has been the simultaneous rise of Tamil nationalism and Sinhala nationalism. These forces are among the consequences of British colonial rule. Both Tamil and Sinhala nationalisms originated in opposition to British colonial practice and policy, which they recognized to be dominating and exploitative. Only later did they develop into mutual enmity. Ethnicity as we think of it today was not an issue in precolonial times because it did not exist. The notion of primordial enmities is viewed by most scholars as a politically motivated retrojection of current antagonisms into the distant past. Nevertheless, both nationalisms, in addition to being shaped by colonialist ways of knowledge, were composed of other streams, whose emergence predated the European colonial period.

These nationalisms became inevitable given the habit of the British rulers to denigrate the ways of life of people they ruled, while at the same time naturalizing the concept that people fit into such neat categories as Hindu or Buddhist, Tamil or Sinhalese.[46] A surprising number of otherwise intelligent people accepted the reality of such either/or categories as applied to themselves, while they could not help but resist the derogatory attributes attached to the categories.

Sinhala Buddhist nationalism arose in the late nineteenth century, in opposition to the activities of Christian missionaries. The missionaries preached that the local variant of Buddhism was savage and abhorrent demonolatry.[47] With support and encouragement from the colonial government, Christian missionaries established schools throughout the country in which children received high-quality education in the English medium, coupled with Christian indoctrination. The missionary schools became magnets for children whose parents sought a cosmopolitan education for their children.

But some Sinhala scholars, themselves with cosmopolitan educations, believed that Sinhala Buddhism was under attack from the missionaries and the British government. The language of the missionaries of the eighteenth and nineteenth centuries certainly substantiates the idea that it was under verbal attack. The Sinhala scholars also considered that Buddhism had declined in Sri Lanka during colonial rule. The community of Buddhist monks, some of whom exhibited powerful rhetorical skills in their debates with Christian missionaries, attracted the attention of Colonel Henry Steele Olcott, the nineteenth-century American spiritualist who subsequently founded the Theosophical Society in Madras, India. Olcott was so impressed with the tenets of Buddhism that he converted to that religion in Sri Lanka in 1880, and he was instrumental in popularizing Buddhism in the West. Olcott was also a good organizer, and he helped found a movement for the reform and revival of Buddhism in Sri Lanka with a vision of a utopian, socially egalitarian Buddhist society. In this society, the monks and the monasteries would be "restored" to their rightful place as chief protectors and teachers of the people.[48]

In the years preceding Sri Lankan independence in 1948, the monks became politically active in an unprecedented way. They agitated for the *sangha* to have a strong voice in government. Shortly after independence, they achieved this goal. As political activists and voters, they could become what Americans call kingmakers. They were the determining force in the election of S. W. R. D. Bandaranaike to the position of prime minister of Sri Lanka in 1956. This victory confirmed the Sinhala Buddhist clergy in their belief that, as a politically organized body, they could get anything they wanted. Some might say it was at this point that the Buddhist religion in Sri Lanka went by the wayside, at least with respect to the activities of monks, and the excesses of unchecked secular power took over.

Tamil nationalism began in India in the late nineteenth century and grew and evolved through the twentieth century. It was born together with what was called the Tamil Renaissance or the Dravidian Renaissance, which was sparked by the (re)discovery of Tamil Sangam poetry. Christian missionaries, most notably Bishop Robert Caldwell and Reverend G. U. Pope, considered classical Tamil poetry to be among the finest composed by anyone at any time anywhere in the world, reflecting the spirit of a great and admirable people. The fact that these men were both Christian clergy gave weight to their strong appreciation of ancient Tamil poetry. Tamil nationalism crystallized around the rich heritage of Tamil poetry and language.

At first Tamil nationalism was part of anticolonial pan-Indian nationalism, but it later split from the Indian nationalist movement in response to its perceived domination by north Indians. In particular, Tamil speakers were offended when Indian nationalists proposed Hindi rather than English as the national language. At least with English as a lingua franca, all Indian languages would be on an equal footing within the country.

Ardent devotion to the Tamil language became ardent devotion to the people who spoke it, by those very people. The movement merging love of the language with love of the people has been called Dravidianism. In the words of one somewhat detached scholar:

The most passionate and radical of all the regimes, Dravidianism routinely elicited from its adherents declarations of willingness to give up their wealth, their lives and their souls for Tamil. It also produced some antagonistic, even violent, attitudes toward other languages and their speakers, as for instance in the following verse published by Bharatidasan: "Our first task is to finish off those who destroy [our] glorious Tamil! / Let flow a river of crimson blood." Its emphasis on fierce public displays of devotion meant that images of battlefields, of blood, and of death proliferate in Dravidianist discourse. True Tamilians are those . . . who show their commitment to their mother-tongue by putting their very bodies on the line, and dying for it, if need be.

The sense of bodily belonging is inherent in such devotion. The notion of race is a bodily notion. Hence, "Dravidianism's driving imperative was a vision of the Tamil community as an autonomous racial and political entity (*inam*), whose sacral center is occupied solely by Tamil."[49]

There were several distinct Tamil nationalist movements, but all of them celebrated the Tamil language as part of the Dravidian linguistic group. North Indian languages, including Hindi, are all part of a larger language family infelicitously labeled "Indo-Aryan." European scholars and rulers of India in the nineteenth and early twentieth centuries considered Aryans to be superior to Dravidians, and those who were classed as Aryans were happy to share this view. Aryans were also considered lighter-skinned than Dravidians — clearly a point in favor of the Aryans from the colonial point of view.

A pan-Dravidian separatist movement was initiated in India by the great Tamil reformer E.V. Ramaswamy, or Periyar (1879–1973). His aim was to unite all the southern Indian states, and all Dravidian speakers, under one banner. Periyar was a staunch atheist and humanist. On the walls of some Tamil houses even today hangs a picture of the bearded old man with a saying in Tamil beneath it: *Kadavulai mara, manithanai ninai* (Forget God, think of Man). A modified version of Periyar's totally antireligious stance emerged in the Self-Respect Movement of the mid-twentieth century. In this view, Tamils could and did practice their traditional religion, but without Brahman priests (who traced at least their religious tradition from north India), and using Tamil rather than Sanskrit in the ceremonies. Many Self-Respect marriages were celebrated. Cross-caste marriages and dowry-free marriages were practiced in a similar reformist spirit.

The pan-Dravidian movement initiated by Periyar is said to have failed because Periyar attempted to unite all of South India against the north, which was an unrealistic aim, and because Periyar rejected all religion, whereas most Tamils are deeply religious. Nevertheless, Periyar's staunch atheism has been adopted by more than a few educated Tamils, and the anticaste and antidowry movements continue.

A specifically Tamil nationalism was championed by the writer and orator C.N. Annadurai (1909–69). The leaders of the Tamil Renaissance were all reformers who promoted a casteless, classless society. All were great speakers and writers. All were charismatic. But Annadurai was the most popular of all of these, inspiring widespread devotion.

In 1964 and 1965, nine young Tamil men took their own lives, six by fire and three by poison, declaring in their last words that their sacrifice was for the sake of Tamil.[50] This collective devotional self-immolation demonstrated the intensity of the young men's *pattu/bhakti;* it mirrored legendary acts of self-sacrificial devotion attested in early literature, and it presaged the levels of self-sacrificial devotion that would later be attained by the LTTE.

But despite the passionate devotion, despite the violent words, and despite the call for a Tamil or Dravidian state independent of India, no armed insurrection and no mob violence ever arose in India from this movement — only violence against the self. In the end, the Indian Tamil nationalists achieved their goals by political means and by the strength of their voting numbers. No insurrection or secession was necessary. The status of their language and their right to speak it were not threatened. They were not invaded or occupied by a government army. They were not forcibly displaced from their homes. And for very few was war or political separation something inherently desirable. The painful lessons of the partition of Pakistan from India had been learned.

Tamil nationalism in Sri Lanka took a different direction. From at least the time of independence, Sri Lankan Tamils distinguished themselves from Indian Tamils. Thus when Indian Tamils in Sri Lanka were denied voting privileges immediately after independence — on the grounds that they had been "recently" imported by the British to act as plantation laborers (even though many of them had lived on the island for generations, and had had voting rights during British rule) — Tamils who identified themselves as indigenous to Sri Lanka raised few objections. Thus the indigenous Sri Lankan Tamils lost an important bloc of allies, who subsequently were granted voting rights again.

For Sri Lankan Tamils, an early and ominous turning point came with the proclamation of the Sinhala-Only Act in 1956, shortly after S. W. R. D. Bandaranaike was elected. This act established Sinhala as the official language of the country. Tamils strongly objected, and Tamil leaders staged a *satyagrāha* in Colombo, which was met with violent repression.

A second move against Tamils came two years later. "In May 1958, a rumor that a Tamil had killed a Sinhalese sparked off nationwide communal riots. Hundreds of people, mostly Tamils, died. This disturbance was the first major episode of communal violence on the island since independence. The riots left a deep psychological scar between the two major ethnic groups. The government declared a state of emergency and forcibly relocated more than 25,000 Tamil refugees from Sinhalese areas to Tamil areas in the north."[51] A third ominous incident came in September 1959, with the assassination of Bandaranaike by a Buddhist monk for his proposal of moderate local concessions to Tamils with regard to the Sinhala-Only Act. This was the same Bandaranaike whom the Buddhist monks had helped put in power three years before. The monk who assassinated him acted under the sponsorship of one of the most prominent leaders of the *sangha*. The concessions for which Bandaranaike was killed included "allowing the opportunity for persons trained in English or Tamil to take examinations in those languages for entry into public service, letting local bodies decide for themselves the language of their business, and giving persons the right to communicate with the government in their own language."[52] The two main political parties in Sri Lanka, the UNP (United National Party) and the SLFP (Sri Lanka Freedom Party), have been careful ever since not to upset the Sinhala ultranationalists, even as they vie for the support of the Sinhala majority.

Subsequent blows to Tamils — particularly Jaffna Tamils — included the introduction in 1974 of a new procedure for allocating university places, which took into account not only exam scores but also regional proportionality. In practice this meant that Tamil communities, for whom education was the only means of advancement and which had always done well on exams, were discriminated against in favor of rural students whose scores were lower. No significant portion of the Sinhala community was negatively affected by this legislation, but Jaffna Tamils found their traditional livelihoods and ways of life both insulted and threatened. For some of them, the last straw was the burning of the Jaffna library in 1981 by one or two hundred rampaging Sinhalese police. The library contained numerous irreplaceable manuscripts.

After 1983

Following the events of July 1983, tens of thousands of young Tamil men and women went to war. Training camps were set up for them in India and some of the Arab countries. The prime minister of India from 1984, Rajiv Gandhi, tacitly allowed and perhaps even actively supported the training camps in India. Some say that Gandhi sympathized with the Tamil militants. Others say he simply wanted to destabilize Sri Lanka.

The Tamil militant movement grew and then split because of a quarrel between Velupillai Prabhakaran and his best friend, Uma Maheswaran. Subsequent splits among the Tamil militants ensued. All of them were armed and trained in combat, and they fought one another fiercely. Some Tamil civilians who remember that time describe it as "teenagers killing teenagers." Each group had its own ideology, but, more than ideology, personal loyalties prevailed. In the end Prabhakaran came out ahead, not least because of his willingness to kill former friends who had betrayed him, along with their followers. Ultimately most of the other Tamil nationalist movements became political parties and joined the Sri Lankan government. A number, however, retained paramilitary groups that fought against the Tigers.

The LTTE developed and refined its skills and knowledge as the years passed. It got very good at blowing things up and carrying out assassinations. It developed an elite corps of Black Tigers (suicide bombers), with more volunteers than could be accepted.[53] It ambushed and killed soldiers and raided army bases and police stations. The Sri Lankan army and other security forces ballooned in size and strength to meet this challenge. Arms and equipment were sold or donated to Sri Lanka by foreign countries, including India. The LTTE, on the other hand, received support from elsewhere.[54] In 1987, the president of Sri Lanka, Julius Jayawardene, signed an agreement with Rajiv Gandhi that Indian peace-keeping troops (IPKF) should come in and settle the discord between the LTTE and government troops in Sri Lanka. The Tamil political party, TULF, welcomed the intervention. However, Jayawardene and the TULF had different expectations of the IPKF. There was concern in some quarters of the Sri Lankan government that India might use its military presence in Sri Lanka to annex the smaller country. The Tamils, for their part, after having joyfully welcomed the IPKF, quickly found that the Indian troops were fighting them and committing human rights abuses (rape and torture) against Tamil civilians. As in 1983, many ordinary Tamil people who did not think of themselves as warlike turned themselves into warriors. Those who could not physically fight supported the LTTE in any other way they could. And again many people fled the country to join the growing diaspora. In 1989, with the backing of the new president, Ranasinghe Premadasa, the LTTE drove the IPKF out of India.

Rajiv Gandhi was killed by a suicide bomber in Tamil Nadu in 1991. Premadasa was killed in a bomb explosion in 1993. Prabhakaran is presumed to have been behind both killings. The assassination of Rajiv shocked the Indian people, and many Indian Tamils who previously sympathized with the LTTE withdrew their support.

In 1994 Chandrika Kumaratunga, the daughter of S. W. R. D. Bandaranaike and head of the SLFP, was elected to the presidency by a strong margin on a promise to end the war and bring peace. She assumed office at the beginning of 1995. Talks between Chandrika's representatives and

LTTE representatives failed, however, and soon the LTTE was back at war with the Sri Lankan military. The SLA staged Operation Riviresa (Sunshine), whose aim was to capture Jaffna from the LTTE, and "liberate" the Tamil civilians there. The LTTE did not put up a fight but moved to the Vanni jungle area south of the Jaffna peninsula. Many civilians fled the advance of the army, joining the LTTE in the Vanni. The Sri Lankan Army occupied (and continues to occupy) Jaffna.

However, because most of the army's forces had been sent to the north to capture and occupy Jaffna, the LTTE was able to take full control of the hinterlands of the eastern Batticaloa and Amparai areas. By 1997, the LTTE had consolidated its control of this region, although the SLA maintained control of the coastal cities. Both the LTTE and the SLA continued to focus on the north. In 1997, the SLA initiated Operation Jayasikurui to capture the stretch of highway from Vavuniya (controlled by the army) through the Vanni (controlled by the Tigers) to Jaffna (controlled by the army). After his easy victory in Riviresa, the commander of the armed forces anticipated that Jayasikurui would be just as easy. But this time the Tigers fought tooth and nail. They were trained, experienced, and committed, and they used all the strength they had withheld during Riviresa.

I entered Batticaloa for the first time in March 1996, right after Riviresa and a little more than a year before Jayasikurui. Chapter 3 tells what I found there. The remaining chapters of this book describe what I learned when I came back to stay longer and Jayasikurui was in full swing.

March 1996

Sister Maria has given me careful instructions for entering the Tiger-controlled area in the hinterlands.[1] Hearing me tell of my desire to meet with Tiger combatants, she has advised me to take great care. She will send a message that I am coming. I should take the bus from the town to a village some miles away and disembark there. Then I should rise before dawn and cycle across the bridge before the soldiers are up and about. She sends a note with me to Sister Ann, telling her to let me stay at the orphanage overnight and the following morning to send me with a boy from the orphanage to the bridge and beyond. The bridge she says I am to cross has no checkpoint. After crossing the bridge, I am to ask for a man named Payyan, who will introduce me to local LTTE officers. Sister Maria tells me that I can identify Payyan by his missing ear.

I wait for the bus in the afternoon. An acquaintance has come with me to tell the driver specifically where to let me off. The bus — which turns out to be just a van — is packed full of people, and I am fortunate to get a seat. The driver lets me off at the orphanage, a beautiful place surrounded by huge, ancient trees, where I meet Sister Ann. She is dressed in a plain dark blue sari and looks about twenty-five, innocent and lovely. She offers me tea and cookies, which I accept, and then she disappears for a long time, leaving a younger girl to look after me. The orphanage is not far from a TELO camp — TELO (the Tamil Eelam Liberation Organization) being one of the several paramilitary groups made up of Tamils who work for the Sri Lankan Army (made up almost entirely of Sinhalese) as spotters, informants, and fighters against the LTTE. We can hear gunshots from the camp. A child says the TELO boys are shooting herons for dinner; they use combat rifles for the purpose. Sister Ann later says that once the firing was so loud it broke the windows at the orphanage.

That evening I sleep in a guesthouse separate from the orphanage building. It is in a cool place under the trees, and I look forward to staying there and listening to the night sounds. My hosts ask if I would like someone to stay with me overnight. When I say no, sleeping alone is fine, they tell me I am brave. The truth is, my mind cannot accept that this is a war zone. The surroundings are too idyllic, the people too kind and trusting. I sleep near the window, lighting the mosquito coil that Sister Maria advised me to bring.

There is no trouble finding a boy with a bike to show me the way to the bridge, but it is late morning by the time they are able to procure a bicycle for me. I promise to come back the same way and return the bike. My escort and I set off down the road. We reach the bridge, where, to my surprise, there is a checkpoint with armed guards and twenty or thirty civilians — some on foot and some with bicycles — waiting to cross. I remember that Sister Maria advised me to cross early in the morning, before the soldiers were up. The armed soldiers search everyone's belongings and ask for identification. I show them my passport. I have also brought my camera and tape recorder. They wave me through the checkpoint. I am again surprised.

The bridge is a rickety affair. I think it would be easier and safer to wade or swim across than to go on this questionable bridge, but I see nobody wading or swimming through the water. Everybody goes over the bridge. We ride our bikes until we get to the village of Kokkadich-cholai. At the time I am not aware that over the past ten years hundreds of people have been massacred in this village, and uncounted others have been abducted and tortured to death. It is midday, and few people are out. We ask men at a tea stall for Payyan. They say he is not there, but he will come. We are taken to an empty building with signs on the walls in Tamil. I do not now remember the content of the signs, but one appears to warn that it would be dangerous to cause trouble to the Tigers. No one else is in the building. The young man who has come with me is looking nervous. He says, with alarm in his voice, "This is the LTTE office!" I guess no one had told him my intentions. Someone asks me what I want, and I reply that I want to meet Payyan and members of the LTTE. After a while, a man who looks in his fifties, unshaven and in a slightly soiled veshtie and shirt, says I should come with him.

"How can I trust you?" I ask, trying not to seem afraid. "You can trust me," he says, looking intently in my eyes, as though this were enough. Both of his ears are intact, so he cannot be Payyan. His breath smells of tobacco. Tigers do not smoke. The young man who has accompanied me from the orphanage now asks permission to be on his way. His relatives live in a nearby village; he says he will visit with them. I am pretty sure he wants to get out of Kokkadichcholai and away from the Tiger office as fast as he can.

And so he is gone. I follow the man with smoke on his breath another mile down the road to the next village. He brings me to a lone building at the corner of two main roads, where a few young men are sitting and talking. One of them, whose name I later learn is Inbam, greets me and asks why I have come. I explain that I want to meet some Tigers. I am taken into the building and into a room empty but for one desk. One of the young men takes a seat behind the desk. I later learn that his name is Alagar. His face is smooth and slightly round, unlined and unscarred. He has big, soft brown eyes. His expression is patient, his manners gentle. Neither he nor any of the other "boys" I meet assume the officious mechanical postures of soldiers. Nothing about them causes me fear. They could be my students in New Zealand. I ask Alagar what his status is. His answer — the exact words I forget — makes me think that he is some kind of district official. He seems too young for that to me, like an officer of a student organization earnestly practicing for a future leadership role. But it could be that the LTTE has many young people in middle-manage-ment positions. If they are like Alagar, that would be good. He shows no trace of weariness or cynicism.

Alagar being the man behind the only desk in the office, I explain to him in as much detail as I can my background and my mission. I hand him a copy of my letter from the vice chancellor of Massey University. He keeps it. I explain that I am not a journalist but an anthropologist. I can stay only a short time now, but I hope to come back again to stay longer. During this visit, I want to meet with some ordinary Tiger combatants, to talk with them, to write about them. In everything I have read, I tell him, the Tigers have been represented as either demons or gods, nothing in between. I want to show the world that the Tigers are neither demons nor gods —

" — but human beings." Alagar completes my sentence.

"Exactly," I say. For this reason, I want to be able to interview ordinary combatants (*cātāraṇa pōrāḷikaḷ* — the phrase comes up often later). "I'm an ordinary combatant," he says. I tell him I would like to tape-record the interviews, and Alagar agrees. As I leave the office, Inbam says, "We will do everything possible to help you; if you need anything we haven't provided, just ask."

Inbam is almost black, with snow-white teeth. He is slender and taller than I am. I guess his age to be thirty. There is something wrong with his right arm; he does everything with his left. How does one record or remember the physical features of a person — the voice quality, the facial expression, the gestures, the walk, the pause in the conversation at just a particular moment — all the things that add up to make you remember that person forever? The imprint in the heart that only one person's image will fit, the mysterious neural pattern that responds to one person only?

Later, Inbam's offer of help must be withdrawn, and I must leave. I am a stranger, after all, and for all they know I could be an informant for their enemies. But for now, the hospitality is overflowing. And also by now, after years in Tamil Nadu, I know that this embarrassing kindness to guests is a matter of course, and I accept it gratefully. They have found a house for me to stay in. Wondering uncomfortably if it has been commandeered by the LTTE for my use, I ask repeatedly if I am not putting people out. But Inbam reassures me, no, it is no trouble at all to the family. They only hope the place will be adequate.

It is just down the road, a five-minute walk from the office. Inbam takes me there. He opens the gate and we enter the front yard. It must be no more than twenty by thirty feet, but every square inch is tended. The ground is all covered in smooth, raked sand. A great palm tree and other smaller trees shade the whole yard. Each plant is healthy; each one is watered and tended every day. There are no weeds or garbage. The family has one rooster and one hen. The rooster crows in the morning only. The hen cackles and lays an egg, and people comment on it. A tiny puppy appears in the yard one day, whining; I comment that it looks lost. They tether it near the house and feed it.

The centerpiece of the yard is a round open well; ten feet away stands what looks like a tree bare of branches about twenty feet high, but at the top is a fork. Another long tree trunk is balanced between the prongs of the fork. One end of the balanced tree trunk has a weight tied to it. The other end is directly above the well, and hanging from it is a long pole to which a bucket is tied. This counterweight arrangement makes it easy to draw water. You can lift the bucket right over your head and dump the water on top of yourself for a bath. It feels great, like standing under a waterfall. I do not know the name of this contraption, but I guess that it must have been invented a long time ago. Everything has been worked out and fits together. Is this what anthropologists used to call "a culture"?

I can see the attractiveness of such a concept, and am sadly amused to find in this place an experience that roughly matches the ideal.

The village has no electricity, and consequently no lightbulbs, no fans, and no power cuts. Batteries have to be smuggled in because the army knows they can be used to make bombs. On the surface, the absence of electricity does not appear to pose a hardship. Children doze off in the evening as they study by dim lamplight.

The contrast with the places I've lived in India — all of them dry and ugly — is stark. The water is good. Every evening an old farmer sits on the veranda of his house, not far from where I am staying, and watches the night fall. Sometimes I join him and we talk, and sometimes we are silent together. The war is all around him; it has badly affected everybody. Landholders are taxed by the LTTE as well as by half a dozen paramilitary groups now working for the army (the main ones are the EPRLF, TELO, and PLOTE; the "L" in all these acronyms stands for "liberation").[2] Cultivation is hampered by shelling and strafing; many fields have been abandoned. Nitrogen-rich fertilizers are not permitted because they, like batteries, can be used to make bombs. All the young men who are not members of any militia are desperate to leave; many have already left or been killed. Yet the old farmer appears utterly at peace.

In the central room of the house a bed has been set up for me, next to a window looking out onto the veranda. On my first day, I lie down on the bed and sleep for a long time. Then I am awakened for dinner, which is set for me on a small table, all alone. Inbam opens the door to the courtyard and enters without asking permission, as though he were a longtime friend of the family. Perhaps he is, but he is greeted with reserve — perhaps because of his LTTE affiliation, perhaps because of his caste. Dinner is offered him, too; he sits down by my side at the small table, and we eat together by lamplight. We speak as we eat, and the conversation turns into a long argument about the war and the LTTE. I object to the senselessness of killing that only leads to more killing, and the loyalty to a leader who seems unworthy of such devotion. To the first objection, Inbam responds with a passionate recitation of injustices committed by the government, the army, and the police. We argue past one another on this point for a long time. I am trying to tell him that two wrongs don't make a right. He is trying to tell me that the government is so evil that it must be opposed by military means; I am attacking the wrong side.

My second objection is that the revered LTTE leader, Velupillai Prabhakaran, is only a man, not a god. The stories I have read of his early life portray him as a killer by preference — not exactly a Nelson Mandela type. If the movement is pinning its hopes on him personally to provide them with its guiding light, is he really suited for the role? And what will happen to them when he dies? I respect the combatants more than their leader, I tell Inbam, who replies that I have insulted the combatants, the movement, and him personally by making this statement. His pride, intelligence, and intensity sadden me. What will happen to him? I wonder. As the argument becomes heated, I begin to fear for this new friendship and even for this new friend. I apologize to Inbam about arguing with him, and explain that I just enjoy arguing for its own sake. He says he enjoys arguing, too. I have learned one thing: this Tiger does not mind my arguing with him, face-to-face.

The next day, again I do nothing but bathe, sleep, and eat, and there is another long conversation with Inbam. When I ask him why he joined the movement, he says that the LTTE asks each family to contribute one person, and he was the designated person from his family. His right arm is crippled. "So you cannot handle a rifle and fight," I conclude. "I am able," he says, "but I am not allowed to go into combat."

· · ·

Monday, 11 March. The household in which I am staying is run by Santhosa. She is young, beautiful, friendly, well mannered, competent, educated, unmarried. She will inherit this house at her marriage, and already it is referred to as hers. There seems to be something wrong here. Why is a young, unmarried woman the head of the household? Why, in her midtwenties, does she remain unmarried? But it would be rude to ask such questions. The answers are contained in another question: Where have all the young men gone?

Trying to sort out the kin ties here is difficult — who is related in what way to whom — because there are so many people coming and going. Trying to keep track in my notebook, I write down, "There are three sons in this family." When Inbam comes to visit, he asks what is in my notebook, and I read him the passage beginning with that sentence. As I do so, the household seems to hold its breath. Later I learn that I have been mistaken, both in the observation and in disclosing it to Inbam. The LTTE keeps track of how many young, fighting-age people live in each household. They expect that each household will "give" one child to the movement. Many parents do not want any of their children, even those over eighteen, to join the LTTE, even if they support it in principle. They do not want their own loved ones to face the danger of combat.

Santhosa's mother has been in the hospital in Batticaloa because of a bad asthma attack. Members of the family tell me that the LTTE, whom they refer to as "the boys," were of great help: they took her to the hospital and got medicine for her. It was not possible to telephone for help, her father says, because the boys took the phone away. "Who took the phone?" I ask. Different people say different things. Santhosa's mother returns from the hospital the day after I arrive. She looks less than forty, but fragile and lost in painful thought; she stays on the veranda, quiet and scarcely moving. I offer her "my" bed, but she declines gently, and so do the other family members, despite my entreaties.

Santhosa's nineteen-year-old brother is living in the house, attending school in Batticaloa town. He is tall and well built, with cheerful good looks, like Santhosa. One day, while we are inside the house, he says to me quietly, "What the boys are doing is good." And then, with an apologetic smile, still more quietly, "But I don't want to join them." He wants to go abroad and work and send money back home.

Last November, he tells me, members of the Special Task Force of the police (STF), which he and the other villagers call simply "the forces," entered the village, destroyed property, conducted roundups, and tortured people. He shows me the scars on his wrists and ankles where his hands and feet were tied. He says he was hung upside down and beaten until his whole body was swollen. He shows me an X-ray that was taken of his chest after he was beaten. No bones were broken. (They torture people in ways that leave small evidence of torture, according to physicians in Sri Lanka who treat the victims.) But he says that his chest still hurts, and his lower right leg is completely numb. He says that the forces also torture people by tying bags over their heads until they are nearly suffocated, or by dunking them repeatedly underwater until they foam at the mouth. Any young Tamil man is automatically suspected of belonging to the LTTE, he says. During a roundup in this village a few months before, the forces took him and tortured him simply for this reason. Every day, when he crosses the lagoon to go into town, he has to go through the checkpoints operated by the STF.

He seems so healthy and relaxed that it is hard to believe that all this really happened to him just a few months earlier. But the roundups, torture, and massacres are all documented. The doctors say that people who are tortured only once suffer less psychological damage than those who are tortured "systematically." Some report that the IPKF tortured their victims more systematically than the Sri Lankan army and STF have done.

Santhosa's mother tells me that things are difficult these days if you have a son in the family. She says they will give money to help the Tigers, because they are fighting for a good cause. Two days later, she has another bad asthma attack and must return to the hospital. There are no medical facilities on this side of the lagoon. Transportation from the village across the lagoon to town is difficult and takes hours: there are no longer any buses to the village, no cars, no taxis, and no phone, as there were before the difficulties. A healthy person can manage, but transporting the sick into town is risky. I ask if the International Committee of the Red Cross (ICRC) cannot help, and the reply is hesitant; I gather that the ICRC is only equipped to assist with war-related injuries, not with ordinary sickness. I suggest that the mother stay in town with a family member until she is completely recovered, rather than go back and forth like this. Within a week the whole family has abandoned their house in the village and moved into town. Before they leave, they tell me regretfully that I too must leave. They are unhappy that they cannot provide for me, but they must look after their mother first. Santhosa's cousin, also an unmarried woman in her twenties, tells me that they have all grown to like me very much, they want me to write, they want me to come back as soon as I can. Santhosa's mother's father puts on a white shirt and a white veshtie in preparation for the journey. "This is my uniform," he says, grimly smiling. He uses the English word *uniform.* "It is for people of this nation [*dēsiya makkaḷ*] — both Tamils and Sinhalese. Trousers are for foreigners."

That afternoon I am moved to another house, the one with the peaceful old farmer. There are no young men in that house at all. The mother is dead, and the house is managed by Thangam, a woman in her late twenties, also still unmarried. She tells me her older sister is staying in town, expecting a baby. She shows me an album filled with photographs of her sister's wedding. As she pores over the album with me, she comments aloud on her sister's beauty and laments her own thinness. She is greatly excited at the imminent arrival of the new baby, which will be her father's first grandchild. A few days later, she brings me the news that the baby, a girl, has been born. I am surprised by the apparent indifference with which everyone else in the house receives this news. My mind runs over possible explanations: the birth of girl children in South Asia is generally not a cause for rejoicing, the family is hiding its pleasure to avoid bad luck, the current "difficulties" (as the war is called) eclipse celebrations.

· · ·

Almost all the people in the Tiger office are men. I hear them called by many names: the LTTE, the boys (in English), the boys and girls (in English, to acknowledge the presence of female combatants), *iyakkam* (the movement), *puḷikaḷ* (the Tamil word for tigers), *viḍutalai puḷikaḷ* (Tamil for "liberation Tigers"), and *poḍiyaṅgaḷ* (mainland Tamil for "little boys," Lankan Tamil for "boys" or "young men").

Some people in the village say that the difficulties started after the movements arose. All the Tamil militias, not just the LTTE, are called movements. I ponder the meanings of the term. Whether Tamil people think of the militias as popular groundswells, the way I as an English speaker think of the things that I call (social) movements; or whether they think of the militias as the moving in opposition to the standing (a dichotomy developed in Saiva religious literature and iconography); or whether the word *movement* just accidentally became attached to the militias is a set of questions to be raised in my next conversations with Inbam and Sister Maria.

The word *viḍutalai*, "liberation," is likewise laden both with specifically modern and Western values, and with Tamil religious ideology. Much has been made, too, of the fact that Tigers (and members of other opposing movements as well) are referred to as boys. Sometimes this nickname has been cited in support of the charge that the LTTE employs child combatants. A few prowar Tamil intellectuals have attempted to demonstrate continuities between the modern Tamil militias and the stylized conventions of early Tamil war poetry, where also combatants were described as very young boys. When the LTTE ran its de facto government in Jaffna prior to 1996, it was in charge of education, and it encouraged schoolchildren to aspire to combat. Now, in 1996, it is not clear whether there has been forcible conscription of children by the LTTE (one other, now-defunct, movement, the TLA, supported by the IPKF, did engage in forcible conscription, with disastrous results), although certainly many young people have joined the LTTE against the will of their parents. Others have sought admission to the LTTE because they see it as a source of shelter, food, and protection. Tiger recruitment campaigns take advantage of the attraction guns hold for many people, including children. Opponents of the Tigers have therefore accused them of brainwashing young children. This is an exaggeration. However, there has been at least one credible report of a preadolescent boy in the LTTE going mad from combat experience and from the things he was made to do.

Anglophone nations also refer to combatants as "our boys." That Sri Lankan Tamils are so often criticized for this same practice bespeaks more than anything else a concern on the part of the government that the LTTE does have the sympathy of Tamil civilians. *Boys* in Sri Lankan Tamil implies youth and tenderness. But there is no word for *man* as distinct from *boy,* and so there is nothing a male must do to prove he is a man and not a boy. This situation is different from that in Israel, for instance, where manhood must be achieved through manly acts. And it is different also from the situation in the United States, where trainers insult military recruits by calling them girls, as though girls were intrinsically inferior and unsuited for combat. The Tigers have female combatants on the front lines; the United States does not. Israel has female soldiers, but they are granted special concessions. The use of language reflects attitudes toward gender and combat.

More significant, perhaps, is the fact that the Tigers are the only Tamil militant movement that chose an animal name. I am inappropriately reminded of my American high school's football team, the Waggener Wildcats. Their logo, too, was the face of a roaring feline. Almost all of the Tamil militias have English names, but the term *Tamil Tigers* is easier to remember than, for example, the Eelam People's Revolutionary Liberation Front (EPRLF, one of the rival Tamil militant groups in Sri Lanka), both because of its alliteration and because of its imagery. The Tiger logo is the face of a roaring tiger with crossed rifles behind it. Sometimes I think that the popularity of the LTTE is partly attributable to its name and icon. But Tiger supporters themselves strongly disagree, arguing that what make the Tigers popular are their accomplishments, not their name.

. . .

There are no pictures on the walls of the Tiger office: no posters, no signs. It is the place where members of the public come if they want to meet with the Tiger administrators. I go there every day with my tape recorder, hoping that one or more of the boys will be available for an interview. Usually I find myself sitting on the bench on the front veranda along with some of the Tigers. We talk informally. They decide they will address me as "Auntie." In Sri Lanka, this is a respectful form of address for an older woman. The term strikes me as amusing, but okay. We can think of no viable alternatives. I call them by their names.

"*Vanakkam,* Auntie!" says Victor with a grin whenever he sees me.

"*Vanakkam,* Victor!" I always say in return, grinning right back. Victor is the only one at the office who does not wear a cyanide capsule around his neck. The others keep them under their shirts and show them to me as proof of membership in the movement.

Inbam is on the front porch the first day I visit the office. Two women in saris are sitting on the bench. One is heavy set, and the other is thin. The thin one's eyes are red. She carries a limp, sleeping toddler over her shoulder. Her younger brother was killed just two days ago. Inbam tells her that four thousand men have been killed in the war, and she must be like a heroic mother and not grieve at the sacrifice. I long to tell Inbam that such words can be of no comfort, but this is not the time for me to speak. When he turns away, the bereaved woman's lips shape silent words; her face is distorted with rage. Slowly she leaves.

The other woman remains seated and calm. I sit down beside her and ask why she is here. She tells me that one of her sons was in the Tigers and was killed; the forces suspected her two other sons of being Tigers and shot them as well. She does not tell me why she is on the porch of the office now.

Inbam walks with me down the road. Another woman is following behind us, scolding us. She says that I am being fed by the Tigers at the expense of the village. She says she has seen everything. Inbam ignores her. She gestures to me to come with her, she will talk with me. I tell her I will come as soon as I can, but later I cannot find her.

Three Tiger women walk past the front of the office. While the men wear unremarkable civilian clothing, the women are conspicuously uniformed in trousers and shirts, an outfit that no civilian woman would wear in this village. The shirts are men's shirts in muted grays and greens, with tails out, belted at the waist. One of the women is wearing running shoes with heavy socks; the others are wearing rubber sandals. Two of them have their hair cut very short; to me they look perfectly natural this way, even cute. The one with the running shoes has two braids pinned to her head. The cyanide capsules hanging by black strings around their necks are tucked neatly into their left breast pockets, with only the string showing. They glance sidelong at me but do not stop or smile. Their demeanor is stern. They seem far more serious and formidable than the men hanging out on the porch.

A few of the men on the porch from time to time make pointedly anti-feminist comments. Kathiravan asks me what work I do and what work my husband does. I tell him that I am a professor, and my (former) husband is a middle-school teacher. Kathiravan replies, "The man should always be bigger than the woman; the woman should always be small." I resist the temptation to point out to Kathiravan that he is shorter than me. He is just baiting me, I guess, and let his comment pass. But there are also pronouncements on the part of assorted male Tigers on the veranda to the effect that women should always wear saris and long hair (my hair is medium length; once I wear a skirt and sleeveless blouse to visit the office and am sternly told that this garb is unacceptable, and I must go home and change). When at last I have an opportunity to speak with Tiger women in the office, the men sit outside on the porch and comment, loudly enough for me to hear, that they think the movement will no longer be letting women into its ranks.

By the time I meet with the female Tigers I have seen, I understand very well why they avoid the men. It is Tiger policy for male and female combatants to keep a respectful distance from one another; in any case, the men do not appear to welcome their female comrades. The women quickly warm up with me. Their apparent sternness I reinterpret as shyness, a veil, a mask for protection, behind which they are themselves. One of the three remains silent and unsmiling through my conversations, but Sita and Nirmala easily break into giggles.

I ask Nirmala's age, and she says, "Thirty: how old do you think I am?"

"Somewhere between sixteen and thirty," I say. "No older than thirty."

"How do you know?" she asks.

I study her face for a moment. "There are no lines," I say. "If you were older, there would be lines."

Nirmala glances at Sita. "Good guess!" she says. "I'm eighteen. My birthday is tomorrow at ten in the evening. Will you come?"

"Of course I will come!" I answer. "What can I give you?"

Nirmala is heavy set and dark, and her hair is cut short. She could be any one of my students or my sons' friends. She tells me I remind her of her mother and that she has two brothers in the movement. I invite Sita and Nirmala to the house where I am staying, just a brief walk down the road. They say aloud that they must have lunch first, but Nirmala whispers to me, "We will come. You go."

I depart alone and head toward the house, glancing back toward the office once or twice. In a couple of minutes, Nirmala leaves on her bike and catches up with me on the road. Sita follows.

Nirmala says, "Give me something beautiful. Have you brought many beautiful things?" I say I have only my clothing and a few other items. I offer her my sari and earrings; she says no to both of these. I offer her my watch, but she shows me that she is already wearing a watch. She glances at my camera. After some hesitation, I agree to give her my camera when I leave. But Sita tells me I should not give it to her. I offer American and New Zealand dollars, which they refuse. I cannot find any appropriate gift to offer them. But when they leave, Sita gently caresses my hand, shows me a smile both laughing and tender, and promises they will come back.

As I am eating my breakfast the following morning, Nirmala and Sita visit me again. Nirmala carries a package wrapped in newspaper. In

English I say to her, "Happy birthday." She gives me the package, which contains bananas, biscuits, and candy. They have also brought a set of tape cassettes with songs about the Tigers, and they play a song about Prabhakaran. Sita asks, "Have you seen him? He is beautiful, isn't he?" She quietly sings along. Then, shyly, she asks, "Do you like our movement?"

After some thought, I respond, "I cannot have feelings for a movement, only for human beings. I like both of you very much."

She smiles. Her hair is carelessly braided and tied up behind. We are two women who don't bother much about our hair. I have seen her in her running shoes and heavy socks, climbing a barbed-wire fence to get into the Tiger compound rather than going around to the gate. She scales the fence easily, her expression happy, as though she is headed off on a hike through the countryside. Did she climb trees in her childhood, as I did, until she was told that she was too old for that? I want to come with her, over the fields and into the jungle.

She is the leader of the women's camp where she stays. Neither she nor any of the other Tigers tell me any more about the camps than what I already know; their location is kept secret to protect them from enemy attacks.

"The girls in our camp have asked about you a thousand times," she tells me.

Now is my chance. "May I come there and meet them? May I come there and stay overnight?"

"Yes. We want you to come," Sita says.

Me, eagerly: "When?"

She, invitingly: "We will come and take you."

I am thrilled at the prospect, but the right time never comes. They would have had to ask permission to take me to the camp, and probably it was denied.

Sita does give me a tape-recorded interview, however. It takes courage for her, as for any of the LTTE members, to do this. Their superior officer, higher-ranking than Alagar, has already expressed reservations about this project, although he has not actually forbidden it, yet. Someone might inadvertently say the wrong thing; the tapes might fall into the wrong hands. A taped interview is more powerful than any signed document. It is a pact of trust.

On the evening of Tuesday, 12 March, Inbam tells me the Tigers have successfully raided a nearby army base the evening before. On Wednesday, 13 March, I am permitted to conduct individual interviews with four of the Tigers I have met: Kathiravan and Jeya in the morning, Sita and

Alagar in the afternoon. All the interviews take place in the Tiger office. As I am interviewing Alagar, we hear explosions in the distance. I check the time. It is about 2:30. The interview continues.

At about 3:00, I meet with Sita. Shortly after we finish the interview, at about 4:00, we hear more explosions. My interview with Sita is serious and thoughtful, not playful. But when I ask the question, "Have you ever shot and killed anybody?" she laughs, probably at the audacity of my asking such a thing. Tamil Eelam has never been formally recognized as a nation, and the LTTE is branded worldwide as a terrorist organization. Effectively, I am asking Sita to confess to murder.

"I shoot only those who come as enemies," she says.

. . .

Every day when I go to the Tiger office, I bring my camera as well as my tape recorder. The first day is a great success for pictures. (Only after I return to New Zealand do I find the whole roll of film is blank because I loaded the camera incorrectly.) Julie is at the office on that first day. When he tells me his name, I ask him to repeat it. "A girl's name," says one of the other men. Obviously, they've been through this before.

Julie becomes special to me partly because his name is easy to remember: some of the others have to tell me their names again and again before I finally remember which name goes with which face and they become fully differentiated in my mind. But, in addition, at our first meeting Julie unwittingly offers a great photo opportunity.

Julie is a little less than six feet tall, of medium build — not heavily muscled, but muscled enough to do farm work. Curly hair, not overly tended. Not a handsome face, but a friendly one, nice smile, slightly broad-nosed. Somehow I remember him now as freckled. If he weren't Tamil, I would have called him Irish. He is dressed in what I quickly come to regard as Tiger combat clothing: a gray and brown shirt and gray trousers. These shirts come in different patterns, all of them undistinguished. You would not know this outfit for a uniform, or even for work clothing. The message it carries is minimal: "Average guy on an average day." Julie is barefoot (message with trousers: "Not going anywhere special"). He is carrying a combat rifle (message with rest of outfit: "We are in Tiger territory now").

I ask Julie if I may take a picture of him with his rifle. He says that would be fine.

"But it's not a problem for you, to have me taking your picture like this?" I ask. "What if my film is confiscated, and the army gets hold of it?"

"They have my picture anyway," Julie says. There is no bravado in the way he tells me this — some resignation, perhaps. "During the ceasefire, we handed our photographs over to them."

"Then, if they have your photograph?"

"I won't cross the lagoon," he says. "I'll be on this side for the rest of my life."

A feeling of imprisonment comes over me, of how it must feel to be Julie. The lagoon and the bridge are a ten-minute bike ride away. Julie must have been back and forth many times before the army came. He must have friends and kin on the other side. Even to me, the thought of not being able to cross brings a shudder of rage at the soldiers. Of course, the lagoon doesn't stretch forever. Julie could take a motorbike and travel around it to the north or south. He could take a bus, as I have. But everywhere that is not fully controlled by the Tigers has soldiers, checkpoints. You can't go anywhere without answering questions, showing identification. The risk to Julie of leaving Tiger territory would be too high. If they caught him, he would be shot. He anticipates my next question. "It's not a hardship. I want to be here," he says. I take a photograph of Julie, barefoot, holding his rifle, and Victor takes another photograph of me standing by Julie's side.

Early Monday evening, Julie appears at the door of a house I am visiting. He is still wearing his combat clothing, still barefoot, still carrying his rifle. Seeing the rifle, the people with whom I have been having tea quickly withdraw into side rooms of the house.

I invite Julie to come in and have tea; he enters and takes a seat in one of the chairs near me. "Is that an AK-47?" I ask, trying to make conversation. He has come looking for me for some reason, and I wonder what it could be.

"A related kind," he says. "There are some modifications."

I don't really care what kind of rifle it is, and Julie seems aware of this. All my life I have disliked connoisseurs of firearms, and people who use them to impress. But clearly Julie has not come to the house with his gun just to impress me. He tells me he is going away for a few days.

"You're going to a fight?" Where else could he be going?

"Chee chee!" he says (Tamil for "Don't even think about it!"). "Just into the jungle for exercises."

"Don't you have any boots?" I don't know what the Tamil word for *boots* is, and Julie seems unfamiliar with the English word.

"Something to wear on your feet. You can't go into the jungle barefoot. Aren't there stones and thorns?" Me playing the protective mother.

"There are stones and thorns," he affirms.

"Well, won't they hurt your feet?" I demand.

He smiles. "They will hurt."

"I want to talk with you," Julie says. "Not now, but when there is time, when we're resting from work."

Recording the stories of combatants is what I have come for, and they all now know that each of them has something of value to me, that they can give or withhold as they choose. They also know that my greatest interest is in child combatants, if there are any. To meet with such a child, to learn his or her thoughts and feelings, is my ultimate goal. But I have accepted the improbability of achieving this goal, because one of the most damning charges against the Tigers is that they use children as fighters. I can only hint at my interest with the adult fighters I have just met, but they are astute. Besides, they have already heard about it from others.

Julie is solemn and thoughtful. "There are very young people working in the camps," he says, gazing downward, as though he were making a difficult confession.

"How young?"

"Fifteen, fourteen, some as young as thirteen."

In previous months, I have studied some literature on child combatants, and have wondered about the reality. My friends in southern India have suggested that child combatants are used because children are easy to control; they fear discipline imposed by adults, and, because of their inexperience, they can be made to believe anything. Westerners venture similar hypotheses. The image of deluded children being sent to die at the battlefront is universally repugnant.

But there are other ways of thinking about the role of children in warfare. They learn quickly. Their small size can be an advantage. They are perceptive, aggressive, and bold. They can adapt to any situation. And although adults think of themselves as the teachers, the trainers and shapers of children, children are also pioneers, testers, who advance the frontiers of culture, dragging their elders behind them. Tigers and other Tamil militant groups have reported that children persistently demand entry into their ranks. Children — most of all young boys of a certain bent — want the guns in their hands as quickly as possible.

The well-cared-for six-year-old girl in the home where Julie now visits me says she wants to join the Tigers so that she won't have to go to school. When I report this to Alagar, and ask what the Tigers would do with such a child, he says, "A six-year-old child? We would raise her and educate her with utmost love and care. We are fighting so that the next generation won't have to fight." When Inbam visits the home, he plays gently with the little girl, pulls her onto his lap, asks her name. She responds with delight. It is part of Tamil culture for grown men to indulge little girls, part of a girl's upbringing to think that her wish is her father's or uncle's command.

Now as this little girl waits silently in a side room with some of her kin, Julie tells me about the slightly older children in the LTTE military camps. I ask Julie what use would there be for thirteen-year-old boys. They are as thin as sticks, some of them. How could they endure combat?

Julie says that they do not fight, but they help in the kitchens, carry food and supplies, and do that kind of work. To my mind come the memories of the very small boys I have seen doing heavy work all day and almost all night in kitchens in Madras, Madurai, all the cities of South India. They do not run away because there is no place to run to, except another kitchen. They are the cheapest, most dispensable labor. Later I learn that boys go to work in the LTTE camps in hopes of being admitted to the LTTE itself after a few years; many LTTE recruits join up this way. And when I visit a local boys' orphanage, one of the teachers there tells me that many of the boys ran away when food at the orphanage was inadequate, and some of them went to the LTTE.

But Julie has not come today to talk about the kitchen boys in the camps.

"Do you have a religion?" he asks me.

"Not really," I say. "I was raised as a Christian. You?"

"I am Catholic," says Julie. "I went to a Catholic school." He takes from his pocket a picture of Jesus, shows it to me. Then he produces a newspaper clipping. "I had two brothers," he says. "Both of them died in the movement. My younger brother died just three days ago." He hands me the newspaper clipping, an obituary. His calm is similar to what my own male kin have shown in coping with a death.

"I'm sorry," I say. "Do you not grieve?"

"No. My heart is locked like this rifle." Before dark falls, Julie is gone.

Julie's visit and departure for the field take place on Monday, 11 March. The following day, in the evening, Inbam visits the house. "What news?" I ask him, as usual.

"Good news!" he announces. "Last night we attacked the army camp and killed twenty-seven soldiers." So Julie had probably lied to me when he said he was not going into combat.

I ask Inbam, "Were any of our people killed or hurt?"

"No. No one killed or seriously wounded. Just ordinary wounds." Our people. Ordinary wounds. The only two phrases that matter, just now. How strange is my rejoicing. Inbam anticipates a question that is not even on my mind: What was the point of killing all those soldiers?

"We brought back a load of weapons. The Sri Lankan Army gets these things from Russia and America, but the only way we can get them is by raiding the army camps."

"But now won't the army retaliate? And isn't there a good chance that innocent people will be killed?"

Inbam is too intelligent not to see the consequences, the simple repeated pattern of Tiger raids on the military and military retaliation against civilians. I know he has no control over military decisions; he does not give the orders. But he offers neither this personal disclaimer nor any sign of remorse.

"We will be having a display of the weapons tomorrow in the next village over. Will you come?"

"I'm not really interested in seeing weapons. But if you'll take me, I'll come."

"I'll come and get you in the morning and take you there," Inbam says. I am not surprised, however, when he stands me up. The next evening he tells me he had so much work he completely forgot our appointment.

Meanwhile, I fret about Julie. Will he come back? Has he been hurt? I am pleased and relieved when I see him arrive at the Tiger office, riding a motorcycle. A broad smile lights up his face, and he wears rubber sandals on his feet. His happiness is infectious. But when he dismounts from the motorcycle, I see that he is limping.

"A lot happened while you were in the jungle," I say. Julie just keeps on smiling. "Why are you limping? What happened to your foot?"

Julie sits down on the bench next to me, and shows me a deep puncture wound on the sole of his foot. It looks like he stepped on a piece of barbed wire. No infection is evident. He should get a tetanus shot, though. "I told you not to go barefoot!" He is oblivious to my admonishment.

· · ·

Sister Beth has been in Sri Lanka for more than a decade. When I meet her, she is not wearing a habit, only a plain housedress. She welcomes me with a handshake, a smile, and an apology for something, although I have just walked in unannounced. I explain my plans and interests to her. Just a few days ago, there was a mysterious explosion in a nearby town. A young man visiting the home of a friend tried to construct a bomb there and accidentally blew himself up. The friend has been wounded and is in the hospital in serious condition. The wife of the friend has been taken into custody, suspected of colluding with the LTTE, because the bomb was constructed in her house. The family wants me to help get her out. They say she knew nothing about the bomb; she is in shock that this happened just weeks after her wedding. Because Sister Beth works to help civilians, I am asking her what I can do.

No amount of prior reading about the atrocities of war could have prepared me for what Sister Beth tells me. There is too much information to absorb, too many horrors one after another, and as she speaks I can see them happening in the quiet streets of the town through which I have walked to the convent, in the verdant rural countryside through which I have come by bus. Sister Beth names the military organizations that have been responsible for civilian deaths: the Sri Lankan army, the STF, the IPKF, a range of outlaw groups. She does not say that the LTTE kills civilians, although she says they used to carry out "lamppost executions" — capturing an enemy, tying him to a lamppost, and shooting him, leaving his body for people to find in the morning. She says they don't do that now, but they have been considered responsible for the recent bombings of electrical transformers in the east.

The army and the STF have conducted roundups of civilians in the area. Although their purpose is to capture Tigers, according to all the civilians with whom I speak, including Sister Beth, the roundups have captured only random civilians, and no one can say whether Tigers were among them. In one recent roundup, the people captured were killed and their bodies burned at a public crossroads in the city. A tire was filled with kerosene and the bodies laid around the tire like spokes in a wheel, with the heads at the center. The tire was ignited and the bodies were burned from the center outward, from the heads to the feet. Sister Beth was a member of a committee that went to investigate the remains of the burned bodies. Some of the feet remained recognizable, and some of those feet, Sister Beth said, were very small feet.

About a year or so ago, a "motorcycle brigade" patrolled the east. They killed five people who they said were Tigers, decapitated the bodies, and stuck the heads on stakes at intervals along a roadside as a warning. The Tigers attacked the motorcycle brigade, according to Sister Beth, and for a while it disappeared, while the Tigers were seen riding new motorcycles. But now, Sister Beth says, it seems that the motorcycle brigade is back.

Mortars fired by the army have landed in a nearby school, making holes in the walls and the floor. Fortunately, no one was killed or injured.

The army denied responsibility, but the teachers are convinced that the mortars were fired from the nearby army base. From the school, they can hear when mortars are fired from the base, although they cannot always hear the explosions when they land. The mortars are fired from the safety of the town into the hinterland where the army believes that Tigers live. Their aim is imprecise, and the mortars often end up killing civilians. Scores of children are playing in the school yard as we speak.

An indeterminate number of young Tamil men in eastern Sri Lanka have been killed by government forces and vigilante groups. "Two graduates of this school have been killed," says Sister Beth. "They both were named Jude." She says none of the organizations to which she belongs support the Tigers in any way. "One of the boys from this school did join the Tigers. His name also was Jude. So we've lost three Judes," she tells me. Is she glad that the third Jude joined the Tigers? "We did not educate them for that," she says emphatically.

. . .

Father Sebastian is a native of Sri Lanka, and a Tamil. He is not entirely neutral with respect to the war. While overseas, I learned that Mahattaya (one of the closest friends of the Tiger leader Prabhakaran, and a popular figure among Tiger supporters) was executed on Prabhakaran's orders for treason against the LTTE. Tiger supporters in India say this is all a lie. I mention the story to Father Sebastian, who tells me that Mahattaya was feeding information to the Indian intelligence agency RAW (Research and Analysis Wing). Mahattaya's own wife discovered his disloyalty and reported it to Prabhakaran. "Imagine how you would feel," he says, "if one of your oldest and closest friends betrayed you like this."

"But these killings at the top," I protest. "Don't they mean trouble?"

"All big organizations are the same," Father Sebastian reassures me. "You should see the folks at the Vatican!"

He warns me, however, that Tigers mean business, in more senses than one. He shows me a letter sent to a local businessman, with the Tiger logo at the top. The letter orders the businessman to deliver a certain amount of money to a certain place at a certain time. "If you fail to do so," the letter concludes, "you will be required to think."

Later, a knowledgeable journalist from the area explained the threat: local businessmen may be held by the Tigers until their families provide the "tax" that the Tigers calculate is "owed" by the person held. Sometimes intermediaries negotiate with the Tigers to reduce the amount required.

Father Sebastian is energetic, but he is in poor health. Once I visit him in the hospital. Suddenly, a nurse comes in and says, "It is time for your operation, Father." They wheel him out. Whatever the operation is, it does not take long. I am thinking I should leave, but Father Sebastian's sister urges me to stay, saying, "He reveals his deepest and truest thoughts when he is under anesthetic. Watch." They wheel him back into his room, still unconscious. He calls aloud, "Tamil Eelam! Tamil Eelam!" The nurse comforts him: "Hush, hush, and rest. We've won, we've won [*kiḍaittatu, kiḍaittatu*]."

Father Sebastian is pleased that I know Tamil, and during our first meeting, when there is time to talk, he recites to me some passages from Tamil devotional literature, repeating certain phrases, inviting me to savor the beauty of them. He is one of many committed and devout Christians who adore Tamil religious poetry. It matters not in the slightest that this poetry was composed in praise of Hindu gods: it's the feeling that counts, and the intense emotion aroused by these hymns could as easily be directed to Jesus as to Siva.

Father Sebastian also reads to me passages from the Vatican II Proclamation, a thick volume he thumps like a Bible. "This book was not composed by human beings," he says. "It was composed through the instrumentality of human beings by God himself. It is the direct word of God."

He opens the book to a place where "God" tells human beings of the twentieth century how they must act in the world. A list of ethical mandates includes the imperative "Fight oppression." Father Sebastian reads the whole passage aloud. "My political actions have been challenged by members of the Church hierarchy. Some say my political work is not in accord with the work of a priest. In answer, I read to them what is said here in the Vatican II Proclamation. It says to *fight* oppression. *Fight*. This is the word of God." Father Sebastian looks up from the book to catch my expression. If my face betrays incomplete confidence, his does not.

• • •

Because I am a woman, people assume that my interest in Tigers centers on female combatants. To a certain extent, it does. This is my first foray into the study of warfare. I have avoided it previously because I have always seen it as a man's game. If you know that much, you don't need to know any more. Women warriors are interesting precisely and only because they are exceptions to the general rule. Female Tiger combatants are this kind of anomaly. To the general public, "Tigresses" are among the three most striking features of the LTTE, the other two being the cyanide capsules and the suicide killings. Since the death of Rajiv Gandhi, the image of the female suicide bomber stands as an indelible memorial to the Tiger mystique.

Sita has a sweet, childlike voice and is just about five feet tall. More often than not she is smiling, and many times she is shyly laughing. As becomes a young, unmarried Tamil woman, she seems embarrassed and almost frightened in the presence of men, never initiating speech with them or answering back when they criticize her. She and Nirmala visit me one evening in the second house where I have been quartered. As we are speaking, Victor unexpectedly enters. Instantly Nirmala and Sita rise to their feet, their backs straight, their faces expressionless. Victor ignores them and strides past us into the kitchen, where Thangam is cooking dinner. Thangam, a young civilian woman, does not attempt to conceal her interest in certain Tiger men. She is always asking me about them and commenting on their good looks. I imagine she hopes to marry one.

As soon as Victor has disappeared, Sita and Nirmala break into hushed giggles. I ask, "Why did you rise when he entered?"

"To show respect," says Nirmala, once again unsmiling. "We respect all the men in the movement as older brothers."

"But I thought you were their equals," I say. "Do they rise when *you* enter the room?"

"We are equals," Nirmala insists, ignoring my question. "They are our older brothers, we are their older sisters. We show respect for one another at all times."

This is Nirmala's military demeanor speaking. During the same conversation, I ask her whether she will allow me to interview her, as I have previously interviewed Sita. With a straight face, Nirmala replies, "I am prepared to answer any question you ask," as though she had been brought in for interrogation. Is she being ironic, as she was when I first asked her age? Was she being ironic in her response to my questions about gender equality among Tigers? It is difficult to interpret such stiff formality on the part of a kittenish girl in any other way.

Kittenish and playful, young enough to be my daughters, are these the sinister Tigresses known to all the world for their determination to kill and die? Dhanu was Nirmala's age when she killed Rajiv Gandhi.

The differences between my Batticaloa Tigress friends and my female friends in Madras are striking. Many of these differences may be attributable to differences between Batticaloa and Madras cultures. Both are Tamil, but the Tamil world is a big place. Other differences may be attributable to the fact that Tiger combatants must maintain a strict discipline, whereas in Madras, discipline yields to survival.

My Madras women friends are so aggressive toward men they sometimes embarrass even me. Not toward all men, but to the men they know well, of whom there are many: brothers, cousins, husbands, sons, fathers, family friends. Certain men are the objects of open and obvious physical affection: women lean on their shoulders, sit on their laps, gaze into their eyes, caress their cheeks. Between a mother's brother and his sister's daughter, no holds (but one) are barred. Shows of affection include hard slaps and blows. More than once I have mistaken such love pats as the beginnings of fights and tried to stop them. My efforts at intervention were met with dismayed protests from all the sparring partners. This is big-family life in a big Indian city, more dangerous in some ways than Tiger-controlled parts of Lanka.

Only once in our casual encounters do I encounter a glimpse of the Tigress in Sita. This is when I meet Sita on the road, in the company of another woman, but without Nirmala. "Where is Nirmala?" I ask. Sita looks up at me with that enigmatic serious face. This time no hint of a smile.

"Nirmala is dead."

"What? How? Where?" Sita is silent. "Are you joking? Is what you are telling me true?"

"True."

"When did this happen? Why did nobody tell me? You are lying, aren't you?"

"Yes, I am lying," says Sita. My body, tense with alarm, relaxes slightly. But Sita still does not smile. "Nirmala has gone very far away," Sita says.

"When will she come back?"

"She will never come back," says Sita.

We part on the road, and I am left not knowing what to believe. But a few days later, when all the Tiger workers are going from house to house collecting donations, I see Sita and Nirmala together, talking over a fence to one of the household women. Nirmala is fine.

Much later I learn something about basic LTTE philosophy. Some of this philosophy reminds me of lessons I learned from my Madras Tamil teacher in 1975, as he explicated for me some passages of Tirumular's *Tirumantiram:*

> Life is always beginning. One life emerges from the next, endlessly.
> The living body is a trellis, the spirit a vine.
> When the trellis falls, the vine falls also.
> The living body is a vessel, containing the fluid spirit. When the vessel
>   breaks, the spirit dissipates like steam.

The living body is full of holes; these holes are open windows. The dead
    body is an abandoned house with all its windows closed.
No good endeavor should be allowed to come to completion.
Marriage is a beginning. Marriage is a conjoining.
Death is an ending. Separation is death.
Never say "die." Say "attain time."[3]

Another verse from *Tirumantiram* says:

The mud is one, as you have seen — the pots are of two kinds.
One is made hard by fire.
The other, when the rain falls,
Melts back into mud again. Thus,
countless people die.

Sita later tells me that Tigers consider they gain a kind of immortality,
a timelessness, by going through fire — the fire of death in battle or in a
suicide attack. Normal human beings, like unfired pots, "melt back into
mud again." The Saiva philosophy expressed by Tirumular holds that to
attain immortality, you must harden yourself in a different kind of fire, the
fire of *tapas* (intense self-denial). But the fire of *tapas* described in Saiva
philosophy and the fire of combat described by Sita have the same effect.

At the same time, vegetative imagery of death and regeneration, not
unlike that of my pacifist teacher in Madras, pervades Tiger philosophy.
One example appeared in the pro–Eelam Tamil newspaper *Kalattil*, with
a prefatory note by the editors:

In the battle of Elephant Pass, Captain Kasturi embraced heroic death. These are
the lines of poetry she wrote at the end but was unable to finish. .

Deathless
Severed hands
grow back fast.
The more they're cut,
the more they sprout.
Like stubborn plants,
sliced hands
bear buds
and mangled ones
burst red.
Strangled throats
in streaks of flame
oppose a ripe death,
screaming.
Burnt lungs

scald the occupier,
and sear him
with their breath
forced free.
"He's dead and gone,"
the enemy mocks,
and in that place,
corpses take life.
You enemies cause trembling agony.
Torture. Kill. What of it?
Severed, amputated,
cut down, warriors sprout.
Our warriors
will not die until
your armies flee
beyond our bounds.
Hands raised for rights
submit to no invasion.[4]

The women's wing of the LTTE is called *viḍutalai paravaikaḷ,* Birds of Freedom. The concept is obvious. But this concept contrasts sharply with mainland Tamil women's conceptions of their own womanhood, according to which they are shackled and bound.

As it happened, just before I traveled to Batticaloa in 1996, I visited the village in India where I had done my initial fieldwork. There a village woman sang me this song:

ammāḍi en manacu cariyillai, nimmatiyāka vāra vaṟiyillai
peṇgaḷ vāṟ kaṇṇīriḍa kaṭaiyai tinamum toḍarvatā ammā
ciṟakuḍaitta paravaiyāka atu tuyaril vāṟvatā
ammāḍi en manacu cariyillai, nimmatiyāka vāra vaṟiyillai

Dear mother, my heart is not well,
there is no way to live in peace.
Is the story of tears that women live a daily, continuing one?
Will they live in pain like birds with broken wings?
Dear mother, my heart is not well,
there is no way to live in peace.[5]

This song expresses the lack of personal freedom that traditional Tamil women must live with. Sita, I believe, along with many of her cohort, was trying to break out of that state.

When I interview Sita on 13 March, I want to learn her personal motivation for joining the LTTE and why she stays. The willingness to die in the service of the movement — indeed, the positive desire to die in combat and in no other way — is a desire I wish to understand, though not to share. Similarly, the unquestioning devotion of LTTE members to their leader, Velupillai Prabhakaran, is troubling to me as a liberal Westerner. It seems inconsistent with the secular socialism that Eelam Tamils envision for the independent state they are fighting for. Do the means justify the end? At what point does total obedience to the leader of the movement leave off and self-determination begin? Finally, how total is the Tiger combatants' renunciation of marriage and family for the sake of military discipline? Does celibacy help them or hurt them? Or could it help some and not others?

The radical aspects of Tiger culture are to some degree explicable within the larger frame of Tamil and other Dravidian cultures. The pendant around the neck signifying submission to a particular discipline (*kadduppāḍu*) is a variform of the marriage pendant signifying, for women, the renunciation of personal freedom in the service of husband and family. At the same time, this pendant signifies a renunciation of family in favor of another, hopefully more liberating, discipline. The same pendant is also reminiscent of the lingam (sign of Siva) worn by Virasaivas as a symbol of their radical ownership of this god in their persons. The adoration of Prabhakaran is in line with the adoration (*bhakti, pattu*) offered to many human beings who are perceived as harboring something divine, whether it is great musical talent, rhetorical powers, or the strength to keep a family together. Harboring the divine is not inconsistent with human imperfections or even with acts of apparent madness. Strange vessels are cherished when they contain unique qualities. Renunciation of family is one kind of strangeness apparent in some such vessels. Deviation from sexual norms in the other direction — a life of devotion to sexuality — may also be allowed to the truly great. The choice of suicide as a means of resolving relational losses, and the old tradition of renouncers seeking individual spiritual freedom and the ultimate termination of selfhood, all come into play.

In Tamil culture, love takes three forms: *pācam* (attachment), *pattu* (devotion), and *anbu* (selfless love). Almost everyone has *pācam*, which is a necessary part of life, but it is a bond that must be broken if any kind of liberation is to be gained. Among the Tigers, *anbu* for the people, *pattu* for Prabhakaran, and the breaking of ties of *pācam* for kin and friends are all fully in accord with wider Tamil cultural values.

The renunciation of natural death in favor of violent death may seem more novel, but is not really. The Tiger does not quietly, slowly dissolve back into the elements in the manner of a conventional organism, but fights natural death by embracing a radical death and deliberately stepping out of biological time. This approach to immortality has strong precedents in Tamil Siddha philosophy, as I have suggested above.

I hoped, through my interview with Sita, to gain a better understanding of Tiger culture. I wanted to know whether Tiger women experienced this culture differently from Tiger men. Was the LTTE just another boys' gang? Was the Eelam war just another man's game? The main topics about which I sought elucidation were the devotion to the leader, the renunciation of family, and the choice to die either in battle or by suicide if captured.

I was initially skeptical of the idea that a woman might attain liberation by joining the LTTE. But Sita convinced me that some women do achieve liberation in certain senses. It is no trivial thing to want a place in history, as opposed to being confined to the realm of reproduction, and Sita saw this quite clearly. In addition, she had achieved a privileged degree of physical power and mobility; she could operate machinery — motorbikes, tractors, and guns — that freed her from some of the constraints of a mortal, gendered body. Most important, perhaps, she was liberated from the helpless anger expressed in the laments of so many traditional Tamil women I knew.

During the interview, Sita quoted a Tiger adage: *Nenjilē nanjai ettiyavar tān tamiḻ īṛam piriyar* (only those who have lifted the poison to their hearts are beloved of Tamil Eelam). The term *nenjilē* can mean both "in the heart" and "on the chest." The poison on the chest clearly refers to the cyanide capsule worn as a pendant, but it may have a deeper meaning as well, for Sita made it quite clear that she and many other combatants were motivated to join the LTTE by frustrated anger at the death of loved ones killed by the army. In the interview, Sita described how she harnessed that anger to turn herself into an effective killer. If she came across to me as a joyfully sweet human being, perhaps this was because she had discovered that vengeance is sweet.

What follows is a transcription of the taped interview.

M: Do you have any brothers or sisters?

S: I have a younger sister in Jaffna.

M: How far have you studied?

S: I studied AL [completed Advanced Level exams, indicating readiness for tertiary education]. My sister studied OL [Ordinary Level exams, indicating completion of secondary education].

M: Where is your sister now?

S: My younger sister became a doctor in Jaffna,[6] and now is in Kilinoch-chi. She has only one leg. When she was on her way to market, in Punakari, she was wounded, and she lost one leg.

M: Do you have any brothers?

S: In 1985, an older brother, when he was coming home from school, the STF pursued him and shot and killed him. Another brother, in 1990, was shot and killed in Vantharumulai University [in Batticaloa District].

M: What happened to you after that?

S: In 1990, after the troubles began, both my sister and I were in the camp [unclear whether she means refugee camp or Tiger camp]. Because of that, we joined the LTTE. We received our training in the camp. Now I am in Batticaloa, and my sister is in Jaffna.

M: What about your parents?

S: Father died in 1976. Mother is still alive.

M: Was your mother unhappy that you joined the LTTE? Having lost her two sons, she would not want to lose her daughters as well.

S: Mother is happy that the two girls have joined the movement, because our two brothers were killed.

M: Does this mean that your mother is now all alone?

S: An elder sister is staying with Mother. Also a younger brother is there, attending school. He is nineteen. He would not leave our mother to join the movement. So we two girls left.

M: Do you think you will ever marry?

S: We will not marry. It is enough to fight for the liberation (*vidutalai*) and happiness of the people.

M: Are you [personally] liberated now?

S: Absolutely! [*Tārāḷamāy!*]

M: What was your life like before the troubles started? Were you happy? Was your family comfortable?

S: We were living happily before. After my brothers died, I decided to join the movement. After my brothers were killed, bitterness and frustration [*virakti*] came upon me. I wanted to die as my brothers died.

M: So you don't want to marry, start a new family?

S: There is an age for that.

M: You are twenty-seven. You must have reached that age . . .

S: I have no thought of that.

M: Have you ever been in combat? Have you ever been wounded?

S: I have been in combat, but I have not been wounded. I went into combat in 1993, and in 1992. In Amparai, in 1990, I was among the first group of female trainees. There were twenty of us. I went into combat for the first time in 1991. Many people attained a heroic death [she uses the formulaic phrase *vīramāna maraṇam aḍainta*]. Only four of us now remain.

M: Have you ever shot anybody?

S: [*laughs*] Only if they come as enemies do I shoot them.

M: Have any of your friends been wounded?

S. My friends have attained heroic death. Only my sister has been wounded. In the Punakari fight [17 November 1993] she was wounded. She has only an artificial leg now. Her right leg. I haven't seen her since that.

M: How is it when one of your friends dies?

S: Oh! It is painful! [*Ayyō! Kavalai!*] We are taught in training how to accept this loss. As one friend falls, another comes to take her place. We cannot grieve too much. If we grieve, we cannot fight. We remember that we too will die. We all will die, and this is a heroic death. But still it is hard. We have a funeral in which each friend reads a poem or essay she has written about the friend who has died.

M: What has been your most important experience in the movement?

S: My most important experience . . . [*She reflects for some moments.*] There were twenty of us in the training camp in Jaffna. During that time, one day, we heard the sound of a supersonic fighter. The army was shelling the town and conducting a roundup. We had only seven training masters with us. The rest of us did not know what to do. Those seven fought with the army and drove them away. Then we went to another place.

M: Have you noticed any changes in your mind or heart since joining the movement?

S: If I were at home, I could not do all these things. I have become even more ready to die. I see the suffering of the people, and I have no fear about fighting and dying for them. Even if I die today, I will be satisfied. When people in the movement die, it is a useful death. If I died in the house, there would be nothing remarkable about that.

M: You live close to death. It could come today or tomorrow. Do you really feel no fear?

S: *Chee!* If I were afraid, would I have joined the struggle? I am just exactly like the men. However the older brothers are [*annāṅgal* — the male fighters], we will be the same way. If we were in the house, we would be confined. But now we are like men, so there is no fear.

M: Do you never wear a sari?

S: *Chee!* We can't go to the field [i.e., into combat] wearing saris.

M: What do you think of Prabhakaran?

S: Oh! A man of goodness, intellect, sacrifice. [*Ayyō! Oru puṇitamāna maṇitan. Tiyāga cintai.*]

M: But you are the ones who have made all the sacrifices.

S: But the ideas. Because of the love he had for the people, he left his home.

M: Your life is not important to you. But your honor. What if someone tried to rape you?

S: Prabhakaran?

M: No, I mean an ordinary person.

S: That will not happen. People respect us. Ordinary people respect us. We are members of an army. So they call us younger sister, daughter.

M: Yes. Ordinary people will not do me or you any harm. But there are crazy men in this world . . .

S: Yes, there are crazy men . . .

M: What if one of them tried to rape you?

S: [*laughs*]

M: Would you fight?

S: I would fight as much as I could . . . ? [She does not seem to understand why I am asking this question.]

M: But what if the army comes . . .

S: Oh! Right, right. . . . They might try, but I would fight, and they would not be able to do it. But otherwise, we have our cyanide capsules [*kuppi*]. No one has gotten caught in the field. They [the army soldiers] can do whatever they want [to our bodies] after we're dead.

M: Is age important? For instance, is there a difference between fifteen-year-old fighters and thirty-year-old fighters?

S: Yes. Fifteen-year-olds are less experienced. They have just joined, just started. Every year you gain more experience, more learning.

M: *What do you expect from other countries?*

S: We want a separate nation. Foreign nations should accept that.

M: *What if you don't achieve Tamil Eelam?*

S: We will not let go until we have it. We will fight down to the last person.

M: *What will Tamil Eelam be like?*

S: [*laughs*] The people will be happy. We must see that the people are happy, make them happy.

M: *What kind of life do you desire for yourself?*

S: I want the life of a fighter. That is the kind of life I like. I don't want an ordinary life.

M: *You don't want a life with husband and children and home and nice clothes and all that?*

S: I don't want it.

M: *Why not?*

S: As soon as you get married, you have to look after children. We will raise our children and grow old. When we grow old, we will die. There is a difference between that kind of death and the death of a fighter. Rather than that kind of death, I would prefer this kind of death. It is a heroic death. A historic death. A sacrificial death. Having joined the struggle, gone into battle, for the sake of the people going into battle . . . we are happy at the thought of our death in battle, because then we become part of history.

M: *Yes, but life is one thing, and death is another.*

S: Life is one thing, and death is another . . .

M: *If I had my way, I would live a normal life but have a cyanide capsule so that I could die when I chose.*

S: [*quoting*] "Only those who have lifted the poison to their hearts are beloved of Tamil Eelam." When we have the poison on our chests, we can finish off the enemy.

M: *Are you of the Saiva religion?*

S: Christian.

M: *Christian? But you are wearing the sacred ash on your forehead.*

S: [*laughs*] In our movement, all religions are one.

M: *When you die, after you die . . .*

S: But it's not like that. To come to an end, it's not like that. When we die, we have no religion. But when we are buried, they read poems as they put some earth on us. Ordinary people also join. There is something called strength [*uruti*]. There is something called words of strength [*uruti urai*]. We speak that to the people. For the sake of the people.

M: *Is there another birth after death?*

S: I don't know.

M: *You have friends? Are they mostly women?*

S: There are men, too, but they are brothers [she emphasizes the word].

M: *When you go to a fight, do you see the enemy's face?*

S: We are hiding, so we can see them up close. When we fight the enemy, how can we not see him? He is standing right there. How can we shoot him if we can't see him?

M: *You see the person?*

S: We see the person.

M: *He . . .*

S: If we see him, we shoot him. If he sees us, he shoots us. Therefore, we have to be careful.

M: *But the person's face and everything . . .*

S: We see.

M: *Seeing it, you shoot.*

S: Yes.

M: *Do they see you, see your face?*

S: Yes, they have seen it. They will have seen it.

M: *What do they do when they see?*

S: Who?

M: *The enemy.*

S: When they come?

M: *When the enemy sees you, what do they do?*

S: For us, the way it is for us is, as soon as we see the enemy, our heart changes. The thought comes that somehow we have to shoot them, and our heart changes.

M: How does your heart change?

S: It . . . When I see the enemy, I think of my brothers, and how they were killed, and how they were captured and beaten, and how they did this to all our people, and the thought comes that if I can get close to the enemy, I can do whatever I want.

M: So, you get angry.

S: Yes, angry.

M: You get angry with the enemy, and you want to shoot him in that way. When he sees you, that you are a woman, is he surprised?

S: Yes. Mmm. The enemy went out and told the people that female Tigers had attacked and beaten and chased them. In Valaichenai and Santhiveli, we attacked them. We were only girls, no boys. We chased and chased and fought.

M: When they see you, are they afraid?

S: Yes.

M: Do they run?

S: Yes.

M: Are you afraid? Do you run?

S: No. We chase them.

M: But if you are ten people and they are a hundred people?

S: We receive training according to the situation. Using that training, even if they are a hundred people, we will shoot them down [*cuḍḍu tān vaippōm*]. We put one person every ten yards. Ten by ten in a hundred places, whereas all of them are in one place.

M: In that training, do they teach you how to use a rifle?

S: We were taught in training camp how to attack a hundred people using ten people. Because of that training, we can attack without fear.

M: Do they teach you how to operate vehicles?

S: Yes. Motorbike, tractor, car.

M: Do you get to choose whether to be Sea Tigers or Earth Tigers?[7]

S: Yes.

M: What is the difference?

S: Sea Tigers are taught how to swim.

M: Can't you swim?

S: Yes, but Sea Tigers are taught how to swim in the sea better.

M: Do you know about the Sea Tigers who were captured?

S: Yes. Some died. But some tried to swallow cyanide, but the salt water kept the cyanide from working, so they were captured. The newspapers reported this, but we still don't know what happened to them.

M: Can't you try to rescue them?

S: Their mother and father must get them released. We cannot do it. We can't go there. The army went and interrogated their mother, and assaulted her also.

M: Why do you think the enemy has done all these horrible things?

S: The army attacks the family so that the family won't send the children. And when they can't attack the Tigers, they attack the people. They cannot control their tempers, so they do this.[8] The enemy fights for his salary. We are fighting for the people, for a separate nation, and for liberation. They have other work to do; why should they join the army just to die? In Mandur, twenty-five people who were in the army died. If they hadn't joined the army, they could have lived to serve their wives and children. If he dies, he leaves behind a poor widow with children. The army thinks all the Tamils are Tigers. But we fight only the army, not the ordinary people. We never kill ordinary people, only the army does. When they see schoolchildren, they catch them and beat them, and this causes the children to want to join the LTTE. In general, this is why people join. Like me, my brothers were killed, and out of frustration, I joined the movement.[9]

CHAPTER 4

Vasanta and Rosa

What Vasanta Said

November 1997. I am staying with Vasanta in her house in the village of Mahiladithivu. Vasanta is a Christian; the walls of her house are decorated with pictures of children and babies and passages from the Bible in Tamil. One of them reads: *Itu e<u>n</u>raikkum nān tankum iḍam, itu nān virumbinapaḍiyāl ingē vacampa<u>n</u><u>n</u>uvē<u>n</u>* (In this place I shall always dwell. In accordance with my liking, I shall make it my home).

Vasanta has mentioned to me several times the massacre on a prawn farm in Mahiladithivu, where her brother was among the laborers killed by the STF. I have asked Vasanta if she will tell me the whole story in detail. She is glad to do so, and on 15 December 1997 she takes me to the cooking hut next to her kitchen, seats me at the doorway of the hut, and tells me the story as she prepares dinner. Her narrative is so absorbing that I do not notice what she is doing in the hut as she talks, but afterward, when she brings me my dinner, she says with a smile, "This is what I was fixing while I was talking to you." The meal includes several dishes cooked from scratch.

Vasanta's narrative is in mixed Tamil and English. She dictates slowly to me as I type and render the narrative into straight English. Often I stop her and ask for clarification. Except for the rendering of Tamil into English, deletion of material she repeated when I asked for clarification, and small grammatical corrections made as I typed, Vasanta's narrative is reproduced here as she told it to me.

The prawn project was an American scheme. Earlier, an EPRLF MP, whose name was Sam Tambimuttu, had a business partnership with an American. While Sam Tambimuttu was working in this partnership, the partners bought some paddy fields for ready cash, cleared the bush, and put a prawn pond there. They bought those fields from poor people. They paid 2,500 rupees per acre. Out of each 2,500, the poor people got 500, and Tambimuttu secretly took 2,000. At that time, the people did not know. They were poor people — they took the 500. A couple of months later, the people somehow found out, and went and told the American partner. Then, that American asked [Tambimuttu]. When he asked, Sam Tambimuttu denied it. Sam Tambimuttu was ousted from the partnership. Then Sam Tambimuttu got angry. Out of anger, he had two laborers plant a bomb in the pump that was used to fill the prawn pond with water.

After that, from the American scheme, the LTTE bought kerosene, diesel oil, petroleum. Sam Tambimuttu told the police HQ in Colombo that there was a connection between the prawn project and the LTTE. Sam Tambimuttu drew a map of the project for them. After that, the STF came here on 2 November 1986. They went and looked at the prawn project scheme. When they looked, they saw the characteristics that Sam Tambimuttu had indicated [in the map he showed the police]. Only laborers were there; the LTTE had run away. Then the STF did nothing to the American partners. When the STF asked the laborers, the laborers said there was no connection between the LTTE and the company. Then the STF, doing nothing there, came into this village and did a roundup of all the men, and took them to that field.

Vasanta nods in the direction of the empty field across the road from her house. "That very field?" I ask. "Yes, that one," she confirms.

There they beat them and told them to show where the LTTE camp was. The people who worked on the prawn project [who did not live in this village] were staying in two rented houses in Mahiladithivu. The STF took two or three of those people [to show them the way] and went and burned those two houses. Then they took all the men of the village to Batticaloa. When they went, they told the people to shout, "We don't want Eelam, we don't want Prabhakaran, we want Premadasa, we want the government, we want the STF." After that, over a period of five days, they interrogated each man individually and released them.

After that, the prawn project was moved. On 27 January 1987, again the STF came here — to Kokkadichcholai, Mahiladithivu, and Arasadithivu. They came by ferries, by bridges, and by helicopter. The army that came by way of the Valaiyiravu bridge lost thirteen men on the spot to a bomb blast. Out of anger, on the way as they came they shot civilians on both sides. Ten people were killed. After that, they came straight here, and went to the prawn project. There, they put all the laborers and officers on a tractor cart and brought them to the junction by this house. Then, on 28 January 1987, the American scheme manager (his name was Bruce), who was living in Batticaloa, did not come on that day. That day was salary day and party day. The assistant farm manager was staying in my house on that day. When the STF was here, the assistant farm manager had gone to work (on the farm). The STF had brought everyone to the junction. They took the identity cards of the permanent officers and the temporary officers.

I had two brothers who were working on that prawn project. The STF came to my house and were cooking meals here [in the house where we are now cooking and eating] for some of the forces. While they were cooking, I heard the sound of shooting. I had two brothers working on the project, but we didn't see both brothers. They were reading the identity cards and calling the name of each person. When we heard the gunshots, we looked over to that side. The STF [those who were in the house] said, "You don't go that way, don't look that side, don't go anywhere." Then my fourth brother's wife came running to this house, with her son. She said, "My husband is there."

One Muslim man gave toffee to her child. My brother's wife said, "Don't want." He asked, "Why don't want?" She said, "My husband is there." That soldier asked, "What is your husband's name?" She said, "My husband's name is Kirubhakaran." She told him, "Three years before, he was living at Boosa Camp." He had been captured and then released. The soldier said after thinking for a few minutes, "I think Kirubhakaran — I don't know if he is alive or dead." We were sad.

My brother's wife was looking that side, and she said, "He is sitting on the road near the church gate." The soldier asked, "Kirubhakaran — who is that?" [i.e., which one of you is Kirubhakaran?] My brother did not speak, out of fear. A gun on the left (pointed at his head), a gun on his right, a gun in front (pointed at his forehead). Slowly and fearfully, my brother stood up. He said, "I am Kirubhakaran." They took my brother and five people back to the prawn project pond. There they took a diesel can and petrol can and old tires (from the prawn project pond) and brought them here to the junction. A tractor was here — a big box and tractor. STF said to put the petrol and diesel and tires on the tractor cart. While my fourth brother was watching, they shot and killed my third brother. Still while he was watching, there were many dead bodies in the tractor cart. The prawn project assistant manager also. Then the STF said, "Go and sit."

That Muslim man came to my home. He said, "Kirubhakaran is alive. In just a few minutes, he will come to this home." While he was speaking, that STF commander came to my home. We were crying (I, my mother, my father, my sister, my younger brother, my brother's wife with son, and an auntie with son near the house). We fell down and touched his feet. That STF commander said to one of the soldiers, "Call Kirubhakaran." Then my brother came back. That STF commander warned, "Don't tell anybody about this incident [the killings]. If you tell, we will burn your home and everybody will be killed."

Just at this moment Vasanta's little baby looks up and smiles, and Vasanta says to her, "*Cirikkiriyā?*" and to me, "She is laughing." She hands the child to her mother and begins to feed her older children fish and rice as she continues her narrative.

The STF officer said, "If you tell even one person we will burn your house and kill you all. Don't tell anyone, and don't go anywhere." Then that commander came and ate his lunch and left.

In all, eighty-five men were killed and the house of the prawn project was burned.

After that, when that commander was gone, we heard some gunshots. About six or six-thirty that evening, a jeep came down the road to this junction.

Vasanta's twin toddlers are crying, and she goes to pacify them. Rocking one of them in her lap, she continues.

The soldiers who came in the jeep — what they said I don't know — but the jeep turned around and went back. After that, the tractor left (with the bodies in the cart). After that, where it went, what happened, what was done with the bodies, we don't know. We still do not know.

Another woman sitting nearby on the porch makes a comment about another incident, and Vasanta picks up on it.

That same day, at Kadukkamunai village near Ambilanthurai, five people were made to stand on the edge of a well, and they were shot, and their bodies fell into the well. That same day, in that town there is an irrigation bungalow, four people were put in that bungalow, and a bomb was thrown there while they were still alive, and they were killed in that bomb explosion. The next day, three new STF camps were set up in Kokkadichcholai, Mahiladithivu, and Ambilanthurai. The prawns that were in that pond were taken by the STF and common people and they ate some and sold others and made a lot of money.

I ask Vasanta if the massacre was ever reported. She says it was reported to the Batticaloa Citizens' Committee, which recorded the details. The American company that owned the prawn project filed a lawsuit against the Sri Lankan government. According to Vasanta, the American company won the case in 1989, two years after the massacre took place. The Sri Lankan government accepted the decision because America provides support to the government, and they don't want to lose that support. After winning the case, the American company gave one hundred thousand rupees to each of the murdered men's families.

I ask Vasanta how she manages to continue after so much hardship. I am careful not to ask how she keeps her sanity, as I want to see whether she will voluntarily bring up the topic of madness. She tells me that the event she described, in which she lost one older brother (brother number three), is just one of a series of hardships. She lists six events, all but one directly connected with the war.

The first hardship came when her fourth brother was captured and kept in Boosa Camp. They had to search for him and had much difficulty getting him out. Eventually, though, he was released. He is now married with children. The second hardship was the death of her third brother in the prawn project massacre. Another brother, who was a polio victim without the use of his legs but otherwise healthy, died of shock after a bombing raid. Her father died of a heart attack after receiving news of another massacre. Her sister was shot by a member of the Security Forces. Finally, her husband had left her for another woman just a few months earlier.

In addition to these personal hardships, Vasanta has watched the hardships of others. From 1987 to 1989, she says, when the IPKF was here, they raped women and tortured people, pulling out fingernails and sticking nails through hands. They forcibly conscripted boys into the Tamil National Army (TNA), a new force created by the IPKF — there was a training camp nearby — and put them into the front lines in attacks against the LTTE, with EPRLF and TELO forces behind. With the IPKF in the area, women could not stay at home alone. They had to disguise themselves as old ladies. Now, with the area under Tiger control, at least they are safe from sexual abuse.

Vasanta is not safe on the other side, however. Whenever she goes into town to buy food and supplies, she has to pass through the STF checkpoints. She does not have to tell me about the harassment; I see it with my own eyes. When we go through the Manmunai checkpoint together, the guards stop us and interrogate us. They go through our bags and ask such questions as, "What's underneath your clothes?" When we return, they produce objects such as medicine vials that they say they have found in our bags and ask us if we are smuggling medicine to the LTTE, an act for which people can be arrested and imprisoned, or worse. In this case, I am mocked and then released, but local Tamil civilians are not always so lucky. One man working at that checkpoint abducted a woman with the help of the army and forced her to marry him.

The people at that checkpoint feign concern for me, saying it is dangerous for me to cross because there are Tigers there. They say I should not go to the other side because I might get hurt if they bomb it. Clearly, they do not care if Tamil civilians are hurt. They say that all the people on that side are LTTE, although they know that this is false.

Vasanta says the guards stop travelers and interrogate them because they just want to talk; they are not really interested in the responses. She says she answers their questions as briefly as possible, because if she were friendly to them, someone else going through the checkpoint might misinterpret this behavior and report it to the LTTE.

I repeat my question: "After experiencing so many hardships, how do you find the strength to go on, raising these three children and all? You seem so cheerful."

"I am cheerful in the daytime," she says, "but at night I remember — [*ninai*] these events, and then I have trouble sleeping. Now I have a lot of work — with my job, and the housework, and these three little ones. When I lie down at night, I am so tired I fall right asleep. This is good."

"*Ninaittāl paittiyam varum,*" she concludes. Roughly translated, this phrase means, "Thinking would make me crazy."

The day after telling me the story, Vasanta brings out a small photo album containing pictures of the prawn project and its workers from before the massacre. A photo of her brother is among them. He is seated on the ground, preparing *pōṇgal* (a ceremonial rice and milk dish), smiling up at the camera. It is hard to think that this gentle-looking young man was shot in cold blood, his body thrown on a tractor with dozens of other bodies and then dumped in a ditch somewhere. What if it had been my brother?

There are also photos of the assistant manager who was killed. Vasanta shows me the pictures of the workers she knew. All of them were killed except the manager, Bruce, who now lives in Singapore, according to Vasanta, and is very rich. In Tamil she says, "He didn't like women, only men." And then in English she adds, "He was a very nice boy."

What Rosa Said

Rosa is Vasanta's younger sister. At present she works as a volunteer head teacher in the nutrition center next door to Vasanta's house, one of several such centers sponsored by the Methodist Church. Rosa is a trained and certified teacher. Sixty-five children, ages five and six, attend the center. All of them live nearby; they spend about three hours a day, five days a week in the center.

The role of the center is to give each child one square meal a day and to educate their mothers in nutrition. But Rosa also teaches the children other things. When I arrive, they are practicing for a Christmas pageant, which is held on the Friday before Christmas. It lasts more than three hours, and there are more than twenty different performances (songs, recitations in English and Tamil, and dances) by individual children and small groups of children. The performances are not, for the most part, related to Christmas or Christianity. The one I remember best involves eight children, four boys and four girls, with wings pinned to their backs: at first I think they may be angels, but it turns out that they are baby sparrows in a nest. They do a carefully choreographed song and dance, with coaching from behind the scenes.

Rosa and her sister both do their shopping in the Muslim town of Kattankudi. When Rosa needs medicine, she gets it from a Muslim clinic there. The Muslims who owned shops in Batticaloa have now moved back there, and it seems that tensions between Muslims and Tamils are greatly reduced. Even so, Muslims rarely enter Tiger-controlled territory, and most are terrified of the Tigers. During my stay, when a Muslim did enter Tiger territory, Rosa reported that a Tiger said to him, "If I came to your town, you would cut me to pieces."

Rosa is known around Paduvankarai as *vedippadda Rosa* (Rosa who got [partly] blown up) or *cudappadda Rosa* (Rosa who got shot) because in 1991 she was shot in the legs, and both her knees were shattered. She is not ashamed of her nom de guerre, although she is obviously not happy to be without kneecaps.

She tells me how it happened. In a church near Vasanta's house the LTTE had laid land mines, and when they exploded two Sinhala soldiers lost their legs. The army came and seized Vasanta's father with the intention of killing him, believing that he knew about the mines, but a TELO boy said he was innocent, and so they let him go. The same soldiers used to come to the house for water, telling each other that "these people are Christians and will not harm you." They harassed the women, including Vasanta and Rosa. The soldier who subsequently shot Rosa in the legs, whose name was Ratnayake, was among them.

What Rosa calls the rice mill massacre is known throughout the region as the Kokkadichcholai massacre. The story is that a Sri Lankan Army tractor with soldiers in it tripped a land mine on the road. The tractor blew up, and several soldiers were killed. The soldiers coming behind them went on a rampage through the village, shooting and killing more than 150 civilians in a few hours. One group of civilians sought refuge in a rice mill, and all of them were killed. Rosa hid in a hut nearby. She was seen by a soldier, shot, and left for dead, but the next morning a village man found her still alive, and she was taken to the hospital.

She was in and out of hospitals for eleven months after the shooting and spent another seven months on crutches. The doctors initially advised amputation of her lower legs, but she refused. She now (in late 1997) walks with a hobble. The bullet scars on her legs are clearly visible. She says her legs are shorter than they were before, and afterward I notice that her legs indeed look a little short for her body. Her pretty face and cheerful smile draw attention away from her handicap.

At one point, Rosa asks me, "Do I seem cheerful [*santōsam*] to you?"

"Yes, you do," I respond. "I wonder how you can be so cheerful after what you've been through."

"My face is cheerful, but in my heart I am hurting," she says, and goes on to tell me that she is sad because she can no longer ride a bicycle, sit down on the floor, walk long distances, climb stairs unassisted, or run.

"After the shooting, did you ever think you might want to join the LTTE?" I ask Rosa.

"Yes. I wanted to join them. But my mother and sister wouldn't let me," she said.

"Why not?"

"They said I was too crippled to fight."

Rosa shows me a newspaper article from the Tamil daily *Vīrakēsari* that she has kept at the home of friends; it recounts her own testimony regarding the massacre. The headline reads: "'An Army Soldier Aimed at Me and Shot Me from Twenty-five Yards Away,'" with the subhead: "A Teacher's Testimony about the Kokkadichcholai Massacre Incident before the Presidential Command Commission." The story, in full, reads as follows.

Batticaloa. "Seeing the soldiers, because of fear, I tried to run and hide in a small hut that was nearby. When I neared the door of the hut, an army soldier twenty-five yards away aimed at me and shot me. When I was shot, I lost consciousness and fell." In these words, the twenty-four-year-old teacher [her full name is given] gave witness before the Presidential Command Commission of Inquiry regarding the events of the Kokkadichcholai massacre. This command commission yesterday conducted its second day of inquiry in the Batticaloa Air Force Camp.

[Name], who was shot during the Kokkadichcholai incident and sustained critical injuries, was taken from an ambulance on a stretcher to the place where the inquiry was being conducted.

Before the Command Commission, she continued to give information as follows:

"In Kokkadichcholai, when the land mine incident happened, I was traveling on my bicycle just a small distance from that place. Then I heard the sound of a bomb explosion. I saw that the soldiers who were coming on a tractor had been caught by it.

"When, because of fear, I tried to go to my home, which was a quarter mile away, I saw soldiers in the way. When I tried to go back to the school by way of the road, on that route also soldiers were standing and shouting. Then I went to Mahiladithivu Colony. On the way I saw soldiers, and I tried to go to a little hut next to the road. When I neared the door of the hut, from twenty-five yards away one soldier aimed at me and shot me. When I was shot I lost consciousness and fell. When I regained consciousness, I was inside the hut.

"Seeing that dawn had broken, I cried out because of thirst. Then I heard somebody calling, 'Sister, sister.' When the person who called that way came near, I recognized the features of my uncle. Seeing my condition, he called other people and spread out a sack and laid me on it and carried me away. They took me to my aunt's house.

"The next day, in the morning, for lack of access to a vehicle, I was taken in a bullock cart to Ambilanthurai, and by way of a fisherman's boat to the opposite bank [of the lagoon]. I was taken on a bicycle on the main road, and arrived by bus at Batticaloa Hospital. There, after getting first aid, I was sent by ambulance at three in the afternoon to Polonnaruwa Hospital. After receiving treatment there for seven days, I was taken back to Batticaloa Hospital. After receiving treatment for twenty-seven days there, because of the lack of basic medical facilities there, I went to a private hospital for treatment. Having returned from there, I am now staying in my aunt's house.

"The surgical treatment I require has not yet been fully completed. To do it will take one and a half lakhs [150,000] of rupees, the people in the private hospital tell me."

Head of the Command Commission: "Can't that be done in Colombo General Hospital?"

Witness: "Because many people have said that in the main hospital of Colombo, not so much care is given, I have not gone there."

Command Commission Member, Judge [*kalānithi*] A.M.M. Sahabdeen: "Did the soldier shoot you accidentally?"

Witness: "When I was fleeing in fear, he shot me."

The legal adviser Kumar Ponnambalam asks some questions.

Question: "Did you work at Red Barn [a Norwegian aid organization]?"

Answer: "Yes. I was a teacher there."

Question: "On a normal day, what clothing would you wear?"

Answer: "I wore a skirt and blouse."

Question: "What was the color of your clothing?"

Answer: "The skirt was red in color."

Question: "Did you see the tractor trip the land mine?"

Answer: "I saw the tractor that tripped the land mine being blown up [*tūkki vīciyatai kandēn*]."

Question: "When the army came following behind, did they say anything about the color of your skirt?"

Answer: "They said something in Sinhala. I couldn't understand it."

Question: "Did you see the soldier aiming at you and shooting you?"

Answer: "Yes."

Question: "How many times did he shoot?"

Answer: "Two times."

Question: "Were both your knees affected by the wounds?"

Answer: "Yes."

Question: "Did you give word to the police in Polonnaruwa Hospital?"

Answer: "Yes."

Question: "Did you say the same things there that you are saying here?"

Answer: "Because of fear, I said that in 'cross-firing' I had been shot."

Question: "If a classification of features and marks were conducted here, would you be able to identify the features of the person who shot you?"

Answer: "No."

Because the witness was unable to continue testifying, the questioning was stopped here.[1]

The Kokkadichcholai massacre happened in January 1991. The inquiry and the reporting of it took place in July 1991. When I meet with Rosa and talk with her, it is December 1997. Rosa now makes statements that she says she was unable to make in 1991. In particular, she says that she could identify the soldier who shot her, but feared doing so in 1991 because several soldiers were looking for her.

In all, twenty soldiers were involved in the massacre, in which, according to Rosa, some 152 people were killed. Friends of the soldiers who engaged in the massacre were still at large in the Batticaloa region at the time of the inquiry, Rosa believes. In addition, the inquiry was held on an army base where she was surrounded by soldiers, creating an intimidating situation for her.

Given that the massacre itself was a reprisal, Rosa had every reason to fear further reprisals if she testified in too much detail; that she testified at all is widely acknowledged as an act of courage. Rosa says that the soldiers involved in the massacre are no longer in the region. She says that they were not jailed or officially punished for their crimes but were effectively punished by being sent to Jaffna (the name is often used to refer to all points north where the fighting is heavy).

Rosa says that the pain in her legs was so intense she begged people to give her poison so she could kill herself. She was neglected and mistreated at the Polonnaruwa hospital because she was Tamil. She did not testify to this in court, however, for fear of making trouble for herself.

When I ask Rosa what has given her the courage to carry on, she answers simply, "Jesus."

CHAPTER 5

About Vithusa

November 1997. I first met Alagar in March 1996, when I visited here for a week. He was a boy of this village who now holds a local leadership position in the LTTE. Civilian villagers had told me that Alagar was the cross-cousin of Valli, a young civilian woman. The implication was that Alagar might marry Valli. It would be a good match: both were personable, educated, skilled, and of good families. This match would have been maintained as a probability all of their lives, until Alagar joined the LTTE. Even then, it was still possible: LTTE men often married civilian women. But when I asked Alagar for something to read, he lent me a book he had been reading, titled *En Iniya Pōrāḷi* (My Sweet Warrior), about two members of the LTTE who fall in love.

Alagar has said to me that for Hindus, killing is sinful. It does not come easily or naturally. "We do not enjoy it," he said. But the gentle and feminine Sita, whom I had also met in 1996, gave me the impression then that she did enjoy it. She certainly enjoyed routing the enemy.

Sita is now married to Alagar, and they have a small daughter. Sita spends most of her time at home with the child, while Alagar continues to do political and administrative work for the movement, sometimes at home, sometimes elsewhere. When Alagar returns from work on his motorcycle, Sita rushes out to the road, laughing with joy, to meet him. Sometimes he takes her and the baby out for a ride. To the extent that I can read the baby's emotions, she seems to look forward to this motorbike ride as the highlight of many a day.

I visit Sita on Sunday, 30 November 1997. She introduces me to the new leader of the Batticaloa-Amparai branch of the LTTE women's division. Like Sita when I first met her, this new leader has the looks of a college cheerleader, the confidence and appeal of a senior-class president. Her glossy dark skin, sparkling eyes, and beautiful smile could make her a winner anywhere (or so my American mind sees her). She is one of several young Tiger women in Sita's house when I first call. These visitors are dressed in the outfit that Tiger women always wear, and one of them holds a rifle as they sit on the veranda, talking with Sita about the baby. One asks if the baby has intelligence (*butti*). A government bus passes by the house with the Sri Lankan lion-with-sword logo on it. People on the veranda can see the bus; people in the bus can see the people on the veranda. The fact that LTTE members are clearly visible to people coming from town, including possible army spies, surprises me. But when I ask the LTTE women on the porch about this, they say it is no problem: the army fears to come here.

Sita has the exhausted appearance of a new mother. Today she is wearing a soiled housedress and ankle bracelets. She has help, however: her own mother (the child's *ammammā*) looks after the child, singing it to sleep with the kind of lullabies (*tālāḍḍu*) I have heard in Tamil Nadu. One of Sita's sisters, Koyila, a civilian, lives with Sita and Alagar and shares in the housework and cooking. She is a young widow whose husband was killed by the army.

Sita's mother raised five sons and four daughters. Two sons were killed by the army, and a third died of disease. The remaining two sons are married with children and live in a town outside Batticaloa. None of the sons ever joined the Tigers, but Sita and one of her sisters joined after their brothers were killed. The oldest daughter lost her leg to army fire; she lives "in Jaffna" (i.e., in the Vanni province just south of the Jaffna Peninsula) and is a member of the movement, like Sita. She too is married to a Tiger, and they have two daughters. Koyila tells me she joined the movement at the same time as Sita and their eldest sister, but she found the experience was not for her. When they took the new recruits and left them in the jungle at night, she was afraid and screamed; a very large snake came; they had to eat sitting in the vegetation and litter of the jungle floor (*kuppai*); and the dark of the jungle was frightening. The next morning she ran away from the jungle and back to her home. Another daughter lives in the same town as her civilian brothers and is the mother of three children.

Sita's father, a wage laborer (*kūli*), died when Sita was four, of a throat problem. Sita's mother was also a member of a large family; one of her brothers also was killed by the army during the same year that Sita's brothers were killed. To say that these men were "killed by the army" is a deceptively simple way of describing what happened. One of Sita's brothers was hacked to death, together with many other Tamil men, by a mob of Muslim home guards assisted by the Sri Lankan Army. Her other brother and her uncle were taken captive during one famous army roundup of Tamils. The army never acknowledged their taking of these prisoners and never released any of them, or any bodies. Thus it is not known for sure whether they are alive or dead. They are classified by human rights groups and civilians as "disappeared."

The civilian members of Sita's and Alagar's families often visit their home. School-aged nieces and nephews like to spend their vacations there. Tiger men likewise frequent the house when Alagar is home. Their friendships appear close and easy. Sita is not shy around the men as she was before she was married. She does not stand up when they enter the house, and she doesn't giggle after they have left. To all Tigers she offers a peer's respect; to senior Tigers she gives honor. People who are neither friends nor members of the movement, however, she keeps at a distance. Toward Alagar she shows total, unaffected adoration. Her love for him touches the heart. It is different from anything I have seen in Sri Lanka or anywhere else.

I ask if Sita and Alagar have wedding pictures. This question provokes some hesitation, but a picture album is brought out. There are pictures of the wedding, including a picture of Sita and Alagar with the mother and father of Valli. *Murai pen,* I comment, referring to Alagar's expected match with Valli, and people smile. Valli's parents, by their presence, show that they have accepted the situation. Valli's father and younger brother visit sometimes. But Valli, still unmarried, and her mother do not.

The album also includes pictures of friends who have died in battle. (The term used for such a death is *vīramaraṇam,* generally translated as "heroic death." It is shortened to *vīrasāvu,* and *vīrasā,* perhaps because the term is used so often. As of 1997, ten thousand Tigers have died in combat.) The pictures are casual snapshots. One shows two young men with their arms around each other's shoulders. Both are now dead. Last year, when I spoke with Alagar, he said, "We are fighting so the next generation will not have to fight." But the war drags on. Ten years from now, fifteen years from now, who will be alive and who will be dead, and what will the children be doing?

They bring out a second photo album, containing pictures of Sita, Alagar, and the baby, whose name is Vithusa, and various friends. "This one, heroic death." "Heroic death." "Heroic death." These are people who died in combat after Vithusa was born; she is not yet one year old.

I have been asked several times, "Will you forget us? Do you remember my name?" It seems important to the Tigers that I remember them. But it is not just the Tigers who feel this way. All Tamil households have their photo albums containing memories. When you visit a house, the album is often the first thing that people bring out to show you as you are drinking your tea.

. . .

Sita has named her daughter Vithusa after a friend of hers who died in battle. At the end of November, when I first visit, the baby is around nine months old. She cannot lift her head; her whole body twitches every minute or so, as though she had the hiccups. She is thin, and her skin is wrinkled. But she responds to people, and she smiles at people she likes. She has definite preferences. Her face is pretty; everyone says she looks like Alagar, and I too can see the resemblance. Lying supine, she arches her back, and it appears to me that she is trying to roll over. I watch and try to encourage her. Later I see her lying on her belly.

Sita and Alagar treat the baby as the most treasured being in the world. Sita cuddles her, smiles at her, and showers affection on her; Alagar and his male friends lie around her on the floor in the late afternoon, propped on their elbows, watching her sleep. Three or four young women at the house take turns playing with the child.

Sita tells me she fell down a couple of times during her pregnancy, and she wonders if this why the child is weaker than she should be. I say I doubt it. I ask was the birth normal? Was the child born by cesarean? Sita says no. I ask whether the baby was born in the hospital, and Sita says no, she was delivered at home. Sita shows me a doctor's report, which includes a printout of something that looks like an electroencephalogram. I am unable to interpret it.

Alagar is not home yet, and Sita seems mildly anxious. When he arrives, he briefly acknowledges my presence, then speaks with Sita. This is the first time in almost two years that I have seen him, and I am surprised to get no more of a greeting than this, but both Alagar and Sita are clearly preoccupied. After a bit he shows me another doctor's report regarding the child. He asks me to read it and to explain what it means.

The report is dated just two or three days prior to my visit. This must be what Sita was waiting for Alagar to come back with. Written in English, it refers to "epilepsy," "retarded milestones," and "jerky movements." (The second term means the baby is not developing at the proper rate; milestones, such as rolling over for the first time, are indicators of development.) The report also says that the baby was delivered at home and suffered neonatal sepsis from the third day. It prescribes clonazepam (a sedative), some medicine beginning with L, and physiotherapy. I ask Alagar what the doctor said about Vithusa's being unable to lift her head, and he responds that the doctor said it would come right over time.

I wonder at what risk Alagar went across the lagoon to get the baby tested and then to pick up the test results and the prescription, but he says it was not a problem. I have to leave by two o'clock, but Sita won't let me go without feeding me lunch. When she asks if I ate in the morning and I say no, she seems genuinely shocked. I tell her it's not a problem, I can eat when I get back to town, she has enough work as it is without cooking for me. She says her mother is cooking. And so I eat lunch.

As I gather my things and prepare to leave, I notice that Sita is also preparing to go out. I fear that she is planning to accompany me to the ferry landing. This really would be excessive. It has been a tough day for her, with the bad news coming from the doctor almost at the same time as my unexpected arrival. She is putting sacred ash on her forehead and a dot of red *kumkum*.

"You're not planning to come with me to the ferry?!"

"No, to the temple with the baby." She can only be going to pray for the child's well-being.

· · ·

Fridays are temple-visiting days. My next visit to Sita is Friday, 26 December. It is midmorning, and Sita has already gone to the temple with the baby. Her mother is going, too, and I decide to accompany her, carrying her on the back of my bicycle. It will not be quite as comfortable as a motorbike ride, but Sita's mother is tough. People carry each other on bicycles all the time around here. Anyone can hitch a ride with just about anyone else. The rider can sit on the handlebars or on the back carrier, if there is one. Sita's mother is embarrassed by my carrying her, though. She protests that this work will surely be the end of me and that we should walk. She is laughing at my foolishness. I keep on pedaling so she won't jump off. It is several miles to the temple, and it will take hours if we walk. The road is smooth and level. I promise Sita's mother that on the uphills we will walk, not knowing how steep they are going to be. We reach them and start climbing. I am standing up on the pedals, pushing hard. At last I give up, and we walk.

We reach a small temple to the goddess Mariamman, where a healing session is going on. People are called by number to consult with the oracle (a live person). Sita is number sixty-four of more than a hundred people, and we wait for her turn. As a tall boy stands before the oracle, he starts to sway and tremble. He appears to be in a trance and in pain. The crowd chants to help him, a single syllable repeated in unison, increasing in volume. The boy collapses into the arms of his caregivers.

The hours pass, with one person after another facing the oracle for healing. Finally our turn comes. Sita's bold mother takes the baby and sits down in front of the shrine where the oracle stands. She states the baby's condition. "What happens if you step on a snake?" the oracle asks.

"It bites," Sita's mother responds. "But what does that have to do with this?"

When we get back to the house, Sita's mother entertains us all with an account of the stupid oracle. Betel was sold near the shrine for people to buy and offer to the deity. The oracle took the offerings and gave them back to the vendors to be sold again, Sita's mother says. We are all laughing. I ask her what the oracle meant about stepping on a snake. She says that it meant that the baby's affliction is the result of snake disease (*pāmbu dōsham*), which is a consequence of something sinful the mother did during the pregnancy. Sita is serious about her temple visits to cure the baby, but it is clear that her mother thinks this particular oracle is bogus.

Karmic explanations of the baby's condition are being propagated among the village's civilians. The villagers here know Alagar well but not Sita, who comes from another town, and is of a completely different kinship network. As yet, the locals have not warmed up to her. God is punishing Sita and Alagar, they say, for the sin of killing people and deer. They say that Sita has it easy: a doctor was summoned to help with the delivery at home, and now she has her mother and sister to look after the child. Her mother is burdened, not Sita. My civilian friend Rosa and I have talked about Sita's case. Rosa thinks Sita may have an inferiority complex (*tāṛnta manapāṇmai*).

Sita's mother defends her and berates her and other members of the LTTE, in an affectionate, funny way, for failures in self-confidence. It is true that Sita's mother does most of the child care and much of the housework, but this is a typical role for the *ammammā* among Tamils in eastern Sri Lanka. Vasanta's mother does the same in Vasanta's house, and Vasanta is a civilian. Vasanta's mother is in general pretty quiet, though she puts in a humorous, gently critical word now and then about this or that. Sita's mother is tough and outspoken. She is seventy-five years old and chops firewood with the strength of a young man. Her teeth are mostly gone, and the remaining ones are stained with the betel she is always chewing. She chastises individual Tigers, whenever, in her opinion, they are not living up to their responsibilities as members of the movement. When I ask her whether young teenagers in the movement are allowed to study, she comments, "Nature is what they study [*iyatkai tānē paḍippu*]. Shooting the army is what they study."

If I ever thought that no good mother could let her children go into battle, Sita's mother proves me wrong. She fiercely supports the Tigers. If she did not, she could stay away. She is the oldest of eleven siblings, who have among them fifty children and more grandchildren than they bother to count. She has borne nine children, of whom six survive. But her Tiger daughter, her youngest child, is the one of whom she is proudest. And of all her many grandchildren, Vithusa is the one she has chosen to raise as her own.

"What's going to happen?" I ask her one day.

"The army will come and shoot us all," she says.

"When?"

"Don't know. Sometime."

"Are you sure they will come?"

"Yes."

But Koyila has told me that if the army comes, the whole family will flee to the jungle. The main worry then will be how to care for Vithusa. The jungle (*kāḍu*) is a wild place where no civilians live. The terrain is rough, there's no food or water, and poisonous snakes and insects abound. Many people who have fled to the jungle to escape army attacks have died there, especially young children.

One hears a lot about children "damaged in body and mind" by this war. The reference is to children who have been physically wounded or psychologically traumatized by exposure to combat. The damage to Vithusa is of another kind, one that is more widespread and more serious. If her mother had been able to get hospital services and decent medical care for the delivery, Vithusa might be a healthy, normally developing baby.

The oracle claims Sita must have trodden on a snake. Maybe that snake was the Sri Lankan Army. The consequences of defying that deadly creature have been exile and impoverishment. The hospitals and doctors are all on the army-controlled side. And, even there, most of the doctors have fled the war to Colombo or foreign countries. The only pediatrician in the whole district is the one from MSF (Medicins sans Frontières, or Doctors without Borders, an organization of medical personnel who work in war-torn and impoverished areas). The STF will not allow any medicine to be brought through the checkpoints to the Tiger-controlled side.

It is hard to tell who suffers more from this embargo on medicines and medical care, the civilians or the Tigers. Civilians say that the Tigers have the wherewithal to smuggle in their own medicines, which is true. But sick or wounded civilians can go to the hospitals in town for treatment; the Tigers cannot.

The walls of Sita's house are decorated with pictures of cute babies and children, as in Vasanta's house. One or two of the posters are even the same. But in this house the people are Hindus and not Christians, Tigers and not civilians. The walls also bear photos of two women Tigers who died in combat. Perhaps one is Sita's friend Vithusa, after whom the baby is named. There is also a poster of Sylvester Stallone as Rambo, combat rifle in hand.

Sita has placed a red *poddu,* or mark of blessing, on the forehead of each pictured child, a garland around the picture of each lost friend. A picture of Velupillai Prabhakaran hangs among the pictures of children. No *poddu* has been placed on his forehead, no garland around his photo. This cannot be for lack of respect or affection. It may be because he is a real, living human being, or because Prabhakaran does not desire deification. Tamil culture draws no distinct boundary between gods and adored persons, creatures, or things: the dead are deities of a kind, and so are children and movie stars. But the LTTE insist that they are a secular movement. Any sign that their leader was being treated as a god would belie that claim.

The men in the movement have showered Vithusa with presents: a large box of clothes, a battery-powered puppy that barks a squeaky bark and hops, an airplane with flashing lights that goes around in circles, a little plastic tank, and a plastic automatic rifle, which hangs slung over one of the pictures on the wall. Vithusa, of course, is too little to play with any of them.

I don't know what to make of these war toys. Vendors in towns and in villages have toy guns on display, but I don't think their purpose is to teach the children martial values. For one thing, children in this impoverished area are rarely allowed to get their hands on expensive battery-powered toys. Neither the toys nor the batteries would last very long if they did. Batteries especially are at a premium because the STF does not allow them into Tiger territory. Like medicine, they must be smuggled in. Hence, on the Tiger side, the people most likely to be found playing with battery-powered toys are adult male Tigers.

Tiger men often come over to Alagar's place in the afternoon and evening. Sometimes they are armed with combat rifles and ammunition vests. The visitors include the most senior Tigers in the region, men in their thirties or even as old as forty. I have a feeling they know what a picture they make as they carry Vithusa around and play with her.

Many children, neighbors and kin, play in and about Alagar's house, but Vithusa gets more love and attention than any other child. It is not just because extra attention is required to ensure that her physical needs are met: everyone smiles and coos at her, holds her and nuzzles her, and she responds with smiles of her own. This affection is striking to me because Vithusa is so badly handicapped, her chances for survival to adulthood so remote. It would not be unreasonable to anticipate that in the severe circumstances of warfare, a child like Vithusa would be neglected. There are plenty of neglected babies in Tamil Nadu, for example, especially girl babies, and female infanticide is endemic there. It is possible that Vithusa's parents and the whole community surrounding them are in denial about the tragic outcome of this rare birth. Sita is the only married Tiger woman in the area, and Vithusa is her first child. The baby must be symbolic of something precious to the local Tigers — of their fundamental humanity, their bringing of new life into the world, to counter their infliction of death. Kuddi, the Tiger physician who has been providing medicine for Vithusa's fever, comments to me that Vithusa's condition is a great tragedy. Kuddi is a sardonic, unsentimental man who has seen many people die. But he plays with Vithusa, too, in full knowledge of what her condition means. And I can only think that the extra smiles and coos for Vithusa are given not in denial, but in faith that the Tigers will beat the odds.

One evening after everyone else is asleep, Alagar engages me in a conversation about the movement. We talk deep into the night, sitting on opposite sides of the sleeping Sita. Alagar has a university education and, although he doesn't tell me about his accomplishments, I know from others that he has read extensively in Tamil about history, biology, ecology, and world politics. His interests are also evident from the stack of books and journals lying in disarray on the table in his house. He asks as many questions of me as I ask of him — more, in fact. He is eager to learn as much as he can. He listens to ideas contrary to his own. He has medical training. But with all his knowledge, as Vithusa's father he may not quite accept what his mother-in-law and his physician and friend both know very well.

Perhaps the most painful daily task Sita's mother has is feeding Vithusa. The baby has trouble swallowing and hates feeding times, struggling, wailing, and trying to push food out of her mouth as her grandmother spoons it in. The grandmother sings a loud, mournful lullaby, holding the baby's wobbly head in one hand and scraping the food off her chin and back into her mouth with the other. She tries to get the task over with quickly and still see that Vithusa gets down and keeps down a cupful of her specially prepared baby food. I suggest other ways, but they have already been tried. The only way Vithusa happily takes in food is by nursing, they say, but the slender Sita's milk has all but dried up.

I think of Vasanta's plump, healthy baby, entirely breastfed, and the fact that Vasanta has too much milk, enough to feed three babies, so that her one baby gets glutted and pushes the breast away before even one has been emptied. Vasanta's baby is well cared for, but her twin siblings, barely a year older, demand constant attention from Vasanta and her mother. The boy twin's favorite is Vasanta's mother; the girl twin's favorite is Vasanta. The youngest one becomes my baby. I hold her and bounce her and sing Christmas carols to her, and she falls asleep with her head on my shoulder. Her plump smooth body and buttermilk smell soothe me as nothing else could. Vithusa, in contrast, doesn't like me to hold her; she twists and squirms when I try. Vasanta's baby sprouts teeth, crawls, and takes her first steps in the months I am there. Vithusa does not change. The contrast between the two babies is engraved in my breast. I feel that some animal instinct in me has rejected the one and embraced the other. It shames me to understand this.

In late December and early January, neighbor children and relatives are visiting Sita and Alagar's house because it is a school holiday. Kili is the daughter of Sita's brother, one of those killed by the army, and Kili's mother lives in poverty now. Sita and Alagar are trying to help Kili and ensure that she finishes school, though they say she refuses to study. She is maybe ten or twelve years old, and tiny.

Also staying there is a fifteen-year-old boy, Sudharsan, who is apparently neither relative nor neighbor. He teases Kili, calling her names. Kili retaliates and chases him off. Kili and I play with the toy tank for a short time, but she ends up outside with the two neighbors' kids, who are making things out of plastic bags and sand and throwing them around for a game.

Kuddi the physician tells me that Sudharsan's mother committed suicide by drinking poison. Why? I ask. Because of fights with her husband. In a commanding voice, which I take as a possible ironic comment on what I am doing, Kuddi says to Sudharsan, "Tell her about this, she is doing research." Feeling obliged to do what Kuddi seems to expect, I ask Sudharsan, "When did this happen?" He says, very quietly, looking away, "1995." That night Sudharsan and I both go to sleep on the floor in the *puja* room (a room used for storage and accommodating guests as well as for prayer). I lie on one side and he on the other, five feet between us. I wake up to find Sudharsan lying close to me. A few days later, he is gone. I never see him again.

The teenage girls visiting Alagar's house make much of me, do my hair, powder my face. The fifteen-year-old is Pattini, who is Sita's brother's daughter. The fourteen-year-old is Mallikai; the twelve-year-old is Tamarai. They are the daughters of Alagar's sister, who is an educator, a civil servant.

Pattini says to me, "Do you want to see the puppy?"

"Sure," I say. She leads me down the road and around the corner and through a patch of weeds to a large structure with incomplete walls. Outside are some animal cages, but they are empty; the puppy has been taken out for a walk. Inside are two Tiger boys playing skittles.

Mallikai and Tamarai take me out into the green fields to take pictures. Tamarai asks me whether I favor the army or the movement. I say the movement. Tamarai describes for me how the army beats Tamil people (clutching various parts of her body and making faces and sounds as though she herself were being beaten) and how the president of Sri Lanka, Chandrika Kumaratunga, has gone to America and lied to the American people. When I ask Mallikai if they are *iyakka piḷḷai* (children of the movement), she first says yes and then no. Tamarai says they like the movement, but they will not join it. They will study.

"Why won't you join the LTTE?" I ask — not to challenge their decision, but genuinely to know the reason. I am here to understand children's agency in war, after all. Agency entails making decisions. When she hears my question, Tamarai's eyes open wide: "We will die!" she exclaims.

"But Sita and Alagar haven't died," I answer.

"They are exceptions," Tamarai replies.

Tamarai is right. Earlier generations who joined the LTTE might not have understood entirely what they were getting into, or the magnitude of the sacrifices that would be made. Many were so aggrieved by the massacres of 1983 and 1991 that they thought only of fighting back. By the mid- to late 1990s, however, the situation is different. Tamarai's eyes are wide open in more than one way. Her generation knows that to join the LTTE means almost certain death at an early age. And some still willingly join. Maybe Tamarai and Mallikai are protected against the pressures of recruitment by Alagar, their uncle. After all, he has said, "We are fighting so the next generation will not have to fight." I think he for one really means it, and I wonder how he responds to the ongoing recruitment efforts, for the LTTE needs more fighters to replace those who have died. These efforts, which have been increasingly resisted and resented by the civilian population, will later lead to fissures in the LTTE. I wonder which side Alagar will be on when that time comes.

. . .

It turns out that Sita's mother is the one who takes Vithusa across the lagoon to the public hospital. During this, my second visit, at the end of December, Vithusa has had a fever for several days, and there is talk of taking her back to the hospital in Batticaloa. I offer to do so, and Vithusa's grandmother immediately takes me up on the offer, saying that we will take her together. Alagar says, however, that I need not do them this favor. Not wanting to be involved in a family disagreement, I tell the grandmother that I can't take the baby to the hospital without the permission of Sita and Alagar.

"This is between you and me," the grandmother retorts. "They have nothing to do with it." I remain doubtful, and the grandmother continues, "We are not doing anything secretive or hidden; this is all out in the open." Finally she says to me, "This is my child, not their child." Persuaded by her forcefulness, I agree to go with her. I too am anxious to hear what a physician will say about Vithusa, as I am not yet convinced that all appropriate medical care has been given.

On the evening before we are to leave, an LTTE meeting is held at a hidden place in the jungle. Alagar and all the other LTTE men are gone, and the house is quiet and rather lonely. I wonder what the Tigers are planning. The grandmother is the one who has told me the Tigers are at a "meeting" (she whispers the word *meeting*), and she also tells me that Alagar will not be back until very late, perhaps not until morning. It is indeed late when Sita and I fall asleep on our mats on the floor (the grandmother has told me to sleep next to Sita), and Alagar is still not home. I awake in the middle of the night to the sound of Sita's gentle high-pitched voice. She is quietly moaning in her sleep with every breath. Then she is tossing from one side to another, clenching her fists, and crying out in pain. I ask what is wrong, and she says her chest hurts and her head hurts. She berates herself for having no more resistance to disease. She gets up and puts on Alagar's trousers and shirt over her nightgown and wraps herself in a blanket, but these measures give no evident comfort. She continues in pain through the night and into the morning, while I sit beside her and watch, feeling totally helpless.

Sita is still sick and Alagar still has not come home at eight in the morning, when the grandmother and I set off. Grandmother and the baby are transported to the ferry on a motorcycle by a Tiger, while I set off on my bike. I am carrying Sita's little niece Kili, who has to go back to her home.

The ferry is almost ready to leave when Kili and I arrive; grandmother and baby are already aboard, and about ten men with bicycles loaded to the gills with firewood are struggling to pack themselves and their cargo onto the ferry. Kili gets on, but I and my bike cannot compete with the firewood vendors. The ferry sets off, and I call to the grandmother to wait for me, I will come on the next trip, but the ferry turns around with its other side facing me, and I get onto that side with my bike. Then the ferry takes off. It is going very slowly, heavily overloaded, and we are inches from the water. I am comforted by the thought that I can swim until I remember the crocodiles.

We get to the other side, walk the short distance to the main road, and catch a very crowded bus into town. We go through three or four checkpoints where all the standing passengers and most of the sitting ones get off and are examined individually. Soldiers board the bus, but they ignore both the grandmother and me. Grandmother has been carrying the baby the whole way — sitting on the motorbike, then standing on the ferry, then walking to the road, now on the bus. I offer repeatedly to carry Vithusa, but her grandmother refuses. I guess I would look too conspicuous if I did carry her: white woman with brown baby.

We get into town and put Kili on the bus to return to her mother's home. Kili is weeping and smiling at the same time. She does not want to go. I want to keep her with me, but her grandmother is stern.

The grandmother wants Vithusa to see the white doctor at the hospital — that is, the MSF doctor. We make our way to the usual clinic, but the MSF pediatrician is not there. Vithusa is seen by a GP who prescribes some medicines for her fever, which has now subsided. The grandmother has brought Vithusa's records, and it is only now that I see that on these the baby has been given a false name. The grandmother uses my whiteness to get us into the ward where the MSF doctor is currently doing her rounds. The doctor notes from the medical record that the baby has been brought in and diagnosed already. There is nothing that can be done for her here; she will have to go to Colombo, where they can do an electroencephalogram, but even that probably will give no useful information.

The doctor tells me that the child is brain damaged, that the epilepsy and other symptoms result from this damage, that there is no treatment and no cure. Vithusa will probably never walk. The doctor says brain-damaged children are common in this country. She adds that it is especially tough for the families because there is no institutional support system as in Europe: the family have to do everything for the child themselves. The only thing they can really do by way of treatment is try and ensure that the child's life is . . . "Happy?" I venture.

"Happy," she says.

When the grandmother asks me what the doctor said, I convey the news as gently as possible. The grandmother repeats my words, "She will not walk," in a matter-of-fact voice, but her eyes are filled with tears.

When we get back to the house, Sita asks the same question, and sadly I give her the answer. I think they have heard this or similar prognoses before, because they have been to this hospital before. The grandmother has also told me she took Vithusa up to Colombo, where they stayed for thirteen days while Vithusa was being tested. (The EEG must have come from there.)

A visiting temple priest who is also an Ayurvedic doctor, however, repeats the prognosis Alagar has reported to me: it will come right. When I first meet him, this temple priest is on the front porch telling the ancient story of Nala and Damayanti to a group of children who sit around him, enthralled. He often visits the family and tells religious stories to the children. He is friendly, and I ask him about his life. He tells me he owns land and is well off, but he has not been across to town in two years because TELO will kill him. He says he has no problems with the army because he is not a Tiger, but he owes five thousand rupees to TELO. He never tells me, as Sita does much later, that his wife and all his children were slaughtered by the army. When I finally ask him about it, he says they were hacked to death. Seeing the soldiers coming, the men fled to the jungle, thinking that the army would not hurt women and children. They were wrong. Civilians in town say that when these men returned and found their wives and children dead, some of them hanged themselves on the spot.

Sita and Alagar still believe the baby will get better over time. They have heard the less optimistic prognosis through at least three channels now — from the earlier doctors, from the grandmother, and directly from me. But their only apparent response is to do more leg exercises with Vithusa, flexing her legs while she lies on her back and holding her in the air so that her legs make walking motions: Alagar lets her "walk" over his face. They laugh with joy whenever her legs seem to try to walk. Some of their friends, Tiger men, hold her so that her feet walk over the ground.

One morning I hear gunshots and ask who is shooting, and why. I am told that some of the Tigers are celebrating New Year's Day by firing their guns in the air. Nothing else happened last night, and I had forgotten that it was the turn of the year. The only other way they celebrate, I am told, is by planting new plants in their gardens. Sita has been setting out plants and tending them, and today she puts out some new ones. They are keeping a rabbit as a pet, and she plants special greens for the rabbit.

As I am bathing at the well on New Year's morning, fourteen-year-old Mallikai asks me if I and my people ever feel sad (*ungalukku varuttam varumā*). Confused, I say yes, we often feel sad — but what do you mean? Mallikai elaborates: "Does your head ever pound and ache? Do you ever get fever?" I realize from this exchange that in Mallikai's vocabulary, there are no separate words for sickness and sorrow. When I check, I find that this is general through the region. Sickness is *varuttam*. Sorrow is called *manavaruttam*. Grief at a death has a separate word, *tukkam*.

Mallikai continues her interrogation: "Auntie, is it true that in your country you can go anyplace you want?"

"Yes."

"No checkpoints? No army?"

"No checkpoints. No army."

She looks at me with wonder and incredulity. "Then there are no troubles there?"

"Not like this."

"There is agreement [*ottumai*]?"

"For the most part."

"Won't they grab [*pidi*] you for doing research?"

"No."

"Are there tomatoes in that country, Auntie?"

"Yes."

"They have all the things there that they have here — isn't that true, Auntie?"

"There are some things here that don't exist there, but you can get most of the same foods."

"But the meals are different, aren't they, Auntie?"

"Yes."

. . .

The young Tiger women who used to come and visit Sita are not showing up anymore. This could be for any of a number of reasons; there is no use in speculating. Sita has been sick for a week. All the people in

Vasanta's house except Vasanta and I have come down with the same sickness. People say it is because of the rainy season. Sita will not take medicine, though amoxicillin provided by Kuddi seems to have cleared up Vithusa's fever. Alagar urges Sita to take care of herself (*kavaṇamāka iru*). His tenderness with Sita makes me love them both. But I never see Sita smile or laugh anymore.

. . .

Alagar is liked and respected by the villagers, even those who are ambivalent about the movement. Sita's sister Koyila has told me how he took her and her mother in when others would have driven them away. Alagar has a kindly face, and in all the time I've stayed at his house, day and night, I've never heard him say an unkind word to anyone. Other Tamil men commonly scold their wives, children, or servants in the presence of visitors. But when I spend the night at Alagar's house I hear him speaking to Sita in the hour before dawn, always gently. Once I find Alagar and Sita bathing by the well together. In his dark, gentle face his eyes catch the lamplight at night like a cat's. I know this simile is a cliché, and I don't know whether it would have occurred to me if Alagar weren't a Tiger, but there it is.

As Alagar is bathing alone by the well one day, Sita asks me, "Don't you think he's beautiful?"

"He has a fine face, a good heart," I say.

Both Alagar and Sita are young enough to be my own children, and I want to protect them from suffering. But I can't. They are proud and do not take me very seriously. The best I can do for them is be a clownish auntie, and provide my own outsider's opinion on this or that matter, when they ask. Sita's mother tells them they should pay more attention to me. She listens to me when they don't. She notices me listening to her as well, and perhaps she appreciates that. But I must always keep in mind that I am an outsider. If they can find some use for me, they will. Alagar thinks that this very book, when published, will be useful to the Tigers. That belief is the reason he lets me stay. It is nothing personal.

. . .

I have brought my first book to Alagar's house to give them an idea of the kind of book I write. Alagar and Kuddi look through it, and Alagar asks, "How many books have you written?"

"Just this one," I say. "It's my greatest accomplishment so far."

"You have written one book about love, and now your second book will be about war," Alagar says.

"That's right," I say.

"But you know," says Alagar, "there is love even in the midst of war."

"Yes," I say, "and war in the midst of love."

. . .

Tai Pongal in mid-January marks the beginning of the harvest season, and this week is harvest time in Kokkadichcholai. Today a small ritual is observed: the first stalks of rice harvested from Vasanta's land are brought to her in a small bundle, which she will put away. Alagar tells me that it has been a good year for rice, and the people are happy about the harvest, although it is hard work. It is late afternoon, almost sunset, and men are coming home from the fields. As Alagar speaks, as though to illustrate his point, a tractor comes down the road with a bunch of men on it who seem to be almost dancing with joy. I bike back as the sun sets and encounter many men wearing straw coolie hats, which I guess they have worn to protect them from the sun. A couple of men tip their hats to me in unison, British style, as I bike by.

After the harvest, across the fields, we see big stacks of burning straw. I ask Alagar, "Why are they doing this? Couldn't the straw be used as fodder or something?"

Alagar explains that farmers burn their straw to stop other farmers' cattle from eating it. If they're going to burn it anyway, I ask, what does it matter? Alagar says that no farmer wants another farmer to prosper, even if it means destroying a resource that both could use. He agrees it is a foolish practice.

"But why don't you stop them, then? The Tigers control this area. Can't you make a rule for the farmers not to burn straw?"

"It's their free will [*avaṅgaḷ cutantiram*]," says Alagar.

At that moment, my respect for him grows. But later I have to think again about this episode. The Tigers represent themselves as ecologically conscious, and I believe they are, as much as they can be under the circumstances. All the more reason for them not to let the farmers burn straw. The explanation of foolish mutual jealousy among farmers is not entirely implausible, although I have never known rural Indian farmers to do this. However, when I discuss this practice with a friend from Batticaloa, now living far away, he points out that burning piles of straw can produce nitrogen compounds to make explosives.

. . .

About two weeks later, on Sunday, 25 January, the Dalada Maligawa temple in Kandy is bombed. Five of the bombers and fourteen civilians are killed. Only the Tigers could have had the skill and the nerve to pull off this act, it is believed. The newspapers and the government are outraged at the desecration of this temple, sacred to Sinhala Buddhists, which houses a tooth of the Buddha. To whoever possesses it, the tooth represents authority over Kandy, and by extension over the whole island. If the Tigers were to capture it, they would, in theory, rule Sri Lanka. But despite the bombing, the tooth is retrieved intact.

The Golden Jubilee Festival, celebrating the fiftieth anniversary of Sri Lanka's independence, has been scheduled to take place in Kandy on 4 February with great pomp and ceremony. The deputy defense minister and head of the army, Anuruddha Ratwatte, has predicted that the Tigers will try to spoil the festival, and so it appears they have done. The president of Sri Lanka calls the bombing "inhuman" and calls on all the civilized nations of the world to condemn the Tigers for it. Ratwatte is really upset because Kandy is his home. He vows that, come what may, the ceremony will not be moved. But the president overrules him and orders the ceremony moved to Colombo. They have only ten days to move it, with all the elephants, special displays, and security guards.

The opposition party hangs Ratwatte in effigy for failing to protect the temple better, and Ratwatte resigns; his supporters agitate for him to stay on as head of the army, and the president declines his resignation. She and some of the newspapers claim that the Tigers bombed the temple to incite Sinhalese to riot against Tamils and thereby increase Tamil support to the Tigers. Rioting against the Tamils, they counsel, would be exactly what the Tigers want. There are no riots. The president officially bans the LTTE, which seems odd to me because her government is already at war with them. When I learn from newspapers that the bombers are said to have come from the Batticaloa area, I wonder whether people I know were involved.

Monday, 26 January. Last night, as I was eating dinner with Vasanta, we talked about the temple bombing. Vasanta says that the LTTE did it to prove that they could penetrate Sri Lankan defenses, no matter how strong. I say I don't see how this could help the Tigers' cause. Vasanta says Prabhakaran has to be convinced of that. I point out that many people write letters to Prabhakaran criticizing him when they think he has done something wrong, but I guess most of these letters come from foreign countries. Vasanta says that here they can't criticize the movement like that; no one knows what would happen if they did. The Tigers do some things wrong and some things right. She pauses. "Many things right," she says with a smile. "Just a few things wrong."

But when I ask Alagar about the bombing, he says the LTTE didn't do it; whenever anything happens, the Tigers get blamed. He asks me if I think their struggle is just. I say I can't give an easy answer. It is right and just and necessary for them to fight the army, but they have to be careful to avoid being labeled as terrorists (*bayangaravātikal*). Alagar nods in agreement.

In support of armed rebellion, Alagar puts forward an argument that I do not think he originated, but he certainly believes it. Tamil people, he says, have the quality of kindness (*irakkam*) and an ancient language and literature. The Sinhala people are neither intelligent nor kind: their religion is a good one, but they do not follow its precepts. The massacres of 1983 are an example: the Tigers killed thirteen soldiers, and in retaliation the Sinhalese killed thousands of Tamil civilians. Before independence, Alagar says, Tamil people ran the country because they were skilled and educated. Now they suffer, while the Sinhala people are happy. The Sinhala people must suffer, too, so that they will be made to think.

Alagar says, "Prabhakaran has said something that you may judge to be harsh, but nevertheless it is true if you think about it."

"What is that?" I ask.

Alagar replies, "The enemy is frightening [*bayangaramāka*]. We must also be frightening to keep the enemy at bay. Now the Sinhala people do not retaliate so quickly against Tamil people when the LTTE kills Sinhala soldiers, even when thousands of soldiers are killed in a single battle, as at Mullaithivu; this is because the Sinhala people have learned to fear the LTTE." His cause-and-effect analysis is exactly the opposite of the president's. The president has claimed that Prabhakaran wants to provoke a backlash, and for the Sinhala people to refuse to respond violently is to deny Prabhakaran what he wants.

As we speak, Alagar is measuring and cutting sections out of a piece of blue poster board. First he cuts large rectangles, then tiny squares, from which he cuts off the corners. When I ask him what he is doing, he says, "*Summā*," and I realize it will be easier for me to watch than for him to explain. A chair is standing in front of the doorway with a rubber flip-flop under each of its feet to keep it from sinking into the sand. Alagar stands on the chair and attaches the cardboard rectangles to the wall above the door with a hammer and nails; the tiny squares are like washers for the nails. He goes inside and brings out a large paper welcome sign. "Do you have any glue?" he asks. When I say no, he asks if he can borrow my bike, "just to go to the corner." I say, sure, of course, and he takes my bike and rides off and is back a short time later with glue. I leave on my bike; when I return the next day, the welcome sign is up, and written on it in a careful hand are the words "Vithusa's Home [*vitusavakam*]."

During this visit to Alagar's house, Koyila says to me, "Sita can't go to the hospital. Do you know why?"

"Because if she did," I answer, "she would be captured and killed. It is dangerous even for Vithusa's grandmother to take her over. If the guards found out who the parents were, they would kill her and her grandmother. You would never see either of them again. She is a brave woman," I say, nodding toward the grandmother.

They look at each other and smile. "She understands," says Koyila to her mother. I am surprised at how little they think I know.

A day or so later (Tuesday, 27 January), Sita's mother suddenly invites me out for a walk. She is carrying Vithusa, as usual. "Go with her," several people in the house smilingly command. I don't know where we are going or why.

As we are walking, she asks, "What did the doctor at the hospital say?"

I repeat what I told her before.

She says, "There is no treatment and there is no cure. That is painful [*varuttamāna*] news, is it not?"

"Yes, it is," I say. "But you are doing everything that can be done. Doctors are not always right," I add, trying to offer some comfort. "She may walk, maybe when she is about four years old or so."

"Four years," echoes the grandmother.

"Except," I say, "for these frequent small fevers, it might be better if you let the child's own body handle them, rather than giving medicine all the time, otherwise —"

"— the medicine will become an addiction [*paṟakkam*]," she says, completing my sentence.

"What do you think?" she asks.

"About the baby? She is brain damaged. It is a natural injustice. Sometimes it just happens this way. But I don't have to tell you these things. You must know."

"I know very well!" she snaps back. "They don't understand [*avangalukku vilangātu*]," she continues. "I have raised nine children, I have experience. But they don't. As you say, it is their first child. They don't see how different she is from other children. I know that all these hospital visits are of no use. But Alagar says I must take the child to the hospital and keep her there as long as they will let me."

I spend the night in the house. Vithusa cries a lot during the night, more than on previous nights when I have been there, and Sita tries to comfort her by singing Tiger songs ("Children are we, of a loving brother, we have left Father, we have left Mother"). Medicine is poured down Vithusa's throat, and she chokes and gurgles, sounding as though she will drown; then she lets out a scream and keeps on screaming. Sita and the others laugh. "How angry she is!" They rock her, show her distracting toys, and sing to her. I roll over on my mat, all hopes of sleep lost. But they have had less sleep than I have. Sita sings another song to Vithusa. It begins, "Now is not the time to sleep, my child."

A group of guests have come to see one of their kinsmen, who is a Tiger, but he is not at Sita's house. One of them tells me that last night in Kaluvancikudi the Tigers attacked a police station, and in retaliation the army killed two civilians. (The bus we are to take today to get to the hospital passes through Kaluvancikudi.) As the guests are talking with Sita and others, an old woman comes weeping to the roadside by the house. She tells me her sixteen-year-old son joined the movement and died within the year.

The same morning, I find Sita's mother weeping as she talks to one of the houseguests, another gray-haired old lady. Then a little while later, carrying Vithusa, she gets on the back of a motorcycle to ride to the ferry. "Meet me at the hospital," she tells me as she leaves.

. . .

Wednesday, 28 January. I visit Sita's mother's extended family in a town a few miles from Batticaloa and stay with Sita's third-eldest sister. She is married and has several children; she and her husband are both civilians. She is not there when I arrive, and I speak with her husband for a while. The husband cheerily tells me that he has recently beaten his wife because she left a gold bangle out unprotected, and it was stolen. During the beating, he burned her foot "somehow." When his wife returns, I see that her foot is bandaged, and she tells me the same story. She does not attempt to defend herself or criticize him for hurting her. I put in that even if she lost the bangle, there is no excuse for a husband beating his wife and burning her foot. They listen politely.

The women and girls take me on a tour to see all their relatives and all the stores in the little town. When we return, Sita's sister decides that I have been subjected to the evil eye because I have gone about in a brightly colored sari in a public place and attracted people's attention. She makes me spit on a piece of iron she has heated up. It steams from my spit, and she makes me breathe the steam.

Such events cause me to think that Sita and her family are old-fashioned villagers. Sita's father, as a wage laborer, would have had no land, no money, and probably no education. That Sita studied and passed the Advanced Level exams means that her parents, like countless other Tamil families at all social and economic levels, sought a better life for their children through education. Alagar comes from a wealthier family in which all the children were highly educated. Though I have seen him in deep prayer before the image of Murugan, the beautiful god of warfare and healing, in his *puja* room, Alagar does not believe in ghosts or the evil eye. He does not visit the temple oracles as Sita and her sisters do. Alagar the Tiger treats his wife as an equal. Sita's sister is less fortunate.

Friday, 30 January. We returned today from the other town —"we" being Koyila and Sita's other sister (who is coming to stay with her mother for a while), Sita's mother and Vithusa returning from the hospital, and me. We crossed on a different ferry, where there are fewer guards. The STF question me for a long time — offering me cigarettes, inviting me to their base, examining all the things in my purse, asking me why I am crossing ("To help a sick baby," I answer) — and then let me go. By the time they release me, the rest of our party has quietly disappeared. I proceed alone to the ferry, wondering where they all are. They appear from nowhere just when the ferry arrives, and we cross over together. A tractor and cart are also on the ferry. All the passengers pile onto the tractor cart and are hauled several miles down the road. The driver lets us off at Alagar's house. Koyila wants to know what the STF asked me, and I tell her. The grandmother announces, "I heard her shouting 'No! No!' at the STF" (in response to the guards' insistence that I smoke with them and have lunch at their base). Both Koyila and her mother reiterate that I should not tell the STF that I have connections with the LTTE, or they will all be killed. I repeat that I know that very well and add that I have been surprised from the beginning at how much trust they have placed in me, a relative stranger.

• • •

Tuesday, 24 February. Yesterday I went to Vithusa's first birthday party. This party would have seemed exotic to me three months ago, for several reasons. It is an extended and elaborate household celebration, lasting for days, with hundreds of guests. Toddlers' birthday parties in my country are simple affairs. A one-year-old cannot understand the concept of a birthday, anyway. Why make such a fuss around her and maybe frighten her? But since I arrived in this region four months ago, I have seen other birthday parties for toddlers, also elaborate, and I think now that the first birthday party must be a celebration of the birth itself, postponed until the mother and child can endure it and maybe even enjoy it. In literature about South Asia, one is constantly reminded that the birth of a girl is a cause for mourning. But here is this tiny, critically handicapped girl being feted like a king, as though there were no tomorrow. But now I am accustomed to Vithusa's being celebrated, and maybe the possibility of no tomorrow is, though never spoken, exactly the point. Celebration in the midst of warfare once seemed incongruous to me. I expected that most people would be miserable all the time, scrimping and saving their last crusts of bread, mourning their terrible ongoing losses, depressed and unable to laugh or have fun. But now I see that celebrations, and lots of them, make perfect sense in the midst of lifelong horror and loss. However simplistic it may sound, celebrations cheer people up. Similarly, I once imagined the Tigers to be solemn people, grimly and single-mindedly devoted to their cause. Now I know them differently.

When I visit the party, about a hundred people are there, Tigers and civilians, male and female. A huge birthday cake is brought on a three-wheeler to the house (called an auto-riksha in India, this vehicle is common throughout South Asia; it is like a taxi, only smaller, more fun, and less costly). The cake appears to be a replica of an amusement park, with a little plastic merry-go-round, pretty houses, and candy grass. Little pink-skinned, blonde-haired plastic dolls in frilly bell skirts are set around the cake. A dozen bowls of fruits and sweets stand artfully arranged about the cake on a big table. On the wall behind the table is a huge poster-photograph of a Bengal tiger above an even larger tapestry of a jungle scene. New pictures of babies and young children appear on the side walls. Spangly streamers loop down from the ceiling, and clusters of balloons adorn every corner. Over the front door is a new welcome sign with roses pictured in the center and charming English-style wooden cottages with flower gardens and messages of peace (in English) on either side. Sylvester Stallone's poster is gone. The toy machine gun is still there, but hung in a different place. The head of one of the LTTE visual arts teams, Satyan, is there with his camera crew, making videotapes and still photos of everything and everyone. Malaimalli, the new regional head of the women's branch of the LTTE, who has her own video camera, videotapes the birthday-cake table, her camera slowly panning over each item, and then over every cluster of balloons and every streamer and the face of each person. Tiger music plays.

As I have come early in the day, I get to watch some of the prepara-tions. Dozens of pastel party frocks have been brought as gifts for Vithusa, as well as some expensive toys. Most of the gifts come from Tiger men. Inbam, the manager of the Tiger political office in Kokkadich-cholai, has given Vithusa a plastic tricycle. Geethan, the second in com-mand (I think) for the whole region, has given Vithusa a frock with at least five layers of petticoats. Sita sorts through these gifts and decides which frocks Vithusa should wear today. She decides that the frock I gave will be worn first. It has a little matching hat.

After the party, a civilian woman comments spitefully that they are try-ing to hide Vithusa's handicap under a lot of pretty clothes, but whatever frock they put on her, she is just the same. Maybe this woman speaks this way because she is resentful of the Tigers, but there is no way of knowing.

Sita's relatives dress her in a gorgeous red and green silk sari, and her hair is elaborately done up with flowers. Rudrakumaran, a Tiger man in his twenties, crippled but still mobile, hangs the streamers and balloons. A goat has been slaughtered, and a feast of biriyani rice, goat meat, boiled eggs, and *pāyasam* (a dessert made with milk, noodles, sugar, cardamom, cashews, and raisins) is prepared for everyone. (Vasanta hasn't come to the party, but she predicted this goat. "Because they are Tigers," she said.)

Parties are not my kind of fun: the stress of being on display wears me out. But I attend this one as a show of support for Vithusa and her fam-ily. There is bound to be lots of picture taking, I know, and so there is, even more than I have feared. I am wondering how the birthday girl will respond to it all.

Satyan or one of his crew takes the pictures. Rudrakumaran tirelessly clowns for Vithusa as she is posed for the hundreds of photos that are taken of her. Like a bride, a girl who has just come of age, a head of state at a public function, or a celebrity at the opening of her first movie, Vithusa must be photographed with as many different people as possible, not all in one crowd, but in groups of two and three. She must be pho-tographed not only in frocks but also in a tiny Tiger outfit that has been made for her. She must be photographed inside the house, outside the house, morning, afternoon, and night. She must be held by one stranger after another and smile. She must lie on her tummy on a blanket, and lift her head up again and again, and smile again and again with each stren-uous effort of her neck, each lifting of her face to meet other faces. Her eyes must look at the camera flash after flash and produce for it smile after smile. And every time a picture is taken, behind the cameraman stands Rudrakumaran, smiling at Vithusa and calling to her. And every time she sees his face and hears his voice, she laughs.

Sita's mother is sick with a fever and looks ready to drop, but she heads the cooking crew, making sure each guest has a fresh meal on his or her plate — several full courses for hundreds of people, as much as they all can eat. Sita is perspiring under the camera lights. Rudrakumaran is perspiring from the work of decorating the house and entertaining Vithusa. In the midst of the photo sessions, Sita breaks down and goes weeping into a side room. Alagar and Koyila go in to comfort her, and soon she is back, red eyed, posing for more pictures. Why do they stage this party? Why do they wage this war? Only Vithusa does not give in to exhaustion.

•   •   •

Wednesday, 11 March.   I came back to Batticaloa from Colombo on Friday night, arriving on Saturday morning.

There was a big explosion in Colombo at Maradana last Thursday, 5 March. It was around noon, a busy time of day at a busy junction. We heard the explosion from the lodge where I was staying. When I asked what had happened, other people said we would just have to wait and see. A man who worked at the lodge said it was a bad time for a bomb blast, because all the schoolchildren would be out and on their way home.

About an hour later, news came. A bus loaded with explosives had blown up at the Maradana junction. The bus was driven by a member of the LTTE. He was evidently trying to drive somewhere else before it exploded, but he was delayed by traffic, tried to drive fast through it, and then was detained for speeding by a policeman at the junction, and the bus blew up there instead. Thirty people were reported killed on the spot, and eight others died later of their wounds; many were injured. We all watched the story on CNN at the lodge. It showed the devastation at the junction, just three kilometers away from where we were sitting. Some high school students on their way home for lunch were killed, as the lodge worker had predicted. The bus that exploded was supposedly owned by a man from Eravur, near Batticaloa. People in Eravur and neighboring Chengalady were implicated. The wife and children of the bus owner were detained for questioning.

At Alagar's house a week later, he and Koyila bring up the bombing obliquely. Alagar says that the Sinhala army has killed innocent Tamils in their fight against the LTTE, and the LTTE has killed innocent Sinhalese in their fight against the Sinhala army. It is certainly wrong (*piṛai tāṉ*), but it is an inevitable part of warfare. The Sinhalese must learn through experience that warfare entails great suffering, and then they will stop. I comment that the Tamil people already know that warfare causes suffering, but this has not made them stop. He acknowledges the point. The women listen intently as I tell them what was in the English-language newspapers. Koyila and Sita say the bus was aiming for another target, not a populated city center. I repeat the observation made in one English-language paper that the driver, when trapped, could have taken his cyanide capsule instead of blowing up the bus. Koyila says they don't have cyanide capsules with them on these missions and that the bomb was timed to explode at a certain moment: the driver had no control over it. Whether or how she knows these things to be true I cannot determine. But, I say, any mission may be obstructed by a variety of unexpected events. The possibility that the bus might not reach its target should have been foreseen. Now the papers are reporting that the Tigers have shown that they are capable of killing even children, and it will be said that the movement is uncompassionate (*irakkam illātu*). They listen quietly and do not argue further.

. . .

Monday, 23 March. Sita sings to Vithusa as I listen. Then she repeats the words of the songs slowly so that I can write them down:

kuṛantaikaḷ nām, kuṛantaikaḷ nām, aṉṉaṉiṉ aṉpu kuṛantaikaḷ nām
tāyiṉaip pirintōm, tantaiyaip pirintōm talaivarait tāṉ aṛintōm
tāyiṉ karuvil tōṉṛiḍum pōtu puliyāy uruvāṉōm
vilaṅgiṉai uḍaippōm vīru koṇḍeṛuntōm vīrarāy nam nimirntōm
paḍattaip paḍikka pallikku cellum pālāka paruvattilē
pakaivaṉiṉ pācaṛai aṛittiḍa viraintōm aḍimaiyāy vāṛa māḍḍōm

[Children are we, children are we, older brother's loving children are we.
Mother we left, Father we left, only the Leader we knew.
In our mother's womb, when we came to be, as Tigers we took form,
We broke our shackles, we arose in rage, as warriors we straightened our
    backs,
Milk-drinking little children who study school lessons,
We rushed to destroy the enemy's camp. We will not live as slaves.]

tālāḍḍu pāḍa māḍḍēn tālāḍḍu pāḍa māḍḍēn tamiṛīṛappiḷḷai eṉpiḷḷai talai
cāyttut tūṅga itu nēram illai

etiriyin koḍiya kuṇḍu vīccilē toḍḍil erintatu en piḷḷai viḷaiyāḍum muttattil iruntu
    pantu carintatu
uraṅgakkūḍātu en makan eṉṟa uṇmai purintatu
viḍutalai pulikaḷ pōrāḍum vēlai makaṉē tūṅgātē
vīramillāp piḷḷai ivan eṉṟu keḍḍap peyarai vāṅkātē
nāṉ enna cēytēṉ tāy maṉṉukkeṉṟu nāḷai ēṅgātē
tāy manam kuḷirap pakaivanai en piḷḷai iru kaiyāl pirivār
tāvi viḍutalai pulikaḷ kannattil muttaṅkaḷ porivāḷ
virittē iruppāṉ en piḷḷai pakaivan iruppāṉām arippāṉ

[I will sing no lullabies, sing no lullabies. The child of Tamil Eelam is my
    child. This is not the time to lay down my head and sleep.
In the enemy's cruel bombing attacks, the cradle burned. On the ground
    where my child played, the ball rolled away.
Then I understood the truth in the words "My son, you must not sleep."
At the time when the Liberation Tigers are fighting, my son, do not sleep.
Do not get the bad name of a child without courage.
Do not wait until tomorrow to ask yourself, "What have I done for my
    mother soil?"
To soothe his mother's heart, with both his hands, my child will crush the
    enemy.
She will leap to shower kisses on the cheeks of the Liberation Tigers.
My child will keep awake. They will say the enemy is here. My child will
    destroy the enemy.]

In the first song, the Tigers represent themselves as children who have left
behind their parents. In the second song, a child renounces his childhood
in order to fight the enemy who has bombed a home and killed, perhaps,
another child. The child's reward will be the love and kisses of his mother.
These songs echo Sita's own experiences. She joined the LTTE in
response to the death of her brother and uncle at the hands of the Sri
Lankan Army. She too has left behind the helplessness of childhood, and
her mother is proud of her for her acts.

The first song represents the fighters as having become Tigers even in
their mothers' wombs. Such images contrast with the metaphors of
other military organizations (such as the Israeli army), in which childhood
is represented as an inferior state and manhood is to be achieved, among
other ways, through prowess in war. In the ideal Tamil home, children are
to be protected and cherished, but they have great power nonetheless.
Children are saviors, the whole purpose of life. Of course, not every
household lives up to the ideal. But Sita's household comes close.

•   •   •

It is mid-May. The Tigers are celebrating with parades and other events the army's failure, after a year of trying, to capture a road through their territory in the north.

After the parade has passed by and we are back in her house, Sita says to me with sorrowful eyes, "One thousand three hundred have died in this fight." She means thirteen hundred Tigers.

"And how many army?" I ask.

"More than three thousand," she says. (The army itself reports only 1,200 casualties in this offensive.)

"Do you think you'll be able to make up your losses?" I ask her.

"I don't know," she answers distantly.

.   .   .

Around mid-June, a rumor reaches me that Sita is four months pregnant. The same rumor says that Vithusa's name has been changed because it was inauspicious to name her after a dead combatant. When Sita and I are alone I tell her of the rumor that she is pregnant. *"Chee!"* answers Sita. "I will never have another child."

"Why not?" I ask.

"There is too much trouble and pain," she says. "Giving birth to Vithusa was very difficult; it took a long time, and they cut me to get her out. It was not a doctor belonging to the LTTE."

Sita's words suggest that, in her judgment, the doctor was rough on her because she was a Tiger. That may well have been the case. But it is also true that competent medical caregivers are very few in this area, and the rate of death in childbirth, even in hospital, is high.

"I do not want to go through that pain again. And then after so much suffering, Vithusa is like this. They say she will never walk. What if I have another child and that child is also that way? I cannot do that. I will not have another child. I am afraid," says this woman who has faced enemy fire and seen her closest friend die on the battlefield.

"Do you think that when Vithusa is older, then, you will go back to being active in the movement? Go back to fighting?" I ask.

"That is my thought," she answers.

.   .   .

In June, a big *kumbābishēkam* (temple renewal festival) takes place in Kokkadichcholai. Thousands of worshippers come and stand in line in the hot sun for hours, waiting their turn to anoint the statues with oil. Late in the day, as I'm visiting the temple, Sita appears unexpectedly.

"Auntie!" she says, looking up at me, smiling. She is dressed in a rich, heavy silk sari, and there are flowers in her hair, but both sari and hair are slightly disheveled, and Sita is strangely stooped and looks tired. I wonder if she has been standing in line. She is all alone.

"Where is the child?" I ask.

"At home with her grandmother."

"And Alagar?"

"He has some work with the movement. When will you come to our house?"

"When should I come?"

"Tomorrow."

"Okay. I'll come tomorrow."

She smiles good-bye, and I see her wending slowly from one statue to another, applying oil to each, like the thousands of others who have come, each with their private cares, their personal reasons for pouring oil on the stones. It makes me sad to see her alone, ornately dressed in the red and gold silk, praying after she has truly lost hope for the one gift that means the most to her. I do not ask if she is praying to be absolved of the sin of killing human beings in battle. For what absolution is there, when your child is afflicted so? But as I leave the temple I see her again, seated with Alagar on his motorbike — he has come to pick her up, I guess — and both of them are laughing.

CHAPTER 6

What Menan Showed Me

No one born in the Paduvankarai area after around 1980 could clearly remember a time without war. A generation was coming of age who could only imagine what peace might be like.

The year 1987 was a crisis point for people here, the time of the prawn project massacre. In 1991 the Kokkadichcholai massacre again brought the war home to the people in the Paduvankarai area in the most horrible way. Between such major disasters, intermittent aerial attacks, shelling, ground attacks, disappearances, and abductions kept civilians in a state of constant uncertainty. What was always surprising to me was the way they were able to live their lives between attacks in a more or less normal fashion. Some young people gave up on schooling, at least for a while, but many — probably the majority — continued to attend the impoverished schools available to them. When I asked them to name the most important experience in their lives, almost all of them answered either "school" or "the incident" of 1987 or 1991, depending perhaps on how they interpreted the question. It was clear from what the students said that many had learned and accepted the revolutionary ideology of the LTTE — its analysis of what the war was about and what had to be done for the Tamil people to achieve their freedom. But they did not necessarily plan to join the struggle.

Several of the students had developed a contingency plan: if the army attacked their area again, they would join the LTTE; if not, they would finish their schooling and live as civilians, or, as one boy put it simply, he would join the LTTE, or he would live (*vāṛvēn*). In fact, the students took it for granted that if they joined the LTTE, they would die. They knew that their siblings and friends in the movement had mostly died. They had seen the bodies of those killed in combat. They had no illusions about what they were in for if they joined the Tigers. Those who actually joined were not much different from ordinary teenagers, and were no less realistic in their view of the movement than those who chose not to join.

Some young people, however, joined the LTTE explicitly because they felt safer as members of the army than as unprotected civilians. This was not so much because the LTTE had the weaponry and the training to fight back as because the LTTE knew in advance (at least sometimes) of impending army attacks, and they could get most of their members to safe places in the jungle before the attacks began, whereas civilians had to fend for themselves. The Tigers may deliberately have left civilians unprotected to induce young people to leave civilian life and join them, but it is equally likely that they could not safely convey to the general populace the intelligence reports they had received. Moreover, they had no means of protecting civilians; indeed, fighting back against an army offensive was almost certain to intensify the siege. Especially when the ranks of the LTTE were depleted, as they were during Operation Jayasikurui, they acted with extra caution to preserve the lives of their own members. Their greatest asset was a trained and experienced fighting force, which takes years to raise.

For those who lived on the "uncleared" (Tiger-held) side, joining the Tigers was appealing because these were people they knew, people of the area. Some were friends from childhood or beloved and admired older siblings. None of the young people I spoke with expressed a desire for revenge or considered vengeance a reason to join the LTTE. Even those who had been beaten by the army, or who had seen relatives killed by the army, did not necessarily respond by joining the Tigers.

On the army side, I was told by many sources, there were no street children, and indeed I never saw any. It was too dangerous to be out on that side after nightfall, when army and paramilitary members were said to prowl the streets. Also, there was a perpetual curfew on the army-controlled side. Anyone who broke it might simply be shot. Students and adults living on the army side told me that boys who became cynical and dropped out of school early joined one of the "movements," for money, for safety, and in order to get hold of a gun.

On the Tiger side, only Tigers had guns. Also on the Tiger side, there were no drugs except alcohol and tobacco, and even these were strongly discouraged. The Tigers confiscated alcohol when they found it and poured it on the ground. Thus two sources of potential violence, guns and alcohol, were absent. On the Tiger side, anybody, male or female, could safely go out at night, and shops in the center of the main village that were closed during the day were open and lively long after nightfall. Although a few bands of young boys roamed these areas, as far as I could tell they were considered a nuisance but not a threat.

Acting in anger was generally discouraged among Tamils. Those who acted with irrational cruelty were described as angry. When I asked why some people behaved that way, one boy said with a shrug, "That's just the way they are." Anger (or an angry personality, such as was attributed to some of the conquering kings of yore) was not attributed in modern times to people one liked or admired. Young people and adults, Tigers and civilians, readily admitted they had experienced anger, but no one bragged about actions they might have taken in anger.

Interpersonal fighting was disdained by civilian students and Tigers alike. Tigers who engaged in interpersonal fighting were punished by the movement. The students said the Tigers told them to be good, study, and not get into fights. This is not to claim that students never fought among themselves, but they wanted me to perceive them as above spontaneous fighting.

In general, civilian culture in eastern Sri Lanka, including Paduvan-karai, is not militant and does not condone violence. For this reason, many civilians expressed profound ambivalence toward the LTTE. Whether Saiva or Christian, they believed that killing was deeply sinful, and the Tigers, however righteous their cause, however evil their enemy, took this sin on themselves whenever they took a life. Some Tigers themselves believed that taking on this sin was part of their sacrifice. Perhaps this is why they did not talk about an afterlife. They did not expect God to reward them for what they had done.

Some Tigers perceive themselves as having no future in this life, either. Their only hope is to be remembered. Some civilian young people seem to share this outlook. The students I spoke with in Paduvankarai did not believe that they would ever see an end to the war. Some said peace would come when the Tigers won, but no one ventured a guess as to when this victory would come about. None of them believed peace was possible under Sinhala rule. Certainly there would be no peace under army occupation: from their point of view, the army was the war.

But, despite the absence of any hope for the future, despite severe poverty and exposure to chronic violence, danger, and displacement, despite the destruction of families, despite the urging of people they admired in the LTTE to join in the armed conflict, these students went on with their lives. Bearing them up under all conditions was the earth beneath their feet, which gave their lives beauty, meaning, and sustenance. The culture of regeneration was strong in Muthalaikuda, where all the families were farming families. The students there were proud of what one boy called "the tradition of all the people here" of cultivation. They loved their family homes and loved growing things. They aspired to be teachers themselves if they were fortunate enough to pass their exams. It seemed to me that they had determined to want only this: to farm the land, even someone else's land, so that they could feed others; and to acquire knowledge, even though they might never use it to advance themselves, so that they could pass it on to others. When I asked them what they wanted to be when they became adults, they never said things like "doctor" or "engineer" — the usual answers one would expect from (for instance) middle-class Jaffna Tamils or Indian Tamils. Even when prompted with such answers by adults who were present, the young respondents did not pretend to set for themselves more ambitious goals. Humility of this kind should not be mistaken for an absence of self-esteem.

From the point of view of many Westerners, the involvement of children in warfare is most horrific because of the physical and psychological damage caused by the experience of violence. Even if a child is not wounded in body, merely to witness severe violence is thought by Western psychologists, and those imbued with Western psychological thought, to be traumatic and to leave lasting internal scars. Exposure to violence is often believed to result in the mimetic infliction of violence on others, thus forming a vicious cycle. The psychological damage of exposure to violence is considered to be greater for children (including adolescents) than for adults.

But I learned during my fieldwork that the most pressing hardship for young people in the war zone of eastern Sri Lanka was not the witnessing of violence, no matter how gory; nor was it the personal experience of such violence. Rather, the greatest hardships of warfare felt by the young were separation from family, loss of loved ones, and loss of personal freedom. These losses were often but not always concurrent.

This war, like many others, is in large measure about the control of territory. The Tigers and the army have fought mile by mile and village by village to gain and establish control over bits of land and the people on them. All the traditionally Tamil-owned areas have been contested. Some towns and villages have been continuously fought over, with both a heavy army presence and a heavy, if covert, LTTE presence.

Civilians have to live their lives in the midst of the fighting. In the Batticaloa area, some try to stay on one side of the lagoon or the other to avoid entering contested areas, borderlands, and no-man's-lands. But others must cross almost daily: to carry produce or firewood into the towns to be sold, to bring back provisions from the towns, to visit relatives, to travel between home and work. Those living in inland villages must go into town to get any kind of medicine or medical care. The crossing is always dangerous because of the checkpoints where they may have their property confiscated, be questioned and perhaps beaten, or be taken captive or killed by the checkpoint guards. However, staying at home is no sure protection, either, because raids on villages and homes by the police, army, and paramilitaries are not uncommon. In addition they have faced the risk of bomb explosions in public places such as markets and commercial buses, along with the frequent shelling of villages from distant ground installations and from airplanes and helicopters. During intense phases of the conflict, people have fled from one village to the next, from house to school or temple, from inhabited area to jungle, from countryside to city, and from region to region seeking safety. Those who can leave Sri Lanka altogether have done so. But many cannot.

Young people, especially young men, are the most likely to be targets of violence or capture by government forces, because they are of an age when they can be active fighters in the LTTE. Women are not exempt from suspicion. And a civilian of any age, even if unable to fight, can still be a Tiger "helper." Still, it is mainly young men and adolescent boys who are suspected and therefore most often detained, interrogated, and worse.

In addition to knowing members of the LTTE, students and older civilians in the Paduvankarai area knew some members of the anti-LTTE paramilitaries, and vice versa. Because they were thus able to identify members of the enemy groups to the LTTE, and members of the LTTE to the enemy, they were vulnerable: whenever a young civilian travelled from the Tiger side to the army side, he or she could be captured and forced to become an informant. Moreover, if any civilian bore a grudge against someone else, he or she could falsely report to the army that the other person was a Tiger. That the civilian community maintained its integrity under these conditions is worthy of note. We must ask ourselves why Paduvankarai has not become another Pine Ridge or Buffalo Creek.[1]

Adolescence is by nature a time of exploration of the world beyond home, and also a time when personal self-determination is uniquely important. Restriction of personal mobility is difficult for anybody. So is forced mobility. But in Batticaloa, young people are exactly the individuals most likely to experience both, and they are the ones most likely to chafe against this loss of personal freedom.

It is easy to identify the specific problems civilian youths suffer as a result of war: one need only ask them. In their interviews and conversations with me, the most frequent and serious complaints from young people entailed loss of control over personal mobility. That loss of control might be enforced at gunpoint or as a result of physical injury. Hunger, of course, is also a serious problem, but only one or two schoolchildren actually mentioned it. (Probably the hungriest were not able to get to school.) Checkpoints were frequently mentioned, and in some ways they represented the worst of the problems that school-age individuals experienced. Everyone who went through a checkpoint was subject to bodily search by armed guards. At the minimum, these checkpoints slowed travel.

Displacement was not an everyday occurrence, but it was probably the most terrifying experience in the children's lives. People who had lived in the area through all the horrors until 1998 would now flee their homes only if they were in immediate danger of attack by the army. Endangered civilians might flee to camps or towns; these became targets for shelling precisely because of the refugee presence there, and then the people had to flee again. Some therefore fled into the jungle, where drinking water, food, and shelter were scarce, and poisonous snakes and other dangerous creatures abounded. Wherever they went, they had to hide. But the worst thing of all was that in the chaos of flight, family members could be separated from one another. For a young person to be lost and alone, even for a few hours or days, could be enough to disable all natural courage in that person for years.

Adolescents were at greater risk of abduction than those in other age groups. Little children and older people would not usually be abducted from their homes or at checkpoints and taken prisoner, but youths would be. Additionally, paramilitary groups would come at night to houses on border areas and capture young people from their homes. The abducted would be imprisoned and interrogated, and many of them would never be found. The young people I spoke with also expressed fears of being trapped in a roundup. Government forces supposedly looking for Tigers would surround a whole neighborhood, leaving no room for escape.

Land mines did not choose their victims; a land mine would explode when anybody set foot on it. For this reason, nobody could walk without fear through open fields, but young people were exactly the most likely to be careless. Land mines thus were another restriction on normal youthful mobility. Moreover, if you did happen to set foot on a land mine, if you were not killed, you would lose pieces of one or both legs and subsequently would be unable to get around easily. It was not the disfigurement, nor even the pain, that caused the most distress to the young land-mine victims I knew, but the fact that they could not bicycle or run swiftly to school, or anywhere, anymore. Other children would laugh at them, and schoolteachers would scold them for being late. (We cannot expect that schoolchildren and schoolteachers will always be compassionate.) Finally, the choice of whether or not to join the LTTE involved issues of mobility. Tamil youths, and youths only, were targets of Tiger recruitment efforts, and some feared that they would be taken unwillingly from their houses to a Tiger training camp far away, there to be trained and sent into combat. Even those who joined voluntarily would be taken away from their families and not allowed to see family members until their commitment to the LTTE was assured. On the other hand, membership in the LTTE promised, for some, a degree of mobility, freedom, and even safety that they did not have in civilian life.

The following narrative describes the experiences of Menan, a boy who lived in Batticaloa.[2] At the time I met him, he was fifteen. Like many young people in the community, Menan understood and accepted the cause of the LTTE. But he did not want to join them, knowing that his life would be further jeopardized if he did so. He was his mother's only child, and he needed to care for her.

At fifteen, Menan was on the cusp between childhood and the dangerous age of deliberate entrapment by one or the other side. He was also wary of entrapment by me. No matter how carefully I tried to explain my agenda and show myself trustworthy, Menan could not know for sure that I was not working for one or the other of the warring parties. But he did know that, as a sympathetic foreigner, I might be in a position to help him out in some way in the future, although I never made any promises in this regard. Maybe he even really liked me and cared for me — not as a mother surrogate, for his own mother was with him and loved him above all others, but as a fun and not too strict auntie. For whatever reason, he often sought me out voluntarily. He kept himself in control of our interactions, catching me off guard many times, but never letting himself be caught.[3]

I gradually realized that I could learn the most about Menan by going with him where he wanted to take me and by letting him borrow my paper and paints when he asked for them, letting him take them away and bring back the finished products when he decided to do so.[4] Through journeys and pictures he showed me the world through his eyes.

My narrative is based on the field notes I took about Menan in 1998. He understood that I was writing about him and that he could ask me to stop whenever he chose. I told him often, and he understood, that he was free to talk with me or not. I gave him my notes about him to edit and comment on before I made them known to others. He seems to have been, and still to be, happy for the recognition.

Menan

Menan is the son and only child of Vasanta's brother Daniel, who was shot and killed in the prawn project massacre. Menan was four years old at the time. Now (in January 1998) he is fifteen years old but looks to my eyes to be around ten. He lives with his mother in Batticaloa, where he goes to school. Vasanta says he is first in his class. It was she who first suggested I should meet with Menan. Because of the way his father died, he is a war-affected (*pātikkapaḍḍa*) child. In general, when I try to explain my research to people here, they assume I am interested only in children who have been affected or damaged (*pātikkapaḍḍa* means both) by the war. I lack the linguistic ability to explain to them that I am trying to avoid assumptions about victimization: I just want to meet ordinary children living in wartime.

Vasanta says Menan prefers to be on this side of the lagoon rather than in Batticaloa with his mother because he has more freedom over here. His mother is always worrying, telling him to watch out for TELO and PLOTE. On the other side are curfews and checkpoints. On this side Menan can come and go as he pleases. Also, in Batticaloa he has to go to school; he stays with Vasanta during school holidays.

Today is the first Saturday of the new year. When Menan turned up yesterday, we decided on the spot that we would take the bike trip into the jungle that we had planned but never taken. I ask Menan where exactly we will go, and he names a nearby low mountain called Thantha Malai, on the top of which is a temple to Murugan. Yesterday, when I told the people in Sita's house that I was going to the jungle, they responded with alarm. They have already told me that I am forbidden to go into the jungle. I tell them I am going to Thantha Malai, and Sita says that is okay; she thought I meant *their* part of the jungle, where the LTTE has its camp. I ask her rhetorically how I can go to their jungle camp when I don't know where it is and nobody will show me the way. But still the people in Sita's house advise against the trip, saying the road is terrible, sandy, muddy, and full of ruts and rivulets. It turns out they were not lying.

One of the reasons I like Menan is that he takes it for granted that I can cycle moderate distances through the sun and rain. Previously we have cycled from the ferry slip at Manmunai to the town of Kalladi, where Rosa's in-laws live, a trip of five miles at most. This ride is more challenging. Today it is only cloudy when we start out, but soon it begins to rain and continues to rain heavily all through the day. We cycle through the rain over the muddy road: it is like playing the game of labyrinth. You have to steer your bike with steady hands through an obstacle course of potholes, mud puddles, and narrow, slippery bunds. Pedaling through mud is like pedaling uphill, except there is no downhill when you come back. Menan does it with ease. I follow close behind him and only fall down twice, landing both times in the foot-deep water of paddy fields. It doesn't help that the brakes on my bike don't work, but probably neither do Menan's. At first we encounter quite a few people biking the other way. They laugh or smile when they see us; some of them ask Menan where we are going and who I am. He shames me by telling everybody I have fallen off my bike. One man says to another that I work with the movement people (*iyakkakkārangaḷ*) — that is, the LTTE — and I wonder whether the LTTE is coming to be seen as a kind of caste. It is certainly part of the village social structure. But it troubles me that even strangers have heard of me and identify me in these terms. It is dangerous to be associated with the Tigers, and I do not want civilians to think of me as a dangerous person. At least, so far, Menan does not mind being seen with me.

Before long, the traffic thins out, and Menan and I are traveling all alone through the rain on this awful road. The landscape is beautiful: there are paddy fields as far as the eye can see, interspersed with groves of palm and patches of thick, wild vegetation.

After we have been biking for about an hour or so, Menan turns off the road onto a path that leads through the paddy to a palm grove where there is a tiny hut. I follow him, not knowing why we have turned off the road but guessing that Menan has decided to seek shelter because it is raining so hard. When we reach the edge of the clearing, Menan calls for someone, but there is no answer. The hut is empty. I glance in and see just a cot and an oil lamp, nothing more. But there is space enough to sit inside and wait until the rain lets up, if this is Menan's idea. However,

Menan beckons me to follow him along a path that leads to another palm grove, with another hut. We go there, and that hut too is empty. Menan says we have to go on down the next path to the next grove. It is still raining heavily, we are about a mile off the road in the middle of paddy fields, and now I am really confused. But Menan says that there will definitely be someone at the next place we are going to. So, with a sigh, I follow.

The next palm grove is larger and contains several structures made of sticks, palm leaves, mud, and thatch. And, indeed, two men are there. They greet us. "This is our land," says Menan. And now I understand why we have taken this detour. He wants to show me his family's land, his land.

One of the two men is Menan's grandfather, whom Menan calls *appappā* (father's father), though actually this is Menan's mother's father. The other man is a neighbor. I have met Menan's grandfather once before, in town, where he was consulting a vet about a goat that was having trouble giving birth. The next time I saw Menan's grandfather, I asked him how the goat was, and he said it had recovered. Now there is a pair of cute kids in the palm grove, but Menan's grandfather says the mother goat has died.

Like all homesteads I have seen in the Paduvankarai area, this one is cleared, and has a yard of smooth, raked sand that is fenced all around. The fence encompasses a square about seventy by seventy feet; the edge between the clearing and the fields is distinct. The homestead is an island in a sea of paddy. The tall palm trees make it look like a fantasy island, and so do the thatched huts: it resembles the pictures of natural landscapes that children and adults often make for me using my paper and paints, or my computer. In the pictures, however, there is always a river. What they call rivers (*āru*) in this area are actually branches of the lagoon that now separates the town and army side from the rural and Tiger side of the land around Batticaloa.

One of the thatched huts has a sleeping room and a covered porch in which there is room to sit. Another is for cooking. Both of these huts have mud walls and thatch that is carefully laid and tied. Stored in the veranda of the sleeping hut is a very rusty bicycle with tires that have not entirely lost their tread. In a corner across the center of the clearing from the sleeping and cooking huts is a thatched goat shed made of sticks, raised above the ground like a rabbit's hutch. Next to the goat shed, a vine grows on a stick trellis with gourds hanging from it. Each gourd has a quarter of a coconut shell tied to its end — so that it will grow straight and not curl around, the grandfather explains when I ask. In addition to the tall palms, there are smaller, younger palm trees and some fruit trees. The whole place is immaculately kept. The only trash I can see lies in a hollow at the base of one of the palm trees: one broken glass jar and a pair of old sneakers. I am not sure whether even these things are trash in the sense of having no use.

Both Menan and I are completely soaked. Menan goes into the sleeping hut and changes out of his wet clothes into an old piece of sari (his grandmother's), which he wraps around his waist. I ask for a sarong and am given one, which I wear while my jeans dry out.

In the sleeping hut we eat the lunch we have brought, and, the rain having stopped, Menan invites me outside. He does not explain what we are going to do; I just follow him. As we go along, he points out every plant and names it for me. He picks a bean for me to eat. He picks a small flower and hands it to me, and later a big flower. "For a bouquet," he says with a smile. We come to a large boulder, and he climbs up to the top and tells me to come up, too. I am tempted at this point to remind him of the age difference between us and certain consequent differences in agility, but I stop myself and simply say to him as I face the steep, wet boulder, "I'm not sure I can."

"Try [paṇṇuṅgaḷ]," he says tersely. Obediently, I make an effort and shortly reach the top. There is a pipal tree growing out of the boulder and a neem tree growing in the shade of the pipal. When I ask Menan whether anyone planted them that way, he says no, they just grew.

The view from the top of the boulder is lovely, and so is the homestead, and so is the landscape as we walk through it, with Menan pointing out all the different kinds of wild and domestic plants that grow in close company on his family's land. I tell Menan how beautiful I find the whole place, and he affirms, "Yes, this is nature [iyatkai]." As we walk back, we come to a tallish lemon tree, and Menan tries to beat a big green lemon down from the top as I wince for the tree. The big green lemon hangs on fiercely, but smaller ones fall, and I gather them up. Around noon we decide to resume our journey and change back into our wet clothes. The rain has started again. There is a shortcut through the paddy fields to the mountain temple we are aiming at, but Menan says he doesn't know the way; he will have to get someone to show us. A man is awakened from his sleep in a hut in a nearby homestead, and he leads us, riding Menan's bike, while I ride my bike and Menan rides the old, rusty one from his grandfather's veranda.

We make our way over ditches and bunds to the rocky hill where the temple stands. It was built only about twenty years ago, Menan says. The climb to the top is easy. Because of the rain, we cannot see far, but we are told that an army camp is nearby, behind a hill. At the base of the temple hill is an ashram where men and women are staying. Some, maybe all, of them are *sannyāsi*s, or renouncers. They feed us a big meal of a rice dish and fruit and insist that we spend the night there. There is no point in going all the way back through the rain; wait until it stops, they say.

We are in what people call the jungle, but surrounding us are all boulders and scrub. A scraggly peacock appears, and some monkeys. It is chilly and wet in the ashram, and we have no dry clothes, so we decide not to stay the night but to return home today. All the while I have been worrying aloud that Menan will catch cold from this trip. If he does, his mother will kill me. He is a small, frail-seeming child, and respiratory infections are a real threat to people here. (For me, the heat is the problem, and the rain is a welcome relief. I could not have made this trip on a sunny day.) But Menan insists he will be fine.

When we get back to Menan's grandfather's hut, the rain has stopped. He too insists that we stay the night and return in the morning. He gives us milk fresh from his cow. It is the only fresh milk I have tasted during my whole time in Sri Lanka. But we decide to return to the village today, so that people won't worry about us. Menan's grandfather accompanies us across the fields toward the main road.

Menan has asked his grandfather for a cuckoo's nest, and so his grandfather takes us to a hedgerow where an abandoned nest is hanging from a tree branch. It is like an oriole's nest, a kind of stiff gourd-shaped bag that the bird has fashioned from straw and glue, with a hole in the side for the bird to go in. Because it is pretty, because it is a small marvel of avian craftsmanship, it is valued, and we take it home.

On our way home, the rain begins again. Menan asks me if I like bicycling in the rain. He says he likes it a lot. I say it is a new experience for me, and that's why I'm not very good at it. He says it is a new experience for him, too, biking over this kind of muddy road in the pouring rain. And that's why he likes it. The people who live here do it every day, he adds.

• • •

I interview Menan the day after the bike ride. He is going to school and studying hard at it, hoping that good performance in school will lead to good employment. I wonder how his fate will compare with that of the unemployed, educated youths of the previous generation.

A good taped interview for me is like gold: it can throw light on people's thoughts, worlds, language, everything; but that happens only if they want to be understood, which not everyone does. I am hoping that Menan will just ramble on unprompted, as many of my informants do, but, perhaps because of the formality of the situation, most of his answers to my questions are brief, sometimes only one or two words.

Menan seems to have been avoiding this interview, and I have not wanted to press the issue: obviously, if he doesn't want to do a formal tape-recorded interview, that is his choice. But he hasn't actually refused or expressed reluctance, although I have repeatedly told him that there is no problem with saying no. Therefore I am not certain that Menan's postponements, disappearances at appointed times, and preoccupation with baby care and new purchases and not-to-be-missed TV programs constitute intentional evasion. So today (Sunday) I wait for a moment when Menan is off guard and completely unoccupied. When that moment arrives, I invite him to Rosa's house for the interview.

In general, Menan is not a talkative boy. And of course he has to be careful what he says. Still he makes some important points. He says his favorite movie is *Atisiya Piṟavi* (Miraculous Birth). His favorite story is a Muslim tale titled *Nītikkup pin Pāsam* (Justice before Love). He tells me the plots of both.

The movie is about a boy who dies prematurely and has to go back to earth, but when he gets back his body has already been burned, so he must choose another. The person whose body he is forced to inhabit has one girlfriend, while the main character who takes over the body has another girlfriend. He is not allowed to tell the truth of his situation, or his head will explode. Thus the movie places its hero in an impossible situation not of his making. He does what he can to escape having to tell the truth, but finally he is forced to do so. Then the highest god intervenes and saves him, and everyone lives happily ever after.

The Muslim story allows a queen who has accidentally killed a commoner to compensate for the murder with money, and to buy her own life in the same act. The story is ostensibly about equality of people before the law, regardless of who their kin may be. But the story also takes for granted that life has a cash value, and this trading of money for life is an event so common for civilians in this area that its fairness is not even questioned — at least not by Menan.

Both the movie and the story reflect to a certain extent the situation of Tamil people caught between two armies. If they tell the truth, they may be killed. And they find themselves, together with Muslims, to be the victims of ethnically biased laws. Menan makes it clear that he has no intention of joining the LTTE. He does not want to fight. But he thinks that the LTTE's reasons for fighting are just. In subsequent communications, he conveys to me his ideological worldview in detail. In general, it is in accord with LTTE ideology, except that Menan does not believe that fighting will solve any problems. He considers the fighting itself to be the problem. His is the pacifist's dilemma. He wants the fighting to end, but he says that "we" can do nothing about it; only "they," the fighters, can end it.

Menan's greatest problem is absence of personal freedom — in particular, the obstacles such as checkpoints that restrict his mobility. Like most adolescents, perhaps, he seeks "freedom from control by others." One of those others might be his own mother, who worries when he goes out that he might be abducted or killed by one of the paramilitaries, and probably limits his freedom for that reason.

When I ask Menan, "What would a truly happy life be like?" he responds, "I could go anywhere at any time, I could see anything without restriction by others. I could travel freely anywhere at night. I could go anywhere that I wanted to go." And the places he wants to visit are exactly those that are forbidden to him: the old fortress in town where the army is now stationed and another area where there are only farms, but where he cannot go because the army thinks the LTTE are there. These restrictions bother him more than the bomb blasts and fighting that are happening all around him. Indeed, it seems that these acts of war (the "problems" or *piraccinai*) are troublesome to him mainly because they restrict his freedom. If the fighting stops, he believes he will have the freedom he wants. The concept of fighting for freedom does not come up in the interview.

As a small child, Menan did not fear the army, because he believed that they would not hurt small children. Now he fears that because he is getting bigger, he might be pulled into the conflict. And he fears the bombing, as anyone would, because no one can tell when or where the next bomb will explode. But his experience with such things seems to mute his fear, rather than intensify it, and any fears he may have are overridden by his great desire to explore his world.

Menan says that he is accustomed to the events of war — in his words, he has experience (*anubavam*) with such events. For him the events of warfare — bombs exploding and so forth — are customary (*varakkam*). Therefore he has no interest (*ārvam*) in them. Adults, he says, have no (previous) experience of the war, and therefore it is interesting to them and they talk about it. Menan says he and his friends do not talk among themselves about the war.

Menan's analysis of the difference between his attitude and that of his elders contrasts with what his elders might say. Menan has grown up in the midst of warfare, and that is what he means when he says he has "experience." His elders grew up in peacetime, and when war came down upon them, it was something new to them. For Menan, new things are exciting and interesting, old things are dull and boring, and he surmises that this is why adults are so obsessed with the war. In one sense I think he may be right. Warfare is exciting — but only because it is so different from what one perceives as ordinary. When it becomes commonplace, it becomes dull. In another sense, however, Menan does not have any real experience with the war. He did not witness the death of his father, and he was too young at the time to understand its import. On the basis of his interview, one might guess that the horror and outrage have never really come home to him. Menan has experienced no serious problems with the army, no problems at all with Sinhala civilians; then again, he has never met a Sinhala civilian except on a school trip. The reasons for the war are abstractions to him.

In addition to finding the war unexciting and uninteresting, Menan finds it depressing. He tells me the most important event in his life was the death of his father, but he does not want to talk about it. Talking about his father makes him sad, and he would rather do things that make him happy. What gives him happiness is making jokes with his friends and laughing.

Menan does think about the war, as he makes clear to me later. But in this interview he says he does not think about it "much." He makes no reference to the war when he talks about his future, about the things he loves and the things he wants to do. He clearly loves his family farm, and when he is on it he strides over it like a king. He does not imagine losing it or abandoning it, and he says he would be "happy" with farming if that was what he had to do. But he considers his future is in learning and teaching. Education is in large part for the purpose of getting a job, and it provides a future in that sense. But there is more to it than just that. For Menan, who is first in his class, and thus a very good student, learning is becoming and growing and discovering the world. So he wants to be a teacher — anywhere in Sri Lanka, not necessarily in his hometown. He wants to share his own experience with small children, and thereby make them happy. When he makes this statement, he must not be thinking of the fact that to date his experience is of a war-torn world without freedom. Menan's love of the family farm, with all its growing things, and his intention to teach small children and make them happy seem to me part of the ethos of regeneration that pervades this area, war or no war.

The interview with Menan was my idea. I asked questions, and Menan answered. But the bike ride was Menan's idea. He led, and I followed. Inasmuch as I was there to understand children's agency, the contrast between the bike ride and the interview taught me an important lesson: if you want to know how children or youths exercise agency, let them take the initiative and make the decisions in their interactions with you. They will understand and decide pretty quickly what their relationship with you is to be.

In addition to this basic lesson, my time with Menan reminded me that some people prefer to demonstrate their thoughts rather than put them into words. During the bike trip we exchanged few words, but Menan showed me a beautiful world.

• • •

I have brought over to Vasanta's house some paper, crayons, and watercolor paints so that children can draw pictures for me. One day Menan asks to have some paper and paint, and I give them to him. Days later he comes back to me with a picture he has made.

The landscape is diagonally divided by a straight stretch of blue water. At the upper left grow tall and perfect trees, and a man is planting another tree there. The bank of the water on that side is clear and clean. The opposite bank is littered with dead tree branches, and the trees in the lower right of the picture are broken and losing their leaves. A man on that side is chopping a tree down.

Menan gives me an essay he has written to accompany the picture. Translated from Tamil, the essay reads:

In the world today, trees are being cut down everywhere. Therefore drought and famine are arising everywhere. The resources [*valangal*] of Lanka are being affected [*pātikkapadukinratu*]. Therefore the environment is affected. The environment is polluted [*mācupadukinratu*]. Because trees are cut down, the light of the sun dries up the waterholes directly, and drought occurs. Therefore today, people and animals are dying for lack of drinking water.

Because trees are cut down, the weather becomes disorderly [*vānilai kurambukiratu*]. In the air, the CO_2 increases. Therefore, the heat in the environment increases. When trees are cut down, in the rare world some species of creatures that grow only in a few places and to a limited degree and rare plants die. Species of creatures that grow in the environment nearby are affected. Even species of creatures that live here are dying.

Beyond the river a young boy is planting a tree. Therefore that environment grows with great flourishing. Therefore on that side all the species of creatures live freely [*cutantiramāka*]. There the natural resources are unaffected. It presents a very flourishing sight. We too should follow that boy's example. We should protect our natural resources.

One may find many connections between what is drawn here in this picture and our country of today.

Here the destruction of trees happens in the north and in the east. In other words, the Lankan government has entered into our region and destroys our species [*ematu inam* — the term in modern usage means "our people," that is, the Tamil people]. Our freedom and our rights are being cut down. Our life's order has been crushed [*cīr kuṟaintatu*]. The Lankan government constrains, suppresses, and destroys the Tamils. It wastes our future. It destroys our relatives. If we are beaten so, why should we stay alive?

As for the other side, the Lankan government makes the region flourish where the Sinhala people [*singala ina makkaḷ*] live. And it bestows upon those people all the rights that are needed. It uplifts the lives of those people. It protects only that category [*inam*]. This is what is happening in Lanka.

If one looks at this picture, one will see the government that runs Lanka. Calling itself a democratic, people's government, it constrains one category of people and plants concessions [*aravanaittu naḍuttukinratu*] for another category of people. In the same way, here the trees on one side are cut down. The trees on the other side are protected. The Lankan government protects one side, that is, the Sinhala people, and destroys the other side, the Tamil people.

Menan signs the essay in English with his full name, age, school, and home village. The essay needs no commentary but for the observation that Menan expresses his thoughts to me more boldly and clearly in writing and painting than in speech.

A week or so later, Menan brings me another painting. A bloodred sea roils against a black sky. Pale human hands reach out from the sea, like drowning people's hands. And, scattered across the sky, in bold white English capital letters, are the words "HELP! HELP! HELP!"

The message could hardly be clearer. But Menan has written a few sentences to explain the picture. He writes:

Here are the hands of Tamils drowning in blood. Why?

Because of the cruelties of the Lankan government. Singing and singing refrains that say, "Peace, peace," the Lankan government destroys poor innocent Tamils.

Because of the army's cruelties that the Tamil, struggling for life in a sea of blood, cannot endure.

Today the Tamil asks the world's nations for help. Hands of the world! Will you not change into helping hands for us?

And later still, when I am soon to leave the country, Menan brings me another painting. It is a night scene, with no colors but white, black, and gray. The river, straight and calm, stretches from the foreground to disappear between black, distant mountains. The full moon shines above the mountains and gleams on the river. Two dark figures, one larger and one smaller, are crossing the river in a boat together. This picture has no text.

CHAPTER 7

Girls in the LTTE

A Brief History of Child Soldiers

Young people have served in military organizations for as long as there have been military organizations. Typically, those who were not fully grown were not regular combatants but served in other capacities. During the United States Revolutionary War, the U.S. Civil War, the First World War, and the Second World War, however, beardless boys found themselves at the combat front, in part because the armies they served had run out of grown-up fighters.

Today the global proliferation of small arms has made it possible for small-bodied people (including women and children) to participate as effective front-line ground combatants on a massive scale. Small, lightweight people can make better fighters than larger people in many combat situations. Throughout the Cold War, the United States, the Soviet Union, and other large countries produced and sold large quantities of high-powered, lightweight assault rifles to countries fighting proxy wars. At the end of the Cold War, many small arms were dumped on the world market. The United States gave away billions of dollars' worth of such weapons, and sold billions of dollars' worth more. Other nations have done the same. The development, production, and sale of increasingly sophisticated, lightweight assault rifles continues. It is a lucrative industry. In modern times, and probably for a long time before, the poor have been more subject than the rich to recruitment into front-line combat. This is because the rich have other, better life options. In many countries, moreover, the poor are more accustomed than the rich to physical hardship, and may therefore be better able to adapt to the hardship of combat than those who are better off. Therefore, on the whole, the poor may make better combatants than the rich.

Among the hardships that the very poor of today's world must suffer is enduring hunger, with the physical consequences of malnutrition. Lifetime malnutrition results in small bodies. Among the poor, those who are most subject to malnutrition are children and women.

The broad causes of world hunger in current times are well known. There is enough food in the world to feed everybody, but it is not distributed to the hungry. Food crops such as rice, as well as nonfood crops such as cotton, are grown for sale and profit. If a crop cannot be sold for profit, it is warehoused or dumped. Economic liberalization programs have caused farmers in poor countries to concentrate on the production of export crops to pay off debts rather than on the production of food to feed local people. Many poor countries are caught in a cycle of debt that results in the increasing impoverishment of the local people, who can no longer feed themselves because they have to grow crops for sale to pay off their own debts.

Armed conflict has been listed as a primary cause of hunger in troubled regions of the world. But hunger is likewise a primary cause of conflict. The prospect of starvation is terrifying, and intentionally starving a population is no less a terrorist act than exploding bombs in their midst. People who are starving are willing to fight for food, just as they are willing to work for food — if they are able. One does not have to be big, strong, or well nourished to handle a modern assault rifle. Additionally, many of the consequences of malnutrition can be reversed if an abundant, nutrient-rich diet becomes available, and a good army feeds its soldiers well, to make and keep them strong. Thus, for those facing starvation, working for an armed organization offers an attractive escape. The combination of massive, man-made famine and global proliferation of military small arms has created the modern child combatant.

Nobody knows how many child soldiers there are in the world today. According to Anup Shah, "In 1998 it was estimated that up to 300,000 children were actively involved in armed conflict" worldwide.[1] A "child" for the purposes of this estimate is anyone under the age of eighteen. Therefore, many of those counted as children are in fact adolescents.

The most comprehensive source of information on the situation of child soldiers in the modern world is a report by Graca Machel published by the United Nations in 1996.[2] According to this report, almost all child soldiers live in poor countries where hunger is endemic. Almost all come from poor families. Most belong to nonstate militias. Some work as porters or slaves; others carry guns and are active combatants. Some are abducted and forced to work for an army or militia; others join voluntarily. Many join for food, or for ideological reasons, or both. For some, becoming a combatant is their best option. The Machel report states that military organizations recruit children because children are more easily abducted than adults, and they are more easily coerced once caught.

Some other reasons for persistence in child recruitment may be suggested. The first, already noted, is that children can handle modern assault rifles as easily as grown adults, so there is no practical reason *not* to employ them in combat. Another is that military and related forms of training are most effective if they take place throughout the human adolescent growth spurt. The best combatants, like the best athletes, may be those who begin training in midadolescence or earlier. During adolescence (the period from sexual maturity to attainment of full adult size) human beings demand more calories and protein than at any other time in their lives. A military organization can commandeer food and give it to people at that stage of their lives, together with training, and receive service in return. By the time such adolescent recruits reach their early twenties, having obtained intensive training, good nourishment, and combat experience throughout their teens, they will be very good fighters indeed. The long-term disadvantage of producing highly effective "killing machines" (if such they become) has been widely discussed in the popular media and elsewhere. Even if they do not become machines, there is still a serious chance that such soldiers may one day turn against the organization that trained them. It has happened with the U.S. Army. It has happened with the LTTE. In short, if one asks why so many child soldiers exist in the world today, the answer is a simple combination of factors: first, because there are so many ground wars and insurgencies in poor countries; second, because there are so many impoverished and hungry children in conflict-ridden areas; third, because children are capable of effectively wielding assault rifles, and therefore are capable of engaging in armed conflict; and fourth, because if training starts in childhood, the resulting product may be formidable. The existence of child soldiers in today's world is inevitable, given all of these factors working together. But it is not inevitable that any given child will become a soldier.

Many people lament the existence of child soldiers as a great evil, and blame the military organizations for which those children work. But only quite recently has there been organized humanitarian concern for the plight of child soldiers. The Geneva Conventions of 1949 make no mention of child soldiers.[3]

Women constitute a special category in all of these conventions. Each of the first three conventions separately states, "Women shall be treated with all consideration due their sex." The fourth convention states, "Women shall be specially protected against any attack on their honour, in particular against rape, enforced prostitution, or any form of indecent assault." However, under international humanitarian law in the mid-twentieth century, the category distinctions combatant/noncombatant, able/disabled, and female/male were the only salient ones. Children were not a protected category under international humanitarian law unless they were also civilian, disabled, or female. Able, male, combatant children were completely unprotected.

The first and most likely reason for the exclusion of male combatant children from protection under international humanitarian law is that until these conventions were established, almost all regular combatants were able-bodied young men. Women were excluded by custom from combat, and boys below a certain size would be excluded as unable to effectively bear arms and fight. A second, related reason may be that signatory countries at the time were more concerned with the "honor" of their women than they were with the lives of fifteen-year-old boys. A third reason may have been that the category of "child" was defined differently then from now. In 1977, after the war in Vietnam, and in light of the lessons learned in that war, two additional protocols to the Geneva Conventions were signed. Protocol I, Article 77, stipulates that children shall be the objects of special respect, not subject to "indecent assault," and should be provided with the care and aid they require. But Protocol I applies only to conflicts between states, not to internal conflicts. And this protocol still assumes children to be noncombatants.

Protocol II applies to conflicts within states. It too stipulates that children be provided with the care and aid they require. However, Protocol II applies only to a restricted category of internal conflicts: those between the armed forces of a "high contracting party" (which usually means a government) and dissident armed forces and other organized armed groups. Protocol II would arguably not apply to the majority of current civil wars. The reason is obvious: few governments are likely to concede that any struggle within their borders amounts to an armed conflict.[4]

Protocol II has been ratified by only 136 states. It contains the same inherent dilemma as Protocol I: namely, it does not state whether a child combatant is to be treated as a "protected person" or as an enemy directly engaged in hostilities. If the former, the child must be spared; if the latter, she or he may be killed on sight. Or should children fighting for the enemy receive special treatment?

The case of the IPKF versus the LTTE illustrates the dilemma. This conflict took place between 1987 and 1989, when the IPKF was invited to Sri Lanka to enforce peace between the LTTE and the Sri Lankan government's military forces. The IPKF was welcomed at first by both sides but quickly came to be seen as an alien occupying force, especially by the Tamils. With the covert assistance of the government, which also suspected the IPKF and the government of India of ulterior motives in sending troops to Sri Lanka, the LTTE drove the IPKF out.

The Coalition to Stop the Use of Child Soldiers proclaims, "The LTTE only began to recruit large numbers of women and children to its ranks after it declared war against the 100,000-strong Indian Peace Keeping Force in October 1987."[5] One may ask why the LTTE did not have large numbers of women and children before. Some hints come from statements by members of the IPKF who participated in the incursion into Sri Lanka:

Located in buildings, treetops and even coconut palms, equipped with powerful telescopic infra-red sights they [snipers] took a heavy toll.

[Whereas our] individual weapons and ancillary equipment were bulky and needed to [be] lightened considerably.

Major A. A. Verghese, the only Tamil speaker in the whole unit, went into a house full of crying women and children to comfort them. As he turned to leave, an old woman shot him in the back.

Sepoy Govindan, Madras Regiment, says, "It was impossible to say who was a Tiger and who was not. Everyone male or female above the age of 10 could be armed and dangerous. We saw little girls producing guns from under their frocks and shooting at us. How do you fight them?"[6]

The LTTE succeeded in routing the IPKF because it used guerrilla tactics, it was on its own territory, and the whole population was involved. Children were supremely useful in this effort, and not only because their involvement as combatants was unexpected. They were fast, agile, and brave. They could climb palm trees with rifles in hand. Lightweight people with lightweight weapons had a distinct advantage. How, indeed, do you deal with an army like this?

The answer has been to invoke morality, by way of human rights legislation. In contrast to international humanitarian law, which applies only to acts permitted or not permitted in wartime, human rights law establishes rights that every individual should enjoy during both peace and war.

The United Nations Convention on the Rights of the Child was adopted by the UN General Assembly 1989. It is the most widely ratified of all human rights treaties.[7] Article 38 says: "State Parties shall take all feasible measures to ensure that persons who have not attained the age of fifteen years do not take a direct part in hostilities. . . . State Parties shall refrain from recruiting any person who has not attained the age of fifteen years into their armed forces."

Still, the convention did not address the issue of child combatants in nonstate (i.e., rebel) armies, such as the LTTE. But these were and are exactly the armies most likely to have children in their ranks, for many reasons. Such nonstate armies were and are also a serious threat to the survival of the sovereign state in a globalizing world. For these reasons, the United Nations Draft Optional Protocol on the Involvement of Children in Armed Conflict was developed. It was adopted by consensus on 21 January 2000, when it was signed by twenty-six states. It became law when it was submitted to the General Assembly in July 2000 but became binding only on those states that chose to sign it after this point. Sri Lanka was among the first to ratify this protocol.

Article 2 of the Optional Protocol says: "State Parties shall ensure that persons who have not attained the age of 18 years are not compulsorily recruited into their armed forces." Article 4 says:

1. Armed groups, distinct from the armed forces of a State, should not, under any circumstances, recruit or use in hostilities persons under the age of 18 years.
2. State Parties shall take all feasible measures to prevent such recruitment and use, including the adoption of legal measures necessary to prohibit and criminalize such practices.

Note the discrepancy here. Articles 2 and 4 of the protocol allow states to recruit volunteers under the age of eighteen. But nonstate forces (rebels) may not even voluntarily recruit under-eighteens and may be criminalized by the state for doing so. This favoring of state forces over nonstate forces is unsurprising, as the United Nations consists of established and mutually recognized sovereign states. Rebel groups are thereby faced with a dilemma: either they relinquish their most valuable human asset or they incur the displeasure of the international community.

To recapitulate the main points made in this section: the conditions for the rise of child combatants in the modern world were set by several major global developments in the last quarter of the twentieth century. These are: the severe impoverishment of a quarter of the world's people; their loss of their capacity to feed themselves and their children; the exacerbation of conditions of social and economic inequality on both the local and the global levels; and the development and proliferation of lightweight combat weaponry. All of these conditions were created by global capitalism. As long as these conditions persist, it remains inevitable that children will be employed in combat organizations, including rebel armies fighting against established states.

Conventional military organizations, including the United States military, are seriously threatened by child soldiers. For instance, a recent seminar report published by the Marine Corps Warfighting Laboratory contains the following observations:

Not only have U.S. forces faced child soldiers in the past, it is nearly inevitable that they will face them again in the future. If a 14-year-old points a weapon at a U.S. serviceman, what should he do? No Marine, no soldier, sailor or airman wants to kill a 14-year-old. But a 14-year-old with an AK-47 is just as deadly as a 40-year-old with an AK-47. If one hesitates, then he and his buddies might be killed; if he shoots, then he might have to deal with the potential psychological consequences of killing a child. This presents a terrible dilemma. . . . (p. 10)

[Jo Becker] explained that on the battlefield, children more readily follow orders, are less inhibited, and are more vicious than their grown-up counterparts. They seemingly have no fear, acclimatize quickly, and often do not play by the rules. (p. 14)

[Child soldiers, compared to mature ones, possess] *increased lethality* [emphasis in the original]. According to the Brookings Institution's Dr. Singer, children on the battlefield add confusion, and ultimately drive up the death toll. He emphasized not to underestimate child soldiers; in many cases they have years of combat experience, and are more battle hardened than their adversaries.

[Major Gray, a Royal British Marine] explained. . . . They don't in any way conduct a maneuver approach to operations. They fight in a very disjointed way. The egocentric nature of children, the fact that when a child is a child, they don't have the ability to think about other people. They have a simple one-step requirement that they fulfill. As you get older, you understand about morality. They kind of fight like this. On the playground, they are harsh to each other, they fulfill their own needs all the time. You give them an AK-47 and it's a whole different story. You combine the fact that they are on drugs, you give them a weapon and they behave as if they were on a playground, and it is terrifying. (pp. 17–18)[8]

Characterized as "vicious," "lethal," and "terrifying" creatures who "don't have the ability to think about other people," child soldiers in this seminar appear as dangerous and irrational as rabid dogs. Indeed, from the point of view of Major Gray, even ordinary children are less than fully human. Like robots, "[t]hey have a simple one-step requirement that they fulfill." "On the playground" they think only of themselves and are "harsh" to each other. In combat, child soldiers act like they are on a playground and this, according to Major Gray, is worse than inappropriate, apparently because, in his view, children are not nice to each other when they play. Moreover, Major Gray has us take as a "fact" that the child soldiers we meet are "on drugs," which we are allowed to assume will exacerbate their viciousness, their irrationality, their "disjointed" behavior, their lack of empathy, and their deficit of humanity.

It is almost as though the speakers in this seminar were trying to find a moral justification to eliminate children from the world under their control—children should either be kept confined and off the orderly adult domain of the battlefield, or, because they are (allegedly) *more* dangerous than adults, they must be killed. *Especially* for child soldiers, no mercy should be shown. Of course, it is war itself that is immoral, and the presence of children on the battlefield threatens to force this fact into the consciousness of soldiers.

Ashis Nandy (2004) argues that violent oppression of children by adults is the prototype of violent oppression of the colonized by the colonizer. In the modern world, the process of transformation from childhood to adulthood is construed as a form of progress, applied to the individual life cycle. The child is imagined as undeveloped and primitive, the adult as developed and civilized. On the basis of this model, colonial powers justified their violent oppression of the colonized as benign paternalism that would develop and improve the colonized, who were seen as both "childlike" and "childish." "The former [the childlike] is circumscribed by those aspects of childhood which 'click' with adult concepts of the child; the latter [the childish] by those which are independent of adult constructions of the child. Childlikeness is valued, sometimes even in adults. Childishness is frowned upon, sometimes even in children" (423–24).

The construction of the colonized as children, Nandy continues, is not only a matter of racism. More deeply, it conveys "a certain terror of childhood . . . [the sense] that children could be dangerous. . . . [Children] symbolize, once we have seen through our constructions of childhood, a persistent, living, irrepressible criticism of our 'rational,' 'normal,' 'adult' visions of desirable societies. . . . Colonial ideology required savages to be children, but it also feared that savages could be like children" (425). Nandy argues further that the construction of both children and the colonized as potentially dangerous savages legitimized the infliction of devastatingly cruel and violent punishment upon both, as the only way to discipline and improve them. Such habits of thought and action have not entirely died away. In the concluding paragraph of his article (439) Nandy asserts, "The ideology of adulthood has hidden the fact that children see through our hypocrisy perfectly and respond to our tolerance and respect fully." My experiences with children in Sri Lanka support Nandy's assertion.

The remainder of this chapter describes my encounters with young female soldiers, some of them under the age of eighteen, and the challenges they face. They are ordinary human beings — if anything, more human than those who describe them as monsters — in extraordinary circumstances.

Vidya and Nalini

Saturday, 24 January 1998. When I was at the office in Kokkadichcholai yesterday, two Tiger girls came to see me. The name of the older one is Anjala. She says she is seventeen, and she looks about that age or older. The younger one, Nalini, says she is twelve years old, but she looks even younger. Both of them were dressed in Tiger outfits, with a cyanide capsule tucked in the left breast pocket.

Today Nalini comes to Sita's house with another girl, whose name is Vidya. Vidya says she is fifteen. They are both carrying cyanide capsules. (The older male members of the LTTE sometimes carry these things and sometimes don't. If they sometimes don't, it must mean that they feel relatively safe.) Nalini says she is the only one in her immediate family who has joined the Tigers; Vidya says an older brother and an older sister were both Tigers and died in battle (*vīra maraṇam*). I ask them whether they go to school, and Vidya says that she has finished school. Sita's mother tells me that fighting is what they study.

I try to follow up on these comments and learn that Vidya has been in battle but has not shot anybody. Nalini, when I ask her if she has ever shot a soldier, replies with a shy smile, "*Chee*" (Tamil for "what a silly idea"). I ask them what work they have today, and they tell me they have no work at all. I ask them how their training was, and, with a bit of coaching from Vidya, Nalini replies that it was fine.

Nalini is cute, with a very dark face and a bright, ready smile; she plays with Sita's baby as any young girl would play with any baby. When I ask about training and whether they have to run long distances (as others have told me), Nalini says no, they just have to run three hundred meters. I ask them if they know how to use an AK-47 (this is still the only combat weapon whose name I remember). They glance at each other, and Vidya says, "She knows!" She asks if I know how to use a rifle. I say I learned when I was thirteen (in summer camp), but since then have had no practice. And it was only a small rifle. They ask about the various scars and wounds on my body, and I explain to them the circumstances in which each one was incurred. They seem to believe me when I jokingly tell them a bear ripped open my chest one time, but I fought it off. Nalini comments that there are bears in Jaffna, too. I have to explain to them that in regard to the bear I was lying (*summā,* just kidding). They don't laugh.

I ask Nalini if she is afraid when she goes to the jungle, and she responds, "No; only here is there fear."

"You mean here in this house you're afraid?"

"Yes," she says.

"Why?"

"The army will come here," she says. "The army won't come to the jungle."

After lingering for about an hour, the two little fighters rise and go. I watch them as they walk away, proudly but maybe a bit self-consciously adjusting their thick broad belts around their young-girl waists to meet their young-girl hips, and straightening their shirttails as they go. Perhaps they are still not quite used to their uniforms.

Monday night, 26 January. It is the day after the bombing of the Temple of the Tooth (Dalada Maligawa) in Kandy. Many of the Tigers in the area around Arasadithivu appear to have gone off somewhere. I am at the Tiger girls' camp (*muhām* — sometimes they call it the base). No one is there except two young Tiger girls who have been left to look after the camp, plus an assortment of adult, apparently civilian, women, some of whom may be servants. One is there for the one-month memorial service of her brother, who died in combat.

Nalini and Vidya came again today to Sita's house, where I was staying. They said they had come to see me, just as they had done when I was at the office. It is rather striking because the Tigers publicly insist that they have no child combatants, yet here are these two uniformed girls openly seeking me out. Sita told Alagar in my presence that at the Tiger office these girls came and stood right in front of my eyes; at that time a comment was made about the absence of proper supervision. But here they are again. The young girls ask me to come to their camp, and so a little later, I do.

A path leading from the front gate to the front door of the camp (a regular village house) is lined with flowering plants, some in pots and some in the earth. The walls of the front room in the house are lined with photographs of Tigers who perished in battle. There is also a picture of Prabhakaran and two pictures of real tigers (one with the caption "I have achieved everything"). There is a portrait of Kittu, the famous Tiger leader who, when captured at sea, blew up the boat he was on. This portrait must have been done here for the recent Kittu Memorial Day. There is also the famous portrait in ink of a Black Tiger, with his face blacked out by stripes.

The girls' supervisor, Malaimalli, arrives, and we talk for a while. Nalini comes into the camp. "Where have you been?" I ask.

"At work," she says, with her usual shy bright smile.

"What work?" I ask.

"Political [*araciyal*]," she says.

Vidya is there as well. The first thing she says to me is, "Do you like us [*engalai virumbukiringalā*]?"

I answer truthfully, "Yes, I like you a lot." I ask her what work she had today, and she says no work whatsoever. I ask her how she has spent her time, and she says she has just been wandering around (*cutti tirikiratu*). What do they do for fun, I ask, and she says they play cricket.

"Where? Here in the village?"

"No, no — in the jungle."

I try to imagine the Tiger girls playing cricket in a jungle clearing. I ask her if she is of the political branch (*araciyal*) of the Tigers, and she says, "No. Military [*rānuvam*]." That means her main job is fighting. She says she has not killed anyone in battle because the enemy were hiding, so she didn't have a chance.

Sita has told me that young members of the movement are not yet experienced enough to fight well. Another Tiger told me that very young boys, some as young as thirteen, work in the camps but are not sent to the battlefront. He was Catholic and seemed to offer this news as a kind of sad confession. Child labor is officially condemned by the government, but in fact it is omnipresent in Sri Lanka. There is worse work than being a gopher for Tigers. But Vidya, fifteen years old, speaks as though she would rather be at the front.

"Aren't you afraid when you go into battle?" I ask her.

"*Chee* — it is play [*vilaiyāddu*]," she says. "A game. On the battlefield we are their equals, and they are ours."

She asks me what I will do if the army comes. I say, "I guess I will do what everyone else does — what will you do?"

"We will fight," she says proudly.

"Will you protect me?" I ask.

This may seem an inappropriate question for a researcher to ask a fifteen-year-old girl. But Vidya is no longer a child, and I have a sense that it is important to her to be treated with respect, as a fighter. I ask the question respectfully. And I want to know, with Vidya's supervisor there, what the "right" answer to this question may be. When a village is raided, the army is looking primarily for LTTE members, who face the dilemma of whether to flee and protect themselves or stand between the army and the civilians, firing back, in which case many more people, including civilians, might be killed. Sometimes just a few LTTE members are left in a village during an army raid. Then the army finds them, kills them, and departs, satisfied. This will happen right in this village seven months after I first meet and talk with Vidya. Then I understand that the LTTE members who stayed in the village during the army raid were effectively sacrificing their lives. But when I talk with Vidya, I have not yet thought all this through, and possibly neither has she.

"Yes, we will protect you," Vidya says. Then she looks to Malaimalli for confirmation. "If the army comes, will we protect?" she asks.

"We will protect," comes the terse answer.

"What do you learn in training?" I ask her.

"We exercise," she says.

"Is that all?"

"We learn how to attack."

"Do you learn how to live in the jungle?"

"The training is *in* the jungle," she replies impatiently.

I remember other people's stories about the hardships they suffer while hiding in the jungle. It is infested with poisonous snakes and insects, and the thick bush and stones make travel painful. Sita's sister said she left the LTTE because of her fear of the jungle. So I ask Vidya, "Is the jungle a frightening place?"

"No."

"Are there snakes in the jungle?"

"Yes," she says. "And ghosts [*pēy*]."

"Ghosts? What are they like?" She makes a scary face, to show me what a ghost looks like. She does not try to hide her contempt of my stupidity. But I persist and ask her, "What kind of ghosts?"

"Ghosts of our people," she says.

And I think of all the people who have died violent deaths around here. Mainland Tamils say people who die violently before their time become ghosts haunting the place where they died. Ghosts can literally scare the life from the living. It is never clear to me what people of Kokkadichcholai feel about this, for they travel every day and night through the crossroads where their kin have been slaughtered, occupy the same houses, and work the same fields where so much blood has been shed. Vasanta, a Christian, once told me not to go out on the road by our house at night because so many ghosts were there. But then she added that she was just kidding, that only the superstitious believed such things.

Malaimalli

Malaimalli is the new head of the Batticaloa-Amparai branch of the women's wing of the LTTE, and she has also been assigned responsibility for the Tiger girls at the base here in town, the old head having been transferred elsewhere. So she has two jobs, at least for now: looking after the girls at the base and attending to her higher-level duties. She has just today come back from the jungle, and I see her at Sita's house. She is exhausted and sick from the three-day-long tractor ride. She is thin. Her face is lined and sad, but she smiles more often than not. Her hair is not cropped but tied up in braids, like Sita's. And, like Sita, she has a gentle demeanor and a sweet voice. The two of them sit talking together, Malaimalli leaning forward facing Sita, holding her hands.

She arrives at the girls' camp after I get there. She talks to me woman to woman, the same way she talks to Sita, trusting in my sympathy and understanding. She has brought a flower vase back to the girls' camp with pretty roses on it.

I ask about her family and why she joined the movement. She is twenty-six years old. Her older sister saw her husband shot before eyes. Her younger sister was imprisoned and tortured: they peeled off the skin on her leg and rubbed pepper in, and pulled off her fingernails. Now she is at home but unable to do anything. Malaimalli says there are sixteen thousand widows in Batticaloa District. Why get married just to become a widow? One must go to war in search of a peaceful life (*nimmatiyāna vārkkai*).

I have noticed that the last three fingers on her right hand have been cut off, evenly, as though by a single knife stroke. They have healed cleanly. She says they were lost in gunfire during the battle of Mullaithivu. I am impressed that she fought in this battle, and I ask her what it was like, but she says she will tell me another day. She is still tired from her long journey, and her head is pounding. During the battle of Paranthan some years ago, a bullet became lodged in her skull, and it gives her terrible headaches, she says.

"A what?" I ask, uncomprehending.

"A bullet," she says. And she instructs one of the teenage girls at the camp to go fetch one to show me. The girl comes back with a thick, pointed bullet, two inches long. The bullet cannot be removed from her head, or she will die, she says. She was treated after that battle at the hospital in Jaffna — this was when the Tigers controlled Jaffna. Now there is no hospital to which they can go to be treated. It feels as though the bullet is floating around inside her head, sometimes behind her eyes, sometimes at the back of her head, Malaimalli tells me. She shows me the spot on her head where the bullet is and invites me to touch it. Bullets also passed through both of her thighs: I can feel the deep indentation on the inside of her right thigh. A ball is lodged in her left knee and another in her left foot. She invites me to touch all these places. I can feel a hard spot that can be pushed around beneath the flesh on the top of her foot.

Tiger girls attend Vithusa's birthday party in February. Malaimalli is busy videotaping the party, but most of the other Tiger girls sit shyly and silently in a corner of the veranda. Among them is the head of the women's camp in the jungle. She is taller than I, with a handsome face, and looks very fit, like an athlete, an Athena. I try to talk with her, and she smiles back but seems shy with me and doesn't say much. She is of the military (*rāṇuvam*) division, and, like others of this division I have met, she seems restless, bouncing her legs as many men do in this country, and she does not sit still very long. She barks impatiently at Malaimalli once or twice, like a Marine drill sergeant.

I feel sad for Malaimalli and wonder what right the jungle-camp leader has to treat her this way. But Malaimalli, displaying no rancor, asks me if I like the other woman. Yes, I do, I say. Malaimalli tells me that a sari-clad, middle-aged woman who is sitting silently amid the Tiger girls lives at the girls' camp with them. She has two sons in the movement, and a third was killed by the army, so the Tiger women have taken her in as a cook.

Malaimalli asks if I have brought her anything from Colombo, and I apologetically say no, I haven't — what would she like? She asks for a shirt like the one she is wearing. I tell her I thought the movement supplied those shirts, and she acknowledges that they do, and says I should bring her anything from my heart.

I ask her why people so often ask for gifts like this. Westerners are put off by the habit. Malaimalli says that asking for gifts is a way of showing love. I tell her that my people show love by giving gifts, and never by asking for them. Here, she responds, it is different.

I am aware of what anthropologists write about gift giving and receiving, and the politics of it all, but this is not what I think about when I try to understand Malaimalli's explanation. We have in common our view that a gift is a sign of affection, a sign of love. If you ask for a gift you are humbling yourself, asking for that sign of love. It is a simple idea; the truth may be more complex. But maybe the simple and obvious is sometimes also the truth.

Around February, a Tiger boy dies of snakebite. At his funeral, his death is said to be *vīrasāvu,* a warrior's death. I am confused about this, because not all Tiger deaths are called warriors' deaths. A Tiger who dies of sickness, for instance, will be honored, but his death is not *vīrasāvu.* I ask Malaimalli about it. She explains that snakebite death and warrior's death have in common a certain quality, but she uses a word I do not know, and she cannot find another way to explain it to me. I can only speculate: it is a violent death, a death by attack, a death by poison, a death inflicted by a most sacred creature.

26 March. Malaimalli is in the backyard of the girls' camp with some of the other girls. She asks if I knew that another person in the movement had been bitten by a snake while sitting on the steps in front of this house at night. After three weeks of sickness, the person recovered. I ask Malaimalli about snakes in the jungle. With this question commences a lesson on jungle fauna. I take careful notes. The other girls sit around listening.

Pythons. When the python sleeps, it lies curled in a big heap (she shows the height of the heap with her hand). When it is sleeping like that, it will not wake up. When it is looking for prey, it will lie with its head in the dust and its body up in a tree until you come by, not seeing it, and then it will chase you. The python moves fast and has fangs on its tail. It wraps around you and then sinks the fangs on its tail into your ear. When you feel those fangs in your ear, you know you will die. A rifle is of no use if a python attacks you, because the snake will hold you so tightly you won't be able to take aim. The only way to save yourself is to cut the snake with a knife. A group of Tigers once came upon a python that had half-swallowed a deer. The front of the deer was visible, and the back was in the python. They shot the python, but the deer was already dead.

Bears. There are also bears in the jungle. The bear is a four-legged animal, but it walks on two legs. Its footprint is like the print made by the edge of your curled hand in the dust (she demonstrates), like a child's footprint. It has hands like human hands. It will stand in wait hiding behind a tree (she demonstrates by standing behind the edge of a door, peeking out). It will not eat anything already dead. Of body parts it will only eat the liver, which it rips from your abdomen while you are still alive. It will pull out your eyeballs and examine them in its palm. If you are dead or pretend to be dead, it will come up to you and examine you, putting its palm in front of your nostrils to see if you are breathing. Then it will go off and climb up a tree and watch you to see if you move. It will watch like that for hours. The best thing to do with a bear is play dead. Once the eastern leader Karuna was attacked by a bear; the bear had him in its embrace, and they were swaying back and forth as though they were dancing together (she demonstrates). Someone shot the bear through the body, and Karuna was also wounded. Then they shot the bear through the head, and it died.

Malaimalli's accounts remind me of stories I heard in my childhood around midnight campfires deep in the woods. Why does it entertain us so to be scared out of our wits? But she seems to have ended her lesson. So I ask her about the big battle at Mullaithivu where she lost her fingers. "What was it like to be there?" I want to know.

She asks, "Do you really want to hear about such things?"

"Yes," I say. She then begins an enthusiastic account.

"We were very happy," she says. "They had large quantities of expensive, heavy weaponry — mortar launchers, airplanes. We had only rifles. But they were huddling in fear. The enemy panic when they are attacked. They don't even aim their rifles. They fire in all directions. We take aim before we shoot, and therefore we hit our targets. I would take aim and shoot one soldier. He would fall. I would walk up to him, put my foot on his body [*she demonstrates*], and shoot him through the head. Then I would go on and do the same thing to the next, and the next." She is smiling, relaxed. Her description makes it sound easy. I am not shocked by anything she says, but much later I learn that the Geneva Conventions call it a war crime to kill a wounded enemy soldier. I wonder how many soldiers have put dying enemy soldiers out of their misery by shooting them through the head. She tells me she appears in the videotape of the Mullaithivu battle. She is up in a tree, wearing a cap.

The subject of marriage somehow comes up. A rumor has been going about among civilians that Ramanan, the head of the fierce LTTE attack group based in Mahiladithivu, has eloped with a civilian girl. According to the rumor, he had been courting her for some time. She was in love with him, but her parents did not approve of the match. So they ran off secretly together, and now he is keeping her in Palugamam, where they had a wedding. Village civilians say he has given his wife a *tāli,* a marriage pendant, with seven ounces of gold.

I ask Malaimalli if all of this is true. She says in irritation that common people always exaggerate like this. The *tāli* has just one and a half ounces of gold. A Tiger girl sitting nearby adds that the *tāli* string was just a simple cotton string dyed yellow with turmeric in the traditional way, not made of gold at all.

During my stay there are several Tiger weddings. All the ones I hear of involve Tiger men and civilian girls. I wonder whether civilian boys could or would marry Tiger women, and I wonder if the shortage of potential husbands is a problem. Late in my stay, I am told that Prabhakaran has ordered that Tiger men can marry only Tiger women, but there is no independent confirmation of this news.

I ask Malaimalli if she knows anything about the recent raid of Tigers against TELO in Arayampathi. She says no. I say, how can you not know, you are in the movement, don't they tell you these things? She says she's been sick and has just come back from the jungle and hasn't had a chance to talk much with people in the village. But she tells me that the raiders went across the lagoon in canoes, killed two TELO and took their weapons, then swam back across the lagoon, leaving the canoes behind. (Rosa or someone has told me that the army took the canoes.) I ask how they could swim back with their weapons. She says they had only pistols. I ask about all the gunfire and explosions. She says that they brought grenades across with them on the canoes; the explosions we heard were grenade explosions.

Karttikka and Kausalya

The grounds of the LTTE police station and the women's camp in Kokkadichcholai are beautifully planted with flowers. The police station is the former political office I visited in 1996. Then it was bare and sparsely furnished. Now it is like a home where people have come to stay: furnished, planted, well kept. The Tiger police, both men and women, wear blue uniforms with Tiger badges on the sleeve. There are at least fifty civilians there on the day I show up. Civilians come to the Tiger police to report complaints against other civilians. Ultimately each case is settled in the Tiger courts. Several civilians have told me that the Tiger police and courts are more fair and efficient than the government courts and police on the other side of the lagoon. I talk for a while with two policewomen while one of them signs forms. They tell me they deal mainly with small complaints.

On a trip into Batticaloa, I stop in a bookstore and pick up some papers and magazines. In one of them, *Frontline,* I discover an article that features the Tiger police station I have visited.[9] The article, about the village of Kokkaddicholai, refers to this village as a kind of experimental Eelam, or independent Tamil state.

Frontline is a major political newsmagazine published in Chennai (formerly Madras), focusing on India but covering events all over the world. The article about Kokkadichcholai is in the section called "World Events." I am pleased and impressed that "my" village has been highlighted there and that the article is not entirely unsympathetic. I first encountered *Frontline* among a bundle of publications in the Kokkadichcholai political office. The old man who worked at the office, who told me he had joined the Tigers mainly to get away from the fighting, also told me that this bundle of publications was going to be sent to Prabhakaran, but I could read *Frontline* while I was waiting to see Inbam. It was like waiting for the dentist, except that the magazines were current. And I felt strangely honored that they let me read the magazine before Prabhakaran got it.

The January article shows a picture of the sign right along the main road; I took a picture of it myself a month previously and was arrested by the police in Colombo for having the photo. It is a sign bearing the fierce Tiger logo and the words "High Court of Tamil Eelam, Batti-Amparai Division." But the word *court* is misspelled (the Tigers later corrected it), and the writer of the article suggests that the Tigers are just pretending to govern. To bring the point home, he stresses the youth of the responsible officials. The high-court judge is a small woman just twenty-two years of age. The police office is also headed by young women, who spend most of their time receiving civilian complaints and filling out forms. The OIC (officer in charge) is interviewed and named in the article. The person responsible (*poṟuppāḷar*) for the political office has also been interviewed and complimented for his skill in answering some questions and parrying others. He has not been named in the article, but I know it is Inbam.

In early February, I take the latest copy of *Frontline* to the police station to show to the people who work there. The officer in charge, Karttikka, greets me with the words, "Why has it been so long since you've visited us?" This is a common way of saying you value a person, but Karttikka says it with a straight face, like an accusation. My reason is that the police station always looks so busy, with civilians always waiting in line to see Karttikka or one of the other officers. But I am hoping that Karttikka will be pleased with my gift of the magazine. Not surprisingly, no one has sent a copy to the people about whom this article is written. Karttikka says she remembers a reporter who came by a month or two ago. She asks me to translate the article for her, and I do. She listens calmly, showing no emotion one way or the other. I am careful to show her that although the reporter is skeptical, at least he represents her as having faith in the movement.

"One has to believe," Karttikka says, almost smiling. Her only other comment is that the reporter has got her name wrong. "Who is this Krittika?" she asks in irritation.

I tell her I've brought the magazine for her and her friends to keep. "Don't you want to keep it?" she asks.

"No, it's for you."

"I'll take it only if you don't need it anymore."

Later, I visit the high court mentioned in the article. The judge is indeed a diminutive young woman. Her name is Kausalya. I am impressed by the pains the Tigers have taken to provide this legal service to civilians, the earnest professionalism of the young people who work in the court, and, not least, the way the buildings and grounds are maintained for the comfort of the people who go there. The police station and the court are perhaps the best things about the Tigers in Kokkadichcholai.

Meena and Anbarasi

Sunday, 8 February. A family of women was weeping all day at the gate of the girls' base for their little sister, who had joined the Tigers. They sang laments of the kind I used to hear in India, begging the girl to return, asking her why she left and where she had gone, as Indian Tamils ask the dead in their songs. Every lament I have heard is also a protest against injustice. Some unfair person or the god of death (always unfair) has taken the loved one away. For all I know, this family could be calling for Nalini, who is not there that day. They would be using her real name, whatever it is, and not the new name she has been given by the movement. The chief singer is very beautiful and black skinned, like Nalini, and they appear from their clothing and demeanor to be poor, "traditional" folk (modern people do not sing these laments), agricultural laborers. I want to stop and listen to their singing, offer them help. But even if they were singing for Nalini, what could I do? I have no influence over the Tigers, no strings I could pull to get her released. I don't know whether she has any desire to return to her family. I long to adopt Nalini and take her home with me, but I know better than to suggest to her that this is even in my mind.

The girls at the base ignore the weepers. Malaimalli says the girl joined of her own free will and does not want to go back; she has been sent to a camp somewhere else.

Meena and Anbarasi have come down from fighting in the Kilinochchi area. Meena, who has a bad scar on her chin from fighting in the battle the army calls Riviresa (the Tamils call it Suriyakatir) tells me, when I ask, that she has been in fifteen battles. Evidently they do keep count. She has been in the movement for ten years. These women are not shy and giggly as the younger ones are, but that might just be their individual personalities. They were trained by Sita, who, despite all her battle experience, remains sweet and gentle.

I ask the girls fresh from the front about being afraid when they go into battle. Meena says they are absolutely not afraid, because they have their weapons. On the battlefield the enemy has his weapons, and they have theirs; they are on an equal footing, and so they are not afraid, she says.

"But aren't the enemy afraid when they see you?" I ask.

"Yes, they are," she says.

As I am sitting at the back of the base with the girls, one of them brings a broken vase, the one Malaimalli bought for the base. It is painted gold and has roses in high relief on the front, but they are all broken, and the vase is beyond repair. The girls say it is beautiful, and they are sorry it is broken. They will bury the pieces in the earth.

Anjala

Friday, 20 March. When I visit the girls' camp, Anjala comes in the front door, greets me with a big smile, and puts her hand on mine. We both look down at our two hands, hers small and black, and mine large and white. She says her hand is not good, and I say no, *my* hand is not good. I turn her hand over. None of the lines on her palm extends as far as the edge of her hand. She touches my bangs and asks if I will cut all my hair short like hers. I say no — it looks good on you, but it wouldn't look good on me. She examines my clothing, my jewelry, and asks where I got each item. Then she asks what I have brought her from Colombo, and I say nothing — what would you like? Anjala laughs and tries to think of something, but she can't. I suggest a shirt, and Anjala says good, but you should only get me a shirt, don't get anything for anyone else. I protest that everyone else will be jealous, and Anjala laughs as though this is an outrageous thing to say. What else besides a shirt? I ask. She asks for apples, and I agree to get some. I end up promising to get shirts for all the girls at the base next time I am in Batticaloa — size 16½, long sleeves, any color I think is nice.

A large radio stands in the front room. Some boys are there listening to it. The girls say they are brothers. One of the boys asks me if I like cinema songs or revolutionary songs. They have been listening to a tape-recorded political lesson. I am unable to frame the words to ask whether this is a lesson about ideology or about how to interact skillfully with people so as to get them to contribute to the LTTE, for this is effectively how Malaimalli has defined political activity. When I first met her and asked her to explain what is meant by "political," she responded by saying that President Chandrika can go to foreign countries asking for contributions, but the Tigers cannot; they have to ask for contributions from the people. I have gathered that political activity at a village level means primarily fund-raising. But later I learn it means a lot more. It all involves interactions with civilians: political workers work hard.

Anjala has borrowed my baseball cap, and the button has come off the top. "You've ruined my beautiful cap!" I say ruefully. But after a search through the house they find a needle and thread, and one of the girls sews the button back on. Anjala asks for the plastic cord I use to hold my glasses around my neck. I give it to her, and she puts it around her neck. Someone comments that it would be good for holding the cyanide capsule, and someone else says no. When I search for Anjala to say good-bye, glancing through the room behind the front room to the back, I see a rifle lying on the couch. When I leave, one girl comments to another, "She is buying shirts for all of us."

Tigresses

Thursday, 26 March. I have come to the women's base in Arasadithivu in midafternoon to deliver five apples because Anjala asked for apples. Anjala is not there, but Malaimalli is in the backyard with some of the other girls.

Malaimalli tells me that Nalini has just come of age (i.e., begun to menstruate). Then she says no, just kidding. I ask what they will do when Nalini does come of age: will they have the usual ceremony? Malaimalli says no, they will do something very simple. I ask them to invite me when it happens. Meanwhile, Nalini is there. She seems to have grown taller. Smiling as always, she lies with her head in the lap of one of the civilian women who work there as the civilian woman delouses her. (It is pleasant to be deloused, like getting a massage). It doesn't seem as though they find any lice. Nalini stretches out her arms and legs each in turn, lithely.

I meet with Father Sebastian on Saturday, 28 March, and we talk about children in the movement. For every five who join, there are five hundred who don't join and live ordinary lives — forced into a mold, as he puts it. The LTTE doesn't drag children out of their homes, he says, and doesn't coerce them, but it does entice them. They join voluntarily. Of those who join, maybe one in three regrets the decision, but it is difficult for them to leave after they have joined. Some do go back home, surrender to the army, and try to lead normal lives. But they are constantly suspected of being still with the LTTE, of being LTTE plants. And the LTTE is also distrustful of them because they may divulge information. Father Sebastian says that the children who join are an inspiration because of the sacrifices they make. They cannot be with other children their own age, and play with them and talk with them in the special way that ordinary children talk (*kataittal*) with one another. To knowingly go to one's death in this way is a sacrifice in the strictest sense of the term.

Father John, of the same Catholic order, has a different view. He says the LTTE are unrealistic because of their concept of *vīramaranam* (heroic death). He believes that the LTTE construction of sacrificial death is deliberate mystification. He knows people who have seen LTTE die in battle, and they die screaming for their lives; they do not want to die any more than anyone else does. What is so heroic about this? he asks. Young combatants are like automatons, he concludes. I guess he means they have lost their humanity, though perhaps not irretrievably.

Both Fathers are Tamil, both are very highly educated, both have extensive experience with helping people in this region deal with the problems of war. Father Sebastian may have more direct experience with people in the LTTE than Father John, but Father John is a trained psychological counselor who works with troubled children and teenagers. The only thing they seem to agree on is that young combatants have lost or renounced their childhood.

Both men are eminently truthful. Yet what I have seen is different from what both of them report. Joining the LTTE is a difficult decision, even for those who support and admire the movement. No one has any illusions about the probability of death, especially in the military section of the LTTE, and no one — whether civilians or LTTE, fighters or others — has described death to me as something desirable or to be sought. The LTTE fighters say, rather, I am going to die someday anyway; better to die this way. We will never know what percentage of combatants die in their first battle. But those who survive and go to battle a second or third or thirtieth time cannot have illusions that death is easy.

Perhaps what the Fathers see are two different extremes, and what I see is closer to the middle. The girls I meet have not lost their adolescence. Nalini is growing out of her childhood, but she has not lost it. What she may lose is the chance to grow up completely. What kind of adulthood might she otherwise have faced? What kind of childhood has she left behind?

Newspaper and TV accounts of the LTTE focus on the "young girls" in the movement. They are said to be "fanatically devoted to Prabhakaran," "sexy" like the lovers of James Bond, but "prudish" and "buttoned up" when it comes to sex. One can well imagine a male reporter coming on to a teenage girl like Vidya or Nalini, being rebuffed, and labeling the girls as prudes. Some writers consider the girls' apparent lack of interest in premarital sex to be evidence of their fanaticism. These kinds of reports make me angry.

Monday, 30 March. In Vasanta's house two Tiger boys from the video team are viewing one of their own videos. Some of the Tiger girls come to see me, and I invite them in, but when they see the boys there they back away, saying in loud whispers, "Brothers [*annāngaḷ*] are there!" Their whole demeanor changes when they see the male Tigers: they become shy, embarrassed, frightened, and giggly. I invite them to come in, and reluctantly they do, but they don't sit down; they stand in a corner watching the video, never relaxing, and soon they excuse themselves and depart.

Tiropathi and Suseela

I set out from Vasanta's house to the base to say a temporary good-bye, as I am leaving for Colombo tomorrow. As I leave Vasanta's I meet Anjala and one of the other girls, who have come on a bike to visit me. Anjala asks have I gotten her shirt yet, and I say I will get her one from Colombo.

But she makes me stop in Kokkadichcholai to buy a shirt at the store there. Villagers look on as we select a shirt. She chooses one in light blue, wrapped in a plastic wrapper, even though I object that it will show the dirt. But it is the prettiest shirt in the store. These are all men's shirts, of course. Anjala takes the shirt to the camp and hides it in one of the rooms, but the other girls find out, and she breaks into giggles.

Nalini is bathing at the well when I arrive. As I sit in the front room of the house, she appears at the window, where the blind is down except for a few inches at the bottom. Wrapped in a wet sarong, with her short hair wet, she laughingly spies on me through the gap.

In the backyard, the girls feed me lunch. "Do you think we are terrorists?" asks Tiropathi ingenuously. Then she shows me some pimples on her face and asks if I know of any medicine for this. I tell her not really, it is something you just have to grow out of, but I have seen some pimple medicine in one of the pharmacies in town, if she wants to try it. She asks me to get it for her. Next time I go to town I buy the pimple medicine in the pharmacy and sneak it back through the checkpoint. I am not sure whether bringing over-the-counter pimple medicine into Tiger territory counts as smuggling lifesaving drugs to the enemy. Tiropathi tries out the pimple medicine and tells me it doesn't work. Months later, at the Tiger celebration of the first anniversary of Operation Jayasikurui (whose prolongation the Tigers count as a victory), I see Tiropathi performing *bārata nāḍḍiyam* (classical South Indian dance) on the stage, and am surprised at her skill.

Near the end of March, at the girls' base, I tell them that I am hoping to travel to Madu in the Vanni. Save the Children is working at a big refugee camp there. Suseela says Madu is under the control of the LTTE, and there are many LTTE there. "But not people like us," she continues. "Big people," she says. I don't know whether by "big" she means older or more important or both.

She says there is a big *Mātā kōyil* (shrine to Mary) in Madu. The army came and tried to get the people to leave Tiger territory. But Suseela says the statue of the Virgin waved her hand, indicating that she did not want the people to leave, and the army let the people stay. All the girls ask me to bring them soil from Madu, because it is supposed to bring good luck.

After many altercations with army commanders in Colombo, I am denied permission to go to Madu because it is uncleared territory. No nongovernmental organizations are allowed there, either, I am told (even though I know Save the Children works there on a regular basis). "If you really want to help the people in Madu," says an irritated assistant secretary over the phone in Colombo, "you will buy us ships to carry them back to the cleared territory, where they want to go."

Farewells One, Two, and Three

13 May. I am back from my unsuccessful attempt to visit Madu. I am deeply disappointed for many reasons, not least of which is that I missed Easter there. People say the Easter ceremony at Madu is attended by thousands because of the famous shrine.

Malaimalli and Anbarasi visit me at Vasanta's house today. Malaimalli is being transferred tomorrow to Vaharai, a short distance north, as is Inbam. Anbarasi, who is about twenty years old, is going back north into combat.

Malaimalli asks me what I will give her so that she can remember me. She has said before that I would not want her to die without me giving her a keepsake. It sounds sentimental, but she is a warrior, after all, and there is a good chance that she really will die in the near future. But I am at a loss as to what to give her. She and other Tigers have rejected expensive gifts. I show her and Anbarasi the costume jewelry I have brought. They find the earrings delightful and funny, but they don't want any of the stuff I show them. Anbarasi settles on her pick of several children's toys, kisses one of them, and pockets it — a tiny plastic teddy bear. Malaimalli finally discovers a set of gypsy beads — thin strands of different colors — that she likes. She says with a smile, "These are what I want," and takes them. She says, "I will keep these until the day I die, and every time I look at them I will see your face." And after that I never see her again.

Friday, 15 May. Vidya and Nalini come to visit me at Vasanta's house. They came yesterday also, but I was sick from traveling. Nalini has been asking me when I will buy her a shirt. She even asked for money to buy it herself, but I said no. When they came I was on my way to Arasadithivu. We went together and stopped in Kokkadichcholai, where I bought both girls new shirts. Vidya chose one of aquamarine blue; that seems to be the fashionable color these days.

On the news the same day it is announced that Brigadier Sri Lal (Larry) Wijeratne has been killed by a Tiger suicide bomber. The Sri Lankan press says the Tamil people loved him, and this act is further proof that the LTTE will not tolerate any rivalry for the people's affection. The LTTE on the Internet says that Wijeratne was instrumental in the Kokkadichcholai massacre and that he favored only the rich and mighty.

I visit the girls' base, bringing with me the remaining costume jewelry and toys. "These are just things for little children," I say apologetically.

"We *are* little children," comes the answer. Two of the girls go through all my offerings with curiosity, delight, and criticism. Most of the stuff is tiny plastic toys, useless to them and probably useless to civilian girls or children. But they find some strings of glass beads they like, and one of them says, "I will take these," and puts them around her neck.

2 June. I am visiting the girls' camp. "We get three meals a day and clothing and a place to stay. If we die, it is not a big thing," says Urvashi. I have brought my camera, and Urvashi borrows it and tells me the names of all the parts and what they are for. She has taken lessons in photography from the movement and is part of their photography team. Because one of her older brothers is a combatant, she explains, she does not have to be a combatant; the movement requires only one combatant from a family. She had an uncle who was also a combatant. He was killed.

While she is there, her civilian sister visits her, bringing a small toddler. The sister is older but looks frail and somehow younger. They talk, and some of the other girls play with the toddler. I ask what other kinds of lessons are available from the movement. Urvashi says you can take lessons in anything, and names video, photography, *bārata nāḍḍiyam,* and politics. I remember that Sayanoli, a middle-aged woman Tiger who was visiting from Vaharai, had taken computer lessons from the movement and knew things like what the delete key was for.

Several of the girls tested their English on me: "Good morning," "Good afternoon," "Good evening," and the names of various things like table, chair, fingernail. One asks me to translate "Hello, how are you?" and asks me the meaning of "hello": it seems like a useless word to her. She guesses that it is just there — *summā.* They ask me what year I was born in. When I say 1948, they observe that that was the year Sri Lanka attained independence. I tell them many countries became independent that year, and they say yes, they know, they have studied all about history. They are proud of their learning.

I have brought with me paper, crayons, watercolor paints, and pens. Some of the girls draw pictures and paint them in. The pictures are of flowers. One has drawn a house with her little brother inside it and a small picture of a bus with people inside. You can see the full figures of the people, and another criticizes the painting, saying that you should not be able to see the people like that. The critic paints a bright red roof on the house. At the bottom of the picture, after I say "1948," she sketches a black rifle, which she says is a 47, an AK-47. Another girl paints bright red flowers with brown stems and green leaves. Sometimes one girl finishes a picture that another has started. Another draws a picture of what look like thick, plantlike tendrils with a girl's head at the end of one tendril, as though it were a flower.

One girl has a deep scar on her chin that she says she got from a fall, not from a battle. Vidya and Nalini are both there. Nalini and some of the girls smile often, but Vidya does not. She has a bandage around her arm with a yellow medicine stain. I ask her about it. She says she hurt herself falling off a bicycle.

First week of June. A temple renewal festival is happening in Kokkadich-cholai, and thousands of people are coming to enjoy the festival and help the gods return to life. On Thursday morning, I start out from Vasanta's house to visit the temple. As I cycle up the road toward Kokkadichcholai, a bus passes me. Nalini leans out of the door and shouts, "Pekkianti! [Peggy Auntie!]" She grins and waves and keeps leaning out of the door of the bus and grinning back at me as the bus disappears down the road. What other teenage girl (or boy, or child or adult) could be so free and saucy?

Anjala and Nalini are at the temple and greet me with their usual enthusiasm, running up to me with cries of "Auntie!" and "Pekkianti!" They have come to worship the god, and they have sandalwood paste and ash marks and *poddu*s on their foreheads. Anjala places a dot of sandalwood paste on my forehead also. "Have you seen Rudrakumaran?" she asks. "I saw him yesterday —" I begin. But then I see Rudrakumaran is here. He takes me around and shows me what I should take pictures of in the temple — the new tower, or *gōpuram,* with its brightly colored figures rising against the blue sky, and then a photograph of Rudrakumaran in front of it. The girls also want their pictures taken, and, though I say I need the LTTE's permission first, Rudrakumaran snaps a picture of them for me. Then I also take another. As soon as the camera is aimed at them, their smiles disappear, and they assume somber expressions. Suddenly Rudrakumaran makes a high-pitched giggling sound, the girls burst into laughter, and I snap their picture.

3 June. Malaimalli has been transferred to Vaharai, where an army attack is expected, and Sivagami is the new head of the girls' base here. She has been transferred from somewhere else. I went to visit her last night, but she sent word that she was too busy to see me. She had to travel to Karadianagar, many hours away by tractor, on urgent business — I don't know what. But she came to Vasanta's house this morning around eleven. She is small, serious, hardworking. I asked her how much she had studied, and she told me she left after the fifth standard.[10] This surprises me because I know that she reads a lot and was given the task of transcribing texts of speeches — a hard, thankless job. She says she left school and joined the movement simply because she could not study peacefully when people were being harassed. She served in the military section against Operation Jayasikurui and was wounded there: she does not volunteer this information, but the scars are visible on the backs of her legs, just above the ankles, so I ask her and she tells me. She is not so badly hurt that she can't fight again, and she intends to do so eventually, but now she is in the political division — resting, sort of. This is the first time she has been the head of a base.

I ask what the job of the political division is. Her answer is different from that of Malaimalli, who talked about fund-raising. She says the people are suffering — they have inadequate food and clothing — and the job of her division is to help alleviate that suffering. I ask if the political division gives out food and clothing. She says it cannot do that yet, because the Tigers are not a government yet; they are struggling to create a government. Meanwhile, to help the people, the political division helps them learn how to advance themselves through work and saving money, rather than spending everything they have as soon as it comes in. When the Tigers have established a government, she says, they will give things to the poor.

Kaveri and the New Recruits

Saturday, 6 June. I pay a visit to the girls' base early Saturday evening. Kaveri is the only regular Tiger girl there. Three new recruits in civilian dresses are with her, and a middle-aged woman who lives next door has come for a casual visit. The rest of the Tiger girls are at the temple. Kaveri welcomes me, invites me to sit down, and sends one of the new recruits to bring me tea.

"Where is the kettle?" the girl asks.

"In the place where we iron our clothes, in back," Kaveri answers.

"Is the temple festival finished today?" she asks me.

"There was a very big crowd today. I think today was the last day for putting oil on the statues," I say. "But I think tomorrow is the official last day."

"Then the festival will be continuing all night," she concludes. "We have guests who have come for the festival."

"*Iyakkam?*" I ask. *Iyakkam* means "movement." It is an informal word for the LTTE.

"Yes," she says.

"How many?"

"About thirty. I have to cook for them, but I don't know when they will be coming."

"Thirty. That's a lot to cook for. Are they just coming to see the festival?"

"No. They're on duty [*kaḍamai*]," she says.

"You mean religious duty or *iyakkam* duty?"

"*Iyakkam,*" she says. "They are recruiting people. We grabbed these two today."

"What? You just grab them?"

"No, no. We look for young people in the crowd and ask them where they are from and how many brothers and sisters they have and if they want to fight."

This evening Kaveri and the new recruits have been wondering aloud whether the relatives of one of the new recruits will come searching for her. The girl thinks they won't. Another girl says in a tone of quiet, almost cheerful, self-abnegation, "No one will come looking for me." I ask her if she told her parents before she left that she was joining the movement. She says yes, and they had no objection. She is the oldest of four; there were three other siblings, but they died young—two of fever, one of snakebite. She says hers is an LTTE family (*iyakkakkuḍumbam*): she has a mother's brother in the movement and a father's sister and a cousin (she calls him affectionately *aṇṇācci*) who was killed in battle (*vīrasā,* they call it for short).

She has a beautiful face, a bright smile with even teeth, and clear big brown eyes, set wide apart. She sits sprawled out like the teenage girl she is (sixteen, she has told me), with one leg draped over the arm of her chair. Her dress is torn, but her skin is smooth and clear, and she speaks of a gold necklace she left at home and gold earrings she has brought with her to the base. "So you're not poor," I say. She just smiles and continues telling her story, evenly, calmly, and pleasantly, as though making small talk at a party.

Occasionally a sadness comes into her voice and her eyes, which wander to the distance as she speaks of people in her family who have died. She seems saddest of all, but her eyes remain clear and her voice does not quite tremble, as she describes the body of her brother when it came home, riddled with bullets and already partly decayed. And she says her whole family were beaten and cut with knives because they were an LTTE family. In response to my asking how much schooling she has had, she says none at all. I ask if she can read, and she says no. She is afraid to go to school because she may be beaten. When she was ten — no, eleven, she corrects herself — she was going to school, and the STF stopped her and tied her hands with a wire and beat her legs. She shows me the scars. She says her family got a letter about the death in battle of her older brother; and at first they did not understand its formal language, but then, as they read it, they realized what it meant. And then she got a letter from one of the local leaders, saying there were only two girls in the movement for every ten boys, and was she going to abandon the movement? So she joined. Her mother has recently got a letter saying she can go to Saudi Arabia to work.

"Why did you join?" I ask.

"I want to fight [*pōrāda vēṇḍum*]," she says. It is almost a formulaic answer. She smiles gently as she says the words she knows are the correct ones. "They will send me for training, and then they will send me to battle, and I will die." Her expression does not change as she tells me this. And then she asks me, "Will they take me for training tomorrow?" And I tell her that I don't know.

"They will take me, though, won't they?" she asks, with a tinge of anxiousness in her voice.

"Yes, they will take you," I surmise. "And I won't see you again because I'm going home soon. But I hope after training they bring you back here to this base."

Kaveri asks me if my sons are as white as I am. I say yes. And she and the new recruit go into the spiel I have heard so often before, about how beautiful white skin is, and how beautiful my nose is because it is long. I tell them I think short noses are prettier and try to explain how white rulers of the past convinced the local people that white is pretty and black is ugly.

Kaveri shows me that she has two lower teeth missing. She says she looks like an old woman now (though to me she just looks like a teenage girl with two lower teeth missing). "How did you lose them?" I ask. She says a "piece" knocked them out. She means a bullet or a piece of shrapnel. This was when she was in the north, fighting in Jayasikurui a few months ago. She also got a piece in her shoulder, which is still there. The doctors did not remove it because to do so would have crippled her arm. She is eighteen, she has been in the LTTE two years, she has been in three battles, two of them during Jayasikurui, and she is worried about her dark skin and two missing teeth. When she learns that I am going to town tomorrow, she asks if she can come with me.

"I would take you with me, but if I did, they would kill you," I say, "or at least take you prisoner."

"The brothers [*annāngaḷ*] go across at night," she says.

"But that is for attacks; they risk their lives: it is dangerous," I say.

"No, they go to visit their families. They wear white shirts."

"If you come across wearing these clothes, the army will shoot you on sight. Wear a dress or something," I say.

"But what about my hair?" she asks.

Her hair is cropped short. It would identify her immediately as a Tiger girl.

"You could wear a wig," suggests the new recruit. They both laugh.

"I want very badly to go to town," says Kaveri. "I want to visit my family."

"Won't they visit you?"

"Yes. But they haven't been to see me recently."

"I can't take you across. You'll be killed," I say.

"It doesn't matter if I die," she says.

"It *does* matter. You are an important person," I plead. Saying these words makes me feel like a youth counselor, inadequate to the task.

"Why am I important?"

"You are *iyakkam*. You are young and brave, and you have a heart made of light." My Tamil fails me. "I know you must fight the army, and in fighting them you may die. But you cannot just throw your life away."

It is getting dark. She is lonely there guarding the camp, with just these new recruits for company, and the neighbor woman, almost three times her age, who has been listening to this conversation and nodding in agreement with me sometimes. There are Tiger boys at the gate, and they have come with no apparent purpose but to flirt with the girl left on guard. Kaveri is laughing as they talk. So are the boys.

"They have come to see you," I say, as evidence that she is a person of worth.

"No, they want to see you, not me," she insists. "They want to know if I can understand what you say."

I have heard the boys teasing her, telling her that with her two lost teeth she looks sixty-seven years old. She seems partly to believe them. I am pretty sure they will not harass her, because the movement is strict about such things. But for some reason she wants to keep me there, maybe just so she won't be left alone on guard at night. I leave with a promise to come back Monday afternoon and stay for lunch. As I pull my bike through the gate, the boys deferentially draw back.

Family Issues

On Tuesday afternoon I return to the base. The girls there say the new recruits have already been taken off for training. Vidya is lying down outside under the shade of the *pandal,* and someone says she has a fever. I put my hand to her forehead and ask her what is wrong. She says she has been thinking about too many things.

"What kinds of things?" I ask.

"Many things," she says.

"Family problems?" I ask. The people around smile slightly. "Won't you tell me?" I ask.

"If I tell you, can you make these troubles go away?" she asks, looking at me with tired, sad eyes.

"Maybe I can try," I say.

"My own brother has been sent to Jaffna," she says. "He has been there for twenty-four days." She and the others know there is a big battle going on now at Mangulam. Vidya has two living brothers: one who was in the movement but left it to get married, and this brother, who has now been sent to the front. A third brother was killed in battle some time before.

A boy comes in. He looks about sixteen or seventeen. Usually when male members of the movement appear, the girls become shy, but not this time, for some reason. "Is this a relative?" I ask.

"A brother," says Vidya. "But a movement brother, not a born brother." A large burn scar covers the lower left half of his face.

"How did you get that scar on your face?" I ask.

He makes a gesture as though pulling the trigger of a pistol.

"A bullet did that?" I ask.

"A mortar shell," he says.

"When? What battle?"

"Jayasikurui." Most of the time he sits quietly, listening to the rest of us talk. But he manages to say something that makes Vidya laugh.

"Do you remember my name?" she asks me.

"Vidya, Vidya, Vidya," I say.

I try to tell Vidya that lots of people have been to fight in Jaffna and come back.

"Do your brothers worry when you go to battles?"

"No," she responds. Shortly afterward she goes inside to lie down.

The neighbor woman has come in: when she heard my voice, she says, she rushed over to see me. She admires my bare feet and says they look like mangoes. There is more discussion of white skin versus dark skin. Kaveri's mother has also come to visit, and there are two very small children who must have come with her. Nalini is there, too. She does my hair in a kind of French braid and searches for lice, exclaiming loudly every time she finds one. Then she comes round and sits very close to me, facing me, looking deeply and intently into my eyes. She grins, bares her teeth, and tells me to show my teeth, so I do. She sticks out her small pink tongue and asks me to show my tongue, so I do, touching hers with my finger first. She writes her name on the palm of my hand in Tamil with a red ballpoint pen and asks me to write my name on her palm in English, so I do. Kaveri has arrived and asks if I will tell them before I leave. I say I will.

"When exactly are you going?" she asks.

"About two weeks from now."

"You will forget us, won't you?"

"No, I will absolutely not forget you."

"Will you write to me?"

"Of course."

"But you don't have my address."

"Here is my address book, write it in here."

Then I turn back to Nalini. Her face is still very close to mine, but her eyes are focused away.

"Will you give me your address, too?" I ask. "I want to write to you, too."

"No," she says.

"Why not?" I ask, surprised and troubled.

"She can't read or write," says Kaveri.

• • •

Wednesday, 10 June. I am back at the girls' camp. I ask Nalini if her parents are still alive. Kaveri answers that Nalini's mother died, and the father married the younger sister. I ask Nalini how her mother died. Nalini answers indifferently: "She took poison . . . she got sick and she died."

The three new girls who were there Saturday have already been taken away to training. But there are two girls at the camp who have run away from their families to join the Tigers. One, who is sixteen (born in 1982), says she has run away because her father beat her. She has never been to school because they live in the jungle, where there are no schools. Her father makes a living by killing chickens and selling them (this is the way she describes it). The other girl is eighteen (born in 1980). She has run away because she failed her O-level exams. Both girls say that there are other people in their families who have joined the movement: uncles (*māmā, cittappā*), aunts (*citti, māmi*), older brothers (*annan*), but no one in the immediate family of either girl. The one who failed her OL is the first girl in her family to join. She has a twin brother and an older sister. The older sister also failed her OL and is now just sitting in the house. She says her father has a lot of love for her and does not beat her, but her mother loves her less. Hers is a family where studying is important. If she goes back, people will shame her (*parippārkal*) for failing her OL. She could take it again, but she doesn't want to. Her brother passed his A levels and is now in university.

The mother of this girl appears at the gate of the base while I am there. She is weeping and shouting. I cannot make out what she says. The two girls hide in a dark side room of the base while one of the Tiger girls, smaller than both of them and no older, goes to meet the mother. While she is talking with the mother, I talk with the girls in the side room. The one whose mother has come will not go and speak to her, even when I suggest that she should. She says if she speaks to her, her mother will not let her stay. She is nervously folding a handkerchief in her hands, but she is not weeping as she hears her mother's sobs outside. She is insistent on staying with the movement. The girl who spoke with the mother comes back. She has told the mother her daughter is not there, and has sent her to the men's camp to talk with them. She speaks with the girl waiting in the back room in a friendly, collusive way. When the girl says her mother has lied, she appears to believe the girl over the mother. At 5 P.M. the same day, I return to the base to be told that the new girls have already been taken away for training.

Beside the new recruits, Vidya, Nalini, Kaveri, and Urvashi are all at the base. Kaveri is writing a letter, which she shows to Vidya, who reads it and laughs. I read it, too. She also shows me a diary she has been keeping of work she has done for the LTTE. Nalini tries to hide the fact that she cannot read, but when I ask her to explain a portion of the letter to me, she can just sound out some of the letters phonetically. She takes my hand and asks me to read her palm. I make up a glorious future for her, saying that she has deep wisdom and will learn many arts and skills as she grows older. I look at her "love line" and tell her that she will have three husbands. She breaks into high-pitched laughter and runs away. "Read my palm," says Kaveri. So I do. And, at Vidya's request, I read hers too.

Vidya was sick yesterday, but when I arrive today she is fine and cheerful. After the mother of the new recruit comes to the gate, and as we silently listen to her arguments and laments outside, Vidya disappears, and I find her lying on the beat-up old couch in the front room, motionless again, her eyes glazed. She has no fever that I can feel, but she says she has a headache. It can only be true that she has many troubles on her mind, but when I ask her what she is thinking, she responds, "What is the use of thinking?"

Vidya has been irritated with me ever since I failed to recognize her at Sita's house after she came back from four months at the jungle camp. When Sita asked Vidya to get me some water to splash on my sweaty face, Vidya made a point of washing her own face first. Sita saw this and mildly rebuked her.

During the palm-reading session, Vidya says in her frank fashion, "There is in fact someone I'm interested in." And she asks me to tell her is he close or far, is he tall or short, is he in the movement or not, does he love her or not? At first I continue to play the game and make pretend predictions ("He is medium height, he is not in the movement, he loves you madly; all the boys in the village love you madly"). But after a point I confess that really I was just making these things up, I do not know a thing about palm reading. "But the things you said about me were all true!" says Kaveri.

When I leave, I ask Vidya if she is angry with me for making pretend predictions. "No, Auntie," she says. "For what you said," and she finishes in English, "thank you."

Nalini remains smiling and affectionate. She knows my fondness for her, and it pleases her, I think. She sits close to me, holds my hand and caresses me, and shows me each of the small scars on her legs, from *kambi* (wire), she says. Small, accidental wounds. Or maybe not. She is wearing a sarong tied around the waist today, with her usual shirt on top. She says she got a wound high up on her leg, and it hurts to wear pants. She does not seem especially bothered by this wound, or the others. She borrows my glasses and my straw hat and runs to admire herself in the mirror. She asks again about the scars on my body, and again I tell her that the scars are from bears and lions, but now she is skeptical. The words she uses are *poy* (lie) and *summā*. When she shows me the scars on her legs, she scratches the blisters of heat rash on the tops of her thighs, hissing each time a small blister pops. Then she scratches the blisters on my shoulders, hissing again with each scratch. We all have this rash on our shoulders, the tops of our thighs, all over our arms. It is an impeccably egalitarian affliction. We enjoy the childish intimacy of scratching the rash of another: scratching feels good, although we are not supposed to do it.

While I am in the dark room talking to the new recruits, Nalini comes in with a round object in her hand. "What's this?" she asks.

"I don't know. What is it?" I ask. It seems like some kind of container or something. I can't make it out.

She plops it into the palm of my hand. "A bomb!" she says, with her impish mischievous smile. I look at it and realize that it is a grenade. I have never seen one before. I hand it back to her, gingerly. "It's for throwing at the army!" she says.

"Is it live?" I ask.

"Yes," she says.

"Do you keep it right here in the base?"

"Yes."

"Aren't you afraid that it will explode by itself?"

"No."

She takes it and disappears from the room, as the two new recruits, much older and bigger than her, look on.

Later Nalini shows me the dog tag around her neck. It has stamped on it the Tamil letters *ta, vi, pu* (standing for *tamiṟīra viṭutalai pulikaḷ* — Liberation Tigers of Tamil Eelam) and a four-digit number beginning with 5. Her name is not on the tag. I ask about her cyanide capsule, which usually hangs on the string together with these tags. She tells me it broke. She asks me for my picture, and I tell her for the dozenth time that I have not brought a picture of myself but will send her one. She brings me a framed formal photograph of about thirty young Tiger women in uniform, each bearing a rifle and looking serious, arranged in three rows. She points herself out in the picture. She looks like the youngest of all, and by far the smallest. There is one man, standing in the center of the back row. She pulls the photograph to her face and kisses his picture. She points out some of the people she knows, some of them in this camp, some of them elsewhere, some of them dead. I ask her how many have died. She goes over them one by one: "This one *vīrasā*, this one *vīrasā*, this one alive, this one *vīrasā*," until all of them, including herself ("this one alive"), have been accounted for. It seems that about half of them are dead.

She asks if I would like to see a picture of her older brother. Yes, of course, I say. She disappears and comes back with three wallet-sized photographs of Prabhakaran, the Tiger leader (who is often called "older brother" — *aṇṇan*).

"He is beautiful, isn't he?" she says — just as Sita said two years ago. And she kisses each photo. She produces a fourth wallet-sized photo: a glamorous model in a silk sari with long, silken black hair and pale skin, with a caption advertising some kind of powder. "This is my mother," says Nalini. And then she says, "This is you."

She turns the picture over, takes a pen, and says, "I will write your name."

"Don't write my name there," I say. "It's not my picture."

But she ignores me and spells out in Tamil letters *pa-ki-ya-n-ti* (Peggy Auntie) on the back of the model's photograph. "Is that right?" she asks.

Farewells Four, Five, and Six

On the same day, 10 June, I visit the temple in Kokkadichcholai, where the big renewal festival is still taking place.

I ask two uniformed Tiger policewomen I know, who are standing guard at the temple, if I may take their picture, and they agree. I take a close-up picture of them. One of them is Karttikka. She asks, in the same unsmiling, interrogatory tone in which she addressed me at the police station, "Why did you take a picture of only us?"

And I say, "I am trying to take pictures of all kinds of people, to show that all kinds of people are here — priests and common people and Boy Scouts and Tigers and everyone." And she says, "Why don't you stand back and take our picture to show the things and people around us?"

And I say, "Do you want me to do that, then?" And she says yes. So I stand back and take another picture of them, this time showing the context.

"Why haven't you been to Sita's house?" she demands.

"I was there just a couple of days ago," I say.

"Have you seen her? She is here," says Karttikka.

"No, I didn't know she had come. Is Alagar here also?"

"No, only Sita. Wait here, I will find her." I wait and wait, feeling impatient. The other policewoman stays and speaks with me quietly about trivial things. Then, out of the blue, she asks, "Are you afraid?"

"No," I answer. Why would I be afraid? The crowd is cheerful. Everything feels safe — to me.

In nineteen days, both Karttikka and her companion will be dead.

On Tuesday, 16 June, I stop at the girls' camp in the morning. Kaveri is in the cooking hut in the back, tending a pot propped on bricks over an open fire. She wants me to stay because she is lonely. When I come back in the afternoon, she is in front on the street, talking to two girls who look sixteen or seventeen. She says they are not allowed to join, and we should not speak. She has assumed a stern demeanor, and I leave shortly after that, not knowing why the girls are not allowed to join. The Tiger girls are literally turning them away at the gate.

On Monday, 22 June, the army attacks Vaharai, where Malaimalli and Inbam have been sent. According to the newspapers of the following day, the army has taken over the town.

On the following Saturday, I find that all but two of the girls who were in the girls' camp have been sent to the jungle camp — whether for protection or preparation for battle, or both or neither, I do not know. Vasanta says Vidya has run away because she feared being sent to Jaffna to fight the army; she feared that she would die. She went to her parents, who supported her and hid her. Now her whereabouts are unknown. The LTTE has taken her mother's brother as a hostage until Vidya comes back. Vasanta says the fighting continues in Vaharai. I never hear any more about Vidya, but I suspect that if she did run away, it was not for fear of dying. Perhaps, as she told me, there was "someone" from whom she did not wish to be parted.

On 29 June, the army will advance on Kokkadichcholai. Karttikka will be trapped in an army roundup and will take her own life by shooting herself. Her bodyguard, trapped with her, will end her life in the same way. An unnamed female Tiger will lose her legs and take her own life, together with a male Tiger. The news will be reported in the Tamil newspaper *Dinamurasu* of 9 July, and also in a letter from Rosa that I receive in August. Both the newspaper and Rosa report Karttikka's name correctly. Sri Lankan Tamils overseas tell me that the unnamed female Tiger was Kausalya, the young high-court judge.

CHAPTER 8

Boys in the LTTE

The boys in the LTTE whom I got to know were actually grown men in their twenties or early thirties, some of whom had been in the movement for ten years or more. Some were just waiting for the time when they could leave the movement, settle down, have families, and lead a regular civilian life. Meanwhile, however, they had to play the role of boys whose only desire was to fight for the freedom of Eelam. I am not saying they were cynical: as far as I could ascertain without reading their minds, their dedication was sincere. But they had other aspirations as well, simple, human ones to do with leading a normal life.

The easiest way to settle into a comfortable relationship with someone in Batticaloa was to develop a kinlike relation with them. And a particular kin term may stick to a person no matter who is addressing them. For most people, I was "Auntie" — somewhere between mother and older sister, but more distant than both. To me, it was funny to be called Auntie, because I had certain old-fashioned images associated with that word. An auntie wears her gray hair in a bun, makes lace, and smells of lavender. I had no clear idea what, in Batticaloa culture, the traditional expectations of an auntie might be. My funny feelings about this eponym probably contributed to the ironic, bantering relationship that developed between me and the boys. In addition, I was, like all civilians, expected to call each male member of the LTTE *annan,* "older brother," but these were people twenty or more years younger than I. I could not help identifying them emotionally with my own two younger brothers or my own two sons (I have no older brothers). This situation led to occasional small problems. Inbam once said to me in exasperation, "I am a grown man, not a little child!" implying that I had been treating him like a little boy. It could have been my own grown-up son saying those words.

From watching the boys I learned the use of irony as a key tactic (in the sense meant by Michel de Certeau).[1] The young men in the LTTE were in some respects powerful people, as they were part of the organization that held military and political control over the region. But in other respects they were as marginal as the rest of us, because they did not make the rules or create strategy. Their creativity was therefore tactical, a matter of making use of whatever materials and opportunities came to hand at a given moment. Certeau says that the only creativity possible in such a situation is putting existing things together in new ways — in other words, being a bricoleur. The boys were masters of bricolage, coming up daily with surprising combinations and juxtapositions that could not help but attract attention. With me, the boys triggered the startle reflex so often that for years after I returned from that long sojourn in Batticaloa, I jumped whenever someone came up behind me. Over there, however, it made me laugh: a sudden fright, immediately followed by the knowledge that it was just a joke. In other contexts, I might have been angry at the tricks played on me, and in one or two cases I was. But in general, laughter was more appropriate, and more agreeable, than anger. And the jokesters were people who had suffered and lost so much already, and the jokes on me were so totally harmless, and so genuinely funny, that I could not help but feel affection, which deepened day by day, for the perpetrators.

Accan

When I first arrived in Tiger territory in March 1996, it was Inbam who met me. But Accan was the one who first met me when I arrived again on the Tiger side of the lagoon in November 1997. I explained my intentions to him, and quickly he arranged for me to stay at Vasanta's house. "A well-educated woman, just right for you," he said at the time.

Accan is a member of the intelligence (*bulanāyvu*) wing of the movement. There are several members of this wing in the area. I presume he has been assigned to keep a discreet eye on me, and this is the reason for his visits to the houses where I spend time.

I can never really connect with Accan. Initially he introduced himself to me as a Muslim from Kerala. He had been a Naxalite (a member of a Marxist insurgent group) and joined the LTTE to assist in the assassination of Rajiv Gandhi, he told me. His story was too incredible *not* to believe, so I believed it. But when I mentioned this story to civilians, they said in irritation, "What a lie! That boy was born in this very village and grew up here. We all have known him since he was a child." Since everybody knows everybody else in this village, and since information is shared all around, Accan would surely have known that I would hear his story contradicted by others. Why did he tell such a whopper, then?

While others may say preposterous things, there is generally a hint of irony and humor in their faces and their voices when they do. Accan looks sincere and guileless when he tells his stories; he reminds me of Huck Finn. And his fooling me reminds me also of the time when Sita told me, with a straight face, that Nirmala was dead. As time goes on, I will discover that my Tiger friends have told me stories dozens of times and fooled me every time. Civilians know how to lie, too, but in my experience, Tigers do it more and better.[2]

Rosa asks me if I think Accan is strange. She says he has staring, scary eyes. She speculates that this is because of all the terrible sights he has seen.

Civilians say that Accan has only a standard 5 education, as though this explains and perhaps excuses his apparent naïveté. Education is a measure of worth, and Tamil people are sensitive and proud about such matters. The Tamil militant movements have grown in large part because of government manipulations curtailing educational opportunities for Tamils. It is not their fault when they lose their chance to study, but it causes them pain. When I ask Accan how long he went to school, he changes the subject.

One day, months after our first meeting, I encounter Accan on the road and greet him. He signals to me that he cannot talk. "Why not?" I ask. He puts his hand to his throat. "You're sick?" He nods. "How long?" He holds up one hand and shows me five fingers three times. "Fifteen days?" He nods. "That's a long time. I hope you get better soon," I say.

But it may be that Accan's fifteen-day laryngitis is caused not by a virus but by a command from above that he not speak to civilians for a while. Maybe something Accan said has landed him in trouble with the movement. Maybe he told the wrong truth to the wrong person. But if he had said or done something really bad, his punishment would be worse. The LTTE is renowned for its internal discipline, but an important feature of this discipline is not letting civilians know what goes on inside the organization, including how discipline is exercised: what acts are regarded as punishable and how they are punished. Secondhand, from civilians, I have gathered that Tiger discipline is a subject of research in itself, a complicated mystery inviting speculative theorizing. Civilians say that Tigers make the punishment fit the crime. Some say that for thieves (including civilian ones) the punishment is being kept in a hole underground, like an empty well. Another Tiger punishment is requiring the offender to cook and wash dishes for a whole group of Tigers for a certain period. Some say that several years ago four Tiger boys gang-raped a thirteen-year-old girl. As punishment, their hands were bound and they were dragged behind a tractor. At the end their bodies were torn up, and they were crying for water when they died. Even though they were rapists, onlookers could not help feeling sorry for them — *pāvam*.

There is no point in even asking the Tigers about this event; they would say that civilians lie and make things up. And of course civilians say the same thing about Tigers. Tigers are said by civilians to shave people's heads as a punishment. But Tigers say the man with a shaved head is a training master expressing solidarity with new recruits, whose heads are also shaved. When a Tiger is transferred to another area, civilians say it was because he was too outspoken, whereas Tigers say he is needed there, that his transfer is an honor and not a punishment. All we civilians know is that there are crimes and misdemeanors, and there are punishments. And maybe Accan really did have laryngitis after all.

Raja

At the end of my first meeting with Sita and Alagar in December, Alagar goes outside and summons a young man passing by on his motorbike to take me to the ferry. I climb behind the young man on his bike, and we're off. As we drive down the road, he advises, "Hold onto me so you won't fall off." And then, "You can also hold onto me if you do fall off."

A little later he tells me that he will have to let me off the bike before we get to the ferry, because if the guards on the other side of the lagoon see him, they will shoot him. He lets me off about a hundred yards from the ferry landing, just before the road turns a corner. As he wheels the bike around, he tosses me a smile and pulls a black cord from beneath the neck of his shirt. I guess he is showing me that he is a Tiger.

In half an hour I will be on the army side of the lagoon. The Sinhala soldiers I meet there are just ordinary people. They have families back home, which they joined the army to support. Otherwise they would not be here at all. How could they kill the boy on the bike? How could the boy on the bike kill them? The ride across the lagoon is lovely. Relaxed, friendly old men run the ferry. How can there be a war going on here?

Later Sita tells me that the young man who gave me a ride is the nineteen-year-old Raja. He is not a Tiger, only a Tiger "helper." He works for Alagar running a small general store in the center of Kokkadichcholai and doing other errands. This is what Tiger helpers mainly do — run errands for Tigers, work for them. But I am confused, because I remember so well the cord being pulled from beneath the shirt, and the flashing smile. Or perhaps I just seem to remember. Or perhaps it was not Raja at all who gave me a ride that day (I mostly only saw his back), and Sita is telling me it was Raja for some reason of her own. Much later, when I meet Raja's sister, she asks me not to tell the army that they are a movement family. By then, I understand that to be a Tiger helper is, in the eyes of the army, the same as being a Tiger. It is a dangerous occupation, even if all the helper does is run a general store.

Sita tells me that Raja won't join the Tigers because he is afraid of the training. Maybe she is trying to shame him into joining. Maybe Raja has other reasons besides fear of training. But Sita's comment causes me to ponder what it is about Tiger training that makes it so awful, that gives it such a mystique. Certainly it must be rigorous. It involves fitness training, which always entails pushing oneself beyond the point where one's body screams for relief. An athlete may vomit from exhaustion. But even I, who never made any team, have done that. In retrospect, it was no big deal. I wouldn't have called it torture.

Do the Tigers beat their recruits until they're bruised and bleeding? Are they in this respect like modern college fraternities? Or worse, like the U.S. Marines? Is this what Raja fears?

The Tigers must learn to live in the jungle, which is dangerous and fraught with hardships, but still presents only familiar challenges that countless people have met as a matter of course. And countless other people (who should know better) seek out exactly these kinds of challenges and hardships, to prove themselves to themselves, or something. Does Raja lack this compulsion? Is this why he will not do training?

As I write, I remember Raja most from an evening when Sita's niece Pattini was visiting her. I was sitting on a chair on the veranda, Raja was sitting on a chair to my right, and Pattini was sitting on the ground to my left, with her hands on my knee and her chin on her hands, smiling up at Raja while the two of them talked into the night. Pattini was not pretty or vain, but she had smooth, pale skin and a gift of a perfect body. She was all of fifteen. And she wanted Raja for a boyfriend, Tiger or not. And there they sat in the lamplight, with me between them. What was I supposed to do? Sita's mother came out and observed this scene and directed her quizzical smile at me.

A Dog

Tuesday, 6 January 1998. Today I am at Alagar's house. A grungy beggar dog hangs around here that people are always driving off with cries of *"Aḍi!"* (vaguely equivalent to English "Beat it!"). Now it has got something stuck in its throat; it is gagging and unable to close its mouth. I observe it for some time and comment to Sita that the dog appears to be dying. I don't expect that much can be done about it. Then I go to Vasanta's house to fetch my clothes. When I come back, Koyila and Raja are scrubbing their arms with soap up to their elbows. They have tried to remove the thing (they call it *muḷ* — maybe a sharp bone) from the dog's throat with their hands, apparently unsuccessfully. Geethan, who is the highest-ranking Tiger here, arrives with Alagar, and I can hear Sita describing the problem to them in a distressed tone of voice. Everyone goes out to see the dog, which is lying under a tree, panting in misery. Raja fetches a pair of pliers and reaches into the dog's throat. The dog screams painfully, I bury my face in my hands, and even Alagar turns away. But then Raja gets the bone out, and suddenly the dog is fine and runs off. I hear Alagar say to Raja, laughingly, "You'll get really good karma for this [*ungaḷukku cariyāna puṇṇiyam kiḍaikkum*]."

And I say to Raja, "I was thinking you might just shoot the dog." There are plenty of rifles around, after all.

Raja looks at me in surprise, and answers simply, "Pavam!" The word *pāvam* is hard to translate. It connotes both sin — as in, "It would be a sin to shoot this dog" — and pity — as in, "How could one shoot this pitiful animal?" And it may also imply that the dog is already suffering enough for whatever sins it may have committed; taking its life would be redundantly cruel, especially if that life could be saved. All these thoughts are summed up in that one word *pāvam,* which I hear spoken again and again in this area. (Warfare is massive *pāvam.*)

Gamani

Wednesday, 7 January. Yesterday we had a lot of deer meat for lunch and dinner. It was tender and tasty, like venison in a good restaurant. The deer had been shot by a Tiger boy from another area who was visiting. I talked with him a little last night. This morning he has come by again, and we talk some more.

He seems animal-like to me. He is smiling, with wide-open eyes locked onto mine in a piercing, unsettling gaze. Wild eyes. But he laughs easily and is cheerful as a lark, as though this conversation is a wonderful and important event for him, as though every moment in his life is wonderful and important. He sits on the edge of his chair, bouncing his legs like a fidgety child. He says he is twenty-four years old and has been in the movement for ten years. But I surmise that these numbers may be approximations.

He asks me about myself. "Do you have a plan?" is the first thing he asks. I explain to him about my research, but confess I do not have a well laid-out plan, exactly.

"Are you here all the time?" I ask him.

"No. I'm here for my work."

"What kind of work do you do?"

"I'm not allowed to tell you that." But the tone of his voice suggests that he might be coaxed into telling. He is watching me in anticipation.

"Well," I say, "in the movement there are all kinds of work. People who work as cooks and people who work as medics and people who work on the video team — you can tell me the general kind of work you do, can't you?"

He says, "I do that kind of work," gesturing toward the poster of Sylvester Stallone on the wall. Stallone is dressed in black, holding a combat rifle, and looking cool.

"You're a movie star?" I ask. He laughs. "Your work is fighting?"

"Yes."

"Do you like your work?"

As we talk, I am convinced that he really does enjoy being a fighter. He is fully in his element. He spends most of his time in the jungle, and says he loves it there. They eat all kinds of wild game in the jungle — not only deer, like the one he has just brought back to us, but wild boars and snakes and crocodiles.

"You eat crocodile meat?"

"It's good, Auntie!" he protests. "And sometimes we even have leopard meat."

"Leopard!"

"It's good, Auntie!" He's enjoying my shocked expression. "Leopard meat is good for asthma and all kinds of lung diseases. I have a leopard skin. Would you like to see?"

"Yes — did you bring it with you?"

"No, I have kept it in the jungle. Next time I come I will show you."

And he tells me they even killed an elephant once, and took a big piece of its flesh for food and left the rest for jackals. He holds his hands wide apart to show me how big the tusks were.

"But," I ask, "isn't it wrong [*aniyāyam*] to kill an elephant like that?"

The smile fades from his face. "We only do it in a strapped situation, when there is nothing else," he says.

He has been to battle thirty-three times, he says when I ask. He did not fight at Mullaithivu, where the greatest Tiger victory so far was achieved, but he names another famous battle, at Paranthan, in which he did participate.

I ask him if the LTTE plan out their battles in advance. Yes. Is planning important to them? Yes. I ask how many fighters ordinarily would go into a battle together. He says about a thousand. He must mean big battles, not small raids and skirmishes of the kind that happen all the time here. I ask him how many enemy soldiers he has killed in battle. He says very many. "How many?" I ask.

"Beyond counting," he says. I ask if he has lost many friends to death in battle. "Many," he says. "Beyond counting." I ask if it is not painful for him to see so many friends die. He says yes, he does not eat for a day or two. But he is accustomed to the sorrow now, it does not show (*kāḍḍātu*). He uses the same word for his parents' sorrow at his having joined the Tigers, and for the thorns in his feet that must be removed one by one with a needle. He shows me the myriad tiny scars. They go into battle barefoot, carrying cream-filled cookies as provisions. They don't wear boots because boots get waterlogged in the wet parts of the jungle. His favorite cookies are Maliban Lemon Puffs. After the battle, they eat a regular meal of rice and curry.

"In battle, have you ever been shot?"

"Oh, yes, Auntie! Many times." He shows me that he cannot bend either leg all the way.

"But you can still fight?"

"Yes, Auntie," he says. "It is not a problem."

I ask him his name, and he tells me it is Gamani. We exchange addresses. He wants me to write to him. He asks if I live in Colombo. When I tell him my home is much farther away than that, he seems thrilled.

A couple of days later, about 7:30 in the morning, I am riding my bike from Sita's house to Vasanta's and see him turn onto the road ahead of me. He is also on a bike, pedaling with legs that do not fully straighten. I catch up with him, and we bike down the road together. He said he hadn't recognized me.

Yesterday Raja told me a long story about his plans to go to Singapore next December. He seemed completely serious, and I warned him of the dangers of overseas travel, gave him my address, and told him I would try to visit him in Singapore, maybe even bring him from there to New Zealand. Then Sita had told me that what Raja said about going to Singapore was all a lie. I felt very silly and was wondering this morning why people lie to me like this all the time. So, while biking down the road with Gamani, I ask him if all the things he told me were true.

"Yes," he says, "all completely true [*sattiyam*]."

"Did you really eat an elephant?"

"No, that was a lie," he says, "but all the rest was completely true."

"Really?" I ask.

"Really," he says.

I explain to him, by way of apology, that I cannot tell in this country when people are telling the truth and when they are just telling me things for fun. He continues with me toward Vasanta's house and points to a mud and thatch house by the road where he says he has relatives. I think he will turn off there, and I start to say good-bye, but he keeps biking with me all the way to Vasanta's house. When I stop at the door, preparing to ask him in, he leaves me there, and we say good-bye. I never see him after that.

Satyan

Late January. The regional LTTE video-production chief, Satyan, has come to Kokkadichcholai to videotape a reenactment of a massacre that happened here. We can watch the process. Rosa is interested because she was part of this event, and now she has heard that a Tiger actress is going to play her role.

Satyan visits homes and plays with babies. He is lively and cheerful. Vasanta, in discussion with him, locates him on her seemingly infinite kinship chart. Both of them comment separately that he is known to this household from long ago, though the details of the acquaintance escape me.

After that, Satyan visits us regularly. The main reason, probably, is that I have bought a TV for Vasanta, and the Tigers' own TV is broken. When it is working, they have to run it off a generator. At Vasanta's house, through some political moves that I do not understand, there is actually regular electricity, so the Tigers bring their VCR and hook it up to Vasanta's TV to view their videos.

One day Satyan brings a video montage of songs and dances from commercial Tamil movies with romantic themes. Only Satyan, as video chief, is allowed to watch such things. Other Tigers can watch only battle movies, with the boy-girl scenes cut out, and the Tigers' videotapes of their own battles. But Satyan's art comes from everywhere, goes everywhere. He says he learns about film techniques from watching a wide variety of films. He wants me to get him a videotape of *Titanic* and a tape with nature sounds on it. I have no idea what he will use these for.

Satyan is planning a sports meet in remembrance of Annai Pupathi, who fasted to death for the sake of Eelam. The anniversary of her death was just this week: the Tigers celebrated this with a procession around Kokkadichcholai in which children were taken around in a tractor cart for their entertainment. I expect this remembrance day to be solemn, but Satyan is planning pillow fights, swimming races, oxcart races, fishing canoe races, tag games, pin-the-tail-on-the-elephant contests, and another game something like a piñata, in which blindfolded people try to break a hanging pot with a pole. I ask Satyan how this event will benefit the movement. He says it will be of no particular benefit to the movement; it is an event for a day when there is neither joy nor sorrow. He asks if I will take him with me to New Zealand. He asks about my sons, whether they write to me and I write to them. He takes two-year-old Mohan for a ride around the block on his motorbike before he departs for the day.

Satyan has a high-pitched, manic laugh, like Mozart in *Amadeus*. He says his laugh sounds like a telephone. I like his laugh. The next time he comes, he asks if I will sing for him. I say I will sing if he will sing, but he says if he sings, his song will cause turmoil in the natural surroundings.

"Will the leaves wilt on the trees, then?" I ask.

And he says, "No, the trees will bud and blossom. But there is such a thing as blossoming too much." At the sound of his voice, they will die of joy.

Someone must have told Satyan about my palmtop computer, because he asks about it, and I bring it out and show him all its functions. He asks if it has a painting program on it. I bring out my laptop, open the paintbrush application, and show him how it works. In a few moments he has painted a lovely picture of a small house with palm trees around it, a river in front, and the sun setting behind the mountains. I express my genuine admiration: his colors are gorgeous, and I like the design. I have never been able to draw the simplest figure on a computer, or on paper, for that matter. I lack the coordination or something.

Rosa insists that Satyan is "in love" with me. I have no independent evidence of this at all, but Rosa enjoys teasing me about it whenever Satyan comes by. "*Antiyai kaṇḍāl pōtum*" (it is enough for him to see Auntie), comments Rosa when Satyan passes the house on his motorcycle.

In a conversation about birthday parties, Satyan tells me his twenty-eighth birthday is coming up. He asks me my age, and I tell him. Later in the conversation he tells me, "Auntie, what you have said is like exploding a bomb." I think he likes such images; he uses them often. He says since I miss my own sons so much, he can be my son in Sri Lanka.

On Satyan's next visit, I show him *Forrest Gump*. The movie includes a scene in which a bomb lands in a ball of flame on top of a crowd of people and bodies fly about, just as the Muppet bodies did in a TV show we have recently seen that parodied warfare. When he sees the explosion and flying bodies in *Forrest Gump*, Satyan exclaims, "Cho!" It is an expression of surprise and admiration. He enjoys explosions so. As an artist for the LTTE, he has painted pictures of fireballs that look like flame-colored flowers. I think to myself that Satyan's response to the movie explosion is just like the refugee children's response to explosions in the Muppet show. The refugee children's response to the puppet carnage is no more or less surprising than a perfectly nonviolent American child's enjoyment of violent computer games. One expects adults — especially soldiers — to comport themselves with more dignity, to suppress their childlike emotional responses, to kill their spontaneity, but Satyan doesn't seem to, and neither do most of the other Tigers I meet. I have been criticized for speaking to Tigers as though they were children, but how can I help it when they present themselves that way?

Satyan asks if I will give him my computer when I go, and I say I will trade my computer for his motorcycle. He says okay. But then I think about this and tell him I don't want to trade, because I can't take the motorcycle with me when I leave. He says he will give me a folding motorcycle that I can pack in my bag.

"Do you know any jokes?" he asks me.

"None I can tell in Tamil," I reply. "Do you?"

"When will peace come?" he asks.

"I don't know," I say.

"Peace will come when Chandrika's son marries Prabhakaran's daughter," he answers. "Peace will come when the Muslims celebrate Sivaratri." In other words, peace will come when pigs fly. Chandrika Kumaratunge is the president of Sri Lanka and the commander in chief of the armed forces. She despises Velupillai Prabhakaran, the head of the LTTE. Sri Lankan Muslims also fear and hate the LTTE, which is blamed for several unprovoked massacres of Muslims. Sri Lankan Muslims' religious identity comes first to them, and it will be many years, if ever, before they observe the Saiva festival of Sivaratri.

Satyan's joke betrays an un-Tigerlike doubt about whether and how the war will end. Of course, he is only joking. Still, to joke about something so central to the movement must surely be dangerous. Other Tigers have told me that their resolve (*uruti*) is a great part of their strength: they will win Tamil Eelam, or they will die. But certainty is no longer realistic in this context. No one can know how or when the war will end. Satyan's very uncertainty makes him more credible. Has he calculated this effect on me? His aim in visiting us, most likely, other than to use the TV, is to win friends for the movement, and not to stir up doubts. But doubts pervade the civilian population. By seeming to share our doubts, Satyan may earn our trust.

He talks with Vasanta about the dilemma of a friend of his. The friend is a Tiger, in love with a civilian girl who is training to be a pastor. The girl and boy love each other, and the parents like the boy, but they don't want their daughter marrying a Tiger. I think he confides in Vasanta about this problem because she is a Protestant Christian. "Is the boy willing to leave the Tigers?" asks Vasanta.

"Yes," said Satyan.

"Then there's no problem," says Vasanta.

Satyan thanks Vasanta for her advice. "That Tiger boy is me," he says. I look up at him, surprised, from where I am sitting on the porch.

On another visit, Satyan asks if I will take him to New Zealand. I say I don't have the power. "Why don't you have the power?" he asks.

I say, "You are a Tiger. I would have to get you a passport and a visa. To get those, you must be able to prove that you are not a Tiger. Can you do that?" I ask. He laughs. "Besides," I say, "aren't you in love with a girl who is training to be a pastor, and aren't you planning to marry her?"

He laughs again. "I was just kidding [*summā connēn*]," he says. (But much later, when I meet Satyan, who has sought asylum overseas with his wife and child, I realize that what he said about loving a woman in training to be a pastor was true. Now they are married and live overseas in the country where they have been granted asylum. Satyan continues his work and his studies as an artist.)

Satyan looks at my notes and tells me my handwriting is ugly. He writes some words and draws some pictures on my notepad. He is completely ambidextrous. One of the pictures is a caricature of me, captioned "*Antiyin Āvi*" (the ghost of Auntie). It is not exactly flattering, but definitely me. He also draws a cartoon of himself, with a cyanide capsule on a string around his neck, a large handlebar mustache (an imaginative addition to his clean-shaven face), and a pipe in his mouth. I wonder if he has ever smoked a pipe.

I purchase crayons and paper in town and bring them back to Vasanta's house to let children draw pictures for me. The children are eager to use the new art materials. They are all poor, but when they leave, not a single crayon is missing.

Satyan and Rudrakumaran come by shortly after most of the kids have gone and use the crayons to draw cartoons. Satyan has said that to celebrate the first anniversary of Jayasikurui, they will have a procession. When the procession comes around, the wagons are painted with big cartoon pictures of Tigers (beautiful) and Sinhala soldiers (ugly) in a style that is unmistakably Satyan's.

Satyan also plays keyboard instruments. He learned his art when he was a teenager and played in a band in Jaffna. I have asked him to tell me his life story, but he says it is so tragic I would not be able to endure hearing it. So I never do. He does mention in passing some of the hardships he, along with other Tigers, has undergone. They were without food sometimes and had to eat tree frogs.

Monday, 11 May. Vasanta says that Satyan brought a peacock egg and gave it to her to put under the hen to hatch. The hen sat on it but kept it apart from her other eggs. It hatched, but the chick died.

In the height of the hot season I become sick. Satyan comes to visit me, to ask if he can help. I say all I want is ice. Less than an hour later, somehow a cooler full of ice packed in sawdust appears. It is like magic. Rosa says Satyan brought it. But when she tries to wash the sawdust off with the well water, the ice melts. I don't have the heart to tell Satyan what happened.

Sudha

Some Tamil boys strike me as wild-eyed. Probably it is just the bone structure of their faces and means nothing. Gamani was one of these. I meet another wild-eyed boy at Vithusa's birthday party in February. He comes up and sits close to me, examining me with intense bright eyes and a vulpine smile, while I, feeling uncomfortable, attempt to make conversation by asking him where he is from. He says, "Polonnaruwa."

I say, "How did you get here from there?"

"By bus."

"That was very brave of you."

"I have a police ID because I was in the police before. And anyway," he continues, "I have my cyanide capsule in case they do catch me."

I am about to say, "But if they see the cyanide capsule, they will surely capture you, and anyway, would you not think twice about putting yourself in a situation where you might have to poison yourself?" when Satyan from across the room says, "He is just saying that for fun" (*summā collurān*), and my conversation partner retorts that Satyan is just saying *that* for fun. I tell him that I have to believe Satyan because I know Satyan better.

I ask the wild-eyed boy, "Are you really a Tiger?"

He replies, "Yes, I really am," and pulls from his trouser pocket his cyanide capsule and dog tag. This is the first time I've seen anyone keep these things in his trouser pocket, but before I have a chance to ask him about the danger of sitting on the glass capsule and breaking it, he is gone.

At the party I also meet Sudha. He is tall, with a gentle, dark, handsome face. No wild eyes here. I have seen him around before, but we have never really talked. He asks if he can borrow my camera to take pictures of the party. He will develop all the pictures for me himself, as he specializes in photography. I say okay, and sure enough, a week or so later, the color prints turn up. I wonder where in the world the Tigers have a color photography lab.

In exchange for the loan of my camera, I ask if I may look at his rifle. He hands it to me. I touch the trigger. With infinite gentleness, Sudha moves my finger. "You must never do that," he says. "You could blow a hole through the roof of the house."

· · ·

Sudha and other Tigers have cautioned me that I must never handle a rifle thoughtlessly, *summā*. The word *summā* is very commonly used throughout the Tamil world, both Indian and Sri Lankan, but it appears to be a key word in Kokkadichcholai discourse. My dictionary defines *summā* as "without any purpose or motive" and "without much effort or care." I translate it as "just kidding" or, as in the banter above, "just saying that for fun."

Etymologically, the word *summā* seems to mean "without any burden" (*summai illāmal*). One can do a thing *summā*, or say a thing *summā*. When one says a thing *summā*, it is always not true. Truth is *uṇmai* (literally "within the heart") or *sattiyam* (true in an absolute sense). But *summā* is not exactly the same thing as *poy* (lie), because to tell a lie, *poy,* is a bad thing to do, whereas to speak *summā* is a form of play, bearing no moral weight. In the world of Kokkadichcholai, to speak the truth is dangerous; it can get you or someone else killed. For instance, if you tell the army that you have friends who are Tigers, you may find yourself forced at gunpoint to identify them. Lies are also dangerous, for they may lead somebody into a trap. Nobody trusts a liar, and trust is essential in Kokkadichcholai. But *summā* speech makes people laugh, and everybody needs laughter.

Inbam

The LTTE political office in Kokkaddichcholai is shaded by tall palm trees and has only a small front yard, but even there a couple of ornamental plants have been set. Playing among them one morning is a puppy the Tigers keep as a pet. It is named Jimmy after one of Princess Diana's dogs. Its long, shiny fur is the palest gold, and it has a delicate face and a fluffy, curled tail. On the inside walls of the political office (a green canvas tent over a cement foundation) are three posters of Bengal tigers that look like Sierra Club prints. One of them has no caption. Another bears the caption "Be friendly with nature," and the third, "Be kind."

The first time I visit the political office, a young teenage boy is there, acting as a gopher. Inbam, who runs the office, pointedly tells me that this boy is a member of the movement.

The older Tiger boys who live nearby are curious, and they crowd around me. We exchange questions. One of them describes their jungle camp for me. It is in a beautiful village, by a great waterfall, with the women's camp on the left side of the waterfall and the men's on the right. They are raising a deer there, and different varieties of wild birds. Peacocks dance in the clearings during the rainy season. I must see them dance, he says. There are also elephants.

I ask him if they go hunting, and he says yes — for deer, rabbits, herons, boars. Before a battle they all bathe together in the waterfall and all have a meal together. These collective baths beneath the waterfall are wonderful fun, he tells me. After every battle, some come back alive, and others don't.

Later I ask Vasanta if there are really elephants in the jungle near here. She says this is not a big enough jungle to contain the elephants; the Tiger boys are just telling stories. I believe her, but later I learn that she is wrong. Pursuing the truth about elephants will become a quest for me.

The Tiger boys' talk of the beauty of the jungle makes me want to go there. But when I ask them if I can visit, they say no, it is for Tigers only. They have built me up only to let me down. And all my other inquiries about the jungle with other Tigers lead to the same blockade. Do not go into the jungle. If you come upon our jungle camp, we will have to shoot you.

The head of the political office, Inbam, I know from my visit in 1996. We had long conversations then, and argued, but it seemed to me that we had parted friends. Now Inbam confronts me with the accusation that I have been married to a farmer from Chingleput. Or rather, he asks if I have. I tell him I have only been married once in my life, to an American, and that was a mistake: I will never marry again. He laughs and says he will never marry, either. But there is some truth in Inbam's charge, and this is what surprises me, for I lived with a farming family in Chingleput (an Indian town) and wrote a book about them long ago. Somehow Inbam has learned about this. Then he asks if I work for the CIA. I laugh. And he asks if I work for the CID (of Sri Lanka), or for RAW (India's Research and Analysis Wing, or intelligence agency). The more he asks, the more I laugh, telling him I am flattered that he thinks I am such an important person. He must be joking. But, remembering how often American social scientists in India are accused of being government spies, I cannot be certain that he is not at least half serious. I try to explain to Inbam that no government would have picked someone as conspicuous as me to be a spy, and besides, my record of opposition to the war in Vietnam would certainly rule me out of the CIA. But still Inbam persists. He stops his questioning only when I say, "You cannot be such great fools as all that." He says his questions were only for fun.

But then, during one of my first visits to the women's camp in the village, Inbam and Geethan appear there fully armed. Both are high-ranking members of the movement, and their visit is unexpected. The young Tiger women, seeing them, scatter like sparrows. The camp leader, smiling and flustered, greets them and invites them in. I guess we have done something wrong, and I shouldn't have come here. I have had long conversations with Inbam on previous days, but have never before seen him armed like this. He comes into the house and sits down beside me for tea with his rifle in hand. The Tiger girls serve us all tea. And Inbam says to me, "I still think you are CIA."

"Are you going to shoot me?"

"We will never shoot you."

"If you do decide to shoot me, shoot me through the heart and not through the head."

"We will shoot you all over your body, in a hundred different places."

I am about 90 percent certain that Inbam would never shoot me unless I did something really bad to the Tigers. But there is that 10 percent of doubt, which the Tigers maintain, I suppose, to keep me good.

When I first came to this region in 1996, Inbam was the person who talked with me most often and most seriously about matters to do with the war, things I really wanted to learn about. He was intelligent and articulate, and when I came here again, I hoped that he would be one of my main "informants," or "consultants," or "interlocutors," or "research participants" (all these euphemisms ethnographers use for people who choose to talk to them and have interesting things to say). But he was probably assigned as my minder back then, and he has other assignments now. Hence, during the whole eight months of my current visit (1997–98), I see very little of Inbam. If we meet by chance at Sita's house, he departs after just a few minutes. He always says he has a lot of work to do, and Sita always confirms this. But it is never clear to me exactly what he does.

I know that Inbam is in charge of the Tiger political office in Kokkadichcholai. It is a small place on a back road hidden among trees, but civilians are always waiting to talk with him whenever I visit. In contrast to the courthouse, which is open and public, in the political office most of the matters discussed with civilians are secret. Karuppayya, the old man who is the office assistant, calls each person into the office with a whisper. After a wait, the person is invited behind a screen that divides the small office further. The visitor talks with Inbam behind the screen. It is all very solemn. But whenever he sees me coming, Karuppayya giggles wildly. I ask him why, and he says it just because he is happy to see me. He insists that I have lunch at the office and takes me behind the screen to wait for Inbam. Then Karuppayya brings a nice hot lunch, and Inbam either appears or he does not. I please Karuppayya by licking my plate, while Inbam elegantly peels a banana with his teeth. In this secret and serious place, we play these silly games to amuse poor old Karuppayya.

I come to the office with the purpose of setting up a serious interview with Inbam, taped or not, as he chooses, on so many questions I have about the LTTE. He knows he does not have to answer any of my questions, but he never allows a space for me even to ask them, diverting me instead with Karuppayya's tasty meals and other such entertainments. But when I report my disappointment to Vasanta's mother, she comments that if the Tigers go so far as to feed me, it means I am their child (*piḷḷai*).

Inbam is more patient with civilians than I would expect. When an old woman in a worn sari appears at the office, grabs his hand, and begs for help, he gives her some cash, which appears to be what she wants. On another day, a shockingly beautiful girl appears, coal-black, maybe twenty, clad in a sky-blue frock. She is accompanied by an old woman. I am sitting in the front of the office with her, and I ask her why she has come. She says she has come to see one of the boys. Karuppayya calls me to the back of the office. Inbam slips in through the back also. He whispers to me, "Pretend I'm not here." So I sit and silently eat my lunch, pretending that Inbam is not there. But the young woman simply comes to the back, looks at Inbam, and says with glee, "What kind of deception is this?" She jokes about bombs. She talks about pleasure for everybody and asks what harm there is in that. It seems that she is trying to seduce him right there on the spot. Poor Inbam sinks back in his chair and buries his face in his hands. "I'll talk with you later, mother," he says respectfully to his assailant. But she insists that he write her a letter. "I have nothing to write with," he says. Thoughtlessly, I hand him a paper and pen. The girl mocks him and teases him. She is obviously not afraid of retribution for shaming a Tiger like this. I tell Inbam I'll come back later, and I leave him with his problem.

Some time later, Koyila and I are cycling to the new base in search of Daya Mohan, one of the local LTTE leaders. Inbam has moved there too, and so has Accan. On the way to the base we encounter the beautiful young woman who embarrassed Inbam at the political office. Now she is biking away from the base with a smile on her face. I think to myself that this bright smile must mean she has suffered some terrible tragedies, because by now I have met too many smiling civilians with the most tragic of life histories. The histories are true, and the smiles are real. I wonder, too, whether this smiling girl has just been to the new Tiger base and whether she has had any success with Inbam. When we get to the new base, Accan is there, bathing at the well, wearing a *lungi*. When he sees us he approaches, still wet, with a smile. Koyila suddenly becomes very shy and quickly makes an excuse to leave. I try to hide my embarrassment at Accan's bare, hairy chest by asking him about some recent, war-related news. Daya Mohan is not there, and I start to leave and tell Accan to say hello to Inbam for me, as I haven't seen him in a long time. Accan, however, says Inbam is just arriving, and he tells me to wait. I see Inbam arriving on the other side of the new house. He is armed, but that is nothing unusual. He disappears and reappears a couple of times, and I don't know whether he has seen me. So I tell Accan to tell Inbam I won't bite, and I head back to Arasadithivu and Kokkadichcholai on my bike.

I visit the political office regularly for a while, hoping for a conversation with Inbam about his life in the movement or anything else enlightening. I have no "teacher" among the Tigers, no one whom I can rely on to answer my many general questions and give me a detailed picture of their world. But after a month or so I give up on the idea that anyone there will take a real interest in my project; I just have to piece together whatever information comes my way.

Das

Jimmy the puppy has a sister whose name is Di, after the princess herself. Di the puppy looks just like Jimmy the puppy, but she is very spoiled. Whenever she comes to Alagar's house, she chases chickens all over the place. She forms a sharp contrast with the beggar dog Raja saved, which is scrawny and hasn't the energy to chase another living creature. Das the Tiger takes care of Di the puppy, and she follows him everywhere. Sita tells me that Das loves to raise animals. He has pigeons, too. Many of the Tigers like animals, especially wild ones, but Das is among the few human beings I know who has a devoted pet.

Das is a quiet man who often spends the evening at Alagar's house. Like so many others, he has bad leg injuries and is partly crippled, although he can still walk and fight. One day I find Das playing with Di in the house with Vithusa's battery toys. Di is hopping and barking around the moving toys as though they were prey.

I know it is stupid to think that a lover of animals cannot be a killer of people. Das has been in combat and probably has killed people, and so have probably most of the other Tigers I know. But this issue of compassion and killing must be examined more closely. We are not talking here about the dictator or godfather who strokes his adored Persian cat while his sadistic, robotlike henchmen shoot down his pleading and sobbing victims. We are talking about ordinary combatants who believe in what they are fighting for and do not necessarily like to kill.

Rudrakumaran

Like Das, Rudrakumaran likes animals. He tells me he has a parrot that he captured from the jungle (parrots are common here), but I never get to see it. I do get to see his monkey. Just as Das walks along the road with Di bouncing behind, Rudrakumaran may be seen walking along the road with his monkey following on a rope. I never learn to what extent the monkey is devoted to Rudrakumaran, but I know one human being who is, and that is Vithusa. Every time she sees him, she breaks into a wide grin, and thus it is Rudrakumaran's job to coax her to smile for all the pictures taken of her at her birthday party.

Rudrakumaran walks with a limp, but the way he swings his game leg as he walks is more like a swagger. Indeed it is months before I realize that he walks like that because he was shot in the leg. Many Tigers are crippled, or are missing an arm or a leg or an eye. So are many civilians. Rosa says the checkpoint guards have accused her of being a Tiger because she has bullet wounds. Only the army would shoot her, they reason, and the army would only shoot Tigers; therefore Rosa must be a Tiger. Rosa somehow has convinced them to let her cross, maybe in part because she is female, but Rudrakumaran can never cross, because with his limp he would be immediately spotted and probably killed.

Rudrakumaran, with his mustache, his swagger, and his salty black humor, seems like a pirate to me. Countless men wear mustaches in this country, but somehow with Rudrakumaran the mustache is key.

But one day Rudrakumaran walks into Alagar's house, and to my dismay I see that his mustache is gone. And I ask, "Where is your mustache, Rudrakumaran?"

And he replies, "We're shooting."

"Who are you shooting, and what does that have to do with your mustache?"

"We're shooting the massacre, and I am a Sinhala soldier." The LTTE video crew is making a simulation of the Kokkadichcholai massacre, and Rudrakumaran is acting in it. Rosa has already told me all about it.

I ask, "Don't Sinhala soldiers have mustaches?"

"I shaved it off as a disguise," he answers. He certainly looks like a different person without his mustache. Now, fortunately, it has grown back. But I can't understand the logic about a disguise. He will never cross to the army side, and so even if he appears in a video that might be shown there, the army cannot use it to identify him unless they come here — in which case there will be no protection for anyone, video or no video.

Moreover, Rudrakumaran is always wanting me to take his picture. I have obliged, and now he is asking for the print. I tell him the picture of him didn't turn out, and a good thing too, because the police arrested me for taking pictures in Tiger territory (they recognized Tiger monuments in the photos) and seized them and examined them before returning them to me.[3] Nobody seems to believe me when I say I was arrested. When I tell Inbam, he responds with the single word "lie" (*poy*). Perhaps I should have brought back some kind of documentation from the police station to prove it. Maybe it would enhance my credibility with the Tigers. But it's too late now.

Rudrakumaran looks through the photos I do have. He asks to keep the photo of a checkpoint security guard, and I give it to him. Rosa has asked for the other photo of the guard, and I gave that to her — I still don't know the reason why, but maybe there is no real reason.

We come to the pictures of the Kattankudi mosque, with its bullet holes. In 1990, more than a hundred people at prayer were shot to death in the mosque by five Tamil-speaking men with combat rifles they had smuggled into the mosque under their robes. The killers escaped and were never identified. The bullet holes in the walls of the mosque are kept as a kind of memorial, and Muslims ask people to photograph them. I say to Rudrakumaran, "They say the LTTE did this." Rudrakumaran is silent. "Did they?" I persist.

"Yes, the LTTE did it," Rudrakumaran replies offhandedly. "There were fights between Muslims and Tamils at that time. Muslims were cutting Tamils, and Tamils were cutting Muslims." I am astonished at this confession, because the LTTE denied that they had committed the mosque massacre and have never retracted that denial, although civilians almost universally think the LTTE did it. But, especially when we talk about shooting and killing, Tigers' conversations with me are ironic. They say something and then contradict it on the spot or later. My conversations with Rudrakumaran are not much different from my conversations with Inbam. I will never know whether the Tigers really suspect me of being a spy.

Once I start to say to Rudrakumaran, "If you have even the slightest suspicion —"

And Rudrakumaran says, "No, no! I have no suspicions at all."

And then, apparently to demonstrate that he has no suspicions, he says, "I am a Tiger [*nān iyakkam*]," and pulls the cord from beneath his shirt and shows me the cyanide capsule. Of course, this revelation is not worth much as a gesture of trust: I already know that he is a Tiger. But previously, when I took his picture, he told me, "We're not Tigers, we're just Tiger helpers," and opened his shirt to show me that there was no cord around his neck, no cyanide capsule.

2 February. I visit the women's base right after the battles at Paranthan and Kilinochchi. I am still at the women's base when Rudrakumaran appears there. Breathlessly, he says to me, "Inbam! Inbam!"

"What about him?" I say with careful indifference.

"Inbam was in a motorcycle accident and is badly hurt!"

"But I just saw him a few minutes ago," I say.

"It just *happened* a few minutes ago," says Rudrakumaran. "He broke his leg!"

"Are you sure it was broken?"

"Yes!"

"Were there head injuries?" I ask, beginning to feel concerned.

"Yes! He was hit on the head and lost consciousness and was taken immediately to Kuddi in Palugamam. There was blood everywhere." All of this Rudrakumaran says in the ironic fashion to which I have become accustomed. But Rudrakumaran says everything that way.

I am invited to the back of the base to talk with the girls, but the thought that Inbam may be badly hurt preys on me. He was driving a motorcycle when I saw him; maybe he really did have a fall. Jeyakuddi, a Tiger shot in a quarrel with another Tiger, died of a loss of blood; the Tiger doctor did not have enough blood on hand to save him. I think to myself that I could give blood if it were needed. After a while, I decide to go to Alagar's house and ask. It is just down the road. I tell them what I have heard and offer to help. But Sita and Alagar say it is all a lie, and Alagar says, "That boy is a chronic liar."

All of this is playful, though Alagar seems mildly irritated with his joke-ster friend. I remember that Rudrakumaran is the same one who told me the massacres of Muslims were carried out by the LTTE. Was he lying then, too? I say to the people in Alagar's house, when you see him, beat him up for me, he has made a fool out of me. I bike back down the road and see Inbam at the gathering of people for the funeral of the Tiger boy who died of snakebite; I smile at him, and he smiles back. At Alagar's house that evening, Rudrakumaran shows up. I smilingly confront him and demand that he beg forgiveness and touch my feet. He asks forgive-ness, also smiling, but does not touch my feet, and Sita's mother chases after him to hit him, but he gets away. Inbam and Accan appear. I am glad of this proof that Inbam is really okay, but someone laughs, "She was even ready to give her blood." And we sit there looking at each other.

．　．　．

Around mid-March, Rudrakumaran declares that if I don't give him my camera, he will never speak to me again. He is joking, of course.

I say to him, "Rudrakumaran — why do you always lie like this?"

And he says, "I don't lie!"

And I say, "Yes, you do!" I remind him of his telling me that the Tigers were responsible for the Kattankudi massacre. Was that a lie, too? A joke? How can I know? After I say this his face grows sober, as though he had forgotten this event, and thought I had forgotten too, and now discovers that I remember things that are said even months ago, things that are important.

And he says, "I only went to school up to the tenth grade. I was not in the movement at that time. It was what civilians were saying." And I realize that Rudrakumaran was a schoolboy at the time the massacres in question took place — recently in my time frame, but long ago in Rudrakumaran's. He is only about twenty-three years old.

On the topic of his jokingly telling me that Inbam had been in a motorbike accident, he says: "We do this among ourselves also. If you have attachment [*pācam*] toward someone, we tease you about it and lie to you to cut [*veḍḍa*] that attachment. We even joke about combat death in the same way."

"But why would you want to cut attachment?" I ask. Rudrakumaran doesn't answer.

The idea of cutting attachments is central to Saiva Siddhanta, the philosophy connected with Tamil Saivism. To attain *siddhānta* ("ultimate victory," the pinnacle of spiritual achievement) one must cut one's attachment to home and belongings, family, and one's life. Saiva Siddhanta philosophy is abstract and complicated, but it is favored by educated Tamils in Sri Lanka. To a certain extent, it fits the Tiger philosophy that combatants must renounce worldly pleasures, including home and family, if they are to be successful fighters. They must also be willing to give up their lives for the higher cause of the Tamil people's liberation from oppression.

Rudrakumaran owns only his clothes, has little education, and probably is not a connoisseur of Saiva Siddhanta. I have never tried to ask him about his family, assuming that he would just tell me some story. For people to love, as far as I know, he has only his friends in the movement, most of whom may well die before they reach middle age.

Rudrakumaran examines my little twenty-dollar camera and asks, "Have you given it to anybody?"

I say, "I was thinking of giving it to Malaimalli."

"Malaimalli! But she already has a video camera."

I ask him, "Do you want my camera, then?"

And he replies, slowly and clearly, enunciating each word distinctly, the way some of them do when they want to make sure I understand something, "I must not ask for or take anything from you."

I say, "If I offer my camera to you, will you accept it?"

"Yes."

"Okay — it's yours." A worldly possession for Rudrakumaran.

It is against Sri Lankan law for anyone to give or sell anything to the Tigers. The minimum penalty is seven years' imprisonment. Moreover, asking for gifts violates the Tigers' own code: by asking, they humble themselves, and Tigers are never to humble themselves before civilians. But small gifts from civilians to Tigers are commonplace; giving something to an individual is different from contributing to the movement; and, despite what Rudrakumaran has just said, some young Tigers do ask for personal gifts, just as civilians do. I have often been asked for gifts in India, and it has happened here, too. It is not only that people want the material object; they also want a sign of friendship from you, a sign that you care for them personally. A moral dilemma: should I break the law of the country in a small way, or should I insult this person who is my research participant and also my friend?

I promise that when I leave, I will give Rudrakumaran my camera, and my crayons and watercolor paints also.

Early in our acquaintance, I made Rudrakumaran promise to give me rifle lessons. But after the incident with Sudha, he seems to chicken out. He shows me how to aim a rifle but never lets me shoot it. Instead, one day he ambushes me, standing behind a doorway, gun held to his chest, as I approach, and then jumps out from behind the door and pretends to shoot me dead, startling me into laughter. His weapon is a toy gun. It is battery powered and bright orange, and it makes various loud noises: a siren, a machine-gun rattle, a bomb falling with a Dopplerized whistle and then exploding, and so forth. You never know which noise it will make when you pull the trigger. Lord only knows where it was made. Rudrakumaran bought the gun for Vithusa at a stall at a temple festival for twenty-five rupees. But Sita, seeing my attraction to it, gives it to me.

And I keep my promise to Rudrakumaran and give him my paints, my crayons, and my camera.

Good-byes

In early May, I learn that Inbam and Malaimalli are being transferred suddenly to Vaharai, a town to the north. I know there are problems up there, but the nature of the problems is vague.

On 13 May, the day before he is to leave, Inbam appears unexpectedly at the door of my room in Vasanta's house. I invite him in, and he gives me his home address and asks me to write.

"You ask me to write letters to you, and I do, and you never respond," I say. "Now if I write a fourth letter to you, will you promise to answer this one?"

"I will certainly answer your fourth letter," he vows. (But he never does.) He studies my face in a bemused kind of way. "My Auntie," he says. And then he is gone.

. . .

Wednesday, 10 June. When I visit Sita, she tells me that Gamani is dead. When we met, Sita reminds me, he gave me his address and asked me to write to him. I ask how he died, and she says he was one of the fourteen who were killed after the attack on the Chengalady army base. The attack was successful: the soldiers at the base were frightened and scattered in all directions, firing randomly, while the LTTE attackers made off with a load of weapons. But the army fired mortar shells in retaliation and hit a different group of LTTE, who were at their base, not even on a mission. About thirteen were killed or took their own lives on the spot. Gamani lost one leg in the shelling; the other leg was shattered, and he had wounds all over his body. Others who were gravely hurt ended their lives immediately by biting their cyanide capsules, but Gamani did not, Sita tells me. He died of his wounds three days later.

That night I try to sleep, but sleep does not come until just before dawn. I dream that a man is attacking me, saying that I am attacking him and he must defend himself. He has a knife. There is just a table between us, and I know he will get around it. I wake up screaming and burst into sobs.

CHAPTER 9

Spectacles and Mysteries

Objectivity and Realism

Military analysts do not like to speak of emotion and imagination as significant components of warfare. For them it is all strategy and tactics, numbers and probabilities, an intellectual game. But it is a truism that once you get on the battlefield, the ordinary world of logic, meaning, order, and reasonable expectation dissolves, and you find yourself in another kind of game. Reports from the battlefield stress the sureality of it, the dreamlike, nightmarelike, sudden, unheard-of, unexpected, officially denied juxtapositions of beauty and horror, cruelty and devotion. I have never been in battle, but representations of it, from the *Iliad* to LTTE videos, tell me this much. We can say that these representations are beyond imagination, that "truth is stranger than fiction," and all we have heard before, and leave it at that. But to get to the heart of war, it may be necessary to go back to imagination, to drama, to play, to dreams and childhood and intense, uncivilized feelings. All of these things are powers, strong potential energies, that are generated from within us —"by" us — and yet we cannot be said to control them, let alone to wield them. And yet, as politicians, we do, we try to control and wield these great human powers in others, to use them to do our will.

Not every battlefield is the same. Cultural acts, emotions, and imaginings are not all the same. So I will not speak of samenesses here, but of differences. On the battlefield of Sri Lanka, or, more exactly, on the edges of the field, just barely over the border between war and not-war, it is possible to discern how different are the emotional and imaginative worlds of people whose sons, brothers, daughters, sisters, friends, and lovers killed and died together in the eighteen-month-long battle over the A9 highway.

In 1997 and 1998, the LTTE in the Paduvankarai area of Batticaloa District were involved in two major activities. First, they were fighting the army, mainly by sending many of their people to the north to fight in Jayasikurui and by attacking the army forces that occupied parts of the eastern districts. Second, they were trying to build and maintain high morale among Tamil civilians at home. The morale-building activities included, among other things, numerous public entertainments and shows. The civilians had been terrorized in waves by the Sri Lankan Army, the IPKF, and the half-dozen anti-LTTE paramilitary groups, as well as, to a lesser extent, by the LTTE itself. Anti-Tamil acts of terror could motivate some civilians to fight directly against the terror by joining the LTTE, but the terror could also immobilize them. Among the rest, many refrained from directly supporting the LTTE. Some feared the danger involved; others felt that by demanding money from civilians who were relatively well off, and by recruiting young people against their parents' will, the LTTE had in a sense betrayed the civilian populace. Some felt that the LTTE cared only about the LTTE. To counter such feelings, the LTTE members who were not off fighting — because of injury, inexperience, or a range of other reasons — spent all their time in what was called political (*araciyal*) activity: interacting with civilians, gaining their trust and friendship, and, not least, entertaining them. The entertainment extravaganzas struck me as a kind of reverse of Bob Hope's U.S.O. shows. Whereas Hope recruited civilian entertainers to lift the spirits of military troops, the LTTE recruited talented individuals from among their own membership to provide public entertainment for civilians.

The entertainments involved some tricky emotional balancing. On the one hand, it was necessary to remind civilians of what the LTTE was fighting for, and, even more important, of what it was fighting against. Some of the spectacles therefore represented, in gruesome detail, the bloody massacres in which so many of their own relatives had died. Such reminders came mainly in the form of colorful paintings. Civilians were also reminded of the sacrifices that LTTE members had made for their sake. Every time an LTTE member died in combat, his or her body was brought home and taken in procession around the villages of the area of his original home before burial. It was hard even for a stranger like me not to weep at the sight of a young person who could have been my own child, whose dead face I had viewed and strewn flowers on, being lowered in a coffin into the earth. And there were reminders, in the form of miles and miles of videotape, of the heroic exploits of LTTE fighters. I saw riveting footage of a Sea Tiger on a suicide mission driving a motorboat full speed to collide with a navy ship, crashing into it, and blowing it up, together of course with himself, while his comrades, following in another boat with the cameraman, cheered, jumped up and down, laughed, and hugged each other at the sight of his victory. Grimly fascinating footage of army corpses strewn on a field after an LTTE victory just a few miles from here just a few days earlier, footage of the Sinhala soldiers' untidy garbage disposal habits, of their officers' half-empty liquor bottles, was made available for the edification of civilians, like some real-life horror movie. At the same time, it was necessary to counter the pain of such reminders with something fun, something that would make people laugh and cheer.

I never heard Tamil people say that fear was the greatest enemy, but civilians and combatants alike often remarked that fear was in most situations a useless emotion. If you were on the battlefield, fear could disable you and keep you from thinking straight. If you were a massacre survivor, fear could keep you from identifying the soldier who shot you. If you were a mother of young children, fear could keep you from feeding and caring for them. Whatever had happened to you in the past, fear could keep you from enjoying the rest of your life. Many pacifist workers from aid organizations gave all their energy to healing children's fears of rival ethnic groups: Muslims and non-Muslim Tamils in the east had been involved in massacres against one another, and children of each side had learned to fear the other.

Far from keeping silent about violent events, civilians engaged in continuous, open discourse about them, including acts by the local LTTE of which the civilians disapproved, or approved, or had mixed feelings, as the case might be. Gruesome public executions, violent interpersonal quarrels, detainments, tortures, abductions, elopements, weddings, birthdays, divorces, ambushes, battles, what boy got shot in what part of the body on what day in what action, newspaper and radio reports of distant and nearby events, the rising price of eggs, army activities across the lagoon, beatings at checkpoints, names and personal habits of the checkpoint guards, and many other topics were part of everyday conversation. Even civilians who had undergone terrible suffering — deaths of relatives, loss of limbs — seemed to relish gossip about the war. On verandas and courtyards they would be found sorting out different versions of a story, questioning official versions, seeking more information.

This is not to say there were no silences, no topics about which speaking was muted, and no moments of horror so great that the scream inside turned to ice. But the general atmosphere of ease and laughter was not what I had expected of a terrorized community, where at any time another young boy or girl might disappear, at any time mortar shells might fall, at any time the army might conduct raids and roundups, at any time a bomb could blow up and pieces of just-living flesh could rain down all around. In fact, there were times of the year when explosions of that sort were commonplace, and yet people continued to live their lives and do most of the things they would have done were they not in the midst of a war. Some said that this was exactly their way of showing that they were not defeated, and we might take their words as a definitive explanation of their relative fearlessness. But the comparison of this situation with what was going on in rural southern Sri Lanka at exactly the same time has made me think again about how people manage terror. Sometimes they hold it within themselves, keeping silent about both domestic and public violence, and valuing fear as the only way to keep themselves and the community under control.[1]

Events and Interpretations

Among Tamil people in Paduvankarai, the political organization of emotion was a matter not of stirring up or manipulating vague and inchoate feelings, but of the subtle and calculated organization of emotional power. Sometimes the force of terror was turned against itself by small, instantaneous acts. Sometimes there were sharp juxtapositions of the terrifying and the playful, the grisly and the lovely, the tremendous and the trivial, the silly and the profound. Sometimes there were contradictions, incredible stories and conflicting incredible stories, that transformed fear and frustration into wonder, amusement, and determined curiosity. Sometimes everyday life presented itself as so strange that the observer or interlocutor (in this case me) was left to feel that nothing was real and anything was possible. I think I myself was in a state of dissociation much of the time.

I am sure people carefully and deliberately attempted to manage my feelings — and those of others — to produce certain effects. It was almost an artistry of the heart. Maybe they were just playing with me for their own amusement. But they were not hurting me; in fact they were helping me by keeping me from being afraid. The emotional jujitsu described here is not the kind of tactic that could necessarily be reproduced in some other cultural context: this community has its own long history, language, and habits, and these events took place within a specific Tamil and Sri

Lankan technology of human power, in which — as I have argued elsewhere regarding Indian Tamils — emotion is accorded primacy of place. And it was not only by human design that I found myself (as others must have found themselves) frequently and rapidly yanked from one strong feeling to its opposite, from one kind of experience to another, incompatible one. Everything happened so fast, in a tightly circumscribed space and time. The whole war was this way. It was the way this whole world was made. Other wars, other worlds, will be different.

To illustrate this surreality of the war, the sense of simultaneous hyperawareness and detachment it induced (a contradictory combination right there), I can offer only descriptions of representative incidents, in no particular order. In some cases I believe the effect was intentionally caused, as a quasi-playful experiment, to see how I would react. In other cases, it may have been part of an effort to divert me from some awkward question I was pursuing or a mystery I was seeking to solve. But in other cases, I believe it involved no deliberation on anyone's part. Then it was a group spectacle; we all contributed to its making, and we all felt outside ourselves, sometimes helpless as babies, sometimes fearless and free.

Razeek's Corpse Display

Early December 1997. Accan has come to tell me that two *iyakkam* (members of the movement) have been killed by the Razeek group in a distant town. The Razeek group is an infamous Tamil paramilitary organization that helps the Sri Lankan Army fight the Tigers. There are several Tamil paramilitaries, all of them aligned with Tamil parties in Parliament. The Tamil political parties (TELO, PLOTE, EPDP, EPRLF, and others) represent themselves as moderate and generally antiwar, but the paramilitary groups associated with them are savage, and international human rights groups have singled them out for condemnation. In the Batticaloa area, the Razeek group, associated with the political party EPRLF, was, at the time I was there, considered to be the worst.

Accan tells me that the Razeek group is refusing to release the bodies of the two Tigers it recently killed, which are quickly decaying in the heat. One of the main jobs of the International Committee of the Red Cross in this area is delivering the dead bodies of combatants back to their respective organizations. The Tigers are supposed to give back the dead bodies of army personnel, and vice versa. But instead, they tell me, the group's leader, Razeek himself, who works for the army, is putting the Tiger bodies on display in his own house for the civilian population to view. Accan asks, calmly and offhandedly, if I want to go and see the bodies. I am not at all interested in seeing rotting corpses, but, desiring to be helpful, I say, "If you *want* me to see the bodies for some reason, I will go."

And he answers, "I thought you would want to go and see them."

"Why would I want to do that?"

"Just as a way to pass the time [*oru poṟutu pōkku*]." He is quiet but earnest as he speaks, as though it would be perfectly natural for me to go look at decaying bodies for entertainment.

He continues, "Razeek is keeping the bodies in his house, and ordinary people like you can see them, but we're not allowed to see them."

"Are you certain they're dead?"

"Yes," he says.

"Well, then, there is nothing I can do for them if they're dead," I say. "Unless there is some reason why you want me to view these dead bodies, I think I would rather not." And so he leaves. But through the night I keep wondering about Accan's corpse story. Maybe they want someone to identify the bodies (but how could I do this?). And then I remember that the Razeek group has a reputation for torturing people before killing them, and maybe the Tigers want me to inspect the bodies for signs of torture.

So the next day I go to the Tiger political office and ask Accan if this was the reason they want me to see the bodies. He says yes. So I say, "If you want me to, I will go over to the other side with my camera and see if I can find Razeek's house, and I will take a picture of the dead bodies. That way you can identify them and also see if they have been tortured. But you have to say if you want me to do this, because it involves some danger to me, and I'm not going to do it unless you actually need it to be done."

"Why is it a danger to you?" asks Accan.

And I say, "Because that Razeek might do something to me if he learns I'm helping the Tigers. Now, should I do it or not?"

"It's up to you," he says.

"No, you tell me, do you want me to do this work for you or not? Please give me some kind of responsible answer."

And Accan says, "No problem [*piraccinai illai*]."

The next day I take the ferry across and then get a three-wheeler into town. I am thinking how easy it would be for a person like me to get in and kill the brutal Razeek. Logistically speaking. Of course, I would be killed in return. Such is my frame of mind at the time: nothing makes sense, and nothing matters.

I have been told that Razeek's house is next to the hospital — Accan said the general hospital, but someone else has told me it is behind a certain private hospital. Accan has said people in the neighborhood will tell me where Razeek's house is. Now I am beginning to feel frightened, wondering what Razeek and his house will be like and what condition the bodies will be in by this time. It is late afternoon, and I will have to be safe inside somewhere by nightfall. So I ask the three-wheeler driver to take me to the ICRC headquarters, and fortunately Alain (a French ICRC worker I have met before) and someone else are there. When I explain what I am doing, Alain says the ICRC returned the LTTE bodies that morning (a Sunday): one went to the LTTE, and the other went to the family of the dead boy. Alain says the Razeek group is the armed branch of the EPRLF (which I already know), and Razeek is not, to his knowledge, a particular person, but is just the name of the group. (Tigers and villagers, to the contrary, say that Razeek is an actual person; I recall reading somewhere that his choice of a Muslim pseudonym is irksome because in fact he is a Hindu.) Alain says that Razeek's "house" is the EPRLF office in town. I ask whether the Razeek group is officially working for the army (because if it is, then the Sri Lankan government would be responsible for human rights abuses, such as torture, committed by the group). Alain says yes. I ask if the ICRC has examined the bodies for signs of torture, and he replies that the ICRC does not look at the bodies it hands over. But how can it not? Am I crazy to think this is strange?

Later in December, I am back at Sita and Alagar's house. This time Sundar, a Tiger I met in 1996, is sitting on the veranda. We talk about technological gadgets and Sundar's ambition to learn English. He tests some of his words out on me, and Alagar joins in. They want to know the difference between "I don't know" and "I have no idea," and to explain "high time," as in "It's high time I saw you." My knowledge of these idioms varies from what they've been taught, and we banter for about thirty minutes or so. But I am impatient to talk about other things.

I ask Sundar, "Did you hear about the boys who were captured and killed by the Razeek group?"

His face changes. He says, "No."

I thought they would all know about this by now. But Sundar apparently doesn't. I ask him if the news troubles him. He says no. He is gazing across the road, across the fields to the mountains. He seems suddenly remote and quiet, and I wonder if he is thinking about friends of his who died under torture. But this is a question I dare not ask. But I also wonder how Sundar could not know about this incident. Yet, if he knew, why would he pretend otherwise?

(In June 1999, I read on the Internet that Razeek has been killed by a suicide bomber on a bicycle. The story includes a picture of Razeek. He was a real person.)

A Murder

Friday, 9 January. Rosa comes to the lodge in Batticaloa where I'm staying for a few days. In the main dining room and lobby, she looks around and tells me in a whisper that the Razeek group meets here. I ask her how she knows, and she says she just does. The information makes me nervous.

She tells me that after I left the village yesterday, one Tiger boy shot and killed another in a personal quarrel. No one knows what the argument was about. They were talking, and the talk became a fight. The dead boy was called Jeyakuddi. He was a nice boy, and everybody liked him. He was engaged to a civilian girl, and they were to be married in a year. *Pāvam tānē?* (It's a pity, isn't it?) He was responsible for LTTE activities in the town of Batticaloa. The killing and the funeral happened on the same day. Rosa tells me I missed it all because I was in town at the time. Her tone is reproving. Again I have missed seeing a dead body.

I tell Rosa that I know a Tiger boy called Jeya, and another boy called Kuddi (the physician). Perhaps the longer name of one of them was Jeyakuddi. Rosa tells me the dead boy is the Jeya I knew. The news troubles me because that Jeya was a quiet and gentle person. I ask what became of the killer. Rosa says the Tigers tied up his hands and feet and took him away. They will write to Prabhakaran about the incident, and Prabhakaran will order the appropriate punishment. The killer will be shot.

Back in the village, Vasanta tells me that the Jeyakuddi who was killed was not the Jeya I knew but someone else. They did take the body in procession around town, as they do with all Tiger bodies, but it did not come down this road, and Vasanta did not see it. I ask what the Tigers say happened; Vasanta says they are saying it was an accident. But her version of the death is the same as Rosa's. She says that Jeyakuddi did not die immediately after he was shot but called out to be saved. Kuddi the doctor tried to save him, but he had lost too much blood, and Kuddi did not have enough blood on hand to replace it. I go to Sita's house the same afternoon and, by chance or otherwise, see both Kuddi and Jeya there. I have not seen Jeya in a long time and am glad to know he is still alive. I do not have a chance to speak with Kuddi.

On one or two occasions, a Tiger I know has told me with a straight face that another Tiger I know has died or is in danger of death. Sita once told me Nirmala was dead, and Rudrakumaran told a similar tale about Inbam. Shortly later I found out that the allegedly dead or dying person was fine, and the story was just a joke — or something. Now Rosa, a civilian, has done a similar thing. To spare me shock and needless sadness, I feel, she should have been more careful. I think they are testing me to see how I respond to death. When the death is real, they will know.

A Land-Mine Victim

People keep directing me toward children who are obvious victims of the war. This is because of the nature of the research I am doing, but still it troubles me because I sometimes feel as though these children are being put on display. I would prefer that they come to me voluntarily, but of course many of them are shy of an adult from a foreign country who speaks oddly. So I have to compromise, go where I am directed, and take it from there.

At the urging of Rosa and others, I visit a little boy whose leg was destroyed by a land mine. He is twelve and looks younger. Rosa takes me to the house. Only the boy is there — the mother has gone to Kokkadich-cholai. The neighbors say she will come to Vasanta's house to see me, and about an hour later she and the boy arrive. Of his legs, I ask the usual questions: how did this happen, what did you do, how do you feel? The mother replies with a brief narrative, describing how horribly the boy's legs were torn up when she found him. It happened in 1995. He had gone to the fields to defecate with a friend and had stepped on a mine. The mine exploded, and the friend ran to the mother's home crying that the boy was dead. The mother ran to see and found that the flesh of the boy's leg had been shredded and was hanging in strips, and the bones were hanging in pieces among the flesh. The other leg also had flesh torn off. She took him to the army camp nearby. They took him to the STF camp at Manmunai, and from there he was taken to the main hospital at Batticaloa and treated. The left leg was amputated at midthigh. A large square of flesh was cut from the right thigh and grafted onto the calf, where much of the flesh had been destroyed. One corner of the graft, near the foot, is now infected and bleeding.

The mother says that whenever she sees the other boys riding their bicycles, she feels sad. She is on the verge of tears as she talks to me. She says the other children tease him and chase him and call him cripple, and once, when he arrived late to school (because he had trouble walking), the schoolmaster sent him home. "A small-minded person," all of us agree.

I ask if the boy was unconscious when she found him, and she says yes; he did not regain consciousness for days. I ask the boy himself if he remembers anything of the events, and he smiles in embarrassment and hides his face behind his hands. A five-year-old girl who is sitting nearby (who has been orphaned by the war) mimics him.

The mother of the boy says the boy is stupid and doesn't remember anything. The boy listens silently while she talks, but his eyes respond eloquently as I look at his face and listen to his mother's words. His eyes assume different expressions during her narrative: I can't give a name to them, but pain is there. I ask who planted the mine. The mother says she doesn't know: the army says the LTTE did it; the LTTE says the army did it.

Rosa tells me to take a picture of the boy. There are already so many pictures of children who have lost their legs to land mines, I say it is not really necessary. I do not want to embarrass the boy any further, don't want to make an exhibit of him, any more than has already been done. But the adults insist. The boy is made to stand, and I take his picture to satisfy them.

Television

Mid-January 1998. Vasanta, knowing the indebtedness I feel to her, asked me to buy her a television. "It will help with the children's education," she said. So I bought one in town, and a relative delivered it to the house. Now the TV has become a center of attraction.

Last night, while I was in my room, two-year-old Mohan and his grandmother were watching TV together. Mohan got interested in something on the screen and asked his grandmother what it was. She told him it was *āmi* (army).

This morning the grandmother dresses Mohan in spiffy new clothes and sends him to preschool next door, and I hear Rosa's voice leading the voices of sixty children in recitations of Tamil nursery rhymes. And later I hear her laughter and the laughter of her friend and helper Selvi, and the sound of water being lifted from the well behind the school. Life on these days seems so normal, so idyllic.

On Rupavahini (the government-owned TV station) I see an advertisement urging viewers to cooperate with checkpoint guards. In the ad, uniformed guards are shown looking through the backs of trucks, and the glossy cars of well-dressed, cooperative citizens, while the voice over describes various places in vehicles where explosives may be hidden. It is somewhat like an ad promoting safe driving in the West. At the end is a picture of a giant explosion to remind viewers of what the guards are there to prevent.

In real life, Tamil villagers perceive the checkpoints and their guards as one of the most noxious daily burdens of the war. The villagers travel by foot, bicycle, or bus, not in cars or trucks. The presence of army or STF personnel on a bus or anywhere means trouble. The STF are suspected by Tamil civilians of planting bombs on buses during their investigations; the army are suspected of setting off bombs at checkpoints and then blaming the LTTE to prove they are needed in the east, so that they will not be sent to the main battlefront. Whoever plants the bombs, civilians die in these explosions.

At checkpoints, the guards interrogate travelers at length, harass women and girls, beat young boys and old men, and accuse all and sundry of being Tigers. Villagers do not dare object to the guards' lengthy and abusive questioning lest they be imprisoned as suspects. Hundreds of people arrested on suspicion by the STF have died in custody. Others have been shot and killed on the spot.

Rupavahini is showing *Yuga Vilakkuwa* — a serialized, fictionalized account of the war. We watch. The show is in Sinhala with Tamil subtitles, but the subtitles flash by too fast to be read. There is a scene with terrorists disguised as army mowing down townsfolk with machine guns. There are shots of dead monks. Another shot shows a soldier offering water to an old, sari-clad woman and being killed on the spot by a Tiger. Most of these incidents are made up, but what viewers will be able to separate fact from fiction? Which images will stay with them?

When I ask Vasanta if she thinks the show is true to life, she says no, and I ask why not. She says that the show depicts the army as nicer than they really are and the Tigers as worse. The Tamil people will not be fooled by this, she tells me, as will be shown by their continued support of the LTTE.

Two-year-old Mohan watches the pretend killings on TV and calls out to his grandmother, Vasanta's mother, to whom he always turns for comfort. He is not happy; he seems frightened but absorbed. His grandmother teaches him to say the words for "army shooting" (*āmi cuḍatu*). Mohan is a quiet, reflective child, and these are among the first words I hear him say.

In Tamil households in India, the first words young children are taught are names of kin and body parts. Here, a child might learn the names of body parts from stories of their being blown off by gunfire or mortar shelling, as in the picturesque expression *kāl parantatu* (leg flew off) — like a hat flying off in the wind.

Mohan's grandmother remembers when the army came through and shot her civilian son. She is more afraid of the sound of explosions and gunfire than younger adults in the household are. I think she wants Mohan to know what he should fear. Months later, when Mohan's little sister is sick with a high fever, and everyone in the household is gathered round her, concerned for her life, Mohan will ask, "Did the army shoot her?" But now, Mohan just tells his grandmother, "Move." He wants her to move out of the way so that he can see what is happening on the screen.

Little boys who seem about ten years old watch Muppet-like creatures on Rupavahini making war and singing what must be antiwar songs in Sinhala. The boys are refugees from another district who came here in 1990, fleeing heavier fighting. On the show, when a bomb falls and puppet bodies fly about, the boys ooh and aah in appreciation — of the quality of the special effects, I guess. They will have seen real bombs falling and maybe real bodies flying. One might think they would be disturbed by these reminders of past traumas, but they are obviously enjoying the mock violence of the puppet show.

Vasanta reports to me that President Chandrika has offered to let Prabhakaran rule the north for ten years, as a trial run. This is discussed at length in the news on Saturday night. But Vasanta misses the point: this was an offer reportedly made by Chandrika in the 1995 peace negotiations with the Tigers. The antigovernment Sinhala press has resurrected this piece of news, and the front pages of several Sinhala newspapers are shown on Rupavahini. The papers are critical of this offer. A good-looking man explains at length on the pro-government TV news that this offer shows the sincerity of the president's desire for peace.

The president does not deny that she brought up this possibility in the course of peace negotiations. She must not have thought about what her enemies in Parliament would make of it if they found out. Maybe she thought at that time that she did not have any enemies. Maybe that is why she is so angry with everyone now.

An old man, a Christian priest who is a refugee from the north, watches the Rupavahini show about the history of the war and says it is all exactly true, this is just the way things were. He calls the LTTE terrorists. Vasanta says he is angry because the Tigers borrowed his son's motorcycle and did not return it. He visits this house often but disappears when Tigers come to visit me or to watch TV.

Another old man, who told us before that weeping does not help, comes in every night to watch the 6 P.M. news. His son was killed by the army in the Kokkadichcholai massacre, and his daughter-in-law died of a heart attack in the same month. Now he is raising his orphaned grand-children himself. He knows that one LTTE helper, Ravi (a young man who lives nearby and comes around when he has nothing else to do), is in the house as he listens to the terrorist talk on TV. As far as I can tell, I am the only one who finds the juxtaposition striking.

"Certain Defeat"

22 January. Yesterday, when I was visiting a nearby school to interview students, we heard what sounded like bombing and rapid gunfire com-ing from the next village. The young boy I was interviewing at the time jumped up and ran off. The teachers said he was frightened by the sound of gunfire because his father had been shot to death before his eyes. I said it sounded to me like firecrackers and cherry bombs going off, and the teachers said no; no fireworks were allowed over here, it must be live fire. But the noises stopped, the students went back to their classes, and the little boy I had been interviewing returned and finished the interview with an eloquent flourish.

Now I have learned that the sounds of gunshots we heard yesterday were the Tiger video production team filming a simulated reproduction of the Kokkadichcholai massacre. Satyan confirms this. In midafternoon, Rosa takes me to the local library, where preparations are under way for the video that is to be made here. No one is in the library but the librar-ian and Tigers working on the video. The library is guarded by a one-armed Tiger. He does not respond to my query as to how he lost his arm, but he lets us into the library without comment.

Rosa cheekily tells the librarian that we have come because I want a copy of last week's *Sunday Observer.* Curious villagers stare over the wall, and an old man tells Rosa in a hushed voice the current agenda for the production. The atmosphere of mystery and anticipation is tangible all through the village. It is therefore somewhat disappointing to learn an hour or so later that the video simulation of the massacre is not going to happen today. Consolation is offered in the form of a street theater per-formance to be staged by the Tigers in a nearby temple tonight at seven. That performance will be videotaped.

Young women gather in a corner of the courtyard and joke about romances with Tigers, ice-cream vendors, and STF guards. They are going to give me in marriage to the ice-cream vendor; Rosa has confiscated my photograph of an STF guard because she says she is in love with him. Saroja is in love with one Tiger boy to whom she is allowed to write one letter a year; he doesn't write back, but their marriage is certain, Saroja says. The group dissolves into uncontrollable laughter. Such group laughing fits happen often in this household, I've discovered. I keep getting the giggles myself. It is strange in this grim environment, where almost every day we hear of another death. As we are talking and laughing like this, a beggar appears at the gate. He is old and scrawny, his beard and hair are long, and he's wearing only a loincloth and carrying a staff. He looks like a holy mendicant. Vasanta tells me he had three sons who joined the Tigers, and all three died. One was a Black Tiger whose bodysuit exploded unexpectedly; two were sent north into combat, where they were killed. Their bodies were never recovered. After that, the father chose to live as a beggar.

We who are laughing are not immune to such losses. And the jokes about love do not come from hearts innocent of this sentiment. Rosa has suffered physical harm at the hands of the army and has also lost brothers. She has confided in me that she once was in love with a Tiger boy. Her family did not know, she says. He was captured by the army, who decapitated him, stuck his head on a stake by the roadside, and tossed his body into the field across from the house. One day Saroja, a solemn, thin young woman, will be walking down the road with me and will ask me with no hint of a smile, "Do you love the Tigers [*iyakkam virumbukiṟīṉgalā*]?" "What do you mean?" I will answer warily. Then Saroja will tell me that she has had correspondences with several Tiger boys, all of whom were killed in combat. Now, whenever she hears of any Tiger dying, she mourns, she will tell me.

It is 10:30 — right in the middle of *The X-Files* — when word finally comes that the Tiger performance is about to begin. This week's *X-Files* is about a town full of babies born with tails, all fathered by an alien morph. I have been explaining the plot to Selvi (aged twenty-two), who has earnestly commented, "This is a good show, Auntie." But she and I turn off the TV and set out to find the Tiger production. Vasanta's elderly mother decides also to come, although she has been sick. The three of us make our way down the village pathways on this moonless night. On the army-controlled side of the lagoon, we could be shot for breaking curfew. But there is no curfew here, and I recall Vasanta's comment of weeks ago to the effect that on this side of the lagoon people can go out at night without fear.

None of us, least of all me, is sure where the show will be held. After several wrong turns, we find it. Two or three hundred villagers are gathered in the middle of what seems like a small pasture. Floodlights illuminate a space in the middle. A Tiger boy wearing an ammunition jacket stands motionless behind the microphone while a video camera is adjusted and his picture appears on two of the four video monitors that are set up in a line before the crowd. Another video camera pans the crowd so that different people's faces appear on one of the other monitors and the audience can see themselves. Satyan is up front, facing the four monitors and manipulating the images from a keyboard. If he is testing the equipment, I wish he had done it before the performance, at least before eleven at night. But even as I think these thoughts, I know that this is part of the performance: Satyan is showing the villagers his technical wizardry. After an hour or so of this play, he comes to the microphone and asks those onlookers who are hidden in the darkness to come into the light. It would be easy for a helicopter flying over this field to drop a few bombs on this illuminated spot; but since the Tigers acquired antiaircraft artillery a couple of years ago, aerial attacks on Tamil villages have diminished. Or at least I find the rumor comforting. The air force hasn't bombed this particular village since I came here ten weeks ago, although they did bomb it a month before that.

The show begins with a drum riff. As far as I can tell, it follows the traditional style of Tamil street theater. The actors are all men: Vasanta thinks that they are all Tigers from one of the nearby villages, but a Tiger tells me later that they are civilians. Each actor plays the role of some famous political person or type. There is Chandrika, the president of Sri Lanka; Ratwatte, the deputy defense minister; Kadirgamar, the foreign minister; some other generals and politicians; Sinhalese soldiers; and Tigers and thugs. They are all dressed for their parts, and each character introduces himself separately and sings out his story in a loud, hoarse voice. The show is a comedy, called *Niccaya Tōlvi* (Certain Defeat) in parody of the army's ongoing northern advance, Jayasikurui (Certain Victory), in which many hundreds of combatants have been killed, including some Tigers from this village. Some of the villains are comic — Ratwatte with his limp and his white floppy hat, trailing his niece, the president, like a male dog trailing a female in heat, and the nervous, cocky thugs with red kerchiefs around their heads, filling the air with cigarette smoke as they puff away like steam engines. The Tigers are running an antismoking campaign, and for the children the sight of public cigarette smoking in Tiger territory is more outrageous than the sound of gunfire. The actors who parody the smoking thugs are rewarded by the unrestrained laughter of the children.

One of the villains grabs a child out of the audience and tosses him gently around; again the crowd breaks into wild laughter, and it seems as though the fragile boundary between actors and audience — so far well respected — will simply dissolve. But it doesn't. The child does not seem to be bothered. The faces of some of the actors roughly resemble those of the characters they play. The Tigers are portrayed as skillful, sober, and committed. They introduce themselves with their own song: "We suffer. . . . We have no home, no lives of our own [*tuḍikkirōm, emakku vīḍum illai vāṟvum illai*]."

The characters dance. Kadirgamar and the government ministers dance like puppets on a string. I don't know whether this impression is intentional, but it could be. The Tigers engage in a combat dance with the army. They are all carrying what look like real rifles. The dance is accompanied by fast drumbeats that sound like automatic rifle fire.

Vasanta's mother asks me if I can understand what is being said and identifies some of the characters for me: that is Rohan Daluwatte (the Sinhala brigadier in charge of Jaffna), that is Sivasittampalam (a Tamil politician). She is more than seventy years of age, yet she is so interested in guerrilla street theater that she will leave her sickbed, walk miles through the dark, brave swarms of bloodthirsty mosquitoes, and stay up until 2:30 in the morning to see the show to the end. Vasanta has not come. She will not support the Tigers. She will not forgive them for taking her mother hostage.[2] But the old woman herself is for some reason more forgiving.

At the end of the show, the (actors playing) Tigers are shown being joined by (actors playing) common people. The latter are represented by two uniformed schoolboys, one small and one big, an aged and bent woman in a sari, and a man who seems to play the role of a household head. This scenario of unity is reinforced by the videotaping of crowd and actors mingling under the same floodlights.

Independence Day Circus with Clowns

THE GOLDEN JUBILEE CELEBRATION

Late January. The fiftieth anniversary, or Golden Jubilee, of Sri Lankan independence from British rule is coming up on 4 February 1998. The president is planning to honor it with a grand public celebration. The deputy defense minister has sworn that the LTTE will be defeated before that day. Meanwhile, Jayasikurui, the protracted military operation, is being waged in the north. This operation and the Golden Jubilee are intimately intertwined spectacles, both designed to impress the Sri Lankan populace with the glory and might of Chandrika's government. The government is intent on making both spectacles a success; the Tigers are equally intent on ruining them.

The Golden Jubilee celebration is to be held in the beautiful mountain city of Kandy, site of the Dalada Maligawa, the Temple of the Tooth. According to Sinhala Buddhist legend, whoever holds the tooth of the Buddha rules the island by divine right. Will the Tigers try to steal it? The deputy defense minister, Anuruddha Ratwatte, a native of Kandy, has sworn that no matter what the Tigers do, the celebration will proceed as planned.

Prince Charles will be the guest of honor. He has come and brought with him twenty-four horses, at a cost of two million rupees each, one villager reports. Another says he has brought only a car. Both newspapers and villagers have commented that it is inappropriate for Prince Charles to be the guest of honor at an event celebrating fifty years of independence from the British. But from another point of view it is supremely appropriate, for the Sri Lankan ruling class remains proudly British in its demeanor, and the celebration is intended not so much to celebrate freedom from the British as to demonstrate that Sri Lanka is thoroughly successful, modern, and civilized.

Meanwhile, however, other Sri Lankans remain in love with Princess Diana, if one is to judge by the many Princess Di T-shirts one sees. There are no Prince Charles T-shirts. At least one beloved puppy in this village is named after Diana, but we have yet to discover a creature named after Charles. If you love Di, you cannot love Charles. The *Dinamurasu* serial *Nights Dissolved in Tears,* about the life of Diana, is a great success among Tamils.[3] Both Rosa and Accan follow it and know all the details about her life and how she was misused by Charles. The same paper carries a serial about the brilliant exploits of the Tigers, which is popular among Colombo Tamils. But the Tigers themselves like the Di series better. They think the newspaper is exploiting their charisma for its own profit. They don't seem to mind that the paper is doing the same thing with Di.

Is the Diana cult in Sri Lanka a trivial thing to write about? In itself, yes. But it may be a sign of something more important, the rejection of elitism.

On Sunday, 25 January, news comes through the village grapevine that a Tiger deserter has been captured. He had left his group of Black Tigers, based in Paduvankarai, and run off with an already married village girl to Amparai District. His captors will take him to the prison camp in Colombo, which is bad, because there they torture people by pulling out their fingernails, Rosa tells me. Except for the last sentence, this news was supposedly reported on the radio. I check with Sita, and she says a Black Tiger would never do such a thing. I still haven't asked her about the murder of Jeyakuddi.

THE BOMBING OF THE TEMPLE IN KANDY

On the same day, a bomb explodes in Kandy, and the first reports say that eight or nine people have been killed. I learn this first from Vasanta — she says five *bhikku*s were killed. Then the news is reported on Rupavahini TV, in Tamil. Babies are screaming, and I can't follow it all. Chittu (a neighbor who often drops in) reports that no *bhikku*s were killed, but one was injured, and several LTTE were killed. He says that earlier the report was eight killed; now it is nine, with twenty-odd injured. He reports that Chandrika will hide the truth to prevent anti-Tamil riots, and in this respect she has acted wisely. I will have to wait for the ten o'clock English-language news to hear the report for myself.

Rosa and Chittu argue over whether there will ever be peace. Rosa thinks the war will go on indefinitely; Chittu thinks there will be peace in Sri Lanka "in our time." He tells me he prays to God for the war to end, and he has faith that God will bring peace. Somehow a way will be found. Neither side can win, he says, so the two sides must talk together. They do not understand one another. Both are bad (*mōsam*).

Extensive newspaper reports about the bombing appear in the papers the following week. Five people, presumably Tigers, drove a small truck to the Temple of the Tooth and detonated a bomb. Part of the temple was damaged, and nineteen people were killed (including the five bombers), but, "miraculously," the tooth of the Buddha remained intact and unharmed. Now the question is whether the Golden Jubilee will still be held in Kandy.

I ask Vasanta if she thinks the Tigers did it. She thinks they definitely did, just to prove they could. She points out how difficult it would have been to get past all the guards at the shrine. We discuss what a big deal has been made of the damage to the temple, yet scarcely a thing has been said about the people who were killed. What is more important, a building or human lives?

On 28 January, I am in a town on the army-controlled side, visiting relatives of people in Paduvankarai. We watch the news in Tamil on the TV. It is hard to follow it all, but it seems as though the government is pledging to crack down on the LTTE after the bombing. Some family members seem worried. I offer my opinion that this is just talk, not really news. The father says they will not succeed. Later I learn that Chandrika has banned the LTTE, and this is what the news report was about.

We read newspaper reports of attacks on two mobile army camps in Batticaloa District last week. About six or eight army people were killed and twenty-odd injured. The newspaper reports that the attacking Tigers included women and the "baby brigade" (what the government calls child combatants in the LTTE). A friend reports the news (from the radio or paper or somewhere) that there was also an attack in Valaichenai, not far from Paduvankarai.

On Friday, 30 January, I am back in Paduvankarai, visiting with Sita and Alagar, when Kuddi, the Tiger physician, stops by. With no provocation, he says to me that all Americans are bad people (*kūḍāta āḷ*) because the American president labels the LTTE as terrorists, and the American people voted this president into power.

I ignore this and ask him whether the Tigers were responsible for the bombing in Kandy. He looks at me and shrugs, with an I-don't-know expression on his face. I guess if there were an official Tiger answer, yes or no, he would give it. So I say, "They won't say they did it, and they won't say they didn't do it." He laughs. I mention reports of an LTTE attack on an army camp in Valaichenai last week and ask if this is why all the Tigers were gone from the village at that time. Sita and Alagar, hearing this, exchange knowing smiles, and Kuddi says yes. He reads me the article in the Tamil daily *Vīrakēsari* about the attack. I ask him if it is more or less correct, and he says yes, then clarifies some of the details for me. When I ask him if anything happened to any of "our" people in the attack, he says only one was killed. Someone he knew? Without looking up from the newspaper, he says yes.

I say there appears to have been a 30 percent turnout for the Jaffna elections (held on Thursday, 29 January). Kuddi says 29 percent and recites the figures from the various municipalities in Jaffna District. I mention reports that the Tigers attacked the EPRLF headquarters in Jaffna and killed some of its cadres. EPDP, Kuddi corrects me. Which party finally got the most votes in the elections? I ask. Kuddi responds that none of the parties got many votes. Only a few thousand people voted.

I say Ratwatte resigned, and he says that was all false. I tell him I believed it at first. For a while we discuss Ratwatte's habit of making grand promises and then failing to live up to them, like the several previous deadlines and the most recent (4 February) deadline for completing Operation Jayasikurui, and his claim right after the bombing in Kandy that the independence celebrations would on no account be moved. Chandrika has moved the celebrations to Colombo, despite her uncle's vow.

I ask Kuddi whether he thinks Chandrika's banning of the LTTE will have any significant effect, and he says no, none at all. And I observe that moving the independence celebrations to Colombo is a small victory for us. He says it is a great victory.

He adds that the Indian courts say the LTTE killed Rajiv Gandhi.

HOW PEOPLE RESPOND TO BOMBINGS

Sunday, 1 February. Daya Mohan says he has a letter for me from Gamani, who is scolding me for not answering his letters. So in the late afternoon I go in search of Daya Mohan to fetch the letter. I first visit the office at Kokkadichcholai where Inbam used to preside, and where Daya Mohan also stayed, but now a new Tiger leader is there with a forbidding expression and an artificial leg. He says they have all moved to Ambilanthurai. So I go to Alagar's house and recruit Koyila to show me the way to the new base. Two armed Tigers show up and politely take away a motorcycle that is sitting in front of the house, despite the protests of Sita, Koyila, and their mother that the bike is out of petrol. An armed boy I haven't seen before, who looks to be in his teens, has also come to the house. He is quite tall and well built, but he has a voice like a girl.

Koyila changes her clothes, and we strike out on bikes for Ambilan-thurai. On the way to the base she tells me that four civilians from Kokkadichcholai were captured by the army at Manmunai (where I usually cross on the ferry) and taken to Colombo as suspects in the Kandy bombing incident. She says the truck used in the bombing came from here, and the army believes these civilians were involved with it somehow. At the base we meet Accan, who says that about twelve civilians were arrested, not only at Manmunai but at all the different crossings, including the one here at Ambilanthurai and the one at Kaluvancikudi.

When I get back to Vasanta's house, it is past six, and people are watching the news on TV, including the old farmer who always comes to watch the news. I tell them about the reports of civilian arrests, and he looks worried; I have never seen him worried before. The news shows a crowd of placard-bearing Sinhalese burning a figure in effigy. We assume that this figure must be Prabhakaran, but later I learn it is Ratwatte. They are angry because he failed to protect the temple in Kandy from being bombed. I comment to the old farmer, "They can burn any straw man they like; as long as they don't harm any real people, what does it matter to us?" And the old farmer smiles.

A few days later, Vasanta tells me, the old farmer confirmed that four people had been arrested (but not for the reason Koyila had told me). One was an agricultural laborer who had gone across the lagoon to sell rice. When he returned with the cash, he was stopped at the checkpoint because it was assumed he was taking the cash to the LTTE. TELO took his money, and he was sent to jail in Colombo.

"And a Tamil person did this. It is a terrible thing to be born Tamil," says

Vasanta. These people were arrested two or three days ago — people coming back from selling the rice from the good harvest, celebrating their good fortune and their hard work. Now anyone who can be shown to have "helped" the LTTE by giving them money, even unwillingly, even perhaps at gunpoint, will be in violation of the law. It will be easier for the STF to arrest people on suspicion of helping the LTTE if those people come back to their homes in LTTE territory with money in their hands.

I visit the women's base after the battles at Paranthan and Kilinochchi (2 February), where hundreds of Tigers have been reported killed. The Tigers undertook a big campaign to take back the army base at Kilinochchi, on the northern end of the A9 road. The outcome of the recent battle is unclear. Some girls at the base have come down from that area. The tone of our conversation is subdued, patient. The girls' honesty about their loss surprises me. Rumors are circulating that the Tigers have captured the army base and raised the flag there, but one of the girls says that only a small part of the Kilinochchi military complex has been captured. The rest remains in army hands.

4 February. Last night after midnight, on the eve of Independence Day, the electricity went off. This is the first power cut we have had since I've been here. We assume it is a deliberate attempt to disrupt the Tiger area to forestall acts of violence on Independence Day. When Vasanta came back from Batticaloa yesterday, she said things were tense there.

From 8:30 A.M. today we hear a series of loud but distant explosions from the east. Little Mohan hears the noise, and his grandmother tells him, "Bombs are exploding [*guṇḍu veḍikkutu*]!" Mohan repeats the words.

Vasanta says the sounds are coming from the direction of the airport, or maybe from an attack on the army camp near the airport. In a few hours we will hear what happened. Maybe my judgment is right to stay in Kokkadichcholai for Independence Day. The explosions are frequent at first, then taper off, but they continue intermittently through the morning. Vasanta tells me that last night the LTTE went to the town of Kannankuda, near the airport, and made preparations to attack the airport. Seeing the LTTE, the residents all fled over to this side at night. The Independence Day celebrations were scheduled to begin at 8:30. To spoil them, the LTTE fired mortars at the airport, beginning at exactly 8:30. The army responded by firing back, presumably at the town of Kannankuda. However, because the people left the town at night, the army didn't know they had gone. Vasanta says the airport is about three miles as the crow flies from here. Nothing much changed when we first heard the explosions, and nothing has changed now. Vasanta has made me a second cup of coffee.

The only person who says she is afraid is Vasanta's mother, but even she continues her morning chores; I can hear her scraping coconut as I have my morning bath by the well. When the army retaliates against civilian centers in response to LTTE attacks, they don't do it right away but wait a few days, Vasanta says. We'll see what happens.

In the afternoon we hear that two civilians have been wounded, perhaps killed, and likewise two army soldiers. We don't know how many Tigers. We don't know the extent of destruction to buildings and property. They say that the power cut is caused by transformers being bombed in Vantharumulai. Accan visits the house and speaks with Rosa for a long time, but when I ask him about the explosions, he says he doesn't know. Later I ask Vasanta why he didn't give us any information, and Vasanta says Tigers are proud; we have to get the news from other sources. Rosa says Accan still suspects me of being CID (a government spy) and wants to know if I like him.

On the Thursday after Independence Day I visit the Muslim town of Kattankudi, just south of Batticaloa, on the army-controlled side. The electricity is still out there and in town as well as in those few parts of Paduvankarai that have working electrical wires, and all areas south from Vantharumulai for I don't know how far. I am in Kattankudi (ironically, I guess) to get an electrical adapter for my tape recorder. Rosa and Saroja are with me. This time, when people ask Rosa where she's from, she says Kalladi (a suburb of Batticaloa on the army-controlled side) rather than Kokkadichcholai (known as a Tiger area). The two of them are tense as they walk through the streets. Rosa says that if there is trouble, the Muslims will rape us and kill us. (The two young women lie about which town they come from, but they make no effort to conceal the fact that they are non-Muslim Tamils.) Rosa is nevertheless her usual friendly and smiling self, talking to the vegetable vendor and sympathizing with him about the high price of vegetables. And she and Vasanta do most of their shopping in Kattankudi. Rosa has come to a hospital here because she says it is better than the ones in Batticaloa. One nurse at the hospital is a non-Muslim Tamil whom Rosa somehow knows. The nurse takes us off to the empty maternity ward and brings us soda, and she and Rosa talk for a long time.

The man at the electrical supply shop says that yesterday on Independence Day the roads going into Kattankudi were closed. No one could get out, so they all went home. And of course the absence of electricity was also a problem.

In Batticaloa the next day, Friday, I ask Father John how Independence Day was, and he says it was funereal. Everyone was even more afraid than usual to leave their houses. A few shells fell in the residential neighborhood around St. Michael's, a big, old Catholic school in the middle of town where Father John works. I ask him which side fired them, and he says the LTTE. About twenty people were injured in the shelling. He was not aware of any deaths.

A couple of weeks later I read in one newspaper that the Tigers have denied responsibility for the Kandy bombing. The article quotes the statement of the official LTTE publication *Viḍutalai Pulikaḷ* in full. Still, most of the news media report the bombing of the Temple of the Tooth as though it were established fact that the LTTE did it. And who will ever know for sure? And if anyone does know, how will they prove it, and who will listen?

Who Killed Rajiv?

Early February. I am visiting Sita's house, and several children are there. Sita motions toward one quiet young girl and says, "This girl's older brother is in jail in India for being involved in the killing of Rajiv Gandhi. He was not involved, but he is in jail." I tell her I know that twenty-six people have been sentenced to be hanged because of their involvement in Rajiv's assassination; I thought the other suspects would have been released.

Meanwhile, Alagar and Sita are preparing to take Vithusa to the temple in Palugamam, and soon they depart. Koyila tells me that four Tigers have died in battle in a town on the army-controlled side, and their funeral will be today. The bodies will be taken around this afternoon.

The next morning, Saturday, I bring a copy of the English-language Indian newsmagazine *Frontline* that carries the story of the sentencing and conviction of the twenty-six people involved in the assassination of Rajiv Gandhi.[4] It includes the names and pictures of all those convicted. Several of the convicted appear to have been only peripherally involved and unaware that they were assisting assassins.

I ask Sita, "What is the name of the girl's brother who was jailed?"

She thinks for a minute and says, "Shankar." I show her the magazine. One of the people convicted is named Shankar, and his picture is there. "Is it him?" I ask.

She studies the magazine and the picture and says, "Yes."

According to the magazine, Shankar was one of the leaders of the group who planned and carried out the assassination, the most important person still alive and in captivity. The other leaders and planners either killed themselves or were never captured.

The magazine is passed around, and Sita shares the news with others there. Sixteen of those condemned to death are Sri Lankans, and ten are Indians, she says. The important ones committed suicide, she says.

I say, "I thought you would have known this already." But it is clear from what she tells the others that she already knew about the sentencing.

She and others leaf through the magazine and ask about various pictures: Who are the women with their faces hidden, being escorted by women police, on page 5? Who is the man whose picture is below theirs? Why have casts been made of three people's heads, shown on page 14? I read the captions and answer the questions. Seventeen-year-old Anjala, a Tiger girl, comments, in apparent mild surprise, on the picture on the cover, "That is *tambi* [little brother]." She means Prabhakaran.

Someone else asks whose picture appears next to Prabhakaran's on page 9, and Sita says, "Pottu Amman" (a famous Tiger leader). Someone else says, "He has grown thin." And they move on to other stories and other pictures. We look at a picture of Bill Clinton being embraced by Monica Lewinsky.

"That's the American president," I say.

"Bill Clinton," says Sita.

The magazine is in Rudrakumaran's hands now. "Is this ganja?" he asks of one picture. "No, cotton," I say. "The cotton crop failed, and fifty-five farmers committed suicide."

"Why would they commit suicide?" someone asks.

"Because the crop failed and they were so badly in debt," I say.

"Would farmers commit suicide?" another Tiger queries skeptically.

"Because of the debt," says Alagar.

"Who is this a picture of?" asks Sita.

"That is a photo of one of the farmers who killed himself, and that is his wife and these are his children," I say. They move on through the magazine.

"There's Bush," says Rudrakumaran.

"That's Saddam Hussein!" I say.

"I know," says Rudrakumaran. "Just kidding."

Who Killed Chinnavan?

Friday, 20 February. I am back in Vasanta's house after having spent ten days in Colombo and on the road. I left for Colombo ten days ago, on the full moon. When I got back to Batticaloa, I took a three-wheeler to Manmunai and had to go to the STF camp near the ferry checkpoint to get permission to take the taxi all the way to the checkpoint, because I couldn't carry my five bags from the place where it would normally drop me off. Walking back from the camp, I passed a house where I heard women weeping and singing laments, and I asked a couple of little boys who were nearby if this was a death house. They said yes, the TELO man Chinnavan had been killed by the LTTE. When? The day before yesterday. Where? Here? No. They indicated a place down the road somewhere and I said, "*Pāvam*," and they said, "*Pāvam tān*" — these words that have become like a litany.

At Vasanta's house, while washing the heat and dirt of the fifteen-hour journey off my body, I mentioned the killing of the TELO boy to her. She said, with a smile that could mean anything, "You know!" and asked me how I knew. She told me I knew this boy — he had asked me to take him with me to New Zealand — and then added, with mild reproach, "But you wouldn't remember." (I was reminded of a time when an old lady in a nearby house died. Vasanta said the old lady had asked me to stay for dinner and I, according to Vasanta, had declined and replied, "Another day." Then she had died.) And Vasanta told me that it is sad when people we know die, but there is nothing we can do about it.

At Rosa's in-laws' house the next day, Saturday, Rosa and I are resting, lying down in a side room. I ask Rosa if she knows about the TELO boy who was killed. She tells me that Chinnavan was married and had two small children, which makes his death more the pity. "*Pāvam tānē?*" Then she tells me that Chinnavan, with the help of the army, abducted his wife and forced her to marry him. The girl's mother went weeping to them to give her back, but to no avail, and eventually the girl became resigned to her fate. There are many kinds of marriage in this area, says Rosa; that is one kind, and she tells me it is common among TELO boys. She knows one girl who was forced into marriage this way. I ask if the LTTE does the same, and she says no, but they do get involved in romances with girls. (Rosa uses the term "make love" [*paṇṇu*], but it doesn't mean "make love" as in "copulate": it means fall in love with someone and court them in person and through exchanges of letters.) Almost all the LTTE — except Geethan and Daya Mohan — are involved in romances, she says. Some have one love in Jaffna and another back home. But she says 90 percent of courtships in this region end in marriage. Ninety percent of the boys — whether LTTE or civilian — live up to their promises to the girls and do not deceive them.

At Vithusa's birthday party, in conversation with Sudha, I mention the killing of Chinnavan. He seems mildly impressed that I know about this.

Sundar asks, "What killing?"

And Sudha says, "Where were you?"

I say, "It is said that he had two children and that he abducted his wife and that he was with TELO."

"PLOTE," says Sudha, correcting me. But the rest of what I say about Chinnavan is true.

"I killed him!" says Rudrakumaran.

"No you didn't," I answer.

"They say the killing was done by a small boy, and a brave one."

Sudha and Rudrakumaran glance at each other. On 26 February, Rosa tells me that another TELO boy has been killed by the LTTE. She gives me his name, his physical description, the number of his children, and their ages, and she tells me where this boy was generally posted. She saw him just a few days ago. The young LTTE boy who shot Chinnavan was also wounded — shot in the stomach — in the shoot-out with TELO. Vasanta comments that this LTTE boy is clever, and that the villagers are happy about this particular killing because the dead boy harassed them. The LTTE think that if they can get rid of TELO, PLOTE, and the other rival groups, it will be easy to attack the army, because it is their rivals who identify LTTE members to the army. The army base is well protected, with a TELO camp on one side and an STF camp on the other. It is interesting to me that gregarious villagers like Rosa are personally acquainted with the paramilitary Tamils that the LTTE picks off. These are not anonymous enemies: they have names, faces, families.

When I see Alagar, I ask him about the killing of Chinnavan and repeat to him what civilians have told me, that the killer was a young boy and a clever one. I do not think, under the circumstances, it was wrong for the Tigers to kill Chinnavan. I express my concern over the news that the boy who killed him was wounded in the stomach in the recent raid against TELO. But Alagar says that the civilians have just made all this up. There was no young boy, there was no wound in the stomach. Some time after that, at Vasanta's house, Rosa points to a boy walking down the road in front of the house and tells me it was that very boy who was wounded in the stomach. Now he has healed.

A month or so later, at Alagar's house, Daya Mohan says the LTTE did not kill Chinnavan at all. Chinnavan was a favorite of the army, and he was killed by a rival out of jealousy. The rumor that the LTTE killed him has been propagated by those who want the movement to be seen as terrorist. Later, Rosa tells me Daya Mohan was lying. The Tigers lie and deceive the people, she says. Which of them am I to believe? How am I to check facts?

Later, when I ask Karan, a former Tiger who now works for the STF, about this, Karan says that the LTTE killed Chinnavan, but really they were after him (Karan) and killed Chinnavan by mistake.

The Newspapers

20 February. Vasanta also reports that while I was gone, the LTTE killed eight home guards in Amparai District, wounded twenty others, and took one captive. She predicts that this news will be on TV, and it is, except for the report about the one captive.

More than once, I have been told to expect a newspaper or TV report of an event I first heard of by word of mouth. It does not always come. For instance, Rosa promised me that the murder of Jeyakuddi would be in the Tamil press, but, despite our diligent searching, we never read a word about his death, although Tiger funerals are public events and Tiger deaths are often reported. Sometimes the Tamil press reports local events in remarkable detail, and I have come to rely on the Tamil papers to confirm or discredit rumors. Certainly newspaper and television reports do not always get the facts correct; but never before, as an anthropologist working in small villages among ordinary people, have I noticed the media reporting on events so close to home. In India, I found that people are affected by the media, but generally not vice versa. Here on this small island, despite government censorship on reporting of events in the conflict zone, there is a close connection between local events and those significant enough to be reported on the media nationally or even internationally.

THE EXECUTION OF BAGEERATHAN

Monday, 23 February. When I come back from Vithusa's birthday party to Vasanta's house early in the evening, Rosa greets me with several items of news — some from media reports, some from village talk. A civilian boy from Kannankuda, named Bageerathan, has been executed by two female Tigers for informing on the LTTE. He was shot at a public junction, and the village people were summoned to watch. His body was left in the sun afterward, and his relatives were not allowed to take it away. The next day, Vasanta says that when his body was finally given over, it was so rotten you could scoop the flesh away with your hands. Rosa says that before being shot, he was tortured by being dragged behind a tractor. He was in love with a female lawyer who lived near here (in Munaikkaadu) but is now studying in Colombo. He was the only son and sole support of his family. He had been taken by the Tigers and kept in their camp and interrogated for eight months. He was said to have "spoken with" the army (or TELO or PLOTE or somebody).

Both Rosa and Vasanta are upset about this event: it is different from the killing of Chinnavan. The villagers all said that Bageerathan was a nice boy, not the kind who would act in an evil way. The temple elders went to the Tigers and asked for his life to be spared. They argued that as a punishment he could be barred from going to Batticaloa; he didn't have to be killed. But the Tigers would not listen.

Vasanta asks why he had to be kept for eight months and then shot in public. Why couldn't he have been killed in the Tiger camp, if they had to kill him? She says both the Tigers and the army interrogate people, and those people out of fear confess to things they didn't do, and then they are killed. These are Tamils killing Tamils, she says, and she echoes Rosa's words of the night before: TELO kills Tamils, and the STF kills Tamils, and the EPRLF kills Tamils, and the army kills Tamils; the Tigers kill TELO and the STF and other Tigers and Tamil civilians. Rosa asked me, "Is there a curse on this country?" It is *pāvam* to be born Tamil, she says. Vasanta says that in my country, people are free, but here they are not. But, she says, an action like this will turn the people against the LTTE. They will not say anything — they can't — but in their hearts they will nurture resentment. Rosa said last night that she wants to cry out in sorrow.

Vasanta asks me if I don't also grieve over this news. I say yes, but I want to know why the Tigers did this. They must have had some strong reason to conduct a savage public execution like this. But Vasanta says sometimes they take scant evidence and magnify it; there is no regular trial, as there is in the West. A Tiger CID (i.e., spy) will report to them that I have been talking to the STF guards in Manmunai. Two more, sent to check, confirm the accusation; then four more will say the same thing, and, on the basis of what their spies say, the Tigers will convict the person. The boy who was recently killed had a brother-in-law who had been in the EPRLF but was no longer a member, though he still had an EPRLF identity card. Maybe the boy went to EPRLF headquarters to make phone calls to his girlfriend, and maybe what he said over the phone was reported back to the Tigers. The Tigers could at least have given a reason, she says. I offer to go to Alagar's and ask for an explanation. She says I should tell them I heard the news (but not from her) and ask them why it was done.

I have talked to Alagar about the villagers' distress at the execution. He says he is not aware that Bageerathan was killed. When I relay this information to Vasanta, she says that Alagar would have known. Alagar is an important Tiger, she says, so he would have been in the group that made the shared decision to kill Bageerathan.

Satyan comes to Vasanta's house during this time and asks me if I think the LTTE is *nalam* (good) or *mōsam* (bad). I say for the most part I think they are *nalam,* but there are some things they do that I can't say I like. He says they do things for reasons — sometimes people don't understand the reasons, and so they disapprove. I reply that they should tell people the reasons they do things, so people will understand and not be upset. It sounds condescending, as though I am talking to a child. But viewing Tigers as children helps keep me from fearing them.

Later, I visit Alagar and ask him if the Tigers would ever kill me, if I made an accidental mistake or something. Alagar assures me that I would have to do something very evil for the Tigers to consider killing me. I tell him that some of the civilians are upset about the killing of Bageerathan. Alagar says there were seven things Bageerathan did wrong. I ask what they were. Alagar lists some but cannot remember the rest.

An account of the execution is in the 9 March *Dinamurasu.* Rosa takes me to the library to show me. The article repeats what Rosa told me, though it does not mention the dragging behind the tractor. Bageerathan was shot by two female Tigers. When the people asked why, the LTTE listed seven things he had done wrong. These are not listed in *Dinamurasu,* but one of them was giving information to TELO. The article says the family are "unsatisfied" with the execution and have written appealing to higher authorities in the LTTE.

The only small grace about the event, and it is not a saving grace, is that the public discussion of it indicates the degree to which common civilians feel able to criticize the movement, more or less in private.

MORE NEWS

Thursday, 26 February. Rosa tells me that war between America and Iraq has commenced. It takes me a while to learn that America almost fired on Iraq but didn't.

The other news of yesterday evening was that a bomb exploded in Batticaloa, but no one was hurt. This news came by word of mouth. The radio and TV report that a Tiger boy involved in the Kandy bombing was captured by the army (the TV reports say he came from Trincomalee, but Rosa says he came from here). The BBC and local TV (Rupavahini) also report that the Sea Tigers sank two big navy ships outside Trincomalee harbor, killing over fifty navy personnel. Eight Tiger boats were also sunk. I did not hear the broadcasts about the sinking of the boats and am looking for today's newspapers to get more news.

5 March. I am in Colombo when a bomb explodes around noon at Maradana Junction in the middle of the city, and more than thirty people are killed. In the lodge in Colombo where I am staying, we can hear the explosion. In later news, we are told that a Tiger driving a bus full of explosives had been detained at the junction, and the bus exploded there, rather than at the intended destination, wherever that was.

The following week, when I visit Alagar's house, we speak about this incident. It seems clear that the Tigers were in fact responsible. I don't want to believe that Alagar and his family would do such a terrible thing. I want it to be some other people, not them. I want Alagar to have opposed the execution of Bageerathan, too. But even if he had done so, he would never tell me; nobody would ever tell me. It is a matter of solidarity, a matter of pride.

Back at Vasanta's house, Rosa brings me the news as I bathe that a farming tractor tripped a land mine in Eravur, and several police as well as several civilians were killed. The man who was driving the tractor gave some excuse and ran away before it blew up. Also in Trincomalee District, the Tigers attacked a police station. Rosa says 170 people from around Mahiladithivu who had gone there as agricultural laborers have been arrested as a consequence; whole families have been arrested, including a family she knows. She says she gets her information from Chittu, who gets his info from a radio station called Veritas that broadcasts from abroad (the Philippines).

There was a brief report about the Eravur events on Rupavahini news. The English-language report says it has not been determined whether the tractor hit a land mine or whether it had a bomb inside it.

Nobody on either side even questions that the bus that exploded in Maradana came from this region. Instead they affirm it. Why? This was a far worse thing than the bomb explosion at Kandy last month.

A Sports Contest and a Firefight

Wednesday, 11 March. There was a school sports contest today (*vilaiyāḍ-ḍuppōḍḍi*) in Arasadithivu, a village near Kokkadichcholai. About three hundred students between the ages of six and eighteen participated in the contest, viewed by a casual audience of about equal size. The audience included civilians and Tiger boys who had come on their motorcycles, bearing arms. The kids were divided into three teams (houses — *illam*) called Chera, Chola, and Pandyan, after the three great medieval Tamil kingdoms. The colors of the three sports teams were blue, yellow, and green, respectively. Each team had built a hut for the occasion, posting its flag, its colors, and a sign in front. In front of the Chera team's hut was a tree decorated with empty eggshells dyed bright yellow; the hut had a thatched roof with yellow straw, which Rosa said Satyan had made. Other Tigers I knew supported the Pandyans. The Pandyan team's sign bore a mosaic (made out of leaves, vegetables, and fruit) in the shape of a fish, with the name *Pandyan* written on it. I photographed this painstakingly crafted sign, with the proud civilian artist standing next to it, and the Tigers videotaped me taking photographs.

I had thought that all the Tigers might support the Cholas, the team named after the kingdom with the tiger emblem.[5] Some historians say that Tigers are inspired by and identify with the great Chola kings of medieval South India. But at the sports meet in Arasadithivu, that was not how it worked. All three teams were equal.

The kids gathered at the huts of their respective teams. The Tiger flag was raised, then the school flag, then the flag of each of the three houses simultaneously — five flags altogether — with the Tiger flag largest and raised the highest. The officials, judges, and prize givers included both Tigers and civilians. The announcer shared a tent with local VIPs, including school principals and Tiger officials. A marching band from each team, dressed in team colors, marched around the playing field to orders shouted by a leader in English: "Left, right, left, right." The kids were careful to keep in step. The contests included foot races and jumping events for the older kids and a balloon-blowing contest and candy race for the under-sevens. In the balloon-blowing contest, the idea was to see which child could pop his or her balloon first, but most of the little children did not blow their balloons to the point of popping them. Toward the end of the afternoon the crowd had thinned out, but some events continued. A hat-passing game was going on: whoever was left wearing the hat when the music stopped was out. The participants were middle-aged men, and young men in the audience were laughing at them. The Tiger video team videotaped everything. A vendor sold popsicles.

Also on Wednesday, 11 March, a group of Tigers from that same village of Arasadithivu went to attack an army base north of Batticaloa. They killed three soldiers, but, as they were leaving with the weapons they had taken, they were ambushed, and a Tiger boy named Kanthappan was shot dead.

We civilians did not learn about the attack on the army camp until the next day. Both the attack and the school sports contest were organized and carried out by Tigers from Arasadithivu on the same day at the same time. There could not have been more than fifty Tigers — probably more like twenty — based in the village of Arasadithivu proper. Those involved in the sports event gave no hint at the time that their friends were out on a combat mission.

A Picnic and Two Funerals

Thursday, 12 March. Rosa and I visit the *vāḍi* of Ravi's aunt — a homestead out in the rice fields. Ravi is a friend of the family and a Tiger helper who really likes the Minesweeper game on my computer, which I have been playing obsessively. *Vāḍi*s in eastern Sri Lanka are peaceful, beautiful places, and people often visit them just for that reason. Indeed, that is the real reason we are here, but the official, social reason is that Rosa has brought me to help celebrate the first birthday of a little girl in this house. Actually, it is a few days after the birthday and the party, but Rosa is bringing me here now because it is the full moon, and she has a vacation from work. It doesn't seem to matter that the party is over. Ravi carries Rosa on the crossbar of his bicycle while I follow on my own bicycle, down the road from Paddippaalai and then across the fields through the sandy paths and over the bunds to reach the village of Thandiyadi. Because Rosa has lost both her kneecaps, she cannot get around easily by herself. She wants to see the Tiger burial ground at Thandiyadi.

The sand is deep and dry and difficult to bicycle through. I don't know how Ravi manages with the ample load of Rosa as well, but it seems to be no problem for him. The men and boys of this area are all accustomed to carrying huge bundles on their bikes that must weigh several hundred pounds — everything from stalks of rice to firewood to high stacks of soda bottles. We stop at the burial ground before going on to the birthday house. It contains perhaps two hundred graves. Daya Mohan is in charge of overseeing the cemeteries. He has told me, and it is common knowledge, that there is a much larger Tiger cemetery in the district, with more than two thousand graves. If you ask him, Daya Mohan will recite the exact number of Tigers who have died in combat in this district, and in the whole country. But he does not know how many live combatants there are — in this village, in this district, or overall. No one knows these figures except Prabhakaran and the Central Committee.

Two houselike buildings across the street from the graveyard are owned by the Tigers and used for storage. The only things inside them now are piles of old plastic garlands. An old man — perhaps the caretaker — brings us water from the well to drink. It is clear and cool and slightly bitter. He tells us that previously the graveyard was a beautiful place, but the army came and broke up the cement pillars and the low cement wall in front of the graveyard. They also beat up the old man. Only when he points out the damage do I notice it: I am so used to seeing broken and crumbling things in this country. A Christian graveyard on the road south from Batticaloa has been bulldozed to make room for an army camp; one can see some of the broken gravestones lying in a neglected corner by the camp. Here, again, the Tiger graveyard has been desecrated and not entirely restored. From a rise in the road a short distance away one can see the army camp from which attacks are launched, and which has been attacked by the Tigers.

A boy who looks about eighteen has been hired by the Tigers to keep the graveyard clean. His legs are atrophied as though by polio, but he can still walk. The concrete structures — the low wall paralleling the road, the pillars, the flagpole — are painted in stripes of equal width — red, yellow, and black, reminiscent of the red and white stripes on Hindu temples. But in Tamil Saiva Hinduism the combination of black and red is inauspicious, because black means death and red means power. Oracles for the goddess say you should never wear black and red together. But for the Tigers, life grows from death, and black is present in all their emblems.

We take off our sandals and leave them at the graveyard entrance. Barbed wire is strung across the entrance to keep cattle out. We remove the top two strands and step over the bottom one into the graveyard. The graves are in even rows, each covered with an oblong of gravel and marked with a wooden headboard giving the name and Tiger rank of the person and the date of death. They are arranged by date. In the morning when we visit, I see the graves of six people who have died since November 1997, when I first arrived in the area. By night there will be two more. There is a corner reserved for Tiger helpers who have died in service to the Tigers. Finding a paper sign lying facedown in the dirt, I turn it over and read it. It says in Tamil that the person was killed by the army when traveling to a clinic on Tiger business. The name, written in red letters, has been washed away. There are recent graves with no headboards.

We continue on our bikes to Ravi's aunt's *vāḍi*. Because Ravi is a Tiger helper, I ask him why he does not join the movement. He looks at me incredulously, as though there were something wrong with the question. "Because I don't want to die," he says.

This is a mud hut, but the birthday celebration appears to have been as elaborate as those for other little children in the area who live in nicer houses. A fancy iced cake sits on the table, still uncut. Above it is a picture of the god Murugan, with the caption *Yāmārkkum payamēn* —"I am not afraid of anyone" — and showing Murugan with his usual serene smile. (Murugan is the Tamil god of warfare, youth, beauty, and healing, among other things. He seems singularly appropriate to this time and this place, the celebration of a child's birth amid both great natural loveliness and a war.) They bring out a photo album full of pictures of this party. It must have gone on for days. Why do they celebrate toddlers' birthdays with such extravagance? And why do they always keep the hundreds of photos of so many different people, kin and friends, at so many different events, in so many different situations?

After we arrive, Ravi's aunt prepares a good meal for us, with meat. It takes several hours, and in the meantime Rosa and I rest on mats under the high palm trees, enjoying the soothing breeze. Ravi's sister delouses him as he lies with his head in her lap. Ravi's aunt, her teeth stained red, offers us betel, and we accept. A boy climbs a tall coconut palm and throws down two coconuts so that we can drink the water. Kids are playing *kabadi,* a tag game, three girls against five boys. The girls are taller than the boys; they must be in their teens. Because it is full-moon day, they don't have school.

The one-year-old, the birthday girl, is Ravi's aunt's first grandchild. The child is tall for her age and looks strong and healthy. The grandmother says she talks, but isn't walking yet, perhaps because she has been carried around too much. She is a good crawler, however. When I arrive, she is playing with a homemade toy — a plastic bottle attached to the end of a stick, with wooden wheels attached to the bottle. She pushes it through the sand. They have also made a wooden walker for her, with three wooden wheels, that she can hold onto and push along on the porch.

The walls of the mud hut are decorated with color pictures from a magazine and white handprints from Pongal. We had intended to visit the local Red Cross clinic, which comes to Thandiyadi once a week. But because it is full-moon day, the ICRC workers are also on vacation. Ravi's aunt questions Rosa about her legs, and Rosa tells her what happened and shows her the bullet scars. Ravi's aunt says she also was shot: a bullet hit her in the right arm and grazed her chest. She too shows us her scars. She says when she was wounded she remained silent, for fear of attracting the army's attention. Many people had fled from the village to that *vāḍi*. Rosa points out black scars on the high palm trees, which she says were made by mortar shells fired by the army. Even the trees are scarred, yet they still grow and flourish, as Rosa does. Vasanta has given Rosa money to buy a chicken so that the children can have eggs. It costs 130 rupees. The boy who climbed the palm tree goes out and brings back a chicken and ties its legs. We decide to carry it home in the basket of my bicycle. We are going to take a shortcut by taking a fisherman's boat across the lagoon, so we have plenty of time. And it is full-moon day, so we don't have to worry about getting home before nightfall; the moon will give enough light to cycle home by.

Around 12:30, as we are resting under the palms, we hear an explosion in the distance. An hour or so later, Ravi receives a visit from one of his Tiger friends, and we learn that there is to be a double funeral today. The LTTE is bringing two bodies for burial. Subhadas of the Ramanan group accidentally blew himself up while preparing a bomb at the base in Mahiladithivu, just a couple of hundred yards down the road from where Rosa and I live. That was the explosion we heard. We just happen to be miles away now. And a funeral will also be held for Kanthappan, who was killed during the attack on the army base yesterday. The bodies are being taken around the villages, and it will be some hours before they arrive at the graveyard.

At about five we take our bikes, our bags, and the chicken and make our way toward the graveyard. The chicken escapes two or three times from under the twine net we have woven to hold it in my bicycle basket, and we have to catch it and retie the twine each time. When we reach the main road we ask a young woman for news. She says the bodies are still in Kokkadichcholai. I wonder how she knows.

Along the way we come to Raja's sister's house. Conversation centers on the chicken and the rarity of eggs and fish. This is the first direct mention I have heard of something I noticed long ago, the scarcity on this side of any kind of animal protein. A photo album is brought out for us to look at, featuring Raja's sister's coming-of-age ceremony and pictures of Raja in various poses. Young men so often strike poses for cameras, quite deliberately, as though it were part of their job description as young men. Around six a tractor load of Tigers rolls by, and we leave and make our way back to the graveyard. I am beginning to worry about whether it is appropriate to take a live chicken to the funeral. I can't just leave it behind in the bicycle because it might escape again. The road in front of the graveyard is crowded with more than fifty Tigers and more than a hundred common people. Many of the Tigers are carrying rifles. There is a bus. Alagar drives past me on his motorcycle. Satyan also drives past on a motorcycle but smiles in greeting when he sees me. Rosa looks at me and all but winks. Sita is there in the yellow *salwar kameez* (tunic and trousers) I gave her, which makes her stand out among the group of female, uniformed Tigers. She alone is weeping; she knew Kanthappan pretty well, I think. Three or four civilian women are also weeping loudly; their hair is loose, they are throwing their hands into the air, then bending at the waist, swaying like trees in a heavy wind as they sob, and some are singing *oppāris* (traditional laments). If I were to carry out this project properly, I would tape-record the weeping and the lamenting, photograph all the events, and interview the little girls whom later I see weeping uncontrollably beside the grave. I don't have the heart to do these things, but one of the LTTE video crew is there, recording everything on his video camera. Their videotaping is an intrinsic part of the event — of the ritual, if you want to call it that — whereas I feel I am even more of an outsider when I take notes and pictures and make tape recordings. I remember only fragments of the lament: "My golden jewel . . . my golden son . . . I ironed your T-shirt again and again. . . . I carried you in my arms. . . . I looked for you. . . . Now you have become a big person. . . . Have you forgotten?"

The bodies are in rough wooden coffins with the lids closed but not nailed. They are carried by pallbearers, Das among them. He is silently weeping, the only man I see weeping. Tenderhearted Das.

When the bodies are brought into the graveyard, the people enter and stand around the open graves. The lamenting women continue their laments here; one of them claws at the pile of dirt from the grave. The Tigers are standing at attention in parallel lines, facing the front, where the bodies are. The graveyard is organized almost like a theater, with a central block of cement on which are written in red the words *punita illam,* "sacred home." Sita and Daya Mohan have told me that a Tiger graveyard is properly referred to as *māvīrarkal tuyilum illam* —"the home where great heroes are sleeping."

A Tiger man who is heading this ritual asks the women to be silent, and they suspend their lamentation while he solemnly, formally, and simply announces to the crowd the names and dates of death and manner of death of the two boys. Then six Tigers standing at attention around the stage fire their rifles into the air one by one. The assembled Tigers shout the Tiger salute — *Pulikaḷin tākam tamiṟiṟam tāyakam!* (The Tigers are thirsty for their motherland, Tamil Eelam!) — three times, raising their fists at the second phrase each time. Then people line up to take handfuls of flowers from a bowl and sprinkle the flowers on the bodies inside the now-open coffins.

The only other LTTE funeral I have attended was that of twenty-two-year-old Prem Kumar, who was shot on his way to blow up a transformer, or so went the story. His face was visible in the coffin, but this time, when I go to place a handful of flowers on each body, the faces are not visible, only flowers. Rosa says that the whole upper half of Subhadas's body was destroyed in the explosion, and only his legs remain; this is why you can't see his face. After all have put their handfuls of flowers on the bodies, the coffins are lowered into the open graves. People line up again to scatter handfuls of dirt on the grave. Some old men go first — I guess they are kinsmen — then the female mourners; then the Tigers, first men, then women; then common people, first men, then women. It is all solemn and orderly and over quickly.

Sita's sister Koyila and a cousin, a young civilian woman, have come. We met them on the roadside before the funeral began. They have suggested we ride back to Kokkadichcholai in the bus. I have explained to Koyila about the bicycle and the chicken. Suppressing laughter, she has said I can take them both on the bus. Someone brings us the bike and the chicken, and Rosa and I press our way through the crowd to the bus. Tigers are crowding onto the bus and milling around it, talking, and we have to duck under rifle barrels to get to the door. The left half of the front window of the bus is gone, and Rudrakumaran is perched in the space. Rosa takes the chicken and disappears into the crowd on the bus.

Rudrakumaran calls to me, "Come aboard, Auntie. You don't need the cycle."

"I *do* need the cycle!" I answer back, pondering how to get it onto the standing-room-only bus, but as I ponder, the bicycle moves from hand to hand and disappears into the bus like a bread crumb going into an anthill. So I climb aboard, and the crowd makes room for me. Only then do I see Sita and Malaimalli in the seat behind the driver. Sita calls for me to sit down beside her, and Malaimalli rises and gives me her seat, despite my protests.

Sita asks me if I've brought a flashlight, and I say no. She asks, "How will you cycle back home at night when the bus lets you off?"

I say, "There's the moon," and she seems satisfied.

She and Malaimalli are both smiling as the bus starts up, lumbers forward, gathers speed, and barrels and rattles down the road. It slows once to squeeze over the top of a narrow culvert, while passengers on both sides of the bus shout instructions to the driver, and I calculate how to escape the crush if the bus topples over on my side. Then it picks up speed again and hurtles through the night with Rudrakumaran still riding shotgun and the driver, like all Tamil bus drivers, a paragon of patience, skill, professionalism, and steely nerves, veined hands gripping the sides of the wide steering wheel, sinewy arms pulling the wheel around bends one way and another with musical grace. The driver's eyes are fixed on the road, and I think that to him this cargo of passengers is like any other cargo of precious lives, even when Rudrakumaran reaches across from his fun but dangerous seat and presses for long moments on the horn.

We have had to slow down again because we have come up behind the tractor carrying another load of Tigers, and there is no room to pass. Rudrakumaran is imperiously honking the bus horn at all his friends on the slower vehicle, mocking them. As soon as there's room, the tractor does move to the side, and the bus passes and goes as fast as it can. I wonder where my chicken has gotten to and look back to see it in Rosa's lap. My bike must be back there somewhere too. I think that if the bus hit a good bump, Rudrakumaran would fall out of his place in the front window space and be crushed under the wheels, but death feels far behind us now, and Rudrakumaran looks good and seems happy right where he is.

More Sports Contests, More Firefights, and Some Movies

Friday, 20 March. I am visiting Alagar's house. A young man whose name I don't know is sitting in the shaded sandy-floored porch in front of the house, trying to confirm or clarify news that the army is coming. He says that the army will be coming right here, searching houses, and the people do not know where to run to. Neither he nor anyone else seems especially alarmed, and I ask whether this is for real (*unmai*) or for fun (*summā*), and someone says *summā*. But someone else says the army has come to Kaluvancikudi and Porathivu. Kaluvancikudi is on the Army-controlled side; Porathivu is just across the bridge, on the Tiger-controlled side.

Also today there is a funeral for three Tigers who died in a fight with the army in Amparai. I have spent several days in town, and again I am chastised by Rosa for missing the bodies that were brought in procession.

She says that one of the bodies was in such bad shape that the face could not be made out.

On Saturday evening, Vasanta's cousin Jeya comes to her house and brings us the news that three Tigers were shot and killed at the army camp in Vavunathivu that they were gathering information about; in retaliation, the Tigers fired mortar shells at the camp from Thandiyadi, and three civilian schoolteachers were killed. Differing versions of this story circulate throughout the day.

Satyan visits late on Sunday and tells us two Tigers were killed in an ambush at Vavunathivu: one died immediately, the other died later of his wounds. The one who died later was buried first (on Saturday) because the Tigers had brought him back from the scene of the ambush. The one who died immediately was buried only after his body had been delivered by the army to the ICRC and thence to the Tigers. No civilians were killed in the counterattack, but several army soldiers were killed.

"This is the truth," says Satyan. "This is what really happened." Satyan has probably heard that I have complained about never being able to find out "what really happened." Why else would he make such a proclamation? I am grateful that he is trying to address my concern.

Monday, 23 March. This month there are sports meets in all the villages. Today there are preliminary events in Mahiladithivu, where I live. In this meet the houses or teams are named Ganga, Jamuna, and Kaveri, after sacred rivers in India. Loudspeakers announce the contests and the winners.

March is a windy month here, just as it is in England or Ohio. On the weekend I saw a white kite with a white tail wriggle up into the bright blue sky. The ferry won't go unless it is fully loaded with people, because otherwise the wind will push it off course. From the ferry one can see hundreds of jellyfish in the water; they signal the arrival of prawns. We also saw a large crocodile basking on the beach a hundred feet or so past the checkpoint. A woman lost her new rubber sandals overboard, and the ferry circled round so that she could retrieve them from the water, and while it was circling we all watched the crocodile as though we were tourists, until the crocodile, alarmed by the proximity of the ferry, disappeared into the water.

Satyan has brought videotapes of recent battles. They are called "attack pictures" — in the same category with American fantasy war films like *Independence Day.* But the videos Satyan has brought are real. Three Tiger boys are in the house watching them when I get back from a visit to Arasadithivu in the early afternoon; meanwhile, the sports meet is going on in the field, and we can hear the loudspeaker announcing events.

The boys in the house watch a videotape of the aftermath of a battle in December that was part of Jayasikurui. The camera moves slowly over a garbage-strewn landscape and then finds first one heap of corpses, then another, then another. The Tigers load the bodies into the back of a truck. The boys who are watching tell me that 350 bodies of Sinhala soldiers were found after this battle. One body is a special curiosity, as the dead soldier is sitting stooped over his gun, as though still alive. One of the Tigers in the film comments in Tamil, "This is good." I think he means it is a good thing to take a picture of, because it is strangely interesting.

The second film shows a recent attack on an army base not far from here. The boys in the house say it is February, which would have been just last month. A hundred or so Tigers sit listening to an officer giving instructions for the attack. He is dressed the same as his subordinates, and he looks fit and tall and young. When he's finished, they get up and walk in single file to the battle site, carrying their weapons and gear. They are barefoot, but their heads are covered by camouflage caps. They cross a river. Then there is the sound of firing, and the picture is bad because of the poor light. We see the Sinhala army base with (again) garbage strewn about and clothing hanging on lines and pegs. But the only Sinhala soldiers the video shows are the dead ones, including a body with just a mass of blood where the head should be.

Later the video shows a head without a body. Afterward it shows the Tigers having their meal of rice and curry, drinking water or tea out of empty biscuit packages, and smiling at the camera. Later there are shots of Tigers posing for still photographs. Perhaps whoever was holding the video camera was interested, as I am, in the way the people froze in stiff poses before the camera and then, as soon as the shutter clicked, relaxed like ice suddenly breaking. In these videos the Tigers appear organized and efficient, whether preparing for battle, marching there, or mopping up afterward. They have their method and they follow it, even down to details such as reusing the biscuit packages. Even the footage of actual battle scenes, though confusing to the viewer, shows the Tigers as businesslike. The carnage is grisly, but it is the most important part of the film: pictures of corpses and captured weapons show that the Tigers have done their job. At the same time, there is no separation between the utilitarian and the aesthetic, between the world of the videotape and the real world of living and acting. The battle was close to us in time and space: some of the combatants may be here in this town. Some of the soldiers killed may at another time have stopped civilians on the road.

The Tigers make these films primarily for their own benefit. From watching them, they can learn and teach one another about waging battle. And for some of the watchers, the films provide the pleasure of seeing oneself on camera, which is particularly prized in this society. (On the same day, another person has brought us a videotape of their wedding.) But the films are also intended to impress civilians: one example is the videotape called *Ceaseless Waves* (*Oyāta Alaikal*), about the spectacular Mullaithivu battle of 1996. There is some kind of visceral pleasure in seeing dead bodies, especially badly mutilated ones. Modern American commercial films appeal to the same sensibilities, whatever their source may be.[6]

As I watch the film, I am reminded of how Rosa and other civilians seem compelled to look when dead bodies come by. They describe without flinching or hesitation the ugly details of death, as though they assume I want to hear. Yet Rosa is no more bloodthirsty a person than I am. She has had more than her share of death and horror. Why would she want to witness still more? Why talk about it? From one point of view, grisly scenes are negations of life. We turn our faces from them so that our dreams will not be stained by the images. But from another point of view, blood and death are part of a show. They are meant to be seen. I don't know why.

· · ·

Wednesday, 25 March. This is the final day of the sports meet of the Mahiladithivu school in the field across the street. Vasanta, her mother, and Selvi got up before dawn to start preparing five hundred *vadais* (deep-fried savory snacks) for the event. The schoolchildren are out in the field. Rosa is next door with the five- and six-year-olds. Schoolchildren come to the house for water. We can hear the horn of the ice-cream vendor and the voices of children playing.

In midmorning the electricity goes off. This has become common, just an annoyance. Around noon, Vasanta calls me to hear the sounds of gunfire and explosions. She has not left her place behind the house, where she is frying *vadais* in a big pot of oil over a wood fire, with the help of a visiting old lady. I come back and listen to the rapid gunfire and explosions. Vasanta says the sound is coming from Arayampathi, a village across the lagoon, about three miles as the crow flies. I look over the back fence, where we can see the road going down to the ferry and the junction by the church next to our house. The people who have gone down to the ferry are cycling back at no great speed, not as though they are afraid. Halfway down the road to the ferry people are talking: those going may be asking those returning for information. Three women are running up the road away from the ferry. It is unusual for women to run like that. Two or three armed Tigers have come to the junction, and several civilians are there also. After a while the armed Tigers disappear, and the sounds of gunfire and explosions cease.

Satyan and Das stop by the house, concerned that there is no one to help with the *vadai*s and the baby. Das carries Vasanta's young baby in his arms while Satyan sits with Vasanta and helps her with the cooking. Vasanta asks Satyan about the gunfighting, and Satyan says he doesn't know anything. I have changed from my old nightgown into a blouse and pants. Satyan laughs and asks if I'm going somewhere. I say I have to be ready to run. Satyan says I should fight, not run. I say I am ready to run or to fight, as required. I am not really serious about the fighting part, but speak my lines with a straight face. Satyan says that to fight, I have to be brave like him. We joke about who is the braver. Perhaps seeing that all is calm in this house (I don't really know why they came), Satyan and Das depart.

A man on the porch, who has come to pay the rent on his land and apparently was on his way back to the ferry, explains that Vasanta has invited him to stay at her place until the fighting is over. Now he also leaves and bikes toward the ferry, which is running again. A few minutes later Vasanta asks if I've heard the news: according to the LTTE, they attacked the TELO office and killed five TELO boys. Vasanta says she doesn't know if the rumor of the deaths is true, but they will have blown up the office. If any TELO have been killed, TELO will beat up civilians in retaliation, so civilians will not be wanting to cross over to Arayampathi.

Around noon the electricity comes back on, and the loudspeaker in the field starts playing a cheerful Pillaiyar song (Pillaiyar is the popular elephant-headed god) to announce that the sports meet is soon to begin. We can hear more machine-gun fire. Vasanta is still cooking *vadai*s. I ask her if this is a typical day, with the sports meet and the gunfire and the *vadai*s and so forth. She says she has grown used to the fighting. Even if the gunfights come right up to the junction, she will not stop cooking her *vadai*s, she says. "War is a part of life," she explains. (But it is not yet a *way* of life for the civilians here, I think.)

Shortly after that, Rosa comes in with the news that three TELO and two civilians have been wounded, and the army has seized the two canoes the LTTE used to cross the lagoon. She names the main TELO boy who was wounded (*paddatu* — the word does not reveal whether he has been killed). The LTTE boys have not come back yet, so we don't know what happened to them.

It is one o'clock. The sports meet, which starts at two, is similar to the one at Arasadithivu. The Tiger flag is raised, there are marching bands, three houses, lots of ceremony. Tiger songs are played on the loudspeaker.

Tiger boys are grouped together on the sidelines, alongside civilian spectators. This meet includes competitions not only for schoolchildren but also for runners from the village athletic clubs. The runners are lean, muscular, barefoot, and fast. Teenage girls in prim white school uniforms race at breakneck speed around the course.

I ask Vasanta if they had these competitions before the troubles, when she was in school, and she says yes, they were just the same. In fact, her own generation started these games about ten years ago. I ask if she played sports, and she says she was on both the volleyball team and the netball team. But she was not good at netball: "I couldn't shoot [*suḍ panna muḍiyātu*] because I was short. I played center."

As the contest proceeds, two Tiger boys from the video section of the LTTE are viewing a film in Vasanta's house on their VCR and Vasanta's TV. The film is an LTTE production from 1996 titled *Dēcattin Puyalkaḷ* (Storms of the Country). It is a dramatic reenactment of an attack on Palaly Airport on 1 August 1994 by a team of Black Tigers. This was the second attempt to destroy aircraft based there. The first was unsuccessful, and thirteen Tigers died. On the second mission, all but one of the Tigers died, but the attack was deemed successful because an airplane was destroyed. "During the filming of this picture," a written message on the screen says, "combatant-artists attained heroic death in battles that took place with the Army on our soil from time to time. To them we offer our heartfelt veneration [*anjalikaḷ*]."

In this film, living Black Tigers play the roles of the now-dead Black Tigers who conducted the attack. The filming took place over several months, during which the actors were also fighting; some of them died in battle before the filming was over. Others died in subsequent suicide attacks. The LTTE actors playing Sinhala soldiers speak Sinhala in the film; the Sinhala speech has Tamil subtitles. There is mood music. A Sinhala soldier is portrayed on watch duty smoking a cigarette. This scene takes a dig at both Sinhala soldiers (who smoke) and cigarettes (which kill). Tigers themselves, of course, do not smoke but playact the villains who do. Of all the ironic situations that Tigers get themselves into, this is a small example.

In other respects, the video is not unlike an American war movie, with the heroes employing all the latest combat equipment, silently moving through water and jungle, and narrowly escaping detection on several occasions. The scenes where they blow up an airplane and then set fire to the air force headquarters are especially exciting. The actor who plays the air force commander does a good job of cursing convincingly in Sinhala and in general being a stereotypical military commander–type villain. One of the Black Tigers is portrayed as having a special need to prove himself because he has a "small body" (the actor who plays the role looks thin and frail) and has been excluded from other missions for this reason. As the show proceeds, the Black Tigers perish in explosions one by one. But the mood of the film is one of triumph.

Several family members and neighbors come in to watch, but the film is long, and most of them drift out again, except for the Tiger boys, me, and an old grandmother from a neighboring house who often visits. This woman, unlike Vasanta's mother, does not really follow the news. The two Tiger boys from the video section patiently answer her questions about the film. "Are those people LTTE or Black Tigers?" she asks. A boy answers, "There is no difference between the Black Tigers and the LTTE. The Black Tigers are a special branch of the LTTE." Both boys are impeccably polite, giving up their chairs to elderly people and to women and playing with the baby. Rosa has brought two commercial films that she wants to watch. Vasanta and Rosa have already asked Satyan to let them use the VCR. The implicit agreement seems to be that Tigers can use the TV if civilians can use the VCR.

The sports meet is still going on in the late afternoon. A costume contest is taking place. The children make up their own themes and design their own costumes, but all the themes are ones that the Tigers would approve. One boy comes dressed as the lame Ratwatte in a wheelchair, dragging two slaves behind him. Another group of children dress as refugees. One small boy with no particular costume convincingly plays the role of a drunk, throwing his clothes around and ordering the other kids off the playground. This boy wins the prize because he is so funny. Even the announcer can't help laughing as the boy continues his clowning while the announcer tries to tell him he's won. But no one, including the announcer, seems to know the boy's name or where he comes from. The kids are high-spirited, breaking into screams of joy and throwing their hats in the air when their team is mentioned by the announcer, and running in pandemonium over the playground to pick up marker flags after the races are finished. Meanwhile, the battle at Arayampathi seems to be over.

The Baby Elephant

Late April. The Tiger boys in the political office have told me there are elephants near their jungle camp. Vasanta has told me this can't be true, but I remain curious. I spend April in Colombo, trying unsuccessfully to get permission from the ministry of defense to travel to the town of Madu in the Vanni. While in Colombo I pick up the latest issue of *Dinamurasu* and find a small article about Kokkadichcholai. The article, translated from Tamil, reads as follows:

Elephants Raised by Tigers!

One of the elephants raised by the Tiger movement in the jungle of Batticaloa has been given by the Tigers as a gift to the Kokkadichcholai *Tān Tōṉrisvarar Ālayam* [the famous temple of Kokkadichcholai dedicated to the Lord Who Made Himself Appear]. The people of the Tiger movement had been giving this elephant daily forty liters of milk plus cooked rice.

At the same time it has become known that the Tigers are raising more elephants in the region of Vaharai. Before attacks on the soldiers, the waving of the trunks of the elephants that are familiar with them, and the sound of their trumpeting, are taken [by Tigers] when they set out as good omens [*narcakuṇamāka*] that the attack will be victorious. It is said they believe that attacks they go on with the blessings of such an elephant are given victory.

I decide to learn more about this topic when I get back. Did the Tigers really give an elephant to the temple? Do they really raise elephants in the jungle? The story fits the image of Tigers as children of nature.

10 May. I ask Vasanta and Chittu about the elephant. They confirm the story but say they expect that the people will probably kill it because it needs so much food. It is just a baby elephant and is fed large quantities of cooked rice and milk. When I ask what happened to its mother, Chittu says the Tigers probably shot it, but he says he is just guessing; he doesn't know. I have asked children to do drawings for me of something happy and something scary. Several of the scary pictures were pictures of elephants.

I am going to visit the elephant in the evening. Vasanta says that Nimal, a small fifteen-year-old boy who often visits the house, wants to come with me. I welcome him. We go on bikes to see the elephant, and I stop in the store on the way and buy twenty bananas — ten for Nimal to feed it, and ten for me to feed it. How much did those bananas cost? Nimal asks. Forty rupees, I say. "You are spending forty rupees on an *elephant?*" he asks in surprise and disapproval.

"It's an important animal," I say defensively. When we find the elephant, I feed it all twenty bananas, as Nimal does not want to come near it.

As we leave, he says, "Let's go back this way," heading off on his bike in the opposite direction from the way we have come. On the way we stop first at his aunt's house, where I accept a cup of what is called "plain tea," then his mother's. Both are tiny mud huts. His mother has seven children. She offers me wild berries (*iccaṅgāy*) from a basket. The family members are all small and thin. The father is a field laborer who has gone to Polonnaruwa to work; I am surprised that he goes that far away. An uncle is there, and he shows me that his hair is falling out in patches. It looks like a disease, not like normal balding. Magazine pages are pasted to the walls of the tiny house as decorations. But at the center of the wall, stuck on a nail, is a child's crayon picture with colorful drawings of different pretty things: a house, a tree, a flower. This drawing must have been made by a child who visited me when I had crayons and paper and was encouraging the children to come over to draw and color.

Now I know why we took the alternative route home: Nimal wanted me to see all this. As we cycle back to Vasanta's, he beseeches me to come with him to the field where his family grows tapioca. If we go fast on our bicycles, he says, it is only an hour away. Even if we go slow, it is only three hours.

But I needn't go see the tapioca, which is a crop grown by the poor on poor soil. I have already seen firsthand that some of the people in this village are starving. Nobody said a word to me about this. Neither Nimal nor his family spoke to me about hunger or shortage of food. But Nimal, like Menan, has made me understand his world simply by showing it to me. His act makes a deeper impression on me than any words ever could.

Monday, 11 May. I invited Menan to come with me to see the baby elephant today. It is kept near the temple in Kokkadichcholai; its name is Ayyappan, and it is nine months old. When I came, it greeted me with its trunk. Its keeper says it is his first experience raising an elephant. I ask how much milk it drinks, and he says no milk, it eats only rice. I ask what happened to its mother. The keeper says she died.

"How?"

"She was shot [*veḍi*]."

"Who shot her?"

"Don't know."

The temple is close to the school. On the grounds between the two I saw a peacock and two deer. On the same road is a sign saying *putiya pōrāḷikaḷ iṇaikkum iḍam* (Meeting Place for New Fighters), artistically drawn, with a sun rising over one of the letters.

Some time later, at Alagar's house, I meet a tall, thin, very dark-skinned Tiger who was part of the group that brought the elephant back. I have never seen him before. He looks as though he spends most of his time in the jungle. When I ask what happened to the mother elephant, he says she was driven away by people and barking dogs because she had entered a paddy field and left her baby behind. They led the baby back by a hook on its ear.

I turn to Das, who is also there. He is quiet and gentle, doesn't lie like some others, and loves animals; he raises pigeons, puppies, rabbits as a hobby. I ask him, "Did the Tigers shoot the mother?"

He replies emphatically, "No. We are forbidden to shoot elephants and peacocks. We can scare elephants away by firing in the air, but we would never shoot them."

I report this to Vasanta. Vasanta responds, "A mother elephant would never desert her baby. And an elephant could not be driven away by dogs." But I decide to believe the Tigers' version of this story.

Another Kind of Birthday Party

8 or 9 May. Chittu says that fears have arisen again that the army is coming (people refer to the army in the masculine singular, as "him"). He says they are amassing troops in Vavunathivu and elsewhere. I ask Vasanta what they will do if the army does come. She says there is a village "far away" to which they will flee. In preparation, we must gather all our valuables ready to take with us. Vasanta's mother hid all my gold jewelry away while I was gone, in case the army came.

10 May. Early this morning, about 5:30, I was outside and heard gunfire as though it were coming from next door. But Vasanta said it was only the Tigers (*iyakkam tāṉ*) shooting for no reason (*summā*). Some people were afraid, thinking it was the army, but were comforted when they learned it was only the Tigers. I wonder if the Tigers do this on purpose.

Schoolchildren came by in the afternoon and said that the gunfire was an ambush. Satyan and Rudrakumaran came by shortly after most of the kids had left and drew some cartoons with the crayons and paper. Rosa has been talking about wanting to see the Vesak lantern show that the army is putting on at the same time. (Vesak is a Buddhist holiday — Jayasikurui was initiated during the week of Vesak.) Rosa told Satyan she was going to see the Vesak celebrations and hence would not be able to attend the LTTE celebrations. (In fact, she attended both.)

The Tigers are celebrating the first anniversary of Jayasikurui, which they say represents its defeat. The army has not accomplished its aim. But the Tigers have not yet stopped the army, either. The conflict is still going on, and the Tigers are in danger of being exhausted by it. Their numbers have been badly depleted by this operation. All the more cause, it seems, for this giant party.

There are three days of celebrations, from 11 to 13 May, with the biggest celebration being on the last day. On 11 May, there was something like carol singing, with a group of men going around on a tractor cart singing songs, and late tonight a short *kūttu* (street play) has been traveling on a tractor to the various villages. I missed the caroling, but I come out barefoot and in my nightclothes to catch the *kūttu*. Come-as-you-are is okay, they tell me.

The tractor cart has been decorated with a color cartoon (it looks like Satyan's work) showing grotesque caricatures of Sinhala soldiers. Across from them a beautiful Tiger girl stands by a mortar launcher, and a handsome Tiger man stands behind her, cheering.

People dressed in black, with white skeletons painted on their black clothing and their faces masked, dance among people dressed as Sinhala soldiers. The soldiers dance limply, as though ready to drop with exhaustion; they are pushed back and forth by village children, who have red and white kerchiefs wrapped around their heads. The skeleton-dancers sometimes rush at people in the crowd and startle them, and we all jump back, and then laugh.

12 May. People on tractor carts come down the road carrying signs proclaiming the defeat of Jayasikurui. In one cart, people lie sprawled and motionless, pretending to be dead soldiers. In another cart President Chandrika sits at a table with her ministers, getting drunk on arrack. Another cart carries people playing the role of prisoners taken by the Tigers. They are standing in a cage.

Inbam came to say good-bye to me on 13 May. That night in Munaikkadu, in the field next to the school, the Tigers put on a six-hour-long variety show. The audience was large. Across the lagoon in Batticaloa, the army had put on a big show for Vesak, with lantern displays, fire dancers, and a thousand packets of free food distributed. Probably many people, like Rosa, attended both, despite the article that appeared on the front page of the 11 May (Sunday) *Vīrakēsari:*

Punishment If Help Given to Tigers.
Warning in the Areas of Paddiruppu and Arayampathi

(Batticaloa correspondent Ai. Nadesan) Because the government has banned the organization called Liberation Tigers, giving them money or other kinds of help is a punishable crime. If anybody transgresses this law and gives them help, they will immediately be taken prisoner and be made to stand before the law and punishment will be given, it was announced via loudspeaker in the areas of Batticaloa under control of the Special Task Forces.

On Sunday morning, loudspeakers were mounted on Special Task Force vehicles and this announcement was issued in the Tamil language. In the villages in the areas from Arayampathi to Paddiruppu this announcement was released. Please give help to the banned organization. If people living in areas under the control of the army bring money and/or things to give to the "Tigers" in Paduvankarai areas (areas under control of the "Tigers") and are caught, that also is a punishable offense, it was announced by way of those loudspeakers.

Starting Sunday, the interrogations at the checkpoints of Manmunai, Ambilanthurai, and Paddiruppu, which are entries to the areas under control of the "Tigers," have been made severe [*tīvirappaḍuttappaḍḍuḷḷana*].[7]

These announcements are clearly intended to discourage people from attending the Tiger performance or providing assistance for it. Nevertheless, the field is filled with thousands of people. Most of them sit on the wet ground through the whole show. No food packets are given out, though I had noticed in Alagar's house the day before large piles of carrots and tomatoes and heard some discussion of whether the *iyakkam* or the people should be fed. Thereafter, for several days, whenever I visited Alagar's house, I got carrot-and-tomato curry with rice for lunch. Later I heard a rumor that the Tigers had captured a truck full of vegetables.

The variety show of 13 May, which the Special Task Force has worked so hard to keep people away from, includes an extensive program:

· Speeches by local Tiger leaders: Geethan, Vicu, Thurai, Ilakkiya, Kausalya (the young female judge of the high court of the LTTE in Kokkadichcholai), and others.
· Poems composed and read by several female Tigers: Myouri, Sivagami, and others.
· Dances by Tiger women in *bārata nāḍḍiyam* style. In one dance, the performers are dressed in traditional *bārata nāḍḍiyam* costume, with saris, jewels, and flowers. In another they are dressed in combat outfits. They are skilled classical dancers. A sign for the Tiger has been incorporated into the *mudra*s (hand gestures) of the dance. The dancer lifts both hands before her, with bent elbows and curled, clawlike fingers.

It also contains signs for determined anger and for firing rifles. These fit well into the angular, percussive *bārata nāḍḍiyam* style of dance.

- A ghost dance by three people dressed in skeleton outfits, like the dancers in the *kūttu* of the night before. A fourth dancer represents a tired and frightened Sinhala soldier, around whom the skeletons dance. In dim light, they dance in a slow, ghostly fashion to eerie music. The music suddenly stops, the dancers stop, and the soldier disappears. Then fast and cheery dance music is played, and the skeletons dance to it, disco style. Then the music stops again, the lights dim, the Sinhala soldier reappears, the eerie music starts up again, and the ghostly dance resumes. Two of the dancers are mediocre, but one is good; Rosa says it is Rudrakumaran. (Later, when I meet Rudrakumaran, he confirms he was that dancer. He calls the dance his death dance. "You have a talent I didn't know about," I say. "I can paint, too," he offers. He tells me he can paint portraits from photographs. He did the one of Kittu at Kokkadichcholai.)
- A mother-son song-and-dance act by two women, in which the son finally convinces the mother to let him go to battle.
- A dance by a friend turned Tiger convincing his non-Tiger friends to join the movement. (In traditional *teru kūttu,* street drama, all female parts are played by men or boys; but in Tamil dance, boys can be played by girls.)
- A dance involving two adult male Tigers, two young boy Tigers, and one young and small girl Tiger — an open admission that the Tigers have very young combatants in their ranks, for here they are playing themselves. (This variety show is part of a recruitment campaign to increase the Tigers' depleted numbers after the casualties of Jayasikurui.)
- A *villuppāḍḍu* performance called *Kanakku Tappu Pōḍātē* (Don't Make Arithmetic Errors), parodying the various false predictions of success by Ratwatte for Jayasikurui.
- A skit parodying the way that checkpoint guards harass civilians. Rosa says the checkpoint scene is true to life: the way the guards let citizens go and then call them back again to ask trivial questions, the broken Tamil they speak, the way they bum cigarettes from each other. The skit shows a poor farmer chasing his runaway cow: delayed by the checkpoint guards, he sadly watches the cow disappear in the distance. It is all sad and funny at the same time. At the end, when the guards are partying and drinking, several Tigers sneak up and shoot them.
- A sequel to the street drama *Niccaya Tōlvi* (Certain Defeat) that played here some months ago, parodying figures in government.

Somewhere around midnight, Inbam appears onstage to thank all those who have helped put on the show. He speaks slowly, his eyes are red, and he appears exhausted and sad. The audience begins to drift away. The new women's leader is Sivagami. Her voice comes on the loudspeaker to tell the audience there are to be more performances still. Around then I realize that Inbam has been the organizer of this event: that was what Sita meant when she said he had a lot of work these days. Now he is being sent to Vaharai to be the organizer of events there, or something. Daya Mohan later tells me that this is a promotion for Inbam: he will be the political head of the town of Vaharai. We should be happy for him. Daya Mohan urges me, in a friendly manner, to visit him there.

About a week later, the army attacks Vaharai and takes it over from the Tigers. This attack was expected, and in fact Inbam was probably sent there to help people prepare. Maybe the Tigers encouraged me to visit thinking that the army would have delayed their attack if they had known I was there. Sita tells me that Inbam is okay, and I wonder what his job will be now.

The Hand Sticking Out of the Ground

Wednesday, 20 May. I am coming back from Batticaloa to Vasanta's house. At the checkpoint, Karan, the Tamil-speaking informer for the checkpoint guards, calls me. I try to walk by, but he says, "You said you wanted to hear my story, and you said you would stop and listen next time you came through." This is all true, and so I stop. Among the things Karan tells me is that there is a corpse half-buried in a village on the Tiger side. The hand is sticking out of the ground. The story sounds silly to me, and I am disbelieving. Karan says, "Find out for yourself."

As soon as I get back to Vasanta's house, I ask her about the corpse. The question seems to take her by surprise. She does not smile and does not seem pleased, this time, that I have independently learned about a killing. She hesitates before answering my question. Then she turns to face me solemnly.

"Yes, it is true," she says. She has not seen it, but people are talking. Nobody knows who is buried there, or who buried him. It appears that the body was buried in a hurry, and this is why the hand is sticking out. The stench of the corpse fills the area. If I really want to see it, she will arrange for someone to take me there.

On Thursday morning I ask Alagar about this. He says he thinks it may be the body of an old man who died recently in Arayampathi and fell into the river; it might be a natural death. Chittu thinks this is possible. Vasanta thinks not, because if the body had been washed ashore by the water, how would it have been so deeply buried?

"Why doesn't anyone do anything about it?" I ask Vasanta. As of Thursday evening the body has not been touched by anyone, and it lies rotting in the same place, still only partly buried, still with its hand sticking out. Chittu stops by that evening and says that he first heard about it on Sunday. He wonders if it is an LTTE torture victim but says he doesn't know.

"Has the LTTE done anything about the corpse?" I ask Vasanta later.

"They will send their boys to take a picture of the grave," she says.

I tell Alagar that the civilians are really worried about this corpse. However it got there, it is your responsibility to do something about it, I say. This is territory under your control, after all.

About a week later, Rosa says the rumor about the corpse is that Tigers from the justice department (*nīti turai*) were interrogating a civilian about a problem to do with money. He died during the interrogation, which was not what the interrogators intended, so they hastily buried him. Now the interrogators have been sent to higher authorities in the movement and will themselves be interrogated. The next news on the killing, delivered by civilians, is that the killer has escaped from Tiger custody.

Near the end of June, as I am preparing to leave , I encounter Father Sebastian in town, and he gives me what I accept as the final version of the corpse story. The corpse turned out to be not one person but two, a husband and wife. They were killed by an LTTE boy who had taken money from them for "tax" and had not given them a receipt. The couple were demanding a receipt and threatening to report the boy to the Tiger authorities. The boy in anger killed both of them and hastily buried them. When civilians saw the body with the hand sticking out of the ground, they were afraid to say anything to the LTTE. As Father Sebastian put it, "The civilians told themselves it would be dangerous to bring this topic up with the Tigers." Eventually, when the Tigers found out about it, the previous commander of the region, Thurai, came down from Jaffna and conducted an investigation among the local civilians to ascertain what had happened. As soon as the killer learned that Thurai wanted to speak to him, he fled to the army side and became an informant for them before the LTTE could take him into custody. Now the LTTE is worried because the runaway has information about the locations of their camps and their plans and he will sell this information to the army.

And indeed, within a week of Father Sebastian's telling me this, the army attacks Kokkadichcholai.

The Temple Renewal Festival

In Kokkadichcholai there is an old, once-great temple, the *Sri Tān Tōnrisvarar Koyil* (the Temple of the Lord Who Made Himself Appear). The temple was partly destroyed in the cyclone of 1978 and fell into disuse after that. Now the people are doing a *kumbābishēkam* — a renewal ceremony. Vasanta says that this temple was supposed to protect all the people in the area from harm, but people in this area have suffered severely, which means that the temple has not been doing its job.

According to Vasanta, the temple got its name long ago, when the area was thick jungle and hunters came looking for honey. They found some at the top of a *kokkaḍḍi* tree and set about cutting it down. When the hunters took an ax to the tree, blood gushed out of the cut. Thus the hunters knew that God was in that place — no one made him come there, he just appeared — so they established a temple there.

During colonial times, white men came and said the temple should be destroyed. The priest responded that there was a real god there, and to prove it promised that if the white men came back in a week, a stone statue of a cow there would eat grass. ("Would a statue eat grass?" asks Vasanta wryly, but she continues with the story.) The priest prayed hard for a week. The white men came back and handed a handful of grass to the statue, saying, "Here. Eat." And the stone cow ate it, produced a plop of manure, and then lay down to sleep.

A new mural has been painted on an inside wall of the temple depicting its origin story. The mural provides further details of the hunter story. The first panel of the mural shows two hunters dressed in skins, looking like wild savages, standing beneath a tree in the middle of the wilderness. The tree is bleeding from an ax cut. One of the hunters looks out at the viewer, his palms turned upward as though dismayed. In the next panel a woman, seeing the wound, removes her upper garment (her breasts remain covered by her blouse) and uses it to bind up the bleeding tree. In the next panel the woman is gone, and a baby *sivalingam* is budding through the bloodstained cloth. In the next, the tree is gone; in its place is a fully grown lingam with low walls around it and a person sitting nearby who looks like a holy man. In the next panel are shown a cowboy-like figure with wide-brimmed hat, horse, and rifle; a Brahman priest with a topknot; and Nandi (Siva's bull). In the next, the priest is praying. In the next the bull is standing, eating grass, and defecating, and the white man's horse is rearing up as though saluting the temple or something. In the final scene, Siva and Parvati are seated within the temple.

The story depicted in the mural is similar to stories found in other Siva temples in India and Sri Lanka from the twelfth century onward. The wounded god is an almost universal theme in these temples, especially the wounded lingam. Sometimes the lingam bleeds, sometimes the devotee, sometimes both. The lingam is cared for like a beloved, helpless creature — like a baby. Acts of human love, of joyful and unselfconscious sacrifice for the god are central to Saiva mythology. In the Kokkadichcholai temple, the lingam budding from the cut on the tree echoes the way plants grow after pruning and illustrates a faith in life reemerging from wounded and bleeding places.

I wonder who painted the mural. It does not look like the work of a professional artist; the painter did not bother too much with proportion, perspective, or shading. The colors are bright and the outlines sharp. I think a local person must have done it. The area around Kokkadichcholai flourishes with bright posters and wall paintings, many but not all of them on LTTE-related themes. The temple mural is similar in style to those paintings. And I see hints of humor. On the face of the hunter who has cut the tree is an expression of guilty, apologetic alarm that says, "How could *I* know this would happen?" The white horse representing colonialism is the work of someone who has never seen a real horse, much less a colonial administrator mounted on one, but who has seen cowboy movies. Suddenly I am convinced this is Rudrakumaran's work.

The *kumbābishēkam* goes from 30 May to 7 June. Paddy is being poured over the lingam, and priests are chanting. Food is being prepared in great quantities to be given to the pilgrims. The baby elephant has been decorated and stands within the temple walls for people to look at and feed if they dare. Dozens of stalls have been set up to sell ice cream, soda, bananas, fried foods, souvenirs, and trinkets. Yogurt and buttermilk are being handed out at the temple and at junctions on the way. Those giving it out aggressively foist it on grateful passersby. Reportedly, Tigers are among the temple servants providing buttermilk to thirsty pilgrims. How many hundreds of gallons of buttermilk there may be, and where it all came from, I cannot guess.

The temple has been completely repainted and renovated, but the temple chariot has not been finished on time. It is old and made of wood with elaborate carvings. One by one its wheels are being replaced, and I have seen one being transported in a bullock cart from somewhere far away. An impossible wooden scaffold stands next to the *gōpuram* with steps going up to the top of it that men are climbing one after another, as in an M.C. Escher drawing. I think how brave and faithful they are to climb such a precarious structure. Later I learn that they are anointing the top of the *gōpuram* with oil.

A sign on the inside of the wall near the entrance describes in detail the cause of the *kumbābishēkam* and the events. *Eelam* is the first word of the text ("In the holy land of Eelam . . .").

Brahman priests are performing the rituals. They are richly dressed with silk waistcloths, gold jewels, colored beads, and sacred threads. They are chanting, and music is being played. Satyan is helping out with the wiring of the loudspeaker. When that is fixed, a Brahman priest chants into the microphone a Sanskrit text that sounds like a list of beings to be worshipped. I hear him say the name of the sun (*sūriya*) and the name of Tamil Eelam.

LTTE police in blue uniforms are standing as sentries at the junction between the main road and the street that goes to the temple. Regular Tigers are standing at crucial places, checking some people who try to pass. Boy Scouts act as crowd-control personnel, and people on the temple committee guide the pilgrims to the sites they must visit. The whole show is impressively orderly.

Other Tigers are there like civilians, worshipping at the temple or just buying things from the stalls and enjoying the festivities. Rosa, although she is a Christian, would not miss this event for the world. She examines all the sights, visits all the stalls, and explores the temple inside and out. She wears a *poḍḍu* and sacred ash, signs of devotion to Siva. We are certain that Jesus will forgive her.

Not everyone is so forgiving, however. Village rumors say that sixty Brahmans have been brought in from India, at great expense, to carry out this ritual. Some villagers, those who do not believe in the temple, might be resentful. But, according to a temple trustee, there are only thirty priests, some from around Batticaloa and some from Colombo — none from India. They are staying in the temple.

For forty days, according to one rumor, the people have been ordered to fast: they are not to eat fish, meat, or eggs, and all the fish and meat stores in Kokkadichcholai and neighboring villages are to be closed. The LTTE has supposedly threatened severe punishments for anyone who violates the order to fast. According to rumor, the fishermen wept when they heard this news.

Alagar and Sivagami, who are both Hindus and both LTTE, say it is a temple order and not an LTTE order. The fast is voluntary, they say, and it is for a week, not a month.

Yet another rumor has circulated that the god has ordered a human sacrifice, and the priests have agreed. The priests do not have to perform the sacrifice; the god will take his own victim in his own way. The god wants a first-born or last-born child, so anyone who fits the description should avoid the temple. Sivagami says this rumor is not true; the people who believe such things are ignorant. She also says it is good for people to practice their religion, whether they are Christian or Hindu, Muslim or Buddhist.

Satyan and Rudrakumaran, both of them Saiva, come to visit during the fast period, and Vasanta serves them lunch. I do not see them eating, but when they have left, Vasanta gleefully tells me that the lunch she gave them was beef curry. I do not tell her my feeling that this was a petty and cruel trick. Satyan and Rudrakumaran have never done anything to hurt Vasanta; she would have told me if they had.

On the evening of 3 June, the swami (a *sivalingam* from the temple) is taken on *ūrvalam* (procession around the villages). The *sivalingam* rides in a cart drawn by a tractor, as in other processions, and a loudspeaker is making an announcement as it goes by. Vasanta says the announcement is about the human sacrifice. According to Vasanta, the announcer is saying it doesn't matter, everyone should come anyway.

Tigers are recruiting from among the youths who come to the festival. The temple is close to the Kokkadichcholai school. I wonder if this is the hidden meaning of the human-sacrifice rumor. Many young people will be recruited to the Tigers during this festival; some of them will be sent into battle, and some will die. Of those, some will surely be first-born or last-born children.

Friday, 5 June, is the most important day of the *kumbābishēkam*. Thousands of people have come — in buses, vans, and tractors, on bikes, and on foot. All day they keep arriving, and the road from the junction to Kokkadichcholai is thick with people dressed in their finest. The main ritual of today involves anointing the images of the gods with oil. The queue to participate is at least a mile long under the blazing sun. Someone explains to me that the ritual absolves you of sins (*pāvam tīrkka*), including sins you may have committed inadvertently. Another says god will do good for those who suffer to come (*kashdappaddu vantu*). I hear references to suffering on the loudspeaker.

One of the temple trustees shows me around. The shrines of the various gods are numbered in the order in which they should be visited: Amman, Pillaiyar, Nagadeva, Murugan with his two wives, Nandi the bull, the *sivalingam,* and Vairavan. At the shrine of Vairavan, the trustee explains that Vairavan protects those who suffer, people here and everywhere. Is he scary? I ask. Sometimes, says the trustee, when he is with his dog. The dog is his vehicle. I want to ask the trustee whether he thinks of the LTTE as being like Vairavan but decide I'd better not. If people are coming in such crowds to this festival in the heart of Tiger territory, they cannot be deeply afraid of the Tigers.

Satyan and Rudrakumaran have told me they are painting a representation of Jayasikurui which will be on display near the temple on 5 and 6 June. Rosa says there is a painting of the Kokkadichcholai massacre and what happened to her then. I am looking for both these paintings. I see boards in a cordoned-off area at the side of the road to the temple, but, strangely, the boards are covered, and only the captions show. The captions refer to the suffering of people because of the war. The display is guarded carefully by about five LTTE boys who say the pictures will not be uncovered until nighttime, so I come back then.

When I return, about a dozen paintings are on display. Most are portrayals of army atrocities against Tamil civilians. I don't know if the paintings have been copied from photographs or drawn from memory or imagination. They are photographic in their realism, and they appear more carefully done than the mural inside the temple. I take pictures of all of them. The most memorable one (to me) shows a young woman lying dead inside her hut. Blood is flowing from her body; bloody bootprints surround the body and lead outside the hut. Next to her body, a very small child is sitting with an uncomprehending look on his face. The caption (in Tamil) reads "Mommy, why can't I have a rifle, too?"

A Couple of Imposters

Monday, 8 June. Tomorrow is full-moon day. It is a time of intense activity for all the local religions. While I am in Palugamam to visit the orphanages, the head of one orphanage invites me to a fire-walking ceremony at the Kannakiyamman Koyil at Koyil Porathivu, a nearby village, that evening. A large log fire is being fanned with neem leaves. The fire walking will not begin till the fire has burned down to white embers, at around two in the morning. The atmosphere is festive. Sweets, ice cream, and pinwheels are sold at stalls, and little boys set off firecrackers and other noisemakers. People dressed in their best clothes are sitting or sleeping in the sand. When we arrive two men are doing hook swinging, swinging from ropes with hooks stuck through the muscles of their backs. They dance sometimes, and a boy who looks to be in his late teens dances wildly, face-to-face with one of the hook-swinging men, like a mirror. They are almost but not quite touching, the boy's eyes never wavering from the eyes of the man with hooks pulling the flesh on his back.

All through the night the loudspeaker announces the names of people who are donating money; people come up to the announcer bringing sums of cash and pieces of paper, which the announcer reads as they come. The first announcements I hear are for large sums of money, but later most of the donations are for ten rupees. Often the announcer says that so-and-so has donated ten rupees to aid the victory of (or protect the life of) his (or her) brother (or sister or cousin or uncle or niece) who is fighting in Jaffna for the soil of Tamil Eelam; or to protect the soul of a relative who attained heroic death in fighting in Jaffna for the soil of Tamil Eelam. Meanwhile, the fire is dying down. As I sit in the sand, watching and listening, five or six young men crouch down beside me.

"Auntie!"

"Yes?"

"Don't you recognize us? From Alagar's house."

I look at their faces and do not remember them. Their speech and gestures are polite, and they are smiling, but their bodies are tense, their eyes are burning and wide open, and their gazes never waver from mine. They remind me of starving children staring at a birthday cake. It's scary to be the cake. What do they want?

"Where do you live?" I ask.

" Arasadithivu. You came to where we live. Don't you remember? The video team. The playing field — you were taking photographs there."

"Are you with Satyan?"

"Yes! Satyan!"

"Will you be walking the fire tonight?" I inquire.

The speaker says no. He goes on to say something I don't understand about there being an army camp nearby and five *iyakkam* being captured and imprisoned there; they need to be saved but cannot be. And for some reason this explains why they cannot walk the fire.

"We walk the fire at the temple at Arasadithivu, but not here."

"Auntie, this boy here" — the speaker gestures toward one of his friends sitting next to him —"is a bad boy. He wants to go back with you to your country. Will you take him?" Aha. So this is what they want. Still, I am afraid of them.

"What will I say to the guards along the way?"

"What will you say?"

"I will say that this boy is my little Tiger brother." They laugh and for the first time look away, then back at me.

"Auntie, you must not say that! Auntie, we are going."

"Okay. Bye."

The civilian boys who have brought me here are silent through this exchange. They have brought a toy automatic rifle, "as a joke" (*mūsh-pātti*). I wonder where it is now.

They ask me, "Did you know them?"

"A little."

"Are they *iyakkam*?"

"Yes."

"That's a lie," says one.

A few days later I visit Alagar's house and am eating lunch there when the same boys turn up on the roadside. They call to Sita for Alagar, and she says he has gone away somewhere. But I know he has gone somewhere else. Suddenly, the boys seem different to me. They do not attempt to enter the house but watch me from the road as I eat my lunch. They are grinning. What could they want?

"Are those boys from the movement?" I ask.

"No, they are just common boys," says Sita.

I close the window so they can't watch me eat.

No End and No Escape

On 29 June, the army attacks Kokkadichcholai. The attack happens as I am on the bus from Batticaloa to Colombo, where I am to gather myself and then fly back home. But I do not learn about the attack until about ten days later, when I pick up a newspaper and read about it. The army probably waited until my departure to go in: neither side wants Westerners as casualties or witnesses of the conflict. I don't know what to do. I am tired and worried and frightened and angry. Instead of going back to Batticaloa, I take the plane I am scheduled to take, back home.

I write to Vasanta and Rosa after I return to New Zealand in July and receive a response from Rosa dated 17 August 1998. It contains this news:

In July the army came and burned the whole police station and courthouse, then they burned the political office in Munaikkaadu too. And also they shot the OIC [officer in charge] of the Police Station, Karttikka, that heavyset girl, and also three women police and two boys in the movement. We all left our houses and ran to a storehouse in a neighboring village.

The army came to our house and broke the windows (of the new house) and plucked many coconuts and destroyed them. Also in M-tivu in one family a shell hit a 14-year-old girl, and she died. That girl's father was wounded in both legs. Her younger sister too was wounded. Both of them are in a Batticaloa clinic. Then on the first of August in Manapiddi a bomber airplane dropped bombs. In that, one boy and nine cattle died. We are living in real fear. Yesterday the army came to Porathivu and returned at night, therefore we are really afraid. Even the children in the house are afraid.

Won't you come here again? If you come, you can stay in our house. Our area is fearful. We thought you might not have arrived at your country. When we saw your letter we were really happy. There is nothing else new.

CHAPTER 10

Look for What You Do Not See

Metaphors Again

Social scientists sometimes talk about power as though it were all that existed or as though nothing else were important. And yet one may argue that the concept of power itself, as a social reality, has not been sufficiently problematized. Max Weber's definition of power as the ability to get another to do your will is simple and clear, but it conduces to the idea of power as a substance or quality that inheres in some individuals or is projected onto them by others through mysterious mechanisms. Foucault's idea of power as one-way knowledge (I see all of you, but you cannot see me) has also proved useful. However, one may question the notion that real power over some Other and real knowledge of that Other necessarily coincide. Did Orientalists see the people they were constructing? Edward Said said no. Orientalists had the authority, within the West, to describe the East, even as they did not actually *see* the people they were describing, let alone hear them, and therefore they had only a false and distorted knowledge of those people.

Both Weber and Foucault use physical metaphors to describe social power. For Weber, social power is like the potential stored behind a dam: an ability to do work, to move things (or people) at the will of the agent who controls them. Pierre Bourdieu's concept of symbolic capital likewise entails the accumulation of a form of energy. For Foucault, power is more like kinetic energy, a rapids shaped by and shaping the structure of stone beneath it, which human agents might ride well or badly but which they can hardly be said to control. Is anything other than a physical metaphor possible for the description of social power? Is the notion of social power itself a mere metaphor?

Adopting the physical metaphor, one might say that power as potential or kinetic energy exists wherever there is a differential. When water flows downhill, the energy of this flow can be captured and transformed into other kinds of power, such as electricity. Electrons flow from places with a surplus of electrons to places with a deficit. The energy of their flow can be captured, channeled, and made to do work, to effect a planned (as opposed to random) physical change in the world. Channels for the flow of electricity can be minutely organized to create electronic devices. A vast differential — between two neighboring clouds, for instance — can lead to an enormously powerful flow of electrons.

In society, also, power may be said to exist only where there are differentials. One person or party has power over another because one has more money, more physical strength, more knowledge, or more favors owed than the other, and so can exert power, *has* power, over the other who has less — but only if the two live in the same cognitive, emotional, and physical world. For power to exist between you and me, there must be a connection between us. No matter how poor you are or how rich I am, I have no power over you unless there is a social connection between us — even if it is distant and mediated by many others. Power can arise only in actual relationships, in a realization of a differential.

There are different kinds of power. If I have more money than you but you have more knowledge than I, the interaction between these opposing differentials (if there is any interaction) will be complex. There are many ways in which stored energy may be used, misused, wasted, or preserved. Right here is a matter to consider. Potential energy, the ability to make changes in the world, is one thing; how this ability is used is another. Something other than power itself acts upon power.

Among human beings, power is not only a matter of measurable differentials. To get you to do my will, I must motivate you, and you must have a will to act in the way that I want you to. We must be in the same game. Power among human beings entails *emotion*. Thus we speak of the power of fear, the power of desire, the powers of laughter and grief, of pity, anger, affection, revulsion, curiosity, and delight. All such feelings move people to act, or to choose not to act, in particular ways.

Such feelings may be evoked, intentionally or unintentionally, and they may be manipulated by others. Through manipulation of emotion, one person may exercise power over another person or over a whole population. You can stir up a crowd to a level of collective emotion that turns it into an enormous force.

But again, sheer quantity is not all there is to power, emotional or physical. Consider the power of a microchip. It enables the accomplishment of work because of its minute organization. Likewise, the power of the human body does not lie in its sheer quantity of substances or energies. It takes the minute interaction and organization of these components on molecular levels in so many different ways, systems within systems and every single system different from every other, for a body to have life and the ability to do those things that living bodies do. The organization and interaction of different emotions on a microlevel likewise make a community or civilization alive in a certain sense. In different communities of people, similar sets of emotions may be intricately organized in different ways so as to comprise overall arrangements as different from one another as hope from despair.

The surreality of Paduvankarai during that year was a constellation of surprising emotional organizations that made one gasp and ponder. The experience of each was ephemeral, lasting just moments, leaving just traces. The power was immeasurable.

Love Quarrels

Amartya Sen (2006) writes that Indians not only love to talk, they also love to argue. Sen demonstrates what many scholars of India have noticed and written about, but have rarely dared to generalize beyond the specific domains of their studies. Sen shows how argument pervades Indian literature, ideology, and everyday life. But the love of argument extends beyond the boundaries of India and pervades Sri Lanka as well, or at least, it pervades Tamil Sri Lanka, just as it pervades Tamil and other civilizations in India. These civilizations are all intertwined, locked in ongoing, generally happy argument. Wives argue with husbands, devotees argue with gods, laborers argue with landlords, children argue with parents, subsistence farmers deprived of water argue with huge multinational corporations, poets argue, theologians argue, doctors argue, people who just met in a train compartment argue, and of course politicians argue. The result of such arguments is generally not the triumph of one point of view and the defeat of another, but the proliferation of viewpoints — although, if it is a matter of will, of one thing being done and another not being done, in practice, in the short run, one argument has to win. In itself, however, performed with no aim, and even if it is performed with an aim, argument arouses passion and hones the intellect. Argument is fun.

Sen laments those situations in modern South Asia in which argument is stifled and distorted to become fundamentalist arrogance, violent conflict, and warfare. In such situations, not only argument, but the very possibility of dialogue dies. People inflict terrible suffering on one another, killing wantonly, dying in torment, or living shorn of all but the barest shreds of subsistence, and sometimes all but the barest shreds of their very souls.

In war-torn Batticaloa, however, argument of the former type continued with full spirit. Journalists argued with government at the risk of their lives; village civilians argued with Tigers, knowing the danger of doing so. I am sure that not everyone argued with military might, but a surprising number of people did. The late D. S. Sivaram's mother argued with him, saying, "You can't argue with a bullet."[1] She was right, because a bullet in itself has no consciousness, but Sivaram continued to argue anyway, to great effect, awaiting his death by a bullet, which came soon enough.

In Paduvankarai, the proliferation of points of view took the form of *summā* narratives, sometimes arguing with each other ("He's just saying that *summā*!" "No, *he's* just saying *that summā*!"), baffling my efforts to know what was the "real" truth, "what really happened," and contributing to my feeling that nothing was real and anything was possible. At the same time, the *summā* narratives and arguments created bonds between us, where otherwise there might have been no relationship at all, and certainly no dialogue. The very fact of my wanting to know the truth behind a story, my aroused and thirsty curiosity, made me want to see people again.

As in Twilight

The people for whom this book was written — the young and the very young — were seen most clearly in peripheral vision, like small, distant stars. When I tried to focus on them, their images changed. They would not be pinned down for purposes of study and examination, and this was as it should be, as it always should be in ethnography. In numerous ways, they resisted my knowing them too well.

Some adults, and all adult Tigers, were much the same way. Individuals' stories about themselves and others blurred whatever might have been the simple truth of each person, even when the story itself, told *summā* — for fun, for no purpose, just kidding — was in fact the simple truth. The whole group's creation of surreal moments — the laminated representations of events found in videos and live performances, the joyful sports contests juxtaposed with planned armed attacks in which people killed and died, the horror turned into laughter — forced the question of what "really" happened into obscurity. All these planned performances were evasive tactics, to be sure, but they were more than just that. They evoked the artistry of civilians and combatants, they fed the soul, and they kept us from going crazy.

Michel de Certeau says that resistance is to be found between official events. Resistance is possible only for those to whom power is not attributed. Resistance alters the flow of power and the habits of vision. It reveals the hidden or partly hidden. Between official events, Nimal led me to see his starving family, Vidya showed me her struggle for love and respect, Nalini showed me her closeness to death, Menan showed me the freedoms that mattered to him, Vasanta's baby Jeyshani turned from her mother to offer me comfort, the baby Vithusa fought being fed. In official events, such as the interviews with high school students, I was shown what I was supposed to see. On the edges of official events, I was enabled to see other things.

Pierre Clastres has argued that certain people on the margins of states actively resist incorporation into state structures. By his analysis, they are natural anarchists. They do not *want* to be part of a larger, official body. Daniel Nettle argues that the very fact of linguistic diversity is a mystery, a sign that people do not *want* to be well understood. Veena Das argues that the figure of the child "haunts theories of everyday life but is never fully accounted for." Maybe children do not *want* to be fully accounted for. Maybe there is some degree of natural anarchy in us all. When one dwells in this anarchy, in the shadows of vision, in the place of not being understood, one finds both the surreal and perhaps the closest one will ever come to what "really" happened.

· · ·

By the time I arrived there to do my research, Paduvankarai was fully globalized. News and pictures from afar came there immediately, and news and pictures from there travelled afar. So did people. New technologies were adopted and adapted to the purposes of the moment; ancient technologies, such as ox-drawn carts, continued as staples of survival. Such an environment fostered unselfconscious bricolage. It also fostered a feeling of surreality in me, as when Selvi, a young village woman with no pretense to cosmopolitanism and no direct experience of life more than twenty miles from her home, immediately comprehended and enjoyed an episode of *The X-Files*. It was surreal to me that she liked this show. And the show itself was intentionally surreal, and this is what made it enjoyable to me and presumably to Selvi. Maybe, having grown up in a thoroughly surreal world, her understanding of the relation between fact and fantasy was more complex than mine. It was almost literally, physically, in my peripheral vision that I saw how familiar Selvi was with the strange modern world.

Tamil Warriors

It was also in my peripheral vision that I saw Das, the quiet man who raised pigeons and puppies, and whom I saw entertaining his golden puppy, named after the princess Di, with the mechanical toys Vithusa could not play with. For Das, his love of animals was not an official event, and not important, and he was surprised when he learned I had written of Di's affection for him. To me it was the most important thing about him. A few years after I met him, I learned that Das had been killed in combat. It is not unlikely that during his life he had killed people, enemy soldiers, as part of his job.

And it was in my peripheral vison that I saw Meena and Anbarasi, young women just briefly returned from combat, going back into combat, wounded and in one case facially disfigured, apparently not concerned about their wounds, and not embarrassed about asking and taking plastic children's toys, tiny signs of my care for them, back with them to the battlefront. That gesture spoke eloquently, in a language I cannot translate, of what lived in the hearts of these girl warriors.

· · ·

The Tiger fighter I knew the best was Sita. No doubt there were many important details about her life that I never learned. But I know for sure it was not what she saw in combat that hurt her most. One might answer — yes, but did she not feel that she might be to blame for her daughter's disability? Did she not suspect that she was being punished by some higher power for the sin of killing? Did the fact of seeing combat not do this to her? But I in turn would say, how many loving mothers do not feel guilt for some serious harm that comes to their child at birth or for that matter much later, regardless of how that harm comes about? And how many soldiers do not feel guilt when they kill? The ones who feel no guilt, no sorrow, no pain are the ones we should worry about. But the absence of certain feelings sometimes escapes even peripheral vision.

· · ·

We in the Western world are familiar with books by and about Western soldiers. We learn that some such soldiers have deep moral reservations about the wars they are fighting in. For some soldiers, combat is a test of manhood, indeed it is the one thing that turns a boy into a man. For some soldiers, war is hell, and yet it is also the peak experience of their lives. Some soldiers experience combat as a time when they are forced to control their emotions, to repress their most deep-seated spontaneous impulses, and such control to be achieved must be practiced before combat and maintained after as a permanent habit. Others experience combat as a time when the chaos within them is unleashed, and they go on killing sprees without remorse, without thinking about who they are killing, or why, or how it feels to die in this way. Some soldiers think they are fighting against absolute evil, and seek to destroy their enemies absolutely. Some soldiers enter combat for glory and excitement, and some find just the opposite, while others find just what they want and continue to seek it and find it throughout the war and perhaps for the rest of their lives. Some soldiers fight for honor, and some for their homes far away. And some soldiers just try to get by, in a situation beyond their control.

Have I missed any? You fill them in. Are all combatants all the world over subject to the same psychologies? To which categories do Das, Meena, Anbarasi, and all the other Tamil Tigers belong? Any of them? Or are there ways of being a soldier that we in the West have not contemplated?

In certain modern Western societies, trained combatants who enter civilian society often experience problems, because in the military they become something the civilian world cannot tolerate. Military life has rendered them sociopathic. It is not only the experience of warfare, but the training to engage in it in a certain way, that changes them, and in some ways decivilizes them. The training is inseparable from the practice, and in actual combat, some soldiers may face the truth that they are not prepared after all. If this happens, they may become doubly crazed. That any such people are able to return to "normal" life bespeaks the strength of human resilience.

But the military branch of a society is not a separate thing from the civilian branch. The military is an outgrowth and creation of civilian society. Military culture is fed by civilian culture, and in turn feeds back into it. Coming home from military service may in fact help heal the serviceman (if he needs healing) precisely because it is home, the place he was before the madness, the place he fought to preserve from the madness (or so he believed), the place he loves (or once did love). And maybe he will be accepted back and loved in return for the love he believed he gave in his sacrifice of himself and enemy others, loved not despite but for the very horrors he has committed on foreign soil (but how foreign is it, really?).

It has been assumed that combatants from the Tamil Tigers go through a similar process. Western NGOs have established rehabilitation, re-education, and reintegration programs for young women who have officially left the LTTE. I don't know if there are rehabilitation programs for young men who leave the LTTE, or for middle-aged people who do so. But often enough, the biggest problem that young female LTTE-leavers face is the fact that civilian society does not allow them to use the skills they learned in the movement, and the additional fact that in civilian society they are stigmatized by their short hair (in traditional Sri Lankan Tamil society, women must keep their hair long). Unlike their male counterparts, many of them have been rejected by the civilian society to which they wished to return. The girls' hair was different, their bodies were different, they had new, nonfeminine skills, such as operating motor vehicles, they had become accustomed to wearing trousers, and they were no longer acceptable as good Tamil women. The men had never ceased to be real Tamil men, thus they needed no reintegration. But the girls had ceased to be what a real Tamil woman is supposed to be. Thus, programs with "a real gender component" — such as sewing or home decorating — are suggested for girls leaving the LTTE.[2] Vocations such as carpentry, masonry, welding, and computer repair are inappropriate to the girls, because traditional civilian society cannot accept a female doing such work.

· · ·

How do the Tigers, the militant branch of Tamil society, manage emotion? How are their selves constructed? What kind of people are they? For this book has been expected to answer such questions.

I did not ask Meena and Anbarasi, who had not left the movement and remained active combatants, whether they had been damaged in mind and heart by their war experiences. (This would have been a stupid question to ask of them in any case, no matter how it had been framed). Their return to the fray may have been answer enough. It may have been that for them as for Gamani (a young man), combat had become their life and that was the life they wanted. Or they may have realized that what they had become would render them unacceptable to civilian society: they could not go back even if they wanted to, so they made the best of the situation in which they lived, as combatants for the LTTE. They would be the best soldiers they could possibly be, and be happy with that.

· · ·

The Tamil Tigers are culturally different from the Americans and Europeans who fought and fight in foreign and domestic wars. This is because Tamil culture is very different from Euro-American culture. Tamil culture contains vast internal differences, and its external boundaries are blurred, if they exist at all. Euro-American culture is the same. I know all that. But I will go out on a limb and assert that the great majority of Tamil people are composed quite differently from the great majority of Euro-American people.

Both Euro-American society and Tamil society are said to be male dominant. But gender hierarchies assume different forms in different societies. While European societies have undergone their own changes, American society has become increasingly militarized since the Second World War, and the American military has become radically masculine — some would say hypermasculine, in a bad way. It is not my aim to prove the hypermasculinity of the American military to my readers. I only ask readers to accept that the American military expects its soldiers to be paragons of manhood, in a certain specifically American way, and the presence of women in the United States Armed Forces has had little if any effect on this ethos.

Men among the Tamil Tigers continue to dominate the movement, but they are not expected to be the kind of men that those in the American military are expected to be. The experiences of women among the Tamil Tigers are therefore different from the experiences of women in the American military. Women and girls who join the Tigers aim "to be like the brothers" — in some cases, like their own brothers who have joined the movement. But what is it about the brothers that Vidya, for one, desires to emulate? This is another question I never thought to ask. But I would guess that it is the strength of their brothers, their courage, and the love and respect they garner that Vidya and girls like her sought and seek to achieve. I do not think it was the joy of killing, if killing can be a joy. Whether Vidya got what she sought from the movement is another matter.

In Tamil culture, manhood is not something to be achieved, as it is in Western warrior cultures. In particular, the "tempering and toughening" that in some other cultures must be applied to turn a "boy" into a "man" and to differentiate a "man" from a "woman" are the regular experience of most ordinary Tamil human beings, especially the poor — men and women alike. The poor live by hard physical labor, and their lives entail bodily and emotional hardship as a matter of course. They risk their lives constantly, and they see their loved ones die and know that they can do nothing. They do not have to be trained to deal with these things. That the Tigers draw most of their combatants from among the poor is not only a reflection of the fact that — as in other countries — the rich can buy their way out; it is also, perhaps incidentally, a consequence of the fact that the poor are better prepared for combat in the first instance. Tiger combatants are drawn not from the poor in general, but in particular from the rural poor, who know better than anyone else how to survive under the harsh conditions in the places they will be fighting. (The survival skills of the urban poor, by contrast, do not necessarily match what modern warfare requires of them.)

·   ·   ·

Just as in Tamil culture, manhood is not a state to be achieved, so childhood is not a state to grow out of. Rather it is a state to be revered. The broken little Vithusa was honored and adored by grown seasoned soldiers. Children in general were adored, but they were not protected from hardship; indeed, in most cases they could not be protected. Some Sri Lankan Tamils told me that a child can endure suffering better than an adult. I imagine this belief may be true. It is supported by the evidence that children do endure so much, and still somehow come out on top. The power of children is in the love they elicit in spite of themselves, and in their play. In Tamil culture, the play of children and the power of gods are the same thing. And gods, like children, are loved without reserve, despite all the trouble they cause.

Notes

1. Introduction

1. Patricia Lawrence (1997) offers a stunning account of ways religious practitioners in Paduvankarai address the horrors of war.

2. I still think of the United States as my own country, although I have been resident in New Zealand for many years.

3. The fact that children act on their worlds to change them has not always been recognized by social scientists. Hence the manifesto by James and Prout (1990: 8): "Children are and must be seen as active in the construction and determination of their own social lives, the lives of those around them and the societies they live in. Children are not just passive subjects of social structures and processes."

4. See Das 1991, Coles 1986, Behera and Trawick 2001, and Jones 2002 (the story of Erica Pratt) for examples.

5. See Qvortrup 2004. Qvortrup argues against the concept of childhood as a state of deficiency and incompletion.

6. See, for example, Ehrenreich 1997; Bloch 1992; Shulman 1993.

7. Carolyn Nordstrom (2004) demonstrates how in wars of our time, these three categories and others have become inextricably mixed.

8. Victor Turner developed the idea of the liminal in his early work *The Ritual Process*. Turner was building on Arnold van Gennep's classic *Rites of Passage* (1909). Both Turner and Gennep employed the concept of the liminal primarily with respect to adolescent initiation rites, which transform a child into an adult. Subsequent authors, most notably Mary Douglas (1966), have developed similar but more general concepts concerning human attitudes to beings who are between, astride, or outside of fixed cultural categories. To such beings is attributed dangerous power, Douglas argues. More recently, however, the concept of fixed cultural categories has been challenged by some leading anthropologists

(e.g., Dirks 2001). In response to that challenge, the concept of liminality may also have to be reconsidered.

9. Mies (1998) argues that modern global capitalism is predicated on a view of "nature" as a passive, infinite resource, there to be used by human beings. In this sense, nature is taken for granted. See also the discussion of Francis Bacon's view of nature in Keller 1985. Bacon feminized "Nature," which in his view was there to be conquered. In both the Baconian view as described by Keller and the capitalist view as described by Mies, the natural world outside the control of mankind (specifically male) has no value in itself.

10. See, for example, Kakar 1979. Kakar posits that in South Asia, childhood is imagined as a kind of golden age; life is all downhill from there.

11. All the information about *piḷḷaittamiṟ* in this book comes from Richman 1997. The interpretation of the genre, however, including the suggestion that it represents a Tamil idealization of childhood, is entirely my own.

12. Richman 1997: 217.

13. To describe the ideal, aspects of which are commonly realized in daily life, is not to deny the fact that terrible child abuse occurs among both Tamils and Sinhalese in Sri Lanka, as it does among New Zealanders, Americans, and many other Western peoples. Child abuse, though it happens, is abhorred by Sri Lankans of all classes, ethnicities, and political parties. It is not the norm in that country, any more than it is in New Zealand. In Sri Lanka, anti-LTTE groups and individuals point fingers at the LTTE for the latter's employment of youths, including some quite young ones, in its war against the government, while supporters of the LTTE criticize the Sri Lankan government for its failure to curb the extensive practice of child sex tourism in Sri Lanka. Neither has openly acknowledged that both parties, in their waging of war against each other, have contributed to the fragmentation of families and the increased vulnerability of children to abuse for this reason.

14. Goff 2004a: 8.

15. The *Kalingattuparani* was composed by the poet Cayankondar to celebrate the successful expedition of the Chola king Kaluttonga's general Karunakara Tondaiman against the armies of Kalinga in about A.D. 1110. The poem is discussed at length in Shulman 1985.

2. The Past

1. Prior to colonial times, the island went by the name of Lanka. The Portuguese called it Ceylon, which remained its official name until 1972. For the sake of consistency, I use *Lanka* or *Sri Lanka* throughout this book, regardless of the period referred to.

2. Tambiah 1986.

3. Nordstrom (2004: 26–28). Nordstrom witnessed the events of July 1983 in Colombo and insists that it was not just men, and not just thugs, who joined in the terror against Tamils. Neither did all, or even most, Sinhalese join in the

violence. Many did not succumb to the madness, but gave shelter to Tamils flee-ing the mobs or did what they could to help in other ways.

Pradeep Jeganathan (1997), who was also a witness of the violence in Colombo in 1983, documents robberies and atrocities committed by ordinary Sinhala people against known and unknown Tamil people during July 1983. Stanley Tambiah (1997) seeks an understanding of mob violence that is ignited by, but goes beyond, political manipulation.

4. Tambiah 1986.

5. Wells 2002: 61–80.

6. Tambiah 1992.

7. Anderson 1991.

8. Dharmadasa 2005.

9. Ramanujan 1967.

10. Masatoshi Nagatomi, "The History of Buddhism." Unpublished lec-tures, Harvard University, 1967. Nagatomi was a great scholar and teacher of Buddhism at Harvard University. As an undergraduate there, I took his year-long course in the history of Buddhism. I still have the extensive lecture notes I took at that time.

11. Everyone adopting the religion of the Buddha must adhere to the Five Precepts. These are, first, to refrain from destroying living creatures; second, to refrain from taking that which is not given; third, to refrain from sexual mis-conduct; fourth, to refrain from incorrect speech; and fifth, to refrain from the use of intoxicating drinks and drugs. In addition to adhering to the Five Pre-cepts, everyone intending to become a Buddhist monk (*bhikku*) must accept the Three Refuges. These are the Buddha (as guide), the dharma (as universal code of behavior), and the *sangha* (the community of monks).

The inference from the passage cited from the *Mahāvāmsa* is that only a *bhikku* is fully human; a person who has adopted the Buddhist path without becoming a *bhikku* is merely half human, and nobody else is human at all.

12. Given the Five Precepts, how can one make war in the name of Bud-dhism? Christian crusaders evidently faced a similar contradiction, for, accord-ing to the Church of Rome at that time, killing was a mortal sin. Recent inter-pretations of the Crusades revive the claim that these wars were indeed ideolog-ical and not only about booty. Knights of the Crusades fully believed that their violation of Christian precepts meant they had some accounting to do before God. To stave off eternal damnation, crusaders went on pilgrimages and made donations to monasteries. According to Joan Acocella (2004: 94), "The rise of the monastic orders in the Middle Ages owes much to knightly guilt." The *Mahāvāmsa* of a millennium earlier anticipates this means of atonement.

13. Shulman (1985) describes the religious dilemma faced by medieval South Indian (Saiva) kings, one of whose main jobs was to engage in warfare and killing. Only Brahmans could take on the resulting pollution for these kings.

14. In the medieval period, there were three great South Indian kingdoms: Chera, Chola, and Pandya.

15. Sivaram 1992b. In *Silappadikāram,* the northern kings are called Aryan.

This nomenclature suggests that the Aryan-Tamil divide is what Senguttuvan's expedition and battles were really about. In other words, South Indian kings were already defining themselves as a body against north Indian kings, despite the tolerance of diverse people, religions, and walks of life evidenced on a popular level in the texts by Ilango and his successor, Sattanar. The *Vanji* section of the *Silappadikāram* was adduced by Tamil nationalists of the early twentieth century as evidence of the martial superiority of Tamils over the people of northern India, who outnumbered and sometimes dominated the people of the south.

During the colonial period, the assertion that Tamils were a fighting people was most important, as the British had defined the Tamils as not a "martial" (therefore not virile) "race" — implying that the Tamils were weak and did not know how to fight, as compared, for instance, to the Gurkhas, Sikhs, Rajputs, and other north Indian groups that were characterized as martial and therefore preferred as military recruits. The notion of Aryans goes back to Vedic times, when Vedic people styled themselves as *arya*s and conquerors of the dark-skinned *dasu*s. The latter came to be identified with speakers of Dravidian languages. As a range of Tamil nationalisms arose, some of them pro-British and others anti-British, the issue of whether the Tamil "race" was essentially warlike (hence capable of armed rebellion) or fundamentally high-minded and peaceful (hence trustworthy and nonrebellious) became highly politicized. Militants favored the martial image, nonmilitants the peaceful one (Sivaram 1992a).

Since World War II, the notion of an Aryan-Dravidian racial divide has fallen into disrepute among scholars. But the slippage between language, culture, and race continues to hold sway in the popular imagination, both Western and South Asian.

16. Tambiah 1976.

17. Ilango 1965: 162.

18. Shattan (Danielou trans.) 1989: 45–46.

19. See for instance Hart and Heifetz 1999, poem 139 (pp. 100–101).

20. From this narrative we learn that starvation was a concern in the Tamil lands even during the Sangam age. Meanwhile, the *Mahāvāmsa* also tells of kings who wish to extend their kingdoms but cannot do so without taxing their people; they are saved by miraculous gifts from the gods. One message one may derive from these stories is that only by a miracle can you expand your kingdom through warfare, and feed the people at the same time. In the post-Sangam age in the Tamil countries, feeding others, especially devotees of Siva, becomes an important religious concern.

21. The fact that Manimekalai is just on the verge of puberty when she realizes the tragedy of being alive and chooses a life of asceticism is reiterated throughout the story. In *Silappadikāram*, to which *Manimēkalai* is a sequel, the courtesan Madhavi makes her debut at the age of twelve. Madhavi later gives birth to Manimekalai. The twelve-year-old girl as the pinnacle of human spiritual power, physical beauty, and moral perfection is a theme common in Tamil poetry of the Sangam age and later.

22. A friend and fellow scholar, better versed in Tamil language and culture

than I, recently commented that as soon as you hear a Tamil man start talking about Tamil "culture" (*paṇbāḍu*), you know that a reference to the ideal Tamil woman is soon to follow. It may be argued that Tamil culture contains strongly feminist strands, even as the murderous abuse of women and girls is endemic to that same culture. For an early effort to make that argument, see Egnor [Trawick] 1978.

23. See Obeyesekere 1984: 3.

24. Tambiah 1992: 133–34.

25. Poets could criticize gods as well as kings. Consider this poem to Lord Jagannath (a form of Vishnu), translated by Narayana Rao and Shulman (1998: 37):

> You're so drunk on wealth and power
> that you ignore my presence.
> Just wait: when the Buddhists come,
> your whole existence
> depends on me.

(The Buddhist monks and literati were adept at logic and argument.)

26. Argenti-Pillen (2003) translates the term *yakkuva* as "creatures of the wild" and argues for the aptness of this translation in the southern Sri Lankan village context.

27. Tambiah 1992: 135, quoting de Silva 1986: 11.

28. Compare this view with that of Clastres (1994), who argues that a "centrifugal logic, which expresses itself from time to time in armed conflict . . . serves to maintain each community in its political independence" (164). He also states: "The nation may consider itself constituted, and the state may consider itself the exclusive holder of power, when the people upon whom its authority is exercised speak the same language as it does. The process of integration obviously involves the suppression of differences. The overriding centripetal force is the state, and all state organizations are ethnocidal" (49).

29. U.S. Library of Congress. n.d. Rise of Sinhalese and Tamil Ethnic Awareness. In *Sri Lanka: A Country Study.* http://countrystudies.us/sri-lanka/6.htm. Accessed 25 April 2006.

30. In recent times, the area containing Anuradhapura and Polonnaruwa, which is part of the dry zone of the north-central region, has become one of fierce contestation between Tamils and Sinhalese.

31. U.S. Library of Congress n.d.

32. See also Tambiah 1992: 138, quoting de Silva. Between the northeast and the southwest areas was a vast jungle belt, and the Tamils and Sinhalese lived in their separate parts of the island, though not totally isolated from each other, until the first quarter of the twentieth century.

33. See Dirks 2001 for a thorough account of British governing strategies in India. Many of these same strategies were also applied in Sri Lanka (then known as Ceylon). Among the many differences between Sri Lanka and India was the relative unimportance of caste in Sri Lanka, whereas in India it came to be seen by the British as well as by colonial and later Western theorists as all-important.

34. U.S. Library of Congress n.d.

35. Scott 1994: 155, 269n.

36. Herring 2001: 140.

37. U.S. Library of Congress n.d.

38. U.S. Library of Congress n.d.

39. Cf. Dharmadasa 2005: "Even today, if somebody wants to come to power, it is very important to cater to the Sinhala-Buddhist opinion. Maybe a majority of people's opinion is formed by politicians themselves. It is difficult to say whether a majority of people approve the kind of nationalism fostered by political interests. Anyway, during voting time, these things influence their thinking."

40. Herring 2001: 146, 148.

41. Gillies 1992: 44, quoted in Herring 2001: 150.

42. Herring 2001: 153–54.

43. U.S. Library of Congress n.d.

44. Argenti-Pillen 2003.

45. Herring and Esman 2001: 36.

46. Even now, one may meet people in Colombo who say they don't know whether they are Tamil or Sinhalese or which language they speak. In precolonial times, there would have been many more such. Marriages between Tamils and Sinhalese are common, and they violate no traditional rules. The kingdom of Kandy was founded on mixed marriages. Tamils and Sinhalese worship at each other's shrines and temples and attend each other's ceremonies — although less frequently now than in the past. The great Katharagama temple in southern Sri Lanka is both Saiva and Buddhist: Katharagama is a god of both the Saiva (Hindu) and Sinhala Buddhist religions. Many Tamils are Christian, and so are some Sinhalese. In the past, some Tamils changed their ethnicity simply by changing their language. You don't have to prove you are Sinhalese or Tamil by tracing your genealogy. Many Sri Lankans are happy with, even proud of, their mixed descent.

47. Scott 1994: 161.

48. Tambiah 1992.

49. Ramaswamy 1997: 62–63. The verse in the quoted passage is from *Kuyil*, 6 December 1960, 6.

50. Ramaswamy 1997: 1.

51. U.S. Library of Congress n.d.

52. Tambiah 1992: 46.

53. Counterinsurgency experts who have studied the Tigers to see what makes them tick aver that Prabhakaran is highly selective as to the people he chooses to join the ranks of the Black Tigers. They must pass many tests before they are selected and undergo rigorous training afterward. Even then, not all of them are given the opportunity to exercise their skills. The idea that Prabhakaran sends deluded children out to blow themselves up is a malicious myth. It does not help adversaries of the Tigers to believe in this myth, although they have sometimes used it for propaganda purposes.

54. Mostly it is said that the LTTE gets its funding from the Tamil diaspora. But laws forbidding residents of other countries to send material support to the LTTE do not appear to have made a dent. The LTTE also is said to own legitimate businesses, largely in shipping, the profits from which it may use to fund its activities. The skills and resources the LTTE has been able to garner are impressive, to the extent that it is widely considered the wealthiest and most effective counterstate military organization in the world. There have been rumors of piracy and one widely publicized act of piracy, in which the LTTE diverted a shipment of mortars destined for the Sri Lankan government into its own hads. But nobody (outside the Central Committee of the LTTE) has been able to determine precisely where the LTTE gets its funding, let alone block the flow.

3. March 1996

1. The names of all individuals I met in the field (except Menan, at his request) have been changed. In some cases, other identifying features have also been changed.

2. TELO is Tamil Eelam Liberation Organization; EPRLF is Eelam People's Revolutionary Liberation Front; PLOTE is People's Liberation Organization of Tamil Eelam; EPDP is Eelam People's Democratic Party. These are the main ones that remained as paramilitary groups while I was there.

3. Translation from Egnor [Trawick] 1978. Tirumular's *Tirumantiram* dates from the tenth century, and is one of the foundational Saiva Siddhanta texts.

4. *Kalattil,* 6 July 1997, 9, my translation. Elephant Pass is the isthmus connecting the Jaffna Peninsula to the rest of the island.

5. Refrain of song performed by Tamizhenti, middle-aged female agricultural laborer, Chingleput District, Tamil Nadu, 10 February 1996.

6. One reader has queried how a person could become a doctor if she has only completed her O-level exams. The answer is that in this war environment, people did not have the luxury of attending medical school. The LTTE provided some individuals with medical training, and they became doctors — one might call them medics or primary medical care providers — for the LTTE. The LTTE trained its medical care providers well, and as far as everyone, Tiger or civilian, was concerned, they were "real" doctors.

The same reader has asked whether this doctor were Sita's only sister and, if so, whether this information conflicted with the fact that later in the interview we learn she has other sisters. The answer is that Sita did not say this was her only sister. Early in the interview, Sita mentioned that she had a younger sister. Later in the interview she mentioned an older sister. Sita was not dissimulating in this interview, nor was she confused about the facts of her family.

7. Sea Tigers are effectively the naval division of the LTTE. They conduct warfare at sea. I made up the term "Earth Tigers." What I meant was Tigers who work and fight on land. Around the time of the interview, a story was running in the Sri Lankan newspapers about two young female Sea Tigers who had been

captured at sea. They had been put in jail and nobody knew what to do with them.

8. Nordstrom (2004: 71–72) quotes the words of a Sri Lankan Army commander who privately confesses to her that his troops behave as Sita, Rosa (chapter 4) and others quoted in this book allege:

It's crazy, it's completely crazy. I can't control my troops. It's awful up there. One of the soldiers [government, largely Sinhalese] is hit by a guerrilla [Tamil], or they run over a land mine, or a bomb explodes, and they go nuts. It's been building up and building up, and they just go wild. The guerrillas have long since melted away, and the soldiers turn their fury on the first available target. Of course, the only people around are civilians. They open fire on everyone, they destroy everything in sight, they rape and torture people they catch on the street or in their homes, they lob bombs into homes and schools, markets and city streets. I've tried to stop them, I try to control the situation. I can't. None of us commanders can — though god knows some don't try. The troops just take off like this and there's no stopping them. We can't discipline them. We can't prosecute them. We can't dismiss them. We'd have no army left if we did. The situation up north is completely out of control, and there isn't a damn thing we can do about it.

9. A shorter version of this chapter was published as Trawick 1997.

4. Vasanta and Rosa

1. *Vīrakēsari*, July 1991, my translation.

6. What Menan Showed Me

1. Pine Ridge is an Oglala Lakota Sioux Native American reservation in the state of South Dakota. "Unemployment on the reservation hovers around 85 percent, and 97 percent live below the federal poverty level. Adolescent suicide is four times the national average. . . . The population on Pine Ridge has among the shortest life expectancies of any group in the Western Hemisphere: approximately 47 years for males and in the low 50s for females. The infant mortality rate is five times the U.S. national average." (Wikipedia 2006). Alcoholism is rampant on Pine Ridge. Young people sniff gasoline to get high. The community has been reduced to this condition as a result of continued oppression, treaty violation, and armed confrontation with the U.S. federal government. After many years of failed efforts to maintain their way of life, their independence, and their dignity, the people seem to have simply given up. A number of books have been written and movies produced about the plight of the Oglala Sioux. The most famous of these is Brown 1970. A brief description of the massacre of Lakota Sioux trying to travel home to Pine Ridge is provided by Strom 1995.

Buffalo Creek was a mining community in West Virginia that was destroyed by a flood from a broken dam in 1972. The failure of the dam was caused by a combination of negligent strip-mining and heavy rains in the area. More than a hundred were killed and several thousand left homeless. Efforts to provide housing and counseling for the homeless failed to meet the needs of the formerly tight-knit community, which effectively ceased to exist after the flood. The best-known book about the Buffalo Creek disaster is Erikson 1978.

2. As of this writing, Menan lives abroad, working with a computer company, for which he designed the website. He is happy with his work. His mother, a lovely young woman with a fine sense of humor, remains in Batticaloa. He keeps in constant touch with her. She read what I wrote about him, we discussed what I wrote, and she laughed about the things he made me do.

3. At the age of fifteen, Menan had almost complete autonomy. His mother and other relatives, despite their concern for his safety, allowed him to navigate the world on his own. Perhaps this autonomy helps explain Menan's apparent ease in the face of hardship. As Jo Boyden observes: "There is some evidence that children who try actively to overcome adversity — by attempting to resolve the problems they face, regulate their emotions, protect their self-esteem and manage their social interactions — are likely to be more resilient than children who accept their fate passively, especially in the long run" (Boyden 2003: 8). The fact that Menan had a strong safety net, in the form of his family and their land and resources, also probably lent him confidence.

4. Coles (1986) and Das (1991), among others, have written extensively about certain children's communication of their thoughts through drawings and bodily demonstrations rather than through words. When the children are in danger or in trouble, these forms of communication are particularly significant. Both Das and Coles also showed how such children exercised agency (changing their worlds and making the people around them pay attention to what they wanted) through bodily action more than words. Both drawing and bodily action, unlike spoken words, involve the use of space. For useful discussions on the meaning of *agency,* see Daniel 1996 and Ahearn 2001. For children exercising agency in situations of extreme danger, see Boyden 2003 and Jones 2002.

7. Girls in the LTTE

1. Shah 2003.

2. Machel 1996. Machel was appointed in 1994 by the UN Secretary General to prepare a report of the effects of armed combat on children, pursuant to General Assembly resolution 48/147, "Protection of Children Affected by Armed Conflicts."

3. This body of law declares which acts are permitted during times of war. Each international law is actually a treaty among signatory states. States that do not sign a particular treaty are not bound by it. The most famous of the laws of war are the four Geneva Conventions, signed in 1949, shortly after the United Nations had come into being.

4. Machel 1996, paragraph 216.

5. Coalition to Stop the Use of Child Soldiers, 2005.

6. Subramanian and Mohan 1999.

7. The United States and the United Kingdom were among the six non-signatories to this convention.

8. CETO 2002.

9. Subramanian 1998.

10. She only said "fifth." I took it to mean fifth standard (fifth year of school), but she could have meant fifth form (tenth year of school).

8. Boys in the LTTE

1. Certeau 1984: xii.

2. Cf. Ondaatje 1982, acknowledgments. I checked this with Inbam, and he laughed but did not deny the charge.

3. Later I took a great picture of Rudrakumaran, which I developed in New Zealand and sent to him. Rosa wrote and told me he was pleased with it.

9. Spectacles and Mysteries

1. See Argenti-Pillen 2003.

2. When the Tigers consider that someone owes them taxes, they take a family member hostage until the person pays up. Vasanta was outraged when this happened to her.

3. *Dinamurasu* is a widely read Sri Lankan Tamil weekly, published in Colombo. Members of the LTTE and their supporters say it is run by the EPDP, one of the enemies of the LTTE. But Accan, who is a Tiger, reads it anyway, and probably so do others. At the time, it made for good reading. I, for one, looked for it each week when it came out.

4. *Frontline,* 7 February 1998.

5. The team used yellow as its color, but it did not use the Tiger emblem. And after all, it would not have been right or fair for the Tigers to support one school and one team more than the others, since they were sponsoring the whole event.

6. In 2005 some American soldiers in Iraq were found to be sending pictures of horribly mutilated Iraqi bodies to an Internet website in exchange for access to pornography. See Goff 2005.

7. Ai. Nadesan, the Batticaloa journalist and author of this and many other *Virakēsari* articles, was killed on 31 May 2004 by the usual "unknown gunmen." Countless reporters have been murdered during the course of this war. Of those who survive, some continue to report the news as they see fit — fearlessly — until they too are killed. Nadesan was one of those. The article cited here may not seem especially courageous. Nadesan seems simply to be reporting what the

STF announced. But the third sentence in the second paragraph of the article — "Please give help to the banned organization" — shows the kind of reporting for which he was killed. It could have been a typographical error, and the sentence might have been intended to read "Please *do not* give help to the banned organization." But, in retrospect, it seems probable that Nadesan made this "mistake" deliberately. While the STF was trying to warn people away from the Tigers, Nadesan's small sentence urges people to help them.

10. Look for What You Do Not See

1. Mark Whitaker, personal communication.
2. Peltzer 2005. In the foreword to her thesis, Peltzer speaks to the former LTTE members with whom she worked.

Finally, I would like to thank the girls. I still remember the first morning when you woke me up shouting "Sister, Sister." I remember your laughs, your smiles, your songs, your complaints of short hair, your surprise knowledge of "Baa Baa Black Sheep," your riding on the back of my bicycle through monsoon-like rains, your painting my nails, your surprised faces when you realized that my legs were shaved and my arms weren't, and the sadness in your eyes when it came time for me to leave and you asked to come with me so you would not be abducted again. Your writings provided an insight into your lives that was hidden by your laughter and I truly appreciate your letting me into your thoughts. I respect your courage and your bravery.

Throughout her thesis, Peltzer cites examples of beautiful, deeply emotional poetry written by the girls with whom she was staying.

Peltzer's experience with girls who had left the LTTE was similar to my experience with girls who were still in it. But a few pages later (p. 8) she cites without comment Niloufer de Mel's assertion that within the LTTE, "a woman loses the ability of emotional expression and the reality of her driving impulses lies in the complete obedience of the will of the militant leadership on whose behalf she struggles" (De Mel 2003).

The girls with whom Peltzer worked were not unhappy with what they had learned in the LTTE. She writes (2005: 17), "In my interactions with the girls I found that the girls often wanted to share experiences with me which ranged from LTTE songs, dances, skills, physical exercises and acquired skills. Unfortunately, the policy I routinely heard from NGOs was that the excombatants' time in the LTTE was not a subject to be bridged with excombatants." Traumatic experiences in the LTTE also were not to be discussed. Even when the girls wanted to talk about these experiences, they were not permitted to do so. Some had been abducted by the LTTE and feared re-abduction. Abductions were traumatic because the girls were separated from their families, whom they loved. The LTTE apparently tried to be a new and better family for the girls, so that their allegiance would be given to the movement rather than stay with their families of birth. One who had been abducted had received training as a medic. Others had developed skills in music, dance, English, art, math and computers.

It would not be unreasonable to surmise on the basis of Peltzer's report that many of the girls remained torn between their love for their families and their pride in what they had learned and become in the LTTE.

Like the girls I knew in the LTTE, the girls Peltzer knew who had left it had no problem amalgamating their identity as soldiers with traditional feminine pursuits: "I saw the adjustments made between these identities as they would demonstrate their abilities to do push-ups or proudly describe their ability to shoot a gun in the midst of them doing each others' nails, trying to make their hair look as long and feminine as possible, showing off their new jewelry, and talking about their boyfriends." Peltzer interprets all this, especially the boyfriends, as a "new sexual identity" that the girls were forbidden in the movement, with which they will now have to cope. What I learned, however, was that girls and boys in the LTTE did engage in romances and letter exchanges, although they were forbidden straight-out premarital sex, just as they were in civilian society.

What the girls in Peltzer's report regretted most about their time in the LTTE was their loss of years of formal schooling. But they were still young and could make this up. They could have received formal education simultaneously with valuable vocational training. Instead they were being taught sewing, despite the fact that INGO and NGOs routinely stated that sewing was no longer a viable employment opportunity (Peltzer 2005: 28).

Peltzer concludes that the girls in the LTTE were not empowered by their membership in the movement because a life within the military did not prepare them for a life outside it. This observation brings us back, however, to Sita's statement in her interview that a civilian life for Tamil women was meaningless, and that was why she preferred the life of a combatant. It may well be that those girls in the LTTE who are trained to want more of themselves and their lives than traditional, limited, female gender roles will have serious problems readjusting to civilian life.

References

Acocella, Joan. 2004. Holy Smoke: What Were the Crusades Really About? *New Yorker.* 13 December.

Ahearn, Laura. 2001. Language and Agency. *Annual Reviews in Anthropology* 30: 109–37.

Anderson, Benedict. 1991. *Imagined Communities: Reflections on the Origin and Spread of Nationalism.* Rev. ed. London: Verso.

Argenti-Pillen, Alex. 2003. *Masking Terror: How Women Contain Violence in Southern Sri Lanka.* Philadelphia: University of Pennsylvania Press.

Bate, J. Bernard. 2000. *Metaittamil:* Oratory and Democratic Practice in Tamilnadu. Ph.D. diss., University of Chicago.

———. 2003. Oratorical Embodiment and the Praxis of Self and Person in Tamil. Paper presented at the 31st annual Conference on South Asia, University of Wisconsin, Madison, 24 October.

Behera, Deepak Kumar, and Margaret Trawick, eds. 2001. Children and Childhood in Metropolitan Cultures. Special issue, *International Journal of Anthropology* 16, nos. 2–3.

Blackburn, Stuart. 1988. *Singing of Birth and Death: Texts in Performance.* Philadelphia: University of Pennsylvania Press.

Bloch, Maurice. 1992. *Prey into Hunter: The Politics of Religious Experience.* Cambridge: Cambridge University Press.

Boyden, Jo. 2003. Children under Fire: Challenging Assumptions about Children's Resilience. *Children, Youth and Environments* 13, no. 1. www.colorado.edu/journals/cye/13_1/Vol13_1Articles/CYE_CurrentIssue_Article_Children UnderFire_Boyden.htm. Accessed 25 April 2006.

Brown, Dee. 1970. Bury My Heart at Wounded Knee: An Indian History of the American West. London: Pan.

Certeau, Michel de. 1984. *The Practice of Everyday Life.* Trans. Steven Randall. Berkeley: University of California Press.

CETO (Center for Emerging Threats and Opportunities). 2002. *Child Soldiers: Implications for U.S. Forces.* Report on the Cultural Intelligence Seminar held on June 11, 2002. Quantico, VA: Marine Corps Warfighting Laboratory. http://www.cetoquantico.usmc.mil/studies/ChildSoldiersFinal.pdf. Accessed 16 June 2006.

Clastres, Pierre. 1994. *Archaeology of Violence.* Trans. Jeanine Herman. New York: Semiotext(e).

Coalition to Stop the Use of Child Soldiers. 2005. Some Facts. www.child-soldiers .org/childsoldiers/some-facts. Accessed 10 December 2005.

Coles, Robert. 1986. *The Political Life of Children.* Boston: Houghton Mifflin.

Daniel, E. Valentine. 1996. *Charred Lullabies: Chapters in an Anthropology of Violence.* Princeton, NJ: Princeton University Press.

Das, Veena. 1991. Our Work to Cry: Your Work to Listen. In *Mirrors of Violence: Communities, Riots, and Survivors in South Asia,* ed. Veena Das, 345–99. Delhi: Oxford University Press.

———. 1998. Wittgenstein and Anthropology. *Annual Review of Anthropology* 27: 171–95.

De Mel, Niloufer. 2003. Agent or Victim? The Sri Lankan Woman Militant in the Interregnum. In *Feminists Under Fire,* ed. W. Giles et al., 55–70. Ontario: Between the Lines.

De Silva, K. M. 1986. *Managing Ethnic Tensions in Multi-Ethnic Societies: Sri Lanka, 1880–1985.* Lanham, MD: University Press of America.

Dharmadasa, K. N. O. 2005. Of Language, Religion and Nationalism. *Frontline* 22, no. 12 (4–17 June). www.flonnet.com/fl2212/stories/20050617003611000 .htm. Accessed 13 June 2005.

Dirks, Nicholas B. 2001. *Castes of Mind: Colonialism and the Making of Modern India.* Princeton, NJ: Princeton University Press.

Douglas, Mary. 1966 [1984]. *Purity and Danger: An Analysis of the Concepts of Pollution and Taboo.* London: Ark Paperbacks.

Egnor [Trawick], Margaret. 1978. The Sacred Spell and Other Conceptions of Life in Tamil Culture. PhD diss., University of Chicago.

Ehrenreich, Barbara. 1997. *Blood Rites: Origins and History of the Passions of War.* New York: Henry Holt and Company.

Erikson, Kai T. 1978. *Everything in Its Path: Destruction of Community in the Buffalo Creek Flood.* New York: Simon and Schuster.

Fuentes, Augustin. 2004. It's Not All Sex and Violence: Integrated Anthropology and the Role of Cooperation and Social Complexity in Human Evolution. *American Anthropologist* 106 (4): 710–18.

Gennep, Arnold van. 1960 [1909]. *The Rites of Passage.* London: Routledge.

Gillies, David. 1992. Principled Intervention: Canadian Aid, Human Rights, and the Sri Lankan Conflict. In *Aid as Peacemaker: Canadian Development Assistance and Third World Conflict,* ed. Robert Miller. Ottawa: Carleton University Press.

Goff, Stan. 2004a. *Full Spectrum Disorder: The Military in the New American Century.* New York: Soft Skull Press.

———. 2004b. Military Matters #25: Rape Culture and the Military. http://freedomroad.org/content/view/163/56/. Accessed 25 April 2006.

———. 2005. War Porn. http://stangoff.com/?p=182. Accessed 1 September 2005.

Hart, George L., and Hank Heifetz, trans. and eds. 1999. *The Four Hundred Songs of War and Wisdom: An Anthology of Poems from Classical Tamil; The Purananuru.* New York: Columbia University Press.

Herring, Ronald J. 2001. Making Ethnic Conflict: The Civil War in Sri Lanka. In *Carrots, Sticks and Ethnic Conflict: Rethinking Development Assistance,* ed. Milton J. Esman and Ronald J. Herring, 140–74. Ann Arbor: University of Michigan Press.

Herring, Ronald J., and Milton J. Esman. 2001. Projects and Policies, Politics and Ethnicities. In *Carrots, Sticks and Ethnic Conflict: Rethinking Development Assistance,* ed. Milton J. Esman and Ronald J. Herring, 1–26. Ann Arbor: University of Michigan Press.

Huizinga, Johan. 1955. *Homo Ludens: A Study of the Play-Element in Culture.* Boston: Beacon Press.

Ilango, Prince Adikal. 1965. *Shilappadikaram (The Ankle Bracelet).* Trans. Alain Danielou. New York: New Directions.

James, Allison, and Alan Prout. 1990. A New Paradigm for the Sociology of Childhood? Provenance, Promise and Problems. In *Constructing and Reconstructing Childhood: Contemporary Issues in the Sociological Study of Childhood,* ed. Allison James and Alan Prout, 7–33. London: Falmer Press.

Jones, Richard Lezin. 2002. Officers Praise 7-Year-Old's Courage in Escape. *New York Times.* 25 July.

Kakar, Sudhir. 1979. *Indian Childhood: Cultural Ideals and Social Reality.* Delhi: Oxford University Press.

Kapferer, Bruce. 1983. *A Celebration of Demons: Exorcism and the Aesthetics of Healing in Sri Lanka.* Bloomington: Indiana University Press.

Keller, Evelyn Fox. 1985. *Reflections on Gender and Science.* New Haven, CT: Yale University Press.

Lawrence, Patricia. 1997. Work of Oracles, Silence of Terror: Notes on the Injury of War in Eastern Sri Lanka. Ph.D. diss., University of Colorado, Boulder.

Machel, Graca. 1996. Impact of Armed Conflict on Children. UNICEF. www.unicef.org/graca/. Accessed 25 April 2006.

Mahanama, the Venerable Thera. n.d. *The Mahāvāṃsa: The Great Chronicle of Lanka.* Translated from Pali by Wilhelm Geiger. Colombo: Ceylon Government Information Dept., 1912. Online version ed. Rhajiv Ratnatunga, August 2002. http://lakdiva.org/mahavamsa. Accessed 23 May 2006.

Mies, Maria. 1998. *Patriarchy and Accumulation on a World Scale: Women in the International Division of Labor.* London: Zed Books.

Nagaswamy, R. n.d. Kalinga Influence on Tamil Literature. http://freehomepages.com/brahadheesh/tamilarts/articles/kalinga_inf_tamil.html. Accessed 15 November 2004.

Nandy, Ashis. 2004. Reconstructing Childhood: A Critique of the Ideology of Adulthood. In *Bonfire of Creeds: The Essential Ashis Nandy,* ed. Ashis Nandy, 423–439. New Delhi: Oxford University Press.

Narayana Rao, Velcheru, and David Shulman, trans. and compilers. 1998. *A Poem at the Right Moment: Remembered Verses from Premodern South India.* Berkeley: University of California Press.

Nettle, Daniel. 1999. *Linguistic Diversity.* New York: Oxford University Press.

Nordstrom, Carolyn. 2004. *Shadows of War: Violence, Power, and International Profiteering in the Twenty-First Century.* Berkeley: University of California Press.

Obeyesekere, Gananath. 1984. *The Cult of the Goddess Pattini.* Chicago: University of Chicago Press.

Ondaatje, Michael. 1982. *Running in the Family.* New York: W. W. Norton.

Peltzer, Angie. 2005. Girls after the Gunfire: A Study of Released Girl Soldiers Rehabilitating in an Eastern Sri Lankan Rehabilitation Center. M.A. thesis, Center for East and Southeast Asian Studies, Lund University, Sweden.

Qvortrup, Jens. 2004. Editorial: The Waiting Child. *Childhood* 11 (3): 267–73.

Ramanujan, A. K. 1967. *Interior Landscapes: Love Poems from a Classical Tamil Anthology.* Bloomington: Indiana University Press.

Ramaswamy, Sumathi. 1997. *Passions of the Tongue: Language Devotion in Tamil India, 1891–1970.* Berkeley: University of California Press.

Richman, Paula. 1997. *Extraordinary Child: Poems from a South Indian Devotional Genre.* Honolulu: University of Hawaii Press.

Scott, David. 1994. *Formations of Ritual: Colonial and Anthropological Discourses on the Sinhala Yaktovil.* Minneapolis: University of Minnesota Press.

Sen, Amartya. 2006. *The Argumentative Indian: Writings on Indian Culture, History and Identity.* London: Penguin Books.

Shah, Anup. 2003. Arms Trade: A Major Cause of Suffering. Small Arms. *Global Issues.* www.globalissues.org/Geopolitics/ArmsTrade/SmallArms.asp. Accessed 12 October 2003.

Shattan, Merchant-Prince. 1989. *Manimekhalai: The Dancer with the Magic Bowl.* Trans. Alain Danielou. New York: New Directions.

Shulman, David. 1985. *The King and the Clown in South Indian Myth and Poetry.* Princeton, NJ: Princeton University Press.

———. 1993. *The Hungry God: Hindu Tales of Filicide and Devotion.* Chicago: University of Chicago Press.

Sivaram, Dharmeratnam. 1992a. The Twin Narratives of Tamil Nationalism. *Lanka Guardian.* 1 September. www.tamilnation.org/forum/sivaram/920901lg .htm. Accessed 25 April 2006.

———. 1992b. The Legend of Cheran Senguttuvan. *Lanka Guardian.* 15 November. www.tamilnation.org/forum/sivaram/921101lg.htm. Accessed 25 April 2006.

Strom, Karen M. 1995. The Massacre at Wounded Knee. http://www.hanks ville.org/daniel/lakota/Wounded_Knee.html. Accessed 26 June 2006.

Subramanian, L. N., and P.V.S. Jagan Mohan. 1999. *The Indian Army in Sri Lanka, 1987–90.* Delhi: Bharat Rakshak. www.bharat-rakshak.com/LAND-FORCES/ Army/History/1987/index.html. Accessed 25 April 2006.

Subramanian, T. S. 1998. An Eelam Outpost. *Frontline,* 23 January, 54–56.

Sutton-Smith, Brian. 1997. *The Ambiguity of Play.* Cambridge, MA: Harvard University Press.

Tambiah, Stanley J. 1976. *World Conqueror and World Renouncer: A Study of Buddhism and Polity in Thailand against a Historical Background.* Cambridge: Cambridge University Press.

———. 1986. *Sri Lanka: Ethnic Fratricide and the Dismantling of Democracy.* Chicago: University of Chicago Press.

———. 1992. *Buddhism Betrayed? Religion, Politics, and Violence in Sri Lanka.* Chicago: University of Chicago Press.

———. 1997. *Leveling Crowds: Ethnonationalist Conflicts and Collective Violence in Sri Lanka.* Berkeley: University of California Press.

TamilNet. 2005. Pirapaharan Extols Jeyanthan Brigade on 12th Anniversary. 5 May. www.tamilnet.com/art.html?catid=79&artid=14818. Accessed 6 May 2005.

Trawick, Margaret. 1990. *Notes on Love in a Tamil Family.* Berkeley: University of California Press.

———. 1997. Reasons for Violence: A Preliminary Ethnographic Account of the LTTE. *South Asia* 20: 153–80.

Turner, Victor. 1969. *The Ritual Process: Structure and Anti-Structure.* Chicago: Aldine Publishing Company.

———. 1982. *From Ritual to Theater: The Human Seriousness of Play.* New York: PAJ Publications.

United States Library of Congress. n.d. *Sri Lanka: A Country Study.* New ed. http://countrystudies.us/sri-lanka/.

Wells, Spencer. 2002. *The Journey of Man: A Genetic Odyssey.* Princeton, NJ: Princeton University Press.

Wikipedia. 2006. Pine Ridge Indian Reservation. http://en.wikipedia.org/wiki/Pine_Ridge_Reservation. Accessed 22 June 2006.

General Index

113, 179, 233; terrorism, 4, 211–213; torture, 54, 62, 80, 94, 159, 212, 215–216, 226, 237, 261, 288n8. *See also* death; warfare

Vīrakēsari, 97, 228, 257–258, 290n7

vīramaranam. See death

warfare, 2–8, 11–12, 14–15, 24–25, 30–31, 38–39, 71, 76, 108, 121–122, 125, 132, 142–143, 195, 210, 243, 273, 276, 279, 283n13, 284n20. *See also* violence

Weber, Max, 270

welfare socialism, 45–46

Index of People

These are people I met in the field; the names are pseudonyms.

Index of Places

Text:	10/13 Galliard
Display:	Galliard
Compositor:	BookMatters, Berkeley
Printer and binder:	Maple-Vail Manufacturing Group